THE GOTHAM LIBRARY
OF THE NEW YORK UNIVERSITY PRESS

The Gotham Library is a series of original works and critical studies published in paperback primarily for student usc. The Gotham hardcover edition is primarily for use by libraries and the general reader. Devoted to significant works and major authors and to literary topics of enduring importance, Gotham Library texts offer the best in literature and criticism.

Comparative and Foreign Language Literature:
  Robert J. Clements, Editor

Comparative and English Language Literature:
  James W. Tuttleton, Editor

The Victorian Imagination

Essays in Aesthetic Exploration

William E. Buckler

New York University Press · New York *and* London

Library of Congress Cataloging in Publication Data

Buckler, William Earl, 1924-
  The Victorian imagination.

  (The Gotham library of the New York University Press)
  Includes bibliographical references and index.
  1. English literature—19th century—History and
criticism—Addresses, essays, lectures. 2. Tennyson,
Alfred Tennyson, Baron, 1809-1892—Criticism and inter-
pretation—Addresses, essays, lectures. I. Title.
PR463.B8   820'.9'008   80-17571
ISBN 0-8147-1032-8
ISBN 0-8147-1033-6 (pbk.)

Manufactured in the United States of America

To

MRB, S.L.

"Where the heart lies, let the brain lie also."
—Robert Browning, "One Word More"

Acknowledgments

I am grateful to the editors of the following publications for permission to reprint portions of this book that originally appeared as articles in their journals: to John Stasny, editor of *Victorian Poetry*, for permission to reprint *"Marius the Epicurean:* Beyond Victorianism," "The Dark Space Illumined: A Reading of Hardy's 'Poems of 1912-13,'" and "Thomas Hardy's 'chronicle-piece' in 'playshape': An Essay in Literary Conceptualization"; to Philip Dodd and J. C. Hilson, editors of *Prose Studies, 1800-1900,* for permission to reprint *"Past and Present* as Literary Experience: An Essay in the Epistemological Imagination"; to Ward Hellstrom, editor of *The Victorian Newsletter,* for permission to reprint *"Déjà vu* Inverted: The Imminent Future in Walter Pater's *Marius the Epicurean"* and " 'The Thing Signified' by *The Dynasts:* A Speculation"; to Michael Timko and Fred Kaplan, editors of *Dickens Studies Annual,* for permission to reprint "Thomas Hardy's Illusion of Letters: Narrative Consciousness as Imaginative Style in *The Dynasts, Tess,* and *Jude. "*

I am also grateful to Professor James W. Tuttleton, Chairman of the Department of English at New York University, for sponsoring the volume and to Professor Tuttleton and Dean Norman Cantor of the Faculty of Arts and Science for cutting through economic impediments.

Many former and current students have been close to my work and have enabled me to talk rather fully about it. I wish particularly to cite three: Professor William Luhr, St. Peter's College; Dr. Kevin Z. Moore, President of the Thomas Hardy Society of America; and Mr. Richard A. Sylvia, New York University.

Contents

1.

The Victorian Imagination:
A Nonpolemical Introduction

English literature has had one great theorist, Coleridge; and it has
hardly known how to use him. Coleridge is inexhaustibly interesting, and our fascination with his critical revelations, both practical
and theoretical, multiplies daily as we gradually gain access to all
the fragments of his intellectual brilliance. For the literary student
interested in following an imperial literary mind in the act of dis-
solving inherited literary frontiers—vertically as regards individual
notions, horizontally as regards boundaries between subject matters and idea-clusters—Coleridge is the incomparable exemplar and
master. And yet, Coleridge has touched the critical models by
which we try to talk about literature in a sustained fashion very
insubstantially, and he has influenced the actual process of making
literature hardly at all. His century recognized him as a great
founder from beginning to end: Wordsworth, Arnold, and Pater
admired him immensely, but took little from him. Between 1817
(*Biographia Literaria*) and 1929 (I. A. Richards's *Practical Criticism*),
Coleridge never really assumed a critical place in the study of
letters, and even now the values at the apex of Coleridge's critical
hierarchy are at the nadir of critical practice. Mill's dramatic pair-

1

ing of Bentham and Coleridge as the two great seminal minds of the century shows Mill moving among the dry thickets of Bentham with the deftness of a native, but his generosity to Coleridge does not disguise his own perceptual disorientation. The essays have come to mean much more to us than they meant to the nineteenth century; and although F. R. Leavis discovered them when they were not quite lost, they are more significant as metaphors of Mill's temptation to alter the structure of his own consciousness than of the genuine proportions of the early nineteenth century. From, say, 1798 *(Lyrical Ballads)* to 1928 (the death of Hardy) Aristotle still had a currency with both poets and critics that Coleridge never enjoyed, and Thomas Hardy continues to shape the form and content of twentieth-century poetry in such pervasive and visible ways as to make Coleridge's fragmentary presence in the continuity of English poetry, by comparison, negligible. For a moment in his middle period, Arnold created a critical phrase—"imaginative reason"—which is rooted in Coleridge and suggests a passing inclination on Arnold's part to absorb into the body of his criticism adapted Coleridgean theory. But the body soon rejected the transplant; and while Arnold passed the phrase on to Pater, it altered the critical mix of neither of them in any significant and lasting way.

As Victorian criticism failed to find a function in its own labors for the admirable deposit of Coleridgean critical theory which it knew and admired, so Victorian literature has refused to absorb the various species of formalist criticism which the twentieth century has developed. The New Criticism, which took large portions of Academe by storm in the second quarter of this century, touched Victorian literature only tangentially and superficially, even though it was a healthy rebellion against varieties of critical depletion which were as detrimental to Victorian literature as to any other. Setting aside the grosser forms of sociological and biographical and psychohistorical diversion from the true text of literature, the post-Victorian aesthetes, ideologists, and neo-humanists had lost touch with the robustness, complexity, distinctiveness, and indispensability of literary experience and needed to be replaced. They were diminishing literature in general, but their influence on Victorian literature was singularly and subtly inimical since they seemed to be the inevitable outgrowth, the legitimate continuity, of a literary intuition with which they had in fact lost touch.

The new critical formalists will eventually have to face up to Victorian literature, and it will be a very different experience from that of their predecessors in the 1930s, '40s, and '50s. At that time, Victorian literature was on the defensive and seemingly defenseless: it could be tutted with impunity, and the failure of a critical methodology to deal successfully with it could be turned into an indictment, not of the methodology, but of the literature itself. The present situation is very different. By one of those ironic convergences that Thomas Hardy has taught us to fancy, Victorian literature has been growing in "stature, grace, and hue" even as the formalist criticism which ignored the earlier phase of its steady reemergence dissolved, redefined itself, and reemerged too. Victorian literature is no longer defenseless. It has drawn to itself one of the largest clusters of gifted, intense, hardworking, creative contemporary students of letters, many of whom caught the formalist bug in its earlier epidemic; and this has reversed the older disposition of things. Now, a critical methodology that fails to take adequate measure of the Victorian experience in literature is itself thereby indicted because Victorian literature has assumed an imaginative presence analogous to that occupied by the literature of the period from Spenser to Milton: it is now a literature of critical arbitration, not exclusively but indispensably. And although it is not quite possible to read the critical future—the whole Coleridge is still in stages of becoming, the new formalism is still somewhat gaseous—it is safe to say two things: the more systematic the theorists become, the more exquisitely enclosed in concepts and terms, the less likely they are to touch literary experience empirically at all or to establish significant contact with a literature that eschewed theory inductively rather than deductively—not because it wanted to, but because it had to; and the more tightly the formalists draw their lines, the further they remove their methodology from the dynamics of Victorian literature, which draws its extraordinary vigor from a multiplicity of practical imaginative fusions and, being shaped by a decision to forego creative monism, is likely to be essentially immune to critical monism.

Moreover, Victorian literature and criticism had, in the very

process of becoming Victorian literature and criticism, already
dealt with the various cultural or philosophical flows of our time
which have shaped themselves or tried to shape themselves into
more or less coherent critical methodologies. The epicureanism of
Hobbes, the epistemological sensationism of Locke, the atomism of
Hume, the dialecticism of Hegel, the transcendentalism of Kant,
the evolutionism of Lyell and Darwin, the rationalism of Des-
cartes, the rationalistic mythicism of Strauss, the positivism of
Comte—all are absorbed presences in the imaginative consciousness of the Victorians; and existentialism is a conditioner of both
Freudianism and Nietzscheanism. The point is not to diminish the
recent growth, codification, and solidity of any one of these critical
matrices, but to suggest that Victorian literature had so subsumed
their elementary implications to other imaginative rubrics, had so
mixed them up with other things, that it would resist any effort to
use any one of them as a singular or "pure" critical strategy for
unfolding its major imaginative secrets. Hegelianism was one of
the Victorian signs of the times, but no major Victorian writer can
be fairly described as a Hegelian; Kant was vastly subordinate to
Goethe as a pressure on the Victorian imagination from Carlyle to
Pater and Hardy; and the Victorians had implicitly expressed
their detachment from the psychological metaphysics of Jung, although Victorian literature is suffused with an awareness legitimately called archetypal. The point is simply that any systematic
cultural or philosophical methodologist is likely to find in dealing
with Victorian literature that, despite all his brilliance and inge-
nuity, his method has led him to the revelation of a "truth" that is
inferior to the truth that is actually there.

The literary experiment which the Victorians undertook with
the urgency of a desperate hope was the salvation of imaginative
letters. This is the current which runs steadily, expansively, sometimes turbulently from Carlyle in the 1820s to Hardy in the 1920s.
The modern world needed a new testament, and literature was the
only mode in which it could be made available. The sense of hieratic intensity was already there: a sacred pungency had been created by Blake, Wordsworth, Keats, Shelley and by the flow from
Germany that was released into England by Coleridge and, in a
more strictly literary fasion, by Carlyle. Goethe reached his English

ascendancy in Carlyle, and Richter, Novalis, and Tieck showed Carlyle how to convert philosophy into literature, thought into organic, profoundly moving dramatic experience. The first four major Victorian writers to be drawn into this highly psyched spiritual-aesthetic atmosphere were Carlyle, Tennyson, Browning, and Newman; but Browning fumbled for almost two decades in his efforts to find a conversional process that worked for him on a major scale, and the specialized involvements of Newman kept him from giving to his imagination a voice strictly literary except in fragments. So it was left to Carlyle and Tennyson to be the founders of Victorian literature.

That Carlyle and Tennyson pair so constructively is an illustration of how two vastly different temperaments and literary personalities blended in a common cause. They were both learned men, though Carlyle let his learning ricochet all over the surface of his writing, while Tennyson stripped his public texts of the signs of erudition and subordinated thought to the experience of thought; Carlyle used a technique of confrontation and challenge, Tennyson a strategy of oblique insinuation. But they read the direness of the present and the bleakness of the future very much alike: a world without faith is a chaos, and a faith without imagination is a delusion. That is the twin perception in which Carlyle and Tennyson rooted the aesthetic imperative of the Victorian and post-Victorian periods. It was admittedly a most precarious imperative, ever threatening to tumble into bald instruction or to collapse into despair. Keats had felt the dilemma keenly in the decade before Carlyle got into motion, and Yeats was to feel it in the decade of Tennyson's death. Arnold, Swinburne, and Hopkins all registered their deep sensitivity to its stresses in the 1860s, Swinburne in his separation of the truth of art for art's sake on the positive side from its falseness on the negative side and Arnold in his recognition in Eugénie de Guérin of the conflict between poetry and religion which Hopkins was to experience at the deepest personal level. But precarious or not, it was imperative: without literature, modern man is without guidance in spiritual renewal, and without spiritual renewal men are doomed to sit, like Carlyle's monkeys on the edge of the Dead Sea, chattering to each other.

Thus Carlyle and Tennyson made some fundamental literary

decisions: they must keep the way open, against such imperious, popular, insular mentalities as that of Macaulay, to the flow of fresh knowledge—Romantic or Classical, native or foreign, present or past; they must turn the energy of their literary imaginations frankly and fully upon the crucial problems of their own day, upon towering topical dilemmas; they must keep literature intact as literature by employing structures that convert topicality into perenniality, fact into metaphor, history into myth; they must use literature as a method for converting man's perception of the world around him as well as his perception of literature itself by showing him that literature is relevant, not only to life, but also to literature, that literature is made of literature, and that his whole literary heritage has incomparable relevance to his whole life in this world. It was not some simple matter of mechanical influence that Carlyle and Tennyson felt so deeply about. It was a translation into literary experience of the concept contained in Carlyle's metaphor of "organic filaments," a concept of spiritual simultaneity by which Time and Space are only "stubborn illusions" (Einstein) and man's experience is taking place in an ever present eternity; more prosaically, it was the expression of a faith in the conversional, hence the salvational, qualities of literature and of the organic unity of the great literary vine. It was through these decisions that Carlyle and Tennyson created the imaginative atmosphere in which Victorian literature, with its endless variations, throve. It is the literary, the imaginative atmosphere in which Browning and Newman, Ruskin, Rossetti, and Morris, Dickens and George Eliot and George Meredith worked; it was renewed but not abandoned by Arnold, Swinburne, and Pater; and Hardy's *The Dynasts* (his "Iliad of Europe") and the relevance of *The Dynasts* to his whole poetic canon shows that, well into the twentieth century, it was still in place.

The literary atmosphere thus created for their time by Carlyle and Tennyson out of influences rich and various and needs urgently felt demanded a critical voice, and it found a critical voice par excellence in Matthew Arnold. It was a stunning concurrence, in Arnold's own terms, of the power of the man and the power of the moment. Belonging to the generation immediately following that which had founded Victorianism, called upon, in part, to give perspective in the 1860s and '70s on what Carlyle and Tennyson had launched in the 1830s and '40s, Arnold brought extraordinary powers of critical empathy to bear upon the age. He was both intimate enough with, and detached enough from, the work of his immediate predecessors to be able to recover, enlarge, and redirect the style and energy of their initial intuition without damaging its fundamental content. He was a generation removed from both the English and the German Romantics; and he saw the former somewhat differently from the way Tennyson had seen them, and he was more skeptical about the latter than Carlyle had been. It was a slight but significant shift having large and positive value: it enabled Arnold to see the many-faceted Goethe in clearer and fuller perspective; it made him more available to the critical brilliance and balance of France than Carlyle and Tennyson had been, introducing him to the French "science of origins" and to the luminous metaphors by which the historical rhythms and cross-currents of Western civilization were beginning to be perceived; it enlarged and gave deeper rooting to his emergent idea of the modern, Europeanizing his consciousness; and it clarified and strengthened his faith in the sanity and relevance of the critical counsel and creative practice of the ancients, especially of Aristotle and Homer. Moreover, there had been a shift in the *Zeitgeist* between Carlyle's era of concentration and Arnold's era of expansion, and what was needed was less Romantic explosiveness and more Classical steadiness and wholeness, less disproportionate feeling and more proportioning thought, less Richter, Tieck, and Novalis and more Goethe reenforced by more Aristotle and corrected by more Homer.

Matthew Arnold as a critic is an emblem of literary Victorianism in its central, most expansive, least brooding, least tortured phase. All of the human negatives are there: ignorance, poverty, violence, injustice, grossly outmoded institutions, bullishly inept politicians, the decay of spiritual coherence, an explosive tension between the individual and the group, the failure of privilege to assume responsibility, the aggressive determination of incompetence to take over the future. But they are there, in Arnold's perspective, *because they are always there.* They are real, individual, threatening, demanding urgent attention; and they must be dealt with in a real manner that touches the real need. They cannot be

vulgarly swept aside by the rhetorical flourish of a Lord Macaulay
or dissipated by the solvent reason of a John Stuart Mill or sublimated by the exquisite metaphysics of a John Henry Newman,
and the Savonarola-impulse of a John Ruskin destroys the man
without solving the problem. Each of these approaches is humanly
representative in the long rhythms of perenniality, and hence real
but metaphoric problems invoke real but metaphoric gestures of
solution, the solidity of the fact being in no way weakened by the
poetry of the perspective. Arnold was able to keep free of the intellectual or emotional provincialism that somewhat tainted the work
even of some of his magnificent contemporaries by keeping in
mind a crystal-clear distinction between the work of the critic and
the work of practical men of affairs; by seeing his own age both
with uninhibited clarity and *sub specie aeternitatis;* by carefully
avoiding the allurements of a system of thought that, by witness of
the history of thought, must eventually become self-enclosed and
by resisting the enticements of definitions that, by virtue of conscientious and hence irresistible pressures toward perfect clarity and
definitiveness, must ultimately become tautological; by relishing to
the full the knowledge-explosion that was swirling around him
without panicking before its infinity of details and without confus-
ing the genuine excitements of an expansive contemporaneity with
an apex of civilization (Mill) or, more vulgarly, with the best of all
possible worlds (Macaulay); and by undertaking, seriously but not
solemnly, forcefully but not dogmatically, Classically rather than
Romantically, the role of the critic in its multiplicity of aspects—
the reinstatement of sound principles for the writing act; the elab-
oration of a fluid, purposeful, conscientious, and experientially re-
warding system for the reading act; the recovery of the original
and invaluable intuitions of the world's great literary texts; the
insinuation into the general consciousness of ways in which to understand and value the distinctiveness and worth of various peoples, cultures, times, both as things in themselves and as
contributions to the general human character; the reexamination
of the bases for a rational, modern, workable social and political
system; the reform and guidance of education; and the recasting of
religion. Thus through Matthew Arnold emblematically perceived,
Victorianism with all its conscientious vigor, experimental bold-

ness, and imaginative *élan* emerges in a metaphor of personal style by which its intense and multitudinous stresses are brought to a point of literary poise, to the sort of chastened reassurance which the perspective of a deep, rich, widely experienced, imaginative mind offers as a realistic antidote to chaos and despair. After Arnold, Victorianism does not move backward toward Carlyle and Tennyson, but forward toward Pater and Hardy; and it was Arnold who effected the transference.

Arnold's literary criticism excels all other Victorian literary criticism in a paradoxical way. It is the natural, organic outgrowth of the needs of literature and culture at his moment in time for fresh critical perspective, for a view that was Olympian and yet eminently practical, for a consciousness that was thoroughly, ineradicably, functionally rooted in its own *Zeitgeist* and at the same time capable of translating the metaphors of its own time and place into that metaphor in which *Zeitgeists* are themselves enveloped. Thus he was both an authentic expression and a redefinition of Victorianism, and he both gave Victorianism an illumined sense of itself and moved it off the center on which he found it, thereby creating a slightly altered atmosphere or ambience in which Pater and Hardy could do their imaginative work and give those cultural metaphors yet another slight but distinctive turning. But while Arnold's literary criticism is the center of gravity in his whole critical consciousnes—the source of its strength and stability, the ultimate reference point to which his intellectual endeavors draw for their coherence—it is not, if given a reasonably narrow academic definition, an adequate instrument for measuring his critical activities and must itself be understood in the light of those larger activites. Arnold knew what literary criticism had been before him, what Dryden, Johnson, Burke, Wordsworth, Coleridge, De Quincey, Hazlitt, and Lamb had done in the way of criticism, and he knew in the end what it had all come to. He also knew the Greek, Latin, Italian, German, and French critics and could measure the very different interconnections between their criticism and the culture in which it rose and flourished. His effort, therefore, to make English criticism move outward was his way of making literature itself move outward. Wordsworth had redeemed poetry for the few, so Arnold was redeeming literature for the many. It was the central "social idea" of his life's work, and in it there is a silent correction to Newman's characterization of the university as the great ordinary means to a great but ordinary end. The study of letters is, to Arnold, the great extraordinary means to a great and extraordinary end, namely, the redemption of life in this world. Without some sense of creativity, life is hardly worth living; and for the present and the indefinite future, poetry is man's new and only testament.

Arnold's efforts to enlarge literature's field of relevance has drawn the fire of those who would replace him in successive phases of an evolving critical tradition. But it is notable that Arnold's detractors have consistently been alienated from the Victorian experience in literature as a whole. Eliot was weary of the Victorians; the word *Victorian* itself seemed to make Leavis in his heyday apoplectic; Frye devised a system that for the most part touches the Victorians irrevelantly or reductively; and the severer contemporary theorists and methodologists can hardly be expected to be interested in, among many other things, Arnold or the Victorians. But since Arnold both enlarged the field of criticism and held it steady at the center, there will always be a deep commitment to his suffusive sanity and an even greater return to it as the social idea of literature reinvades our consciousness and displaces our contemporary romance with anarchy.

What Arnold did for literary criticism—and what no predecessor or successor in English has ever done—was to bring the critical act so close to the creative act that criticism's generative analogue is clearly visible in the creative work itself, while at the same time he preserved impeccably the discrete distinction between the work of the critic and the work of the creator. He brought the suffusive empiricism of the modern *Zeitgeist,* with its reenforcing counterpart in Aristotelian Classicism, to the service of literary experience. And he did this in two ways: by drawing the intuitions and practical rules of his criticism only from literary experience itself, from a wide, deep, oft-repeated, wholly experimental proofing of the world's great literary texts; and by communicating to his readers the proven, verifiable *"ground* and *authority"* of literature's, especially the greatest books', call on them. Thus Arnold's very mission as a critic was rooted in an irrefragable faith in the organic, transformational, conversional affectiveness of that literature which was itself rooted in just such experience. His temperament, the character of his education, his sense of mission, the peculiarities of his life-history, and the *Zeitgeist* had removed Arnold from the confessional mode by which Wordsworth, Coleridge, Carlyle, and Newman gave literary exposure to this sort of conversional experience; but the fact that he used an Aristotelian rather than an Augustinian or a Rousseauistic mode of discourse does not disguise the fact that his personal transformation through literary experience undergirds the character and intensity of his devotion to letters and brings it close to the sort of revelation in which literary experience is itself centered.

A's Aristotelianism

This closeness to the power, crux, and distinctivenss of literary experience saved Arnold from the various traps to which literary criticism, even criticism which is learned and eager, is always prone—from philosophical criticism, which is drawn into a system, especially a stystem of terms, and is measured by the integrity of its system rather than by its practical relationship to literary experience; from scientific criticism, which imposes on literary experience a methodology that is alien to it and either misses the literary work's total impression or gives a wrong impression of it; from critical impressionism, which centers attention on the reader rather than on the object read; from historical criticism, which values a literary work on critically tangential grounds; from genre criticism, which is the conventional criticism of the belletrist and often fails to look beyond the signifier to the thing signified; from myth criticism, which dismantles one set of metaphysical dogmas while it erects a new metaphysics of its own; from critical provincialism, whether of time or place, which is the criticism of those who either have not read enough or have read to little purpose and which tends to be vapid or violent according to the temperament of the critic.

But his closeness to the very best literary experience available contributed far more importantly to the constructive character of Arnold's criticism, and this can be illustrated in one of his most elaborate yet succinct statements on the demands of literary criticism:

> This literary criticism, however, *is* extremely difficult. It calls into play the highest requisites of the study of letters;

great and wide acquaintance with the history of the human
mind, knowledge of the manner in which men have thought,
of their way of using words and of what they mean by them,
delicacy of perception and quick tact, and besides all these, a
favourable moment and the "Zeit-Geist." *(Literature and
Dogma,* VI, v)

This is what Arnold's literary experience had taught him, and this
is what he brings to the art of criticism. Applied to the way in
which the Arnoldian critical canon actually works, it reminds us of
his perpetual habit of looking before and after, of the kinetic simultaneity of all of his literary reference points; it points to the care
and attendance which he gave to man's varied and never-ending
effort to identify the answer to the human riddle, to work upward
through the *Zeitgeist* to the metaphor in which the *Zeitgeist* is itself
enveloped, and to all the prismatic analogues, the infinite variety
in unity, by which their discrete efforts in different times and
places draw to a common center called literature; it instructs us
anew that to Arnold the language of poetry, the language of literature and eloquence, has its own special character and function, is
language in motion, searching out its insights in a fluid, approx-
imative fashion that is different from the manner in which the
language of philosophy and science absorbs and gives off the
qualities of definiteness and exactness aspired to in those disci-
plines—is language constantly undergoing the renewal of a dynamic creative context with a significance that is inseparable from
that context; it asserts that unless the critic has refined to the
utmost his apparatus of literary perception through the effects on a
large, rich, deep, imaginative mind of immersion in the finest literary experience, he will be inadequate to the task of recovering the
original intuitions of the world's great books; and it puts in place
Arnold's persuasion that, in criticism as in creation, movement is
possible at one time that is just not possible at another and that the
critic who would be more than a journeyman must be deeply in
touch with his own time and with the literary experience of the
past that, recovered through a sound criticism, can make anew its
grand creative contribution.

Thus, Arnold can be fairly called the critical voice of the Victorian imagination. Like his early and late contemporaries, he was a great experimentalist in the quality of modern life; like them, he turned all his creative energy—and the style in which that creative energy functioned—upon the stresses with which human nature in his time was struggling and dealt with them both literally (as current and real) and imaginatively (as metaphors of man's perennial condition for which the great literature of the past has genuine relevance). Arnold adopted as a cardinal principle of his critical endeavors a sentence from Isaac Newton—*"Hypotheses non fingo,"* I *do not invent [my] hypotheses;* and it was that principle which enabled him, like his contemporaries, to discover empirically both his motive and his method in the verifiable experience of the human spirit trapped and shrunken in the literalnesses of its own time and space and then freed into perceptual light and expanse of spirit through the deliverances of the world's most trustworthy revelation, its greatest books.

2.

Past and Present as Literary Experience: An Essay in the Epistemological Imagination

It is not sufficiently noted by those who look to the whole cloth in Thomas Carlyle that each of his major works is a distinctive literary experiment and that, more than any other of his numerous and abundant characteristics, a truly creative experimentalism enabled him to dominate the British literary scene for at least a quarter of a century. Despite the energy that has been expended on the explication of his ideas, Carlyle was not an ideologue. He was, as George Meredith said, "an artist in his work," and his conscientiousness as an artist "cost him his health . . . swallowed up his leisure." [1] As an artist, as an innate and practiced man of letters, Carlyle knew that literature was transformational, moved experience (including ideological experience) to a new *locus* so that it could be perceived afresh and with more stunning affectiveness. Like nineteenth-century artists generally but with the awareness and timing of a literary founder, Carlyle's profoundest contribution was to the *how* of modern life rather than to the *what*—to new ways of seeing, to the apprehending consciousness, to what Arthur Henry Hallam, with reference specifically to Tennyson's early poetry, called new "modes of knowledge and power." [2] Carlyle can fairly be called the

14

great original even among a century of great originals, and almost every thought-ripple stirred in us by such a notion draws upon the *how* rather than the *what* of the man—upon his function as an artist, not as an ideologist. The relationship of poetry to truth was one of the controlling concerns of Carlyle's major period just as it was one of the controlling concerns of Browning's *The Ring and the Book:* how men suppose and state facts, including how men may learn to suppose and state facts, is a crux in the modern artist's modernism, and Carlyle contributed incomparably to the definition and workability of a modern epistemological aesthetic.

What was at stake when Carlyle emerged as a major man of letters was the worthiness (including the quality) of modern life. Machinery had replaced Nature and God as the most conspicuous symbol of man's condition: industrialism, having taken a quantum leap as a result of the hardware needs of the Napoleonic war, had become systemic. The social, economic, and political stresses of this new era of industrialism, capitalism, and democracy not only threatened current chaos but also promised, from more than one serious point of view, permanent unmanageability. This was the imperious ambience that Carlyle understood so vividly and, for his purposes, so accurately as to enable him to move modern literature to the central stage of modern life.

The unique combination that Carlyle brought to this undertaking was a fully developed aesthetic and a well-fueled social conscience: this intense coupling enabled him to deal positively and successfully with the issue of modern literary relevance. Being a learned man fully versed in modern history, he had as firm a grasp as anyone of the imperatives of historical development; and not being a fool, he knew that neither poet nor prosist could impede the wave of the future or divert its course. But he knew too that in a world going quickly into drabness and distress of spirit, the imagination became more and more indispensable as a human resource and that, having spent most of his adult life exploring the meaning and uses of the literary imagination, he had here a major role to play. He played that role most consciously and completely in *Past and Present,* the book at the center of Carlyle's special career as literary guide to his generation.

There can be no reasonable challenge to the unparalleled importance of *Past and Present* to our access to and understanding of the spiritual (social, psychological, aesthetic) dynamics of the nineteenth century in England. Despite the rather numerous "signs of the times" pamphlets and the several contemporary testaments of social lamentation, *Past and Present* stands forward as the first full-bodied, densely textured, imaginatively confrontal challenge to the *soi-disant* imperatives of a revolutionary century. The only document of an importance even comparable to that of *Past and Present* emergent from the same time-womb is Friedrich Engels's *The Condition of the Working Class in England in 1844;* but Engels's book, though long considered a "great socialist classic," [3] is not a literary classic and from a literary point of view is certainly not "full-bodied, densely textured, imaginatively confrontal." Engels is an imaginative dullard compared with Carlyle and obviously assumed a very different role from that assumed by Carlyle; but *The Condition of the Working Class in England* is an extraordinary book looking boldly forward to the methodology of modern urban anthropology, and it does share with *Past and Present* a fundamental radicalism.

Behind Engels the statistician, case-student, expositor, orderer, and ideologue and Carlyle the apocalyptic orchestrator, aesthetic organicist, and jubilarian of the imagination is a basically comparable motive—namely, the remaking of modern man. Both Engels and Carlyle reject specifically the conventional wisdom of their epoch and press their readers toward new definitions, especially new self-definitions. The men of the 1840s particularly, but modern man generally, had been trapped within a system that had shaped itself with revolutionary rapidity. The system had been put in place within a few short decades and in a spirit of ready justice and had been rationalized and reenforced through a relentless program of propagandistic brainwashing by both Church and State so that disbelief in the system could be looked upon as both an act of treachery to God and country and a symptom of mental instability. What both Carlyle and Engels had embarked upon was the dismantling of the conventional wisdom—the cluster of culturally induced imperatives—of their age. In order to achieve this, they had to provide a way out of the trap, a way out of the system; and since the system itself was a point of view, a way of looking at one's self in one's universe, they had to create an alternative perceptual reality. The common denominator of their otherwise very different methods was a radical empiricism, the authority of the eye put to relentless social uses, a look-see so fearless and searching as inevitably to give the lie to the false perceptions out of which the conventional wisdom of the age was fabricated.[4] Engels and Carlyle came from very different backgrounds, belonged to different generations, were possessed of fundamentally different life-illusions, experienced radically disparate senses of self and self-role, and were destined to leave very different marks upon the modern world. But in *The Condition of the Working Class in England* and in *Past and Present,* respectively, they sent out analogous signals: modern man is locked into a false and self-destructing myth based upon the manipulative misvision of established thought-controllers, and the indispensable key to his survival is a purification of his vision so that he may see himself (his present, his past, his universe, his nature) as he really is and shape his cultural structures accordingly. The "facts" are not in dispute between them: Engels quotes from both *Chartism* (1839) and *Past and Present* (1843) in verification of his own observations, and the facts he appeals to—"facts of historical development and facts of human nature" [5]—are the central concerns of Carlyle. Where they differ so dramatically as to be hardly comparable is in their *imaginative sense of fact,* with the result that, whereas Engels can hardly be said to provide a literary experience at all, Carlyle employs a harrowing social condition to provide one of the most complex and influential literary experiences of the century—indispensable and, it would appear, inevitable.

Anyone who takes even the least of his cues regarding the special nature of literary experience from Walter Pater [6] will quickly perceive that the special spiritual involvement that the author of *Past and Present* invites the reader to participate in is aesthetic rather than sociological. Carlyle has created a formal structure through which the reader is asked to look at the incipient anarchy of modern life and has created a voice which appeals to the reader, to an extraordinarily high degree, "to catch [his] spirit," to participate in "his peculiar intuition of a world, prospective, or discerned below the faulty conditions of the present." More conspicuously than any other nonfiction prose text of the first half of the century, [7] *Past and*

Present represents "the finer accommodation of speech to [the] vision within" and makes its essential appeal as a piece of literary fine art.

It is as an impassioned editorialist that the narrator/commentator of *Past and Present* makes his appeal to the reader: the experiences that he relates are suspended in the medium of his distinctive consciousness; what we see is not the raw data but a deeply moved witness to the data. Hence our essential experience is not objectively historical, but subjective/objective-subjective perceptual: we perceive (subjective) him (objective-) idiosyncratically perceiving (subjective). Perception itself (how he supposes and states fact) is the pattern of experiential learning that the book provides. Thus, with a necessary accommodation or two, [8] one can fairly see the imaginative process of *Past and Present* as analogous to that of the individual monologues in *The Ring and the Book:* what the speaker tells us is who he is, what eye he has brought to the seeing of reality; and what he implicitly urges us to do is to reconsider these matters with particular reference to ourselves (who we are, how the world looks to us). Seen in this way, *Past and Present* assumes the character of one of the generic literary formulations of nineteenth-century literature—namely, a narrative objectification of a formally confessional process through which a *persona,* real or imaginary, tells the reader how it is/was with him and reveals in the telling the insights his experiences have taught him.[9]

Like Browning and Pater, too, Carlyle keeps his reader persistently aware of the indispensable role of literature in shaping and conditioning man's awarenesses. Indeed, implicit in the book's method is the assumption that *Past and Present,* like literature generally, is made of literature. The most conspicuous illustration of this is the literary transformation of Jocelin's Chronicle: it provided the *how* that enabled Carlyle's book to come into existence, showed him a way to convert a seared social conscience (a naked heart) into a meaningful literary experience (controlled, interpretive, transformational). Jocelin's mythohistorical narrative became the imaginative catalyst for Carlyle: seeing the past through Jocelin's eyes enabled him to see the present *through Jocelin's eyes,* renewed for him, as it were, the literary (mythohistorical) mandate to see things *sub specie aeternitatis,* to convert topicality into perenniality, to rise afresh to the perceptual realization that all facts are symbolic. Thus, literature becomes something totally functional for Carlyle: it is assumed into the very texture of his language, and its ancient meaning is fully capable of mediating present difficulties.

That there is an explicatory analogy between Jocelin and Carlyle seems likely enough: they are both poet-chroniclers of human affairs in their brief moment of time, in their "narrow section of the world." Like the narrator/commentator of *Past and Present,* Jocelin is a way of looking at life and, through language, illuminating it; in a real sense, he is rarer even than a Samson, as a Homer is rarer than an Odysseus, or an Aeschylus is rarer than an Agamemnon. Thus in introducing Book II, Carlyle uses a literary device that, if not exclusively novelistic, was habitually needed and employed by nineteenth-century novelists. This is the device of conditioning our acceptance of the protagonist (in this case, Abbot Samson) by the careful prior establishment of the dependability, through explicit qualifications, of the narrator (here, Jocelin).[10] Thereby Carlyle answers the question which "Readers and men generally are getting into strange habits of asking all persons and things," namely, "in God's name, what *art* thou?" (II, i)—a question directed not only at simple, shrewd, quick-witted Jocelin, but also at the author-editor, at the reader, and at "men generally." It becomes thus a central question posed by *Past and Present,* and upon the answer it provokes depend many of the affective qualities of the work: Who are *you,* and what do *you believe* about this "two-legged animal without feathers?"

The catalogue of Jocelin's qualifications (II, i), apparently very casually trotted out before us, has in fact a highly significant order with far-reaching implications and is worth schematizing.

(1) *He knows authoritatively what he is talking about:* he was " 'chaplain to my Lord Abbot, living beside him night and day for the space of six years;'—which last, indeed, is the grand fact of Jocelin's existence, and properly the origin of this present book, and of the chief meaning it has for us now."

(2) *He is an especially open-ended fellow, both as a human being and to things human:* "an ingenious and ingenuous, a cheery-hearted, innocent, yet withal shrewd, noticing, quick-witted man . . . has looked

out on this narrow section of the world in a really *human* manner
. . . is of patient, peaceable, loving, clear-smiling nature; open for
this and that."

(3) *He is a truthful man:* his veracity is of a "simple," "natural"
kind "that goes deeper than words."

(4) Though no erudite Dryasdust, *he is what may be called a learned
man:* he has "read his classical manuscripts, his Virgilius, his Flac-
cus, Ovidius Naso; of course still more, his Homilies and Brevi-
aries, and if not the Bible, considerable extracts of the Bible."

(5) *He is a deeply religious man:* " 'a man of excellent religion,' ":
" '*eximiae religionis, potens sermone et opere.*' "

(6) *He has a peculiarly fetching literary style:* his chronicle is "written
in its childlike transparency, in its innocent good-humour, not
without touches of ready pleasant wit and many kinds of worth,
[which] . . . men liked naturally to read."

(7) *He is a man with a special talent of relevance:* "The good man, he
looks on us so clear and cheery, and in his neighbourly soft-smiling
eyes we see so well our *own* shadow."

(8) *He is a distinct individualist:* he "will not answer any question:
that is the peculiarity of him, dead these six hundred and fifty
years, and quite deaf to us, though still so audible!" "How inter-
mittent is our good Jocelin; marking down, without eye to *us,* what
he finds interesting!"

In this significant portrait of the artist, Carlyle suggests how
literary experience is distanced and distilled: it comes to us at "the
remove of form and idea" and exists only in that state; [11] but such
"form" and "idea" as literature has is conditioned by the personality through which it is filtered. Argument and observation are
given perspective through character: what we know is a gesture of
who we are. Hence, affective literary experience functions at a
deeply personalized level—*who he is* negotiating with *who we are.* In
Carlyle's case, as in Browning's and Pater's, imaginative knowledge is "instracted" knowledge, functioning at a level of personal
absorption. Literature, in both its inception and its affectiveness, is
inseparable from life-style.

But perhaps the most startling index to the literary (as distinct
from the sociological and ideological) rooting of *Past and Present* is
Carlyle's use of what I will call a *"Metamorphoses* analogue." It

would have been surprising if, in a work so clearly devoted to the theme of metamorphosis (degeneration/renewal), Carlyle had not glanced at the most compendious treatment of that theme in the Western literary tradition. And indeed both versions of the Midas myth that Carlyle uses in the first chapter of the book are to be found in Ovid, Book XI. Midas as the father of the "cash nexus" idea, together with the disastrous results that ensued therefrom, is wholly appropriate to Carlysle's concerns, and by introducing his theme of transformations by means of this particular myth, Carlyle suggests the level of "religious" experience which his book, like Ovid's, will pinpoint: as Midas has "insulted the Olympians," so man with his new-old cult of Mammonism has "insulted Apollo and the gods"—his own highest nature, Nature herself—and has introduced an isolating factor that forces him into alien and antagonistic roles, makes his society atomistic, and induces asphyxia as a spiritual condition that necessarily feeds on itself. But this deplorable state of contemporary England (topical) upon which *Past and Present* seems so exclusively to turn is really only a localized version of a perennial human propensity upon which Ovid's book also turns (mythic):

> The land, which had previously been common to all, like the sunlight and the breezes, was now divided up far and wide by boundaries, set by cautious surveyors. Nor was it only corn and their due nourishment that men demanded of the rich earth: they explored its very bowels, and dug out the wealth which it had hidden away, close to the Stygian shades; and this wealth was a further incitement to wickedness. By this time iron had been discovered, to the hurt of mankind, and gold, more hurtful still than iron. War made its appearance, using both those metals in its conflict, and shaking clashing weapons in bloodstained hands. Men lived on what they could plunder: friend was not safe from friend, nor father-in-law from son-in-law, and even between brothers affection was rare. Husbands waited eagerly for the death of their wives, and wives for that of their husbands. Ruthless stepmothers mixed brews of deadly aconite, and sons pried into their fathers' horoscopes, impatient for them to die. All proper affec-

tion lay vanquished and, last of the immortals, the maiden
Justice left the blood-soaked earth.[12]

The links between Carlyle's portrait of man and Ovid's are too
crucial and numerous to be accidental: [13] the enclosing of the common lands, the central significance of corn, the hellish wealth, the
warring conditions incited by competition and the discovery of
new warlike materials, the selfish plundering and the atrophy of
the ordinary social and domestic affections resulting therefrom, the
departure finally from such a violent human situation of "the
maiden Justice"—all of these are as central to Carlyle as they are to
Ovid.

Recognition of this *Metamorphoses* analogue in *Past and Present*
helps to monitor our critical judgment of what Carlyle is attempting to do in the book. It suggests, for example, that mythohistoricism affects every aspect of the book—that "The Modern Worker"
has mythic coordinates as surely as do the tales of Midas and the
Sphinx and the metaphoric narrative of Abbot Samson and his
twelfth-century microcosm. That in Book III the narrator/com-
mentator is dealing with facts is a matter of the first importance to
the aesthetic experimentalism of *Past and Present:* the imaginative
transformation of fact from one state of relevance to another requires the preimaginative existence of the fact itself. But how one
copes with these facts, how one organicizes empirical knowledge,
introduces the point at which epistemology and imagination
merge. The relationship of *Dichtung* (poetry, imagination) to *Wahrheit* (truth, fact) is a central creative concern of Carlyle in *Past and
Present,* as it is a central creative concern of Browning in *The Ring
and the Book,* of Tennyson in *In Memoriam,* and of Victorian literature generally: how one order of truth (fact) can be transformed
into another order of truth (also fact). Knowledge, especially a
finer than intellectual knowledge, is the basic goal, but the process
by which this conversion takes place so coalesces with the imaginative process through which it is being explored that the two become essentially one, and the epistemological imagination
emerges: the imagination as an authentic way of knowing (as perhaps the only authentic way of knowing some kinds of facts) is
counterpointed with more prosaic ways of knowing, and such per-

ceptual coherence as modern man can find in his complex, secu-
larized, modern universe is sustained by experience of and faith in
imaginative reality.

> How much in Jocelin, as in all History, and indeed in all
> Nature, is at once inscrutable and certain; so dim, yet so indu-
> bitable; exciting us to endless considerations. For King Lack-
> land *was* there, verily he; and did leave these *tredecim sterlingii,*
> if nothing more, and did live and look in one way or the other,
> and a whole world was living and looking along with him!
> There, we say, is the grand peculiarity; the immeasurable one;
> distinguishing, to a really infinite degree, the poorest historical
> Fact from all Fiction whatsoever. Fiction, 'Imagination,'
> 'Imaginative Poetry,' etc. etc., except as the vehicle for truth,
> or *fact* of some sort,—which surely a man should first try other
> ways of vehiculating, and conveying safe,—what is it? (II, i)

Like Browning, Carlyle appeals to lovers of live truth [14] and, again
like Browning, sees truth (fact) imaginatively vehiculated as just
one fact the more. Both of them recognized that a new knowledge
explosion was one of the defining characteristics of their time.
They knew, further, that empirical knowledge (scientism) in their
time appeared plausibly to induce points of view about man and
his needs that were basically either apoetic or antipoetic. But they
also knew that scientism (social, physical) was, like democracy, one
of the imperious demands of the age. So they saved the present by
means of the past: having accepted as facts the most empirically
observed brutalities of the present, they made them organic with
man's historical experience by concentrating in more refined ways,
not on raw facts, but on facts as perceived, humanized facts. In this
way, human awareness became the common denominator, and the
myths by which that awareness had reached its highest imaginative expression became a model both of an authentic way of rising
above a welter of present facts and of a wholly human strategy for
coordinating present reality with the past, however distant and
dim.

Literature (poetry, imagination) is a persistent theme in *Past and
Present.* In the dense fabric of literary allusion the theme is re-

lentlessly insinuated into the reader's consciousness that world literature is an indispensable access route to living truth, and the
point is made quite explicit with reference to the sudden termina-
tion of Jocelin's Chronicle:

> And Jocelin's Boswellean Narrative, suddenly shorn-through
> by the scissors of Destiny, *ends*. There are no words more; but
> a black line, and leaves of blank paper. Irremediable: the mi-
> raculous hand that held all this theatric-machinery suddenly
> quits hold; impenetrable Time-Curtains rush down; in the
> mind's eye all is again dark, void; with loud dinning in the
> mind's ear, our real-phantasmagory of St. Edmundsbury
> plunges into the bosom of the Twelfth Century again, and all
> is over. Monks, Abbot, Hero-worship, Government, Obedi-
> ence, Coeur-de-Lion and St. Edmund's Shrine, vanish like
> Mirza's Vision; and there is nothing left but a mutilated black
> Ruin amid green botanic expanses, and oxen, sheep and dilet-
> tanti pasturing in their places. (II, xvi)

Our only hold on that mythohistorical miniature of a Teaching
Priesthood (Jocelin) and a Governing Priesthood (Samson) has
been a literary hold, and when that ends, history itself ends: without literature, man's very presence on the earth is lost in a dark
void, as if he and his polity had never even been created. All that is
left is vegetal encroachment and a sort of bovine picturesqueness.
On the other hand, there is "a small Poet" in each of us that is
taking "counsel of the Unseen and Silent" and is trying to create
"a thing which never hitherto was" and to give it "real visibility
and speech" (III, xii). Whether man's origins are "two hairy-
naked" apes or two "fig-leaved Human Figures," speech is the
miracle of his identity: it is that toward which he has struggled
"with gaspings, gesturings, with unsyllabled cries, with painful
pantomime and interjections" until he could, like Dan Chaucer,
shape and coin words—"what thou callest a metaphor, trope, or
the like? For every word we have, there was such a man and poet"
(II, xvii). Work is prayer, but work is poetry too; indeed, poetry
and prayer become one in a genuine act of creation:

The first man who, looking with opened soul on this august Heaven and Earth, this Beautiful and Awful, which we name Nature, Universe and such like, the essence of which remains forever UNNAMEABLE; he who first, gazing into this, fell on his knees awestruck, in silence as is likeliest,—he, driven by inner necessity, the 'audacious original' that he was, had done a thing, too, which all thoughtful hearts saw straightway to be an expressive, altogether adoptable thing! To bow the knee was ever since the attitude of supplication. Earlier than any spoken Prayers, *Litanias, Leitourgias;* the beginning of all Worship,—which needed but a beginning, so rational was it. What a poet he! Yes, this bold original was a successful one withal. (II, xvii)

The centrality of aesthetic considerations to *Past and Present* can also be seen in the way crucial chapters are handled. For example, the last chapter in Book II ("The Beginnings," Chap. XVII) and the first chapter in Book III ("Phenomena"), though they look in opposite directions structurally, are closely linked thematically and processively: the thoughts induced in the narrator/commentator by the delightful history of Abbot Samson and his near-forgotten world exaggerate the contrast when he turns to the too too present world of the "modern worker." Both chapters deal with the subject of formulae—habits, customs, conventions, human footpaths—the former in the spirit of creation and emergent light, the latter in anxiety over chaos and approaching darkness and doom. "The Beginnings" stresses the unsung labors of untold millions of men who moved creativity from the noninstrumental stage to the creation of St. Paul's Cathedral, from a nonverbal world to the *Iliad* and *Robin Hood's Garland.* Each craft, each human need—worshipper, lawyer, engineer, architect—found, in a past about which the record is wholly *silent,* its poet, its authentic perceiver, its "hero" who moved a universal awareness forward to a word that men would adopt and forever hold usable. So language was made, so religion, law, habitable civilization. Poetry emerged from men's anxiety "no longer to be dumb, but to impart themselves to one another"—the poetry of language, industry, order. Samson was such a poet-worker, and there have been millions like him who did not find their miniature Boswell, through whose writings we get to know somewhat about a few. But the human record shows nonetheless that they existed and that our debt is near-immeasurable to many an "audacious original."

"Phenomena," on the other hand, portrays a remnant world of surreal sterility, a world in which the authentic origins of man's institutions have been forgotten and worship, governance, and work have all moved into a medium of phantasmagoria, a Hieronymus Bosch world of tragic dislocation and exaggeration. It is a world of Pandemonium (by analogy with Milton) and Dunces (by analogy with Pope). It is a parable of fools—a nightmarish world in which some devil seems to have said, *let there be darkness, let there only appear to be light.* Men have lost their authentic imaginations, hence their will to create, indeed their ability to create—to feel the need that stirs the gesture. Instead, they play-act, pretend, sham. The narrator/commentator's metaphor for what has happened is that "our religion is gone," "we 'have forgotten God.' " But this metaphor is translated to include all aspects of faith, particularly faith in the authentically creative self. The paths of old have become the "broad way" of the present, along which a disbelieving generation is hurrying toward "precipices, devouring gulfs." "Puffery, Falsity, Mammon-worship and Unnature" have taken the place of "Faithfulness, Veracity and Valour." Something more basic than the currency of numerous absurd slogans has taken place, and something deeper than socially cosmetic change is needed. Faith, truth, courage as sources of man's moral energy have been sapped because his imagination has been sapped, because his mind's eye has been blinded. That is the fundamental source of his current malaise, and it is imperative that his imagination—his interpretive, myth-making, conversional apparatus—be fired again as the only available strategy for moving him off the center of his existential inertia.

The narrative curve followed by the chapter entitled "Morrison Again"—the last chapter of Book III, "The Modern Worker"—is extremely revealing. The chapter begins with an address to an audience identified as "O Advanced Liberal" on the subject of a "New Religion," and it ends with a "rhythmic word," namely, a translation of Goethe's *Symbolum* celebrating, not a new modernist "religion," but an ancient awareness of the integrity of life, its labors, its meaning, the centrality to it of choice: thus its movement is from rationalism to poetry. The theme of moral awareness implicit in the narrative curve evolves also on the argumentative/expository level: the purpose of religion is moral preservation; on the levels of both social order and religion, pill-taking is no solution because it is a simplistic substitute for action and has no relevance to the inner spiritual renovation needed; and social order and religion share the central human concern of moral (just, creative) action. Self-denial, in the manner of St. Simeon Stylites, is not the answer either; self-renewal, especially of the imaginative awareness, is the more relevant answer. At this point Carlyle creates rhetoric "in a [higher] strain" designed to induce a state of imaginative being in the reader as a device for persuading him of the imaginative possibilities with which he is generally concerned.

> "Work is worship": yes, in a highly considerable sense,—which, in the present state of all 'worship,' who is there that can unfold! He that understands it well, understands the Prophecy of the whole Future; the last Evangel, which hast included all others. *Its* cathedral the Dome of Immensity,—has thou seen it? coped with the star-galaxies; paved with the green mosaic of land and ocean; and for altar, verily, the Star-throne of the Eternal! Its litany and psalmody the noble acts, the heroic work and suffering, and the true heart-utterance of all the Valiant of the Sons of Men. Its choir-music the ancient Winds and Oceans, and deep-toned, inarticulate, but most speaking voices of Destiny and History,—supernal ever as of old. Between two great Silences:

> > "Stars silent rest o'er us,
> > Graves under us silent!"

> Between which two great Silences, do not, as we said, all human Noises, in the naturalest times, most *preter*naturally march and roll? (III, xv)

This orchestration of reader imagination is followed immediately by a citation, "in a lower strain," from Sauerteig's *Grand Key to Esthetics (Æsthetische Springwurzeln)* drawing "cunning symbolic" wisdom from the household proverb that cleanliness is next to godliness. Into this imaginative aesthetic context he then places the labors of David Friedrich Strauss *(Leben Jesu)* as a technique of nonargumentative deflation: while Strauss and his kin, in the name of rationally analysed historical myths, are essentially de-mythicizing (and in the process destroying) man's imaginative structures, people like Goethe, the German Romantics, and Carlyle himself are mythicizing (and thus creating anew) even the most domestic phenomena; for example, washing the body. By reducing the "sacred word" to analytically perceived patterns of myth, Strauss is dismantling both belief and the apparatus of belief; by translating phenomena into symbolic perception, Carlyle and his guides are re-creating belief and the apparatus of belief and are thus restoring the sacredness of "the word." Thus the chapter leads inevitably toward the "Poet Goethe and German Literature" be-cause, as the French Revolution is the conflagrative symbol, the German poet-philosophers have brought forth (engendered) the procreative symbol of a new sacred religion purified by fire and become "white sunny Light" grander than fire:

> A French Revolution is one phenomenon; as complement and spiritual exponent thereof, a Poet Goethe and German Litera-ture is to me another. The old Secular or Practical World, so to speak, having gone up in fire, is not here the prophecy and dawn of a new Spiritual World, parent of far nobler, wider, new Practical Worlds? A Life of Antique devoutness, Antique veracity and heroism, has again become possible, is again *seen* actual there, for the most modern man. A phenomenon, as quiet as it is, comparable for greatness to no other! 'The great event for the world is, now as always, the arrival in it of a new Wise Man.' Touches there are, be the Heavens ever thanked, of new Sphere-melody; audible once more, in the infinite jar-goning discords and poor scrannel-pipings of the thing called Literature;—priceless there, as the voice of new Heavenly Psalms! Literature, like the old Prayer-Collections of the first

centuries, were it 'well selcted from and burnt,' contains precious things. For Literature, with all its printing-presses, puffing-engines and shoreless deafening triviality, *is* yet 'the Thought of Thinking Souls.' A sacred 'religion,' if you like the name, does live in the heart of that strange froth-ocean, not wholly froth, which we call Literature; and will more and more disclose itself therefrom;—not now as scorching Fire: the red smoky scorching Fire has purified itself into white sunny Light. Is not Light grander than Fire? It is the same element in a state of purity. (III, xv)

Again Carlyle turns to rhetorical magnification, to imaginative awareness experientially induced, to distinguish between very different apprehensions of "the word." The new "word" of Strauss and other "Advanced Liberals" who speak a "new religion" is glossed by juxtaposition to "Poet Goethe and German Literature," where one hears quite another "word," a "word" releasing a "new Sphere-melody." The contrast between a Strauss and a Goethe drawn here is closely parallel to the contrast drawn at the beginning of this article between Engels and Carlyle himself: it is essentially a literary (poetic, imaginative) difference by which fact is dramatically distinguished from an imaginative sense of fact, by which the voice of analytic historicism is distinguished from the mythohistoric "voice of new Heavenly Psalms!"

Language is seen as an Apollo-gift throughout *Past and Present,* powerful for both good and evil. Hence it exists in a state of tension between truth and sham, between poetic veracity, on the one hand, and cant and jargon, on the other. The narrator/commentator is virtually obsessed with language, as if he were determined to shake the dust and cobwebs off of words. Language is a central symbol of the transformational processes of the book: language is everywhere being created.[15] Words themselves are given a past and present: words, like myths, go through a morphological process. They are renewed by being put in touch with their purer origins, by being returned to the root and undegenerate meaning of their poetic birth, while at the same time they are being employed in new senses. Thus they emerge with a double freshness—of antiquity and of neologism. Like the concepts, proverbs, historical facts and fables that they vehiculate, they are being conceived (imagined) afresh. That the whole past must be recovered from the deface-ments of language is the burden of the first chapter of Book IV, "Aristocracies." Between the modern pioneer in the past and the " 'Bible of Universal History' " stands a veritable age of misread-ing, three or four generations of "higher critics" of this Bible of History who have tried, like Strauss, to dismantle the authentic past and reduce it to the size of their own limitations:

> The Dryasdust Philosophisms and enlightened Scepticisms of the Eighteenth Century, historical and other, will have to sur-vive for a while with the Physiologists, as a memorable *Night-mare-Dream*. All this haggard epoch, with its ghastly Doctrines, and death's-head Philosophies 'teaching by example' or other-wise, will one day have become, what to our Moslem friends their godless ages are, 'the Period of Ignorance.' (IV, i)

The " 'Philosophic Historian' " has brought to the past his own godlessness, an "eye [that] sees in all things 'what it brought with it the means of seeing.' He it is who has induced the grotesque con-temporary stand-off: as a culture-apex modernist, he has rejected the past as barbaric and, feeding the inflation of contemporaneous-ness in this "best of all possible worlds," he has blinded himself and his generation to the momentous human misery staring across his philosophical barricades. This it is that makes it so difficult for modern man to get in touch with his more primitive heroisms, the more naked truths of his nature and his universe, why his teaching priesthood is still mumbling over phenomena long extinct and the governing priesthood of the future finds its vocation inaudible: a veil of opaque language hangs over his present, obscuring both his past and his future; a so-called Age of Reason and Englighten-ment, but in fact a godless age and great " 'Period of Ignorance,' " has left him impacted in spiritual obscurity. It is, in a genuine sense, from a prison of plausibility induced by language that mod-ern man must free himself if he would rediscover the faith, truth, and courage with which to renew himself and his civilization.

One of those quickest to recognize what Carlyle was essentially doing—to see to the center of his new transformational apprehen-

sion—was Emerson. In his journal Emerson characterized Carlyle's
efforts in *Past and Present* as "rhetoricising the conspicuous objects";
this is what, in Emerson's view, Carlyle was "doing now for England & Europe." [16] And in his review of the book in the *Dial*, he
again saw it as the conversion of an era into a style: "Carlyle is the
first domestication of the modern system, with its infinity of details, into style. . . . Carlyle is a poet who is altogether too burly in
his frame and habit to submit to the limits of metre. Yet he is full
of rhythm, not only in the perpetual melody of his periods, but in
the burdens, refrains, and grand returns of his sense and music." [17]
It is one's sense of the brilliant aptness of Emerson's judgment here
that disinclines him to be patient with assertions like the following:
"At bottom, Carlyle is not certain whether his book is an artifact
or a social program, visionary literature or self-help manual." [18]
The uncertainty is in the critic, not in Carlyle, who is determined
that the reader shall not only see the topical problem in a new
light, but also develop a new epistemological mode, a new apparatus for perceiving himself and his problems. Hence he deals with
the most heart-rending and discouraging problems facing modern
man, deals with them with vivid particularity, while at the same
time inducing his reader (encouraging him, training him) to perceive these problems through the illuminative structures of myth/
fable/history. [19] The central retrospective episode employed in the
book ("The Ancient Monk"), though valid as history, is also valid
as myth: its lineaments are both singularly true and generically
refractive. Thus it seems to be Carlyle's point that only when history *(both past and present history)* is seen mythically is it energized
and creatively usable because it thereby reaches a level of imaginative self-reproductiveness and perpetuity that makes it genuinely
methodological—a condition of the way in which the imaginative
perceiver percieves. [20]

The style, or "rhetoricising," of which Emerson speaks is clearly
an experiential key to the book: what it "does" to the reader, the
metamorphosis it induces in him, is inevitably a measure of the
book's success, and such affectiveness is largely a function of style.
That it is a tough style, almost every initiate will attest; and the
critics repeatedly speak of the density of its verbal texture and the
elaborateness of its verbal structures. According to John Holloway,

"whatever its defects, it has an elaborate symmetry, and a closely woven rhetorical structure." [21] G. Robert Stange speaks of it as a "prose . . . densely allusive, organized according to an elaborate scheme of interwoven symbols, fiercely magnifying for satiric purposes the impedimenta of everyday life." [22] Such consciously heightened stylization as clearly marks *Past and Present* is itself one of the book's major statements: it represents a way of dealing with drabness of aspect and distress of spirit. But it should be noted that the symmetries and structures that are identifying marks of the book's language strategies are the result, not of careful, conscious, individual monitoring, but of a whole method of and faith in creation: these closely knit, dense, mind-startling patterns emerge from an imaginative energy released rather than from a virtuosity manipulated. These patterns emerge because Carlyle gives them spiritual space in which to emerge. They are not "organized" and "schematic," but surfacings in a prose of imaginative motion, a prose validating the author's premise that chaos rightly looked at reveals order, though a too orderly, rational, schematic way of looking at reality is likely to reveal a phenomenal rather than a noumenal order. *Past and Present* is stylistically organic at the level of conscious faith rather than conscious reason: even its virtuosities parade *as virtuosities* rather than as rhetorical disguises. The insight that Carlyle, through style, contributed to the English-speaking consciousness is essentially his faith that whole realms of excitement can be released by an energy that is not intellective but imaginative, not so much ordered as simply freed.

Let the final point be tied to Emerson too: Carlyle, "giant-like and fabulous," was the first literary domesticator of "the modern system, with its infinity of details." It is, frankly and fully looked at, an astounding assertion: Carlyle is the first modern man of letters, the first English writer to perceive the modern threat of literary irrelevance, the first to do battle with and tame an incipient cultural rebellion against letters. And yet, Emerson's assertion thus extrapolated is confirmed by abundant facts that Emerson could have known nothing of at the time he passed the judgment: not a single imaginative writer in England in the balance of the nineteenth century escaped Carlyle's influence; the very sense of their role as writers was deeply affected by Carlyle, especially the

Carlyle of *Past and Present,* in the cases of Tennyson, Dickens, Browning, Ruskin, Arnold, Meredith, Mrs. Gaskell, William Morris, and a dozen others; though the Victorian aesthetic was chiefly articulated by Ruskin, Arnold, and Pater, it was shaped, deep into the twentieth century, in the unwithdrawing presence of Carlyle.

Why? Because, especially in *Past and Present,* Carlyle showed that, even in a nigh-intolerable present, his ultimate faith lay with the sacred word of a conscientious, an engaged, literature. The renovation of man and his social institutions was an acute contemporary need, as it was an acute need perennially. And the chief hope Carlyle saw for getting that renovation started in his own time was through the culture of individual imaginations as a way of rising above an "infinity of details" and seeing the "modern system" for what it in fact was—a dehumanized, denatured machinery of systematic injustice and a threat perennially to every generation unless it keeps in touch with human possibilities as mirrored in those literary artifacts which see man under his generic aspects. What we have in *Past and Present* is literature (Carlyle's) made of literature (Jocelin's), and what we are promised is literature available for transformation, a sort of evolving literary organicism which is a highlight of our imaginative past (e.g., the Bible, Ovid, Shakespeare, Milton) and a model for our literary future. So what Carlyle does here is very complex and very literary: he does not simply say that the past is instructive for the present in the shaping of the future; nor does he simply say that culture in its societal sense is organic, evolving itself out of itself, absorbing elements of its medium; he says that once we get in touch with our imaginative realities, the past *is* the future in the sacrament of the now; then spiritual realities merge, energize themselves, reach out in all possible directions, and Space and Time do verily become modes of consciousness. Carlyle is doing through Jocelin's Chronicle, for his purposes, what Pater will do four decades later with Apuleius' story of Cupid and Psyche, namely, make literature out of literature and in so doing tell us something indispensable about the uses of the imagination. He will thus verify Arnold's theme that as religion becomes less and less, poetry will become more and more because the genius of our culture has embodied our unconscious poetry in our conscious religion; and as the "facts" of our religion (hardened poetry) fail us, our living poetry will reassert itself and enable us to save our souls.

Notes

1. *The Letters of George Meredith,* collected and edited by his son (London: Constable & Ltd., 1912), II, 332.
2. "On Some of the Characteristics of Modern Poetry," *The Englishman's Magazine,* August 1831. Reprinted in *Victorian Prose and Poetics,* ed. W. E. Houghton and G. R. Stange, 2d ed. (Boston: Houghton Mifflin, 1968), pp. 848-860. Carlyle demands comparison with Turner perhaps more even than with Rembrandt.
3. See "Editor's Introduction," *The Condition of the Working Class in England,* ed. and trans. by W. O. Henderson and W. H. Chaloner (New York: Macmillan, 1958), p. x.
4. What we have here is an ironic collision of empiricisms: both the classical economists and their critics (here Carlyle and Engels) claimed to have built their generalizations on observed behavior.
5. P. 335.
6. The reference is particularly but not exclusively to the essay on "Style." The following quotations in the rest of this paragraph are from Pater's essay, "Style."
7. *Sartor Resartus* is here accepted as a novel.
8. The speaker in Carlyle's text is not normed against other speakers, as is the case in *The Ring and the Book;* and measured fallibility has not been established as an expectation of *Past and Present* as it has been in Browning's poem.
9. *In Memoriam, Great Expectations,* and *Apologia Pro Vita Sua* are obvious examples.
10. Later in the 1840s, Emily Brontë does this, very much in the manner of Carlyle, in *Wuthering Heights.* The text of *Past and Present* followed below is that of the Centenary Edition, ed. H. D. Traill.
11. The phrase is R. P. Blackmur's.
12. *The "Metamorphoses" of Ovid,* trans. Mary M. Innes (Harmondsworth: Penguin, 1955), pp. 32-33.
13. It is worth noting, too, that a knowledge of Ovid is shown as part of the education of Jocelin.
14. Thus his running banter with Dryasdust. It is not Dryasdust's facts that distress the narrator/commentator of *Past and Present;* it is his wholly unimaginative way of apprehending those facts. See also note 20 below.
15. John Holloway has some discussion of this matter. See *The Victorian Sage: Studies in Argument* (London: Macmillan, 1953), pp. 41-47.
16. *Journals and Miscellaneous Notebooks of Ralph Waldo Emerson,* ed. W. H. Gilman and J. E. Parsons (Cambridge, Mass.: The Belknap Press of Harvard University Press, 1970), VIII, 408.

17. *"Past and Present." Emerson's Complete Works* (London: The Waverley Book Co. Ltd., 1893), XII, 247-248.

18. Albert J. LaValley, *Carlyle and the Idea of the Modern* (New Haven and London: Yale University Press, 1968), p. 230. Commitment to the book's aesthetic orientation redirects our thoughts about another subject peremptorily dealt with by LaValley: "the most reactionary idea of the book: Carlyle's opposition to democracy and to extending the franchise" (p. 228). Carlyle recognized and asserted repeatedly that democracy was the modern inevitability—that democracy was an irreversible historical imperative of his time and of the immediate future. What he is attempting to do, then, is not to reverse history, but to enlarge and chasten perception. The problem with democracy is not democracy, but false perceptions of democracy—how it reflects human nature, what it can in fact do for modern man. It is the democracy of the second-raters that Carlyle is attacking, the democracy of the *porro unum* school, the democracy of the shibboleth-throwers, of Morrison's Pill-pushers.

19. Metaphorically, emblematically, typologically.

20. The author's satiric quarrel with Dryasdust is relevant here. Carlyle in fact repeatedly uses the facts set forth by Dryasdust; it is the statistical historian's ignorance of the "soul" that inhabits the people and epochs with which he meticulously deals that draws Carlyle's banter. Dryasdust has been an efficient machine in the field of data-collection; but lacking the historical imagination, he lacks the one essential quality for making those data significant. It is an ironic paradox: man needs a sense of the past to gain perspective on himself, and history as a learned discipline has in fact emerged in part in response to this pressing need. But it has emerged blind and unavailing to man in his modern travail because it has been subsumed to his condition of imaginative myopia. It is that condition that provides Carlyle with his peculiar literary apostolate.

21. Holloway, p. 46.

22. "Refractions of *Past and Present*", in *Carlyle Past and Present: A Collection of New Essays*, ed. K. J. Fielding and Rodger L. Tarr (London: Vision, 1976), p. 106.

3.

The Tennysonian Imagination

Alfred Tennyson was not a poetic theorist in any significant meaning of that term. He did not, like Wordsworth, tirelessly hone an aesthetic vocabulary or shape his poems experimentally around theoretical concepts.[1] Whereas the two-volume Blake concordance has more than three hundred entries on *imagination* and *image* and their closest variants, the Tennyson concordance has twenty-seven, only three on *imagination* itself, compared with Blake's eighty-five.[2] And there is no indication that the Tennyson letters, when completely available in printed form, will reveal any urgent poetic theorizing comparable to that of Keats. Tennyson was removed by two generations from the imposing eighteenth-century tradition of aesthetics which was still in place when Blake, Wordsworth, and Coleridge founded a new theory to go with a new poetic practice, and he did not need to redo what the Romantics had done so conscientiously and so well. Moreover, for Tennyson and his literary generation, the most demanding need was weighted somewhat differently from what it had been for the Romantics: though they, too, aspired to create a new poetry and to revitalize "the great vine of *Fable*" (*Timbuctoo*, 218),[3] they worked under increasing pressure, much of it self-induced, to be both innovative and relevant. Arnold's inaugural lecture as Professor of Poetry at Oxford was essentially the confirmation of a point of view that had been current for a generation: relevance is the primary test of modernism in poetry.[4] All the force and intensity of Carlyle had focused on it, and from his Cambridge days Tennyson had never doubted it, though he sometimes saw (or perhaps imagined) its demands as too imperious and probed repeatedly the inescapable temptations to turn away from it.

The hieratic character of the Romantic poet was not at issue, nor was the solemn sacredness of his trust. Indeed, the Spirit of Fable in *Timbuctoo* enunciates a bardic faith that is quintessentially Romantic:

> "There is no mightier Spirit than I to sway
> The heart of man: and teach him to attain
> By shadowing forth the Unattainable;
> And step by step to scale that mighty stair
> Whose landing-place is wrapt about with clouds
> Of glory' of Heaven."
>
> (191-196)

And it is quintessentially Tennysonian too: in *Idylls of the King* he is still "shadowing forth the Unattainable" through fable, and *In Memoriam* is the myth of a *persona* who discovers, in the process of working through his imaginative fiction, new foundations for an old belief, "That men may rise on stepping-stones / of their dead selves to higher things" (*In Memoriam*, 3-4). Thus, James Heffernan's climactic summary of the "core" of Wordsworth's poetic faith is just as applicable to the long curve of Tennyson's poetic career as it is to Wordsworth's: "Seizing the infinite through the finite, the eternal through the temporal, and the invisible through the visible, the exercise of imagination was for Wordsworth an act of faith, a mode of apprehension that yielded 'the sensuous incarnation' of 'ethereal and transcendent' truths."[5] It is a poetic faith that, allowing for the secularization and deflation of language, persists right through Yeats, Eliot, Stevens, and Lowell as the archetypal Romantic faith.

Still, there is a difference which we all sense between the Romantic and the Victorian imprints on English poetry, and since it is not a difference of essential faith, it is likely to be a difference of practice and the motive for practice. Here again *Timbuctoo* provides useful guidance. The spokesman for Romantic faith speaks also for Romantic anxiety:

> "Oh City! oh latest Throne! where I was raised
> To be a mystery of loveliness
> Unto all eyes, the time is well-nigh come
> When I must render up this glorious home
> To keen *Discovery:* soon yon brilliant towers
> Shall darken with the waving of her wand;
> Darken, and shrink and shiver into huts,
> Black specks amid a waste of dreary sand,
> Low-built, mud-walled, Barbarian settlements.
> How changed from this fair City!"
>
> (236-245, Tennyson's emphasis)

This penetrating sense of the doomed imagination has a sharp new edge to it. To the lamentation over the final passing of the last frontier of the fabulous is added the clear recognition of a new and genuine magic, not more true, but more powerful to insinuate its images into the mind of modern man. *"Discovery"* is the new imaginative imperative, "keen" and in charge of the future; and with its ascendancy, miracles will have to be redefined, truth will require new bases (bases more like those implicit in Goethe's question, *"But is it true, is it true for me?"*) , and the poetic imagination, if it would be affective, must find new functional modes.

Despite Tennyson's inclination to shrug off this undergraduate patch-poem, *Timbuctoo* is a foundation-text for the student of the Victorian imagination, a paradigm of poetic perception and procedure. It is a process poem in which an imaginary emblematic *persona* moves through a mythic action by which his whole sense of himself, of his world, and of his role in that world is altered. And so, whatever reasons Tennyson may have had for dissatisfaction with it—its gross technical imperfections, its youthful inflation, its seeming exposure of self-measure, the self-intimidating promise of

Miltonic high seriousness implicit in it—*Timbuctoo* is the prototypical Tennyson poem, the imaginative configuration upon which his whole canon works endless variations. The metaphors vary, and each fiction has its own curve and terminus, but *Timbuctoo* is "an image of the mighty world" in one of its specialized aspects. The fictional structure, as distinct from the special fiction, is renewed in *In Memoriam, Maud,* and *Idylls of the King;* and it is a simple pattern of that used by Swinburne in *On the Cliffs* and *A Nympholept* and by Pater in *Marius the Epicurean.*

The speaker of *Timbuctoo* is characterizing a present in terms of processive stages in a vividly recollected past. The moment at which the poem begins is multiply twinned—East-West, twi-light, fused appearances, memory within memory. It is a sacred moment in which the consciousness opens up to yet more sacred depths of retrospection:

> much I mused on legends quaint and old
> Which whilome won the hearts of all on Earth
> Toward their brightness, even as flame draws air;
> But had their being in the heart of Man
> As air is the life of flame: and thou wert *then*
> A centred glory-circled *Memory,*
> Divinest Atlantis. . . .
>
> > (16-22, emphasis added)

The consciousness thus imaginatively engendered is transformed to a state of ardent expostulation, a prayer of praise, and a cry for enlightenment. The epiphanic moment thereby induced leads to two sharply contrasting awarenesses—that the speaker's " 'sense is clogged with dull mortality/ [His] spirit fettered with the bond of clay . . .' " (81-82), but that, once released, the spirit, in a jubilee of sight, sound, and "piercing, trackless, thrilling thoughts" (113) perceives reality, both in its minutest and in its most cosmic proportions, at "an unimagined depth / And harmony" (106-107):

> My thoughts which long had grovelled in the slime
> Of this dull world, like dusky worms which house
> Beneath unshaken waters, but at once

Upon some Earth-awakening day of Spring
Do pass from gloom to glory, and aloft
Winnow the purple, bearing on both sides
Double display of starlit wings which burn,
Fanlike and fibred, with intensest bloom;
Even so my thoughts, erewhile so low, now felt
Unutterable buoyancy and strength
To bear them upward through the trackless fields
Of undefined existence far and free.

(146-157)

It is in this spiritual / imaginative ambience (lyrical / epical) and after having seen Timbuctoo at its inner, most brilliant depths that the speaker gets his chastening instruction from the Spirit of Fable. He has been anointed in his bardic role—

"I have given *thee*
To understand my presence, and to feel
My fulness; I have filled thy lips with power.
I have raised thee nigher to the spheres of Heaven,
Man's first, last home: and thou with ravished sense
Listenest the lordly music flowing from
The illimitable years"—

(209-215, Tennyson's emphasis)

and then he has been informed of a new dispensation in the affairs of man which has left him "alone on Calpe, and the Moon / Had fallen from the night, and all was dark!" (247-248). Those are the resonances of the personal and mythic past and that is the carefully defined contemporary situation with which modern imaginative man (say, the Victorian or the modern poet) must cope.

If we can assume that an awareness like that defined by *Timbuctoo* constitutes a serious effort on Tennyson's part to pinpoint an altered cultural condition for imaginative man and if we can hold steady in our view that it signals a new weighting rather than a difference of dramatic degree or of kind, then we have a basis on which to consider the difference in practice and the motive for practice among the literary Victorians. By inheriting the peculiarities of their age, they had inherited the obligation to modernize literature by making their own literary creations and man's whole historical and literary past relevant to those peculiarities. They did not need to narrow literary experience to mere topicality, but neither could they ignore the fact that, to the popular imagination, contemporary relevance, at first flush at least, tended to mean contemporary subject matter. That was, admittedly, a weakness of the popular imagination, but it provided writers like Carlyle, Tennyson, Browning, Dickens, and Arnold a very special opportunity that left defining marks on much of their work: by dealing with contemporary topics emblematically, seeing even current events *sub specie aeternitatis,* they could both catch the popular ear and transform the popular imagination, thus putting one of the peculiarities of the age to constructive imaginative uses.

Again Matthew Arnold is a just indicator: *The Function of Criticism at the Present Time* (1864 / 1865) is built in part on Arnold's assumption about the immediate prospects for poetry, and his effort to clear away some of the cultural debris which impeded a full creative flow suggests that, in an age stammering before, or doing such rough justice to, an infinity of details, purifying men's perceptual powers was also a primary function of the contemporary poet, as it was a function of both critic and poet to make men more fruitfully available, not just to some future creative renaissance, but also to the present and to such grand literary epochs of the past as, being perennially relevant, were perennially modern. In the parabolic manner of poetry, Tennyson had dealt with the subject in its poetic aspects almost twenty years earlier: *The Princess* (1847) is Tennyson's *The Function of Poetry at the Present Time.* In *The Princess,* Tennyson's primary concern is to show the relevance of the literary imagination to an acute contemporary problem—women's education and the battle of the sexes—and he pursues this primary literary object in such a rich variety of ways that his characterization of the poem as "A Medley" has its principal reference point in the multiple maneuvers of the imagination itself.

At the center of *The Princess* is a frozen imaginative artifact, grand and tragically faulted. It is the creation—the translation of a myth or illusion into image and action—of a heroic rebel against the injustice of the community, and behind its façade of an im-

pressively justified high-mindedness, there are disquieting remnants of revenge and echoes of the literary formulation in which
the rebel against community got imaginative exposure, the revenge
tragedy. Princess Ida, the female protagonist, has in fact "builded
better than [she] knew," and therefore dimensions of her authentic
self which have been submerged in the furor of her fantastical
adventure (her false mythic action) gradually and painfully reemerge and reproportion her perspective on life before irremediable catastrophe overtakes her and all those she touches. That
authentic self—the "heart" that, according to Gamma, her mother
was so sure she had—has been preserved in a shrunken state by her
steady affection for Psyche; but she has absorbed more than a little
of the stern schooling of Lady Blanche, who has played to her the
role of Sir Austin Feverel, her frighteningly plausible system of
education being rooted in hurt and the hatred of her husband
extrapolated to include all males. The child Aglaïa casts some
warm illumination into the imperious rigidities of Ida's consciousness, and the various appeals of her father, her brother, the soul-
mate of her youth, Lady Psyche, and her memoried mother,
coming on the heels of the shattering of her imaginative artifact,
gradually enable her to reknit herself to a remote but healthier
personal past; and her slow surrender to her love for the Prince and
his new-old myth of humble creative harmony of the sexes gives
promise, at least, of her reconciliation to a vastly altered perception of the future. Thus, Princess Ida combines in a fresh, original
way the haughty monism of the soul in *The Palace of Art* and the
complex, delusive self-myth of Guinevere; and though the fundamentally comedic character of the poem saves her from the mad
derangement of the one and the austere tragic apprehension of the
other, both possibilities, in what might be a slightly altered fiction,
are seeded in the imaginative consciousness of the reader.

Thus, women's education and the equality of the sexes is an
urgent contemporary topic transformed into a metaphor of contemporaneous topicality itself, placed by the poem in the larger
perspective of imaginative perception; and the parable (fiction,
myth, story-line) in which it is configured is absorbed by a larger
parable at whose center is the more general subject of the games
people play in confronting their problems and the function of po-

etry in casting a "white sunny Light" among the dark shadows of
human self-deception and manipulation. All of the chief characters
are more or less imprisoned in a myth (Ida, the Prince's father,
Cyril, Lady Blanche) or are fellow-travelers in someone else's myth
(Gamma, Lady Psyche, Florian, Melissa). The Prince himself is a
partial exception, and this is what enables him, though at the price
of utmost self-jeopardy, to function as a metaphor of solvency in
the poem. He cannot prevent the collision of rigid myths enacted
in the metaphoric battle, which includes the traditional battle of
the sexes but reaches far beyond it; but he does embody a chivalric
renmant that decentralizes the contention and keeps the saving
option open. The Prince's curse is his ultimate glory: not knowing
the "shadow from the substance" (I, 9), he cannot freeze perception into an icon of the aggressive self; and though he "come[s] to
fight with shadows and to fall" (I, 10), it is a fortunate fall, and
such hope for human renewal as the fable promises is centered
there. The "weird seizures" which he experiences are his form of
what Samuel Butler in *The Way of All Flesh* will describe as the
strategy of fainting: when the perceptual conflict becomes insoluble, his psyche retreats into catalepsy instead of leaping into confrontal psychic action, and thus he is enabled to await the better
event. His love for Ida, rooted in a romantic adolescence of which
she has been deprived, is too chivalrous to allow him to condemn
her, but neither is he blind to the grotesque disproportions which
the Amazonian role which she has assumed has worked in her
humanness. As the poem reaches its climax, the Prince and the
Princess move toward each other from widely displaced points of
romantic vagueness and doctrinaire solidity. Both have matured
toward a center of vulnerable but authentic humanness, weak as
yet but full-bodied. His "haunting sense of hollow shows" (VII,
328) has been killed, and she has told herself some truths harsher
even than those of the community injustice against which she had
rebelled. But this resolution would have been impossible without
their individual strengths and susceptibilities and without that
"spiritual love [that] acts not nor can exist / Without Imagination . . ." (*The Prelude,* XIV, 188-189).

The outer parable of *The Princess* is the parable of poetry's way,
and its burden is the function of poetry at the present time. It is a

complex interweaving of imaginative strategies; and though it is indispensable to a serious consideration of the Tennysonian imagination, only the broad outlines of its real presence in the poem can be given in the present context.[6]

The Princess begins and ends with literature. The inspiration and character of the piece are generated by "the gallant glorious chronicle" which the poet-*persona* finds at Vivian-place, in a manner reminiscent of the effects of Jocelin's Chronicle on Carlyle's *Past and Present;* and its climactic imaginative anchorage is in *Paradise Lost,* prophetic of that poem's place in Dickens's *Great Expectations:*

> "O we will walk the world,
> Yoked in all exercise of noble end,
> And so through these dark gates across the wild
> That no man knows."
>
> (VII, 339-342)

Thus, a central consciousness of the work is that poetry is organic and, like the past, " 'Melts mist-like into this bright hour' " (VII, 334). Further, *The Princess* exemplifies metaphorically the evolution of a canonical poetic text: the "sevenfold story," itself a fundamentally aesthetic act, results in a single written poetic composition which is an amalgamation of seven oral contributions to a parabolic tale rooted in an inherited literary tradition, a noble and imaginative past. By combining this device of the "sevenfold story" with the fairy-tale, the poet does something highly imaginative: he draws into his fluid structure one of the chief literary renewals of the century—the Kunstmärchen inventiveness of the German Romantics, by which folk-tales are put to the most sophisticated literary uses—and he fuses the reading act with the writing act. The "mouth-to-mouth" method of the symbolic community creation requires that the participating listeners (readers) give a writer's attentiveness to the reading act into which they have been drawn and in which they must in turn function as writers, building on what they inherit; and the fairy-tale, being the freest form of the literary imagination to which people of all age groups and backgrounds are most wholly available, is as nearly innate to the way human creativity works as a literary form can be and is thus

a real mouthful

the form in which the reading act and the writing act seem to merge in the human imagination. By placing a child at the center of this imaginative community creation, the poet employs yet another discovery of his century—the usability of the child to the literary imagination; and this crucial metaphor, like the fairy-tale form, has deep-flowing psychological implications, drawing frozen contentious adults (both the tellers and the told-of) toward those "spots of time" when reality was still in solution and they were building their reality structures in a free, open, imaginative, and generous way. The problem of neither parable is childish, of course: both the reconciliation of the sexes and the indispensability of genuine imaginative awareness are matters of utmost seriousness. But poetry is an art, not an argument; it tells its truths obliquely, creating an imaginative ambience through which the apparatus of perception can be purified and strengthened rather than confronting arguments argumentatively and becoming thereby a dimension of the problem instead of a perspective on solutions. Thus the "strange diagonal" in which the canonical poet finally moves between the male-"mockers" and the female-"realists" is a metaphor of form, an imaginative realization that if the serious implications of a subject like women's equality, generative of so much confrontal intensity of both the derisive and the fanatical sort, are to have any chance of surfacing, poetry must function in poetry's way, and the poet must look carefully to the formal structures (the *personae,* the myths, the actions) by which, through a technique of indirection, he hopes to bring brightness, joy, and bloom to human confusions. The poet moves in a "strange diagonal" in yet another sense in *The Princess.* Although he employs a fairy-tale in which there is a formal collision of myths, *The Princess* is not a myth-poem as such. Like "the gallant glorious chronicle," it is "Half-legend, half-historic," and both the subject of the inner parable and the carefully designed Prologue and Conclusion root it deeply in the here and now. By providing full and explicit exposure of the way in which the imagination translates topicality into fable, by thus moving diagonally between fact and an imaginative sense of fact, between history and myth, the poet brings all history and all myth into creative relationships and illustrates what the contemporary poet and the contemporary man can do in dealing with the subject matter or problems of his own or any time. Finally, both the intercalary songs, added to the third edition (1850), and the blank-verse lyrics, part of the original publication, support in a fundamental way the perception that the function of poetry at the present time is the poet's primary concern in *The Princess*. The chief relevance of the intercalary songs is much larger than simply to the topical subject matter of the inner fable. They touch lyrically the process of imaginative restoration in men and women generally, a process that is germane to all the metaphors of stress and conflict which human beings may encounter in life. The blank-verse lyrics all center around Princess Ida and, through their individual character and her reaction to or relationship with them, figure as crucial aesthetic measurers of her imaginative transformation. For example, the "volume of the Poets" (VII, 159) from which she reads "Now sleeps the crimson petal, now the white" and "Come down, O maid" enables her to break through to the true truth (VII, 212-230) and, by leading her imaginatively from a painful imprisonment to a renewing self-disclosure, makes it possible for her to save both her sanity and her soul.

Even thus sketchily analyzed, Tennyson's *The Princess* emerges as one of the crucial literary texts to the student of both the Victorian and the Tennysonian imagination. It converts into poetic parable both an acute contemporary topic and the larger question of topicality itself. And in so doing, it fully justifies at least three generalizations: that the Victorian poet recognized and accepted the inescapable relevance of the importunate issues of his age to his work as a poet; that this new subject matter compelled him thoroughly to reexamine the imaginative structures that had come down to him and to adapt them to the imaginative uses to which they must now be put; and that he was yet determined to preserve his sacred trust by doing poetry's work in poetry's way.

As *The Princess* moves debate into fairy-tale that gradually develops sublimely epical resonances, *In Memoriam* moves the pastoral elegy in the direction of the epic. It begins with an epic invocation, finds its chief analogue in Dante's *Divina Commedia*, expands its time-frame to the symbolic dimensions of a cycle of human life, takes as its theme the discovery of new spiritual foundations for the race, places its hero (naked existential man) under the stern, relentless patronage of Urania, the heavenly one, and centers its contest in the commonest and most imposing of all human mysteries, Death. But what makes *In Memoriam* so imaginatively extraordinary is the singular way in which the poet has located the dynamism within the poetic text itself through the creation of a poet-*persona* who has a disposition to believe, an imaginative capacity to transform one order of reality into another order of reality, and "A centred glory-circled Memory" (*Timbuctoo*, 21) by which all the manifestations of human experience can be tested for their authenticity and magnitude. Having done this—having, as Arnold said, taken "a fitting action" and penetrated himself "with the feeling of its situations" [7]—the poet can allow the poem to take on the appearance of working out its own curve through the manipulations (the forward and backward motions, the looped circles) of its own inner consciousness. Thus, the epic outreaches of the poem have an entirely personal, confessional center, the *persona* being himself a lyric poet who lets his feelings, thoughts, strategies come as they will in "Short swallow-flights of song" (XLVIII, 15); and *In Memoriam* invests Everyman's most internalized problems with the full dynamic range of the literary imagination—lyric, dramatic, epic-narrative.

If *The Princess* is a self-conscious commentary by a poet on the method and importance of a poet's work, *In Memoriam* is not. Here there is no parable of poetry's way other than that implicit in every poem that is in itself a "way." Nor is the poet-*persona* of *In Memoriam* so specialized a figure that he has doubtful relevance to the nonpoet. He is, rather, a poet-figure in the Wordsworthian tradition—"a man speaking to men, a man . . . endowed with more lively sensibility, more enthusiasm and tenderness, who has a greater knowledge of human nature, and a more comprehensive soul. . . ." [8] But Tennyson is very careful to bring the level of experience and the level of the language with which the poet-*persona* reveals his feelings, thoughts, and strategies to as common a basis in identification and comprehensibility as the imaginative processing intended by the poem will allow; and although the *In Memoriam* stanza is a work of the simplest but most exquisite artifice, it brings that artifice as close to an illusion of prosaic action and self-reflection as the highly wrought artifice will itself sustain.

In Memoriam is supposed to function for its reader, and that functional quality is a dimension of its imaginative integrity. The function of poetry is not its explicit subject, but it is its imaginatively monitoring goal.

At the heart of *In Memoriam* is a theme of creative fluidity—not perpetual indecision, but a matured willingness not to settle for even the most refined dogmatic solutions available from outside the organically processed self, but to await the better event, the ultimate illumination within. This theme is fused with the poem's revelations of the organic use of the imagination, and thus *In Memoriam* embodies the story-line (plot, mythic action) of a gifted but representative *persona* whose profound personal needs gradually enable him to "rise on stepping-stones / Of [his] dead [self] to higher things" by drawing on his imaginative resources and, through the purification and strengthening thereof, to discover a truly dependable faith in a strengthened and purified self. Being an organically evolutionary process (and, in its total curve, an imaginative critique of the more mechanical evolutionary theories current at the time), the *persona*-fiction of *In Memoriam* is built on a metaphor of indispensable if indefinable relevance: every thought and feeling that the speaker has under varying degrees of stress or momentary relief from stress is a strategy of self-definition and survival, and the poem's hundred and thirty-one cantos are emblems of a process that is (or could be) as long as life itself. But it is also an aesthetic structure, and by the rules and privileges of art it employs various *loci* by which its process as an art-piece is measured. Tennyson speaks of the three Christmas seasons and of the nine natural groupings by which the poem is ordered, and one can readily point to XCV and CIII as the climactic cantos of the poem and to cantos CIV-CXXXI as the poem's grand mythic dilation. These are indispensable *loci,* certainly, and any commentator dealing expansively with *In Memoriam* would devote considerable attention to each of them.[9] But there are three sequences in the poem's *Bildung,* or *persona*-formation, that rather clearly reveal the refinement of the imagination with which the poet is dealing and hence the delicacy of the fusion of imagination with the search for solutions to the profoundest human problems.

In the first sequence (**XXXVI-XXXVII**), the poet-*persona* provokes a stern rebuke from his chief patroness Urania by his temptation to panic in his search for a truly authentic personal faith and to settle instead for that offered by the Christian gospel. It is, in effect, a temptation to despair both of discovering for oneself the "truths" that "in manhood darkly join" and of the strength for that quest of "poetic thought." Urania calls this mere "prating" and presumption and instructs him instead to stay true to himself, an earthly poet, and close to nature:

> "Go down beside thy native rill,
>   On thy Parnassus set thy feet,
>   And hear thy laurel whisper sweet
> About the ledges of the hill."
> (XXXVII, 5-8)

In the next sequence (XLVII-XLIX), there is a shift in the metaphors of presumption, and the "prating," though more personal and subjective, is also more abstract and inflated. The speaker has moved away from the homelier gospel revelation and focuses instead on the subtleties of scholastic idealism, invoking a variation on the spiritual imagination. The result is apt enough imaginatively, but it is also a bit pagan and a bit absurd:

> Eternal form shall still divide
> The eternal soul from all beside;
> And I shall know him when we meet:
>
> And we shall sit at endless feast,
>   Enjoying each the other's good:
>   What vaster dream can hit the mood
> Of Love on earth?
> (XLVII, 6-12)

But the resonances of the word "dream" measure the distance the speaker has moved; and although Urania's rebuke is still implicit in the self-redaction of canto XLVIII, it has now been internalized and is more trustworthily operative within the transforming self. As a result, he has become genuinely available to the imaginative

fancy working within his consciousness and to the whole cluster of
forces—art, nature, "the schools"—by which the human imagination has traditionally been nurtured, purified, and, from time to
time, miraculously magnified. The third sequence (LIV-LVIII) is a
rather stark miniature of the whole process of *In Memoriam*. Here
the word "dream" (LIV, 17; LVI, 21) is critiqued so brutally that
it releases an avalanche of devastating possibilities—nature shriek-
ing against man's fantasies, man "sealed within the iron hills,"
man a presumptuous rebel and, by his self-deceptions, made inferior to "Dragons of the prime / That tare each other in their
slime" (LVI, 22-23). Here the poet's "earthly Muse," his Melpomene, panics in despair; and the poet-*persona* himself tries to
soothe her, while admitting, with a "terribly pathetic" allusion to
Catullus, [10] that he "shall pass; [his] work will fail" (LVII, 8). He
has again grown measurably stronger, bringing inner imaginative
steadiness even to the most cataclysmic imaginings; and thus he is
susceptible both to Urania's gentler chiding for having broken, in
fitful moments, the peace of those who have not moved as he has
moved and to her firmer reassurance:

> The high Muse answered: "Wherefore grieve
>   Thy brethren with a fruitless tear?
>   Abide a little longer here,
> And thou shalt take a nobler leave."
>
> (LVIII, 9-12)

No archetypal ideological contention has been resolved, certainly;
but the poet-*persona*'s psyche has reached a turning point and has
begun to draw its strength from within and to be dependent upon
a renewed self in which love and knowledge can fruitfully merge
and where he can ultimately build a serviceable understanding—a
personal myth—of Nature, God, and the Self.

The imagination is clearly the indispensable transformational
resource of the poet-*persona* of *In Memoriam*, but it is not apprehended theoretically or abstractly by either Tennyson or his
poet-creation; and although one might legitimately and successfully extract a theory of the imagination from the language and
episodes of the poem, such definition was not the poet's primary

concern. The very fiction of the poem implies that every man has his own degree of imagination and that his most pressing need is for the faith in that degree of imagination that will enable it to grow stronger and become the inner foundation upon which he will build, not dreams, but the myths that will sustain coherent beliefs even in invisible realities. The word "imagination" is used twice in *In Memoriam:* "Imaginations calm and fair" (XCIV, 10) and "To feel once more, in placid awe, / The strong imagination roll" (CXXII, 5-6). Calm, fairness of prospect, awe-inspiring insight, and strength—those are the qualities that the imagination, believed in and nurtured, can bring to modern life; and for a man given neither to despair nor to fantastic dreams, it is, in the age of "keen *Discovery*," the chief personal hope.

"imag" as used in IM

If, as has been implied thus far, Tennyson came very early to the conclusion that the crucial need of his time (or perhaps of any time) was for the purification and strengthening of man's imagination and that one way to do this was to bring the reader to a new or reiterated awareness of the emblematic or even archetypal character of his profoundest contemporary problems, then one would expect the Tennyson canon as a whole to manifest that sort of imaginative coherence which a fundamental and unwavering motive would give it. And such is in fact the case: the representative pieces in the corpus of Tennyson's work mirror all the other pieces, just as the individual cantos of *In Memoriam* and *Maud* mirror all the other cantos and the individual idylls mirror *Idylls of the King* as a whole. Even the occasional pieces and verse exercises are only partial exceptions: they reflect the cast of his mind and his unwavering attentiveness to craftsmanship. Tennyson was one of the most inventive of poets, constantly enlarging his framework and keeping his chord finely tuned and full-bodied, building close pairings, mighty opposites, and infinite variations in-between; but the threads that pass out beyond one design are rewoven in other designs until a grand tapestry emerges which can never be completed, and the threads then pass out beyond the whole. Like Arthur, Guinevere, and Lancelot, they are often absent but always present too; and like the Arthurian fiction, there is no ultimate closure.

The unity of effect in the Tennyson canon derives from several

chief sources, and the three most important ones were identified by
Arthur Hallam in his review of *Poems, Chiefly Lyrical* (1830): Tennyson's "vivid, picturesque delineation of objects, and the peculiar
skill with which he holds all of them *fused* . . . in a medium of
strong emotion"; "the variety of his lyrical measures, and exquisite
modulation of harmonious words and cadences to the swell and
fall of the feelings expressed"; and "the elevated habits of thought,
implied in these compositions, and imparting a mellow soberness
of tone. . . ." [11] But the variety implicit even in these sources of an
over-all unity of effect is sustained through the strong symbolist
flow in Tennyson's poetry, by which he sought to make "the
thought within the image . . . much more than any one interpretation" and which led him to characterize poetry as being "like
shot-silk with many glancing colours"; [12] and it is sustained also
through two other characteristics noted by Hallam: "his luxuriance of imagination, and at the same time his control over it";
and "his power of embodying himself in ideal characters, or rather
moods of character, with such extreme accuracy of adjustment,
that the circumstances of the narration seem to have a natural
correspondence with the predominant feeling, and, as it were, to be
evolved from its assimilative force." [13]

This rich variety within an over-all unity of effect gives us a
practical key both to Tennyson's basic concept of the imagination
and to the chief formula by which he translated that basic concept
into the practical work of making poems; and while it would be
disastrous to pounce on either the concept or the formula as if they
were, for the poet or the critic, childish simplifications of one of the
most complex processes known to man, their relevance to an ultimate understanding of the Tennysonian poetic experience is undeniable.

By dividing "luxuriance of imagination" and the "power of embodying himself in ideal characters" into the two primary but separate characteristics of Tennyson's poetry, Hallam is implying a
distinction between the imagination itself and Tennyson's chief
mode of imaginative implementation. By imagination, Hallam
means "the ruling passion of the whole mind," [14] that "leading
sentiment in the poet's mind" [15] which enables him to conceive
"every part" of a poem "with reference to some other part, and in
subservience to the idea of the whole." [16] It is the power of "perfect

keeping" that "aids the illusion of thought, and steadies its contemplation of the complete picture," the source of a poem's unity in variety by which it makes its "final disclosure." [17] The poet's mode of imaginative implementation, on the other hand, his translation of this basic concept into an imagination-centered poem, is implicit in Hallam's comment on *Supposed Confessions of a Second-Rate Sensitive Mind:* "Ordinary tempers build up fortresses of opinion on one side or another; they will see only what they choose to see; the distant glimpse of such an agony as is here brought out to view, is sufficient to keep them for ever in illusions, voluntarily raised at first, but soon trusted in with full reliance as inseparable parts of self." [18] Whether or not Hallam's interpretation of the poem's ultimate intention and effect is right and whether or not one finds that intention edifying, the illustration is still perfectly apt: the poet has created a *persona*-centered poetic fiction in which there is a "final disclosure," through the metaphor of a poem, of an integrated reflection of his "whole mind's" "ruling passion" and has thereby lent his imagination out as an affective pressure on the imagination (ruling passion, leading sentiment) of the reader. By "embodying himself" in an "ideal character," he has illuminated a fragment of reality in a meaningful way through a momentary flash of his own imagination.

[margin note: function of T's persona]

Two very brief passages from Tennyson himself bear upon these issues in a crucial way. The first is from Part II of *The Lover's Tale,* a portion of the poem written about the same time as *Timbuctoo:*

> Alway the inaudible invisible thought,
> Artificer and subject, lord and slave,
> Shaped by the audible and visible,
> Moulded the audible and visible. . . .
> (101-104)

The second is from *Gareth and Lynette* (1872) and is spoken by Merlin in explanation of the phrase "the Riddling of the Bards":

> " 'Confusion, and illusion, and relation,
> Elusion, and occasion, and evasion.' "
> (280-282)

The two passages embody, respectively, Tennyson's basic concept of the imagination and the chief formula by which he translated that basic concept into the practical work of making keenly relevant poems.

The abstract character of the concept of the imagination contained in the first passage can be excused on the grounds of the very special *persona* who enunciates it: he is "supposed to be himself a poet," [19] but of a very self-conscious and imaginatively extravagant sort. Still, the concept itself seems to be intact. The imagination is a deep-seated presence in the inner consciousness of every man, perhaps the alpha and omega of that consciousness. However, it is stimulated into an activity of which one can become aware only by the impingement on it of images which have qualities of sound and sight, and then, once activated by such images, it in turn molds them in a very distinctive way, giving them shape and meaning according to the individual character of the "inaudible invisible thought" itself. Thus, there is a perpetual interaction between this inner consciousness and stimuli external to it; and since this deep-seated presence is both "Artificer and subject, lord and slave," its own character is affected by the images which set its transformational powers into motion, and it is subject to a process of both strengthening and purifying according to the stimulants brought to bear upon it. Thus, the poet has an available process by which to cleanse and invigorate his own imagination, as does every man; and he, like others, can also, through misdirection or carelessness, pollute it. But in any case, whether or not he is a poet as such, the character of his imagination will be in a degree distinctive, homogenization except in the stereotyped habitual sense being ultimately impossible. A poet who uses imaginary *personae* as a poetic device will recognize that they will be only as strong and pure as his own imagination can conceive of them and his own craft shape them; and he will recognize, too, that they cannot be quite like another and that no reader can possibly perceive them in quite the same way as he does. So the imagination involves the poet-as-poet and the reader-as-poet in a complex of approximations which, however strict each may try to be, will always be open-ended in the individual consciousness, though always in some state of stimulation too. And if the poet-as-poet would be fully and trustworthily serviceable to the reader-as-poet, he has an obligation to type the finest and most restorative human imagination in himself and to "lend out," according to his individual capacity, a healthy mind.

The quotation from Merlin in the second passage describes a "bardic subtext" which has the very widest applicability to Tennyson's mode of imaginative implementation. It is a formula of the process by which men in this world, even men with a dwarfed or polluted imagination, attempt to deal, however unsuccessfully, with their affairs. When a person is faced with a sense of distress, mild or acute, in the coordinates of his life *(confusion)*, he adopts or creates a personal myth *(illusion)* in order to give his life a more desirable sense of order and proportion *(relation)*; and by translating that myth into action *(occasion)*, he tries to redirect the erosive effects of an unhappy set of pressures *(elusion)* and to avoid having his life become a self-destructive shambles *(evasion)*. But such a process, however universal, is in and of itself neutral, so that a person may follow it to the letter in a ritual of self-destruction; or he may, through the strength and clarity of his imagination, create a mythic action of such a wholly serviceable character and quality that it will in fact be "the one bright thing to save / [His] yet young life in the wilds of Time" *(Maud,* I, 556-557). And since this psychic/mythic patterning, this customary imaginative self-processing, is so universal in its operation, it becomes the most fundamental and far-reaching avenue of access by which a poet-as-poet can reach a reader-as-poet at the deepest and most crucial inner level and enable his own transformed imagination to function transformationally.

Tennyson uses the bardic subtext throughout his poetic career but in such a great variety of ways that it never appears formulaic; and it can be an instrument of despair, of hope, of dull neutrality, or of transformation from one state of being, good or bad, to another, restorative or destructive, depending on the character of the myths exhanged and the actions they lead to. The speakers in *Timbuctoo* and *Supposed Confessions,* for example, are caught in a collision of perspectives out of which, in the poems' narrative curves, they are unable to create a myth upon which to base an action. Our dissatisfaction with *The Two Voices* as a *persona*-narrative stems from our impatience with the nonorganic manner in which the transformation from one state of being to another takes place, and we salvage the poem by concentration on the resourcefulness of the debate or, perhaps more appropriately, by a concession to the speaker's innate incapacity to discover a truly sustaining myth that will enable him to break out of an endless rhythm of depression and mania. *Œnone* is a poem of panic premonitions which the speaker does not understand, and Œnone's lamentation for her lost shepherd is a lyric/dramatic narrative of the dismantling of her personal myth and of a mythic millennium, the death-song of both Œnone and Pan.[20] Readers of *The Lotos-Eaters* have traditionally challenged the authenticity of the new myth *(illusion)* by which the mariners seek to bring some personal order *(relation)* out of their lives of perpetual external bombardment *(confusion)* and, by taking an action *(occasion)*, to avoid the continuing chaos *(elusion)* that promises nothing but willy-nilly self-destruction *(evasion)*. Their new myth-making has been adjudged a manifestation of psychological fatigue with a patina of moral turpitude, and the mariners have been implicitly admonished by armchair Odyssean commentators to stick with their old myth of return *(illusion)* even if it does keep them strapped to *confusion* "worse than death." [21] Though the fineness of the speaker's imagination in *Locksley Hall* is a pervasive issue, the poem is the self-revelation of a protagonist attempting to clean up the debris of a collapsed myth of romantic love *(confusion)* and to create a new myth *(illusion)* that will give renewed order *(relation)* to his life and, by translating that new myth into action *(occasion:* "I go"), to push aside lacerating memories and fantasies *(elusion)* that, if clung to, will make him "wither by despair" *(evasion)*.[22] The parallels between *Locksley Hall* and *Maud* are frequently noted, and the bardic subtext has fundamental application to them both, though their *personae* and their fictional curves are very different.[23] At the center of *The Princess* is the slow building of an authentic myth and the traumatic dismantling of a false myth that is rigidly in place, and the poem ends at the point at which the Prince and Princess type themselves as representatives of a renewed human race and undertake to translate their new myth *(illusion)* into an action *(occasion)* that will turn discord into harmony *(elusion)* and prevent the strident battle of the sexes (the old destructive myth) from making life in this world intolerable *(evasion)*. In *In Memoriam,* there is a subtle and gradual exchange of myths. The old myth (the traditional, latter-day, socialized Christian myth) has not been false so much as routine, and its dependability has exploded for the speaker in the face of an awful wasting. In the process of the poem, the *persona* gradually creates a new myth that is wholly organic with the self, borrowing from all available sources but using none as a substitute for inner imaginative growth; and he emerges with a new capacity to cope with the blows and shocks of life because his myth is an authentic outgrowth of a transformed self, and from that radiant center he can in a real sense create his universe afresh and perceive God and Nature meeting in that personal mythic light.[24]

Finally, *Idylls of the King* is essentially a mighty measuring of the human imagination through the myths *(illusions)* that these emblematic representatives of humanity create and the actions *(occasions)* by which they convert those myths into life and style. This is the "ruling passion" of Tennyson's "whole mind," the "inaudible invisible thought / Artificer and subject, lord and slave" which had been shaped by all his experience of literature *and* life and which in turn molded that complex experience into "an image of the mighty world." *Idylls of the King* is the modern imagination, the Tennysonian imagination, in one of its grandest and most complex manifestations. It is the story of man in this world emergent out of mystery and destined for a mysterious end. Those insoluble mysteries or origin and doom suspend the whole in a medium of mysticism; but although the mind occasionally and inevitably and hopefully touches a reality to which even the finest of our sensuous knowledge is merely symbolic appearance (Arthur) or translates that reality into sensuously incomprehensible action (Galahad), Tennyson's story of man centers on the tableland of life and is rooted deeply in individual men and women, "their own peculiar natures and circumstances, their selfishness, the perfection or imperfection of their [idealism]," [25] the character and quality of their imagination.

Arthur is himself an inscape of the most refined and steady human imagination: from the day in *The Coming of Arthur* when, in the throes of his love-epiphany, he inscapes his universe and himself, his imaginative insight does not falter, and it survives the existential chaos of that "last, dim, weird battle of the west." The "inaudible invisible thought" at the deepest center of his consciousness has been touched by the "fairest of all flesh on earth," and his imagination, being transformed, transforms in turn all the appearances of things into an awe-inspiring reality that gives to man and his universe a fair prospect that will enable the calm strength of the imagination to convert into light a "dark land" and into life a "dead world" (*The Coming of Arthur,* 74-99). That is Arthur's myth *(illusion)* by which he hopes to bring order *(relation)* out of chaos *(confusion)*. He then converts this myth into an action *(occasion),* the Order of the Round Table, dedicated to the eradication of heathen wildness *(elusion)* and the salvation of man from the imperious imprint of his lower, more bestial self *(evasion)*. Both the myth and the action built upon it have a quality of simple magnificence, and against a vivid background of remembered distress, they work well for a while.

But there are other myth-makers in the world besides Arthur, and a subtle, pervasive confusion of myths begins to sap the strength and purity of Arthur's simple mythic model. It is an inevitable outcome: although the poet has typed the finest and most restorative human imagination in Arthur, he knows that the imaginative type cannot be imaginatively stereotyped; and although the poem traces the decay of community from an imaginative ideal, that decay is centered in imagination itself, and its progress, in the open-ended way characteristic of the imagination, is through the individual consciousness. Gareth's mythic action, though faulted by his collusion in deception, is a close approximation to Arthurianism; Bedivere's loyalty, despite a momentary mythic defection that threatens a catastrophic conclusion for him and for the whole Arthurian model, ultimately reaffirms the Arthurian ideal; and the first curve of Pelleas' story, though takingly naive and disquietingly rigid, mirrors Arthurianism at a literal, bookish, fundamentalist level. But these are widely separated surfacings, and for the most part, the imaginations of the individual characters (the ruling passions of their whole minds, their myths, their actions) lead them by different paths away from that deep-centered consciousness embodied in Arthur.

Guinevere will not accept the authenticity of the Arthurian myth and sets up an ingratiatingly delusive alter-myth having deep roots in old patterns of human strategy. It is the myth of the courtly love tradition by which she becomes the center of a highly ritualized passionate approach to life in this world, the grandest lady with the greatest and most gallant of lovers. Her myth is an orchestration of life as a May-game, of the " 'garden rose / Deep-hued and many-folded!' " (*Balin and Balan,* 264-265). It has an unmistakable quality of magnetic luxuriance. It is so affectively delusive because it seems to fulfill the aspirations of the most romantic of human imaginings, and it is so lethal because the difference between it and true Arthurianism appears to be so narrow. Geraint's myth is an inversion into romantic parody, with many melodramatic, coarsely epical resonances, of the Guinevere myth. Geraint, a gay Lothario *manqué,* has a minimum of imagination, and thus the rituals with which he attempts to institutionalize his male chauvinism and would-be urban sophistication are blunt, stupid, and, except for Enid-Psyche's watchful eye, catastrophic. *Balin and Balan* carries the implicit theme of "man against himself" in the Geraint-idylls center-stage; and since Balin also derives his myth from Guinevere, "man against himself" assumes increasing solidity as the Guinevere theme of the poem. Balin's myth—that the Queen's "crown-royal upon shield" (196) will enable him to " 'forget / His heats and violences' " (185-186)—is, like King Pellam's iconolatry, absurd; but it is the desperate act of a sundered imagination that cannot make him or his world whole, and it measures at a gothically grotesque level the distance we are traveling from Arthurian authenticity. Merlin's myth is a shambles. Long before Guinevere, he has seen the yet larger writing on the wall, and he suffers from the vulnerability of a psyche too fatigued and too depressed to make any more genuine myths. So he falls prey to such a transparent self-delusion that it shapes itself as the most paltry and pathetic of myths, an ancient man's final sexual touching. Vivien is also a Guinevere-figure: she too worships the sun that warms the earth, and the relentless fidelity with which she pursues her myth of perfect hate is a gloss on Guinevere's false myth of a "perfect" love, which will also imprison man in a wholly natural, spiritually comatose state. Elaine's myth is the creation of a finely tuned but childishly inexperienced imagination. She, too, is a Guinevere-figure, at a simpler, more primitive, more horrifying level. Her fixation on Lancelot is no self-indulgent May-game, but real, frozen, and fatal. If she cannot realize her myth in action, then she will de-create herself; and although her story induces in Guinevere and Lancelot realizations that shatter the false myths by which they have locked in their lives, her story is pathetic at such an excruciatingly painful level that it threatens to blind us to the yet sterner demands of an authentic tragic apprehension. Tristram's myth converts Geraint's shabbiness to a new level of tawdriness. He is the fallen priest of the piece, turning the knowledge gained within the walls into an attack upon the institution itself in a dogmatic gesture of self-justification. His is one strategy of revenge, as that of Pelleas alias the Red Knight is another; and the " 'flat confusions and brute violences' " of the revenge tragedy released by Pelleas' public rebellion against community injustice follow Tristram's quasi-private rebellion to a quasi-private but horrifying end. Tristram, like Pelleas, has come late out of barren lands, and he plays with Arthurianism like a wide-eyed provincial. When, after a time, it fails to satisfy his needs, he creates a more commodious myth *(illusion)* to give coherence *(relation)* to his rudderless life *(confusion)*. But the myth made by the dull inner eye of the hunter and the harper and the amorous rover promises only a lucky-breaks life-illusion; and when Tristram's luck goes sour, when the life-action *(occasion)* built on such an imaginatively myopic life-illusion gets caught in the natural turbulences which are a part of the reality in which his illusion is rooted but which it has largely ignored, he becomes the inevitable victim of a chaos that he did not *elude* and a destruction that he did not *evade*. And as the story of Pelleas reduces Arthurianism to a rigid, dogmatic literalism that is shattered with devastating after-shocks, so the story of Tristram reduces the Guinevere motif to the lowest, least attractive, ugliest personal level.

At the heart of *Idylls of the King* is the myth of the magic wand. *The Holy Grail* is a re-casting of the twin metaphors of self-creation / self-destruction upon which the whole poem turns. It gradually fills us with an awe-inspiring understanding of how men, in varying states of imaginative debility, can turn their backs on a

wholly trustworthy illumination and, in an overwhelming enthusiasm for talismanic self-renewal, march toward self-destruction. _The
Holy Grail_ is perhaps the very saddest of the idylls. Arthur's initial
cry, " 'Woe is me, my knight' " (275), echoes through its lines, and
there is a breath-taking tableau of the Arthurians first coming face
to face with the Grailities:

> And many of those who burnt the hold, their arms
> Hacked, and their foreheads grimed with smoke, and seared,
> Followed, and in among bright faces, ours,
> Full of the vision, prest. . . .
>
>   (264-267)

It is a painting worthy of Goya.

Lancelot's great sadness is penetrating, as is that of Bors; and
Arthur's stern lessoning of Gawain for deafness and blindness re-
verberates throughout the story of a quest undertaken by his greatest knights because, having eyes, they did not see, and having ears,
they did not hear. Even Galahad's incomprehensible success leaves
a blind spot in human apprehension. But Percivale himself is the
bearer of the poem's most pervasive melancholy. Percivale has borrowed his myth, lacking the inner resources to create one of his
own; he is not a myth-maker, but the propagandist for somebody
else's myth. He has borrowed an identity—that of being his famous
sister's brother; and he has clung unto the final hour to Galahad's
coattails. Like all the knights, he bears the image of the King, but
he shows no understanding of the Arthurian ideal. He lacks the
capacity to love, and the only proof he has that he exists is his role
in the Grail-quest. He is without Galahad's spiritual imagination,
Ambrosius' warm humanity, Lancelot's moral grandeur. Percivale
is all style and no substance. He is the hollow man of _Idylls of the
King,_ the disillusive androgyny who backs out of life; and as narrator of _The Holy Grail,_ he induces in us a subliminal disinclination to
yield ourselves to the myth of the magic wand.[26]

Arthur's speech at the end of _The Holy Grail_ provides the aptest
conclusion to these remarks on the Tennysonian imagination. He
talks there about the authority of the eye, the fundamental concept
in Victorian aesthetics, whether one thinks of Carlyle or Ruskin or

the Pre-Raphaelites or Dickens or Browning or George Eliot or Newman or Arnold or Hopkins or Pater. The training school of the eye is life is this world: until we can see things as they in fact are, man as he in fact is, I as I in fact am, we cannot rightly be said to see at all. But having trained ourselves truly to see, having penetrated to the level of significant form, to the level of inscape, to *itness*—having put "keen *Discovery*" to *its* ultimate creative uses as "*Discovery*" of nature, man, and ourselves—then we may occasionally, in our most favored moments, make the imaginative leap into the consciousness of a reality that absorbs into itself all of the individual tactilities to which we have brought the authority of the bodily eye and which gives them full place as sensuous symbolic gateways to a reality different in kind from themselves, making even Time and Space mere modes of consciousness. That, both as concept and as process, is the essence of the Tennysonian, and of the Victorian, imagination.

Notes

1. See James A. W. Heffernan, *Wordsworth's Theory of Poetry: The Transforming Imagination* (Ithaca: Cornell University Press, 1969).
2. This is perhaps not a wholly refined comparison, the Blake concordance being a work of meticulous, inclusive modern scholarship, but the point is still intact.
3. All references to Tennyson's poetry are to *The Poems of Tennyson,* ed. Christopher Ricks (London: Longman, 1969). Citations are given in parentheses in the text as appropriate.
4. "On the Modern Element in Literature" (1857), in *The Complete Prose Works of Matthew Arnold,* ed. R. H. Super (Ann Arbor: University of Michigan Press, 1960), I *(On the Classical Tradition),* 18-37.
5. Heffernan, p. 271.
6. I have worked the matter through in considerable detail in Chapter VIII, "Tennyson's Function of Poetry at the Present Time: A Parabolic Reading of *The Princess.*"
7. Preface to *Poems* (1853), in *The Complete Prose Works of Matthew Arnold,* ed. R. H. Super (Ann Arbor: University of Michigan Press, 1960), I *(On the Classical Tradition),* 7.
8. Preface (1802) to *Lyrical Ballads,* in *The Prose Works of William Wordsworth,* ed. W. J. B. Owen and J. W. Smyser (Oxford: At the Clarendon Press, 1974), I, 138.
9. I have done so in Chapter IX, "*In Memoriam* in Aesthetic Context."
10. Tennyson's phrase, in Ricks, p. 913n.

11. "On Some of the Characteristics of Modern Poetry . . . ," *Englishman's Magazine* (August 1831), as reprinted in *Tennyson: The Critical Heritage,* ed. John D. Jump (London: Routledge & Kegan Paul, 1967), pp. 34-49 (p. 42). I subscribe to the view that this essay reflects, despite its light strategies of denial, Tennyson's and Hallam's common thinking at the time.

12. These remarks had particular reference to *Idylls of the King*. See Ricks, p. 1463.

13. Jump, p. 42.

14. Jump, p. 37.

15. Jump, p. 39.

16. Jump, pp. 42-43.

17. Jump, pp. 43-44.

18. Jump. pp. 46-47.

19. Tennyson, quoted by Ricks, p. 300.

20. I have given expansive treatment to this perspective in Chapter V, "Enlarging the 'miniature epic': The Panic Subtext in Tennyson's *Œnone.*"

21. I have given a fundamentally different reading of the poem in Chapter VI, "Tennyson's *The Lotos-Eaters:* Emblem of a New Poetry."

22. I have elaborated the process of the poem and its *persona*-locus in Chapter VII, "In Defense of *Locksley Hall.*"

23. I have dealt with *Maud* extensively in two Chapters: "Tennyson's *Maud:* New Critical Perspectives" (Chapter X) and in the final section of "Tennysonian Madness: Mighty Collisions in the Imagination" (Chapter IV).

24. In Chapter IV, "Tennysonian Madness: Mighty Collisions in the Imagination," I have attempted to show the genuine applicability of this bardic subtext to the following other Tennyson poems: *Rizpah, The Lover's Tale, Lancelot and Elaine, Guinevere,* Lancelot's story in *The Holy Grail, Pelleas and Ettarre* and Pelleas' role as the Red Knight in *The Last Tournament, Balin and Balan, Lucretius, The Lady of Shalott, The Palace of Art, The Vision of Sin,* and *Maud.*

25. Quoted in Ricks, p. 1661. Tennyson's statement has particular reference to *The Holy Grail,* where Christianity has a central symbolic significance. In applying it to the poem as a whole, I have substituted "idealism" for "Christianity" as having larger metaphoric significance.

26. Anyone reading Percivale's character and life-story more sympathetically can, of course, see the Grail as his myth *(illusion)* and monasticism as his action *(occasion)*. But the basic *confusion* of his life (that he does not know that he does not know that he exists) is not brought into a creative order thereby *(relation);* and since there is no indication that his monkhood effects an increase in his contemplation or his piety, it is hard to see that he has done anything but elude *elusion* and evade *evasion.*

4.

Tennysonian Madness:
Mighty Collisions in the Imagination

poet of experience & personality

Tennyson's fascination with "The abysmal deeps of Personality" is pervasive in his poetry. From his earliest known poem *(The Devil and the Lady)* to the last poem he finished *(The Dreamer)*, he was a poet of human experience, perpetually probing distinctive, often strange, states of being through the placement of an imaginary *persona* at the heart of a processive human action that enables that character to gain an original perspective on the human condition and enables the poet thereby to purify and strengthen the imagination of the reader. Tennyson, of course, experimented with almost every turning of the poetic art as exemplified in both the English and the Classical literary traditions, and hence one would hesitate to characterize too broadly and simply such a large, experimental, and varied canon. Still, the human consciousness in motion is a fair phrasing of that central imaginative current in which Tennyson's chief poetic successes flow.

Madness is one of the "abysmal deeps" to which the human psyche is vulnerable, and we know that to Tennyson the man it was an ever present reality, a defining, cautioning outcropping in the Tennyson family. But it is curious how little of this deep per-

sonal experience of madness finds its way into the work of a poet
who has been so persistently searched for autobiographical implants. Instead, Tennyson very early distanced his acute awareness
of this special vulnerability of the human spirit to an imaginative
construct on which he worked many variations in his long poetry-
writing career. The chief lineaments of that imaginative construct
and the process through which it gradually passes in the Tennyson
canon can be clarified through a comparative look at an early and
a late poem, *Sense and Conscience* (written in the late 1820s) and
Rizpah (written in 1878).[1]

Sense and Conscience, called an "unfinished allegory," is an ambitious Miltonic imitation. The poem is narrated by the unidentified Spirit of Man, the minister or steward of Time. The
contention is between Spirit and Sense; and man woos "the Arch-
Enemy *Sense,*" who prospers "at the court of Time," by stealth
drugging "Great Conscience," "boldest of the warriors of Time,"
offspring of *"Reason* and *Will!"* Though drugged by Sense, Conscience cannot die, but lying helpless in "deep shades," he struggles
subconsciously in an all-enveloping atmosphere of sensuous invasion. Finally, Memory, now in mourning weeds, comes upon him,
and he is reminded of what a "fair vision" she once was:

(The woof of Earth Heaven-dipt, in orient hues
Storying the Past which charactered in fire
Burned from its inmost folds). . . .

(80-82)

But Conscience is too weak to rise, and he merely wreaks havoc
among the images of beauty in this unwanted Bower of Blissless
Bliss. He does at last escape into the deep interior, where he lives
on "bitter roots which Memory / Dug for him round his cell" (111-
112). Finally, he is caught up in the rhythms of madness:

One solemn night
He could not sleep, but on the bed of thorns,
Which Memory and Pain had strown for him,
Of brambles and wild thistles of the wood,
Lay tossing, hating light and loathing dark,

And in his agony his heart did seem
To send up to his eyes great drops of blood,
Which would not fall because his burning eyes
Did hiss them into drought. Aloud he wept,
Loud did he weep, for now the iron had come
Into his soul: the hollow-vaulted caverns
Bore out his heavy sobs to the waste night,
And some the low-browed arch returned unto
His ear; so sigh from sigh increasing grew.

                                                          (112-125)

Here we have a simple paradigm of madness as it surfaces repeatedly in the Tennyson canon. A *persona* of considerable emprise
is caught in a collision of forces—a distinctive individual in a conflict of motives and actions—between which he struggles and at the
center of which is the subtler conflict of desire and an unyielding
recognition of the falseness of the desire, creating in the *persona* a
magnified psychic collision. This leads to madness, but it is a madness made inevitable by the very refinement of the *persona*'s imaginative sensibility. Memory, a raw but imperious presence in the
early poetry of Tennyson, will be later integrated and submerged
into the texture of poetic action, but its role as "Mother of the
Muses" and chief igniter of the imagination will, though subdued,
persist.

   Rizpah is a penetratingly sad poem, but its effects are positively
exhilarating too. Here madness is not just a crippled state, but a
heroic solution. A mad, impersonal society is confronted in a mad
personal way, as Rizpah works out for herself and her son a "supreme Dénouement" that functions for her so successfully that the
murky waters of a debilitating pathos are cleansed by her diminu-
tive but relentless grandeur. *Rizpah* is thus a fit illustration of how
Tennyson maintained the Aristotelian, Wordsworthian, Arnoldian
principle "that the feeling therein developed gives importance to
the action and situation, and not the action and situation to the
feeling. . . ."[2] The central irony of the poem is that Rizpah outwits
a brutally dehumanized socio-ethical system through coordinates
of that same system in which she is herself imprisoned. She rectifies
the gross injustice of society's hanging of her son in chains, high for
the world to see and for "the hell-black raven and horrible fowls of

the air" to pick clean, by gathering his bones as they fall and laying "him in holy ground." She thus makes an imaginative transfer from "the cursèd tree" upon which Willy was hung to the blessed tree upon which Christ was hung. Ironic, too, is the discrepancy between the milder predestinate fundamentalism of her Methodist-Calvinist visitor and the desperate faith and unlimited courage of mad Rizpah.

Any number of forces could, in the course of the events, account for the initial madness of Rizpah—overwhelming grief, monstrous injustice, devastating shame. But the poem itself pinpoints the boy's last-minute cry that leaves her with a haunting and unbearable sense of incompleteness—the "something further" that he had to say which she "never shall know" but which her memory and imagination cannot relinquish. That memory / imagination is what torments her unremittingly through years of confinement and beatings (the eighteenth century's version of shock treatment) until she grows "stupid and still." That memory / imagination, too, is what shapes her furtive apostolate: maybe what he was going to say was, " 'Mother, O mother!—[see that I am buried in holy ground!]' " But even if that was not it, the possibility thereof becomes her only way, by the mad internalization of the mad belief of the times, of ever getting to know. The frantic strategy built on that possibility by Rizpah, isolated from the world's understanding and sympathy and carrying on only when protected from the world's spying by the extreme darkness and inclemency in which the most furtive of body-snatchers work, becomes the action by which she effects a tenuous truce with the mighty collisions in her imaginative consciousness.

The grim bardic quality that is domesticated in Rizpah's cunningly imaginative madness seems to translate into the structure and movement of this poem Merlin's "Riddling of the Bards" in *Gareth and Lynette* (280-282):

> " 'Confusion, and illusion, and relation,
> Elusion, and occasion, and evasion.' "

Rizpah is monitored by this "bardic subtext" as follows. Faced with an infinity of insuperably chaotic conflicts *(confusion),* the protagonist creates a private myth or fable *(illusion)* by which she can script into her real-life dilemma a manageable order *(relation)* and thereby sidestep the crushing effects of a shapeless chaos *(elusion)* by creating an action *(occasion)* in which something can be done instead of yielding to circumstances in which everything is to be endured *(evasion)*.

The simple, early paradigm persists: the imagination, fed by memory, attempts to cope with such turbulent inner conflict that the *persona* is driven mad. In *Sense and Conscience,* there is a complete failure to cope; in *Rizpah,* the efforts of the mad old woman to cope are notably successful through the evocation of and perseverance in a private myth that enables her to achieve a grim "salvation" for herself and her son. And although Tennyson did not slavishly subordinate his poetic structures to these two models, both have relevance to all his poems of madness.

In *The Lover's Tale,* for example, a poem of strange imaginative energy and fascinating in the way Browning's *Pauline* is fascinating, the strained, unsuccessful efforts of the poet-protagonist to create a truly functional bardic subtext—or the duplicity with which he attempts to insinuate a false subtext—seem to explain the state of exacerbated vagueness in which he exists. And while one would not call it a successful poem, *The Lover's Tale* establishes an extraordinary space in the young Tennyson's poetic history that otherwise would not be poetically defined. The poet-protagonist of *The Lover's Tale,* for all his lyrical resource, fails through his incapacity to shape an action by which, like the protagonists of *Rizpah* and *Maud,* to achieve at least an eclipsed success. Despite his ingenious psychic maneuvering, he does not evade a situation in which everything is to be endured and nothing is to be done: he merely repeats forever the telling of his tale, the "telling" thus becoming the central metaphor of the "tale's" experience.

Madness is a pervasive insinuation rather than an explicit declaration of *The Lover's Tale,* and this fascinating inconclusiveness is one of the tantalizing, almost subliminal aspects of the poet's imaginative apprehension, as if the highly gifted teller has ingeniously suspended the tale at an indifference point between madness and sanity. At some junctures, the reader is even led to wonder if the tale is really true, if Camilla is not one of the "witching fantasies" to which Conscience is subjected in *Sense and Conscience*

(66-69), and this haunting suspicion is reenforced by the imaginative inflation of the speaker's language, the impreciseness of the narrative situation—place, time, audience, occasion—and the peculiar way in which he selects his narrative episodes. For example, he magnifies in the most erotic way the cradle-cuddling about which he admittedly has no personal memory (I, 243-262), and yet he omits entirely, except for a disturbing reference to the death of her father and "how we found / The dead man cast upon the shore," the eighteen-year period when young love would presumably have been in flower.

After the collapse of the myth of romantic love, which he has created with such imaginative flamboyance and "fantastical merriment" in Part I, Julian attempts to implant in his story the first *illusion* by which to ground his psychic turbulence *(confusion)* and to bring the coordinates of his life into supportable *relation:*

> Love's arms were wreathed about the neck of Hope,
> And Hope kissed Love, and Love drew in her breath
> In that close kiss, and drank her whispered tales.
> They said that Love would die when Hope was gone,
> And Love mourned long, and sorrowed after Hope;
> At last she sought out Memory, and they trod
> The same old paths where Love had walked with Hope,
> And Memory fed the soul of Love with tears.
>
> (I, 803-810)

It will not hold, of course, since it is an attempt to substitute a state of feeling for an action; and although it is effectively said, it is so abstracted beyond flesh and blood that it suffers from a haughty imaginative hysteria, the "mock-disease," perhaps, of the schizophrenic manic-depressive.

At the center of Julian's consciousness is a mighty imaginative collision. His love for Camilla is incestuous, not so much literally as by imaginative conversion. He has refined their closeness in every possible way, prevented only by the historical facts themselves from making them issue simultaneously from the same womb; but his frenzied imagination will not consciously accept the taboo against romantic incestuous love. It is as though he would give Hermaphroditus erotic as well as aesthetic privilege:

> Why were we one in all things, save in that
> Where to have been one had been the cope and crown
> Of all I hoped and feared?—if that same nearness
> Were father to this distance, and that *one*
> Vauntcourier to this *double?* if Affection
> Living slew Love, and Sympathy hewed out
> The bosom-sepulchre of Sympathy?
>   (II, 25-31, Tennyson's emphasis)

Thus the nightmarish visions that he suffers after being hopelessly separated from his love-object (II, 70-100, 163-205; III, 1-58) are all filled with psychosexual images of love and death, weddings interwoven with funerals, bacchanals rising from biers, sexual aggression met with horrified rejection, his efforts to imprint "Colour and life" upon Camilla's "naked forms" resulting in a wild surrealistic turbulence:

>   round and round
> A whirlwind caught and bore us; mighty gyres
> Rapid and vast, of hissing spray and wind-driven
> Far through the dizzy dark. Aloud she shrieked;
> My heart was cloven with pain; I wound my arms
> About her: we whirled giddily; the wind
> Sung; but I clasped her without fear: her weight
> Shrank in my grasp, and over my dim eyes,
> And parted lips which drank her breath, down-hung
> The jaws of Death: I, groaning, from me flung
> Her empty phantom: all the sway and whirl
> Of the storm dropt to windless calm, and I
> Down weltered through the dark ever and ever.
>   (II, 193-205)

Thus the guilt which Julian has so imaginatively masked from his consciousness surfaces in nightmares impregnated by both unyielding desire and relentless conscience.

Part IV *(The Golden Supper,* called "the sequel") [3] relates Julian's efforts to modify the bardic subtext by creating a genuine action, but this, too, fails since the action is rooted in a haughty imaginative self-deception which he cannot quite hide even from himself; and this forces him to abandon the role of "teller" and reenforces the centrality of the metaphor of telling. The key to the explicit falseness of the action *(occasion,* "event") by which he hopes to rise above the darkening chaos of his life *(elusion)* and avoid an unendurable future *(evasion)* resides in the parable by which Julian traps Lionel into affirming that Camilla, "by all the laws of love and gratefulness" is his "body and soul / And life and limbs, all his to work his will" (IV, 275, 279-280). The sexual imperiousness has clearly not abated, and the parallel between the master and his servant and Lionel and Camilla is patently false, as is that between Julian and the savior-figure of the parable. But it is on such falseness that he erects his new myth *(illusion)* of material and spiritual grandeur, in whch he actually arrogates to himself the godlike role of taking into his hands the destinies of others, as in Part I he had attemptcd to mythicize a god-goddess role above human imperatives for him and Camilla. His "action" in Part IV is a mere inversion of his own guilt and psychic turbulence into an ornate grandeur that does not cleanse him of his flamboyant hubris, but only compounds it.

Thus the connection between madness and imagination is made explicit in *The Lover's Tale.* Julian's imaginative frenzy is an attempt to reorder moral imperatives in violation of his own attenuated moral conscience, and it leaves him ultimately companioned with his mental sickness. His theory of the imagination is intact enough:

> Alway the inaudible invisible thought,
> Artificer and subject, lord and slave,
> Shaped by the audible and visible,
> Moulded the audible and visible. . . .
>   (II, 101-104)

But such a theory is morally neutral, and when Julian uses it to support essentially immoral willfulness and aggression, it creates a might collision in his imagination that, by the very keenness of his sensibilities, drives him mad.

Looking again to the later Tennyson, to *Idylls of the King,* we find variations on the same imaginative construct. In *Idylls of the King,* which is too frequently read as a morally apothegmatical poem, characters are in fact measured by the quality and force of their imaginations. Thus Arthur's love-epiphany, by which he suddenly inscapes himself and his universe, imprints its truth upon him so indelibly that he can see his world explode around him without ultimately betraying that initial vision. Leodogran resolves his weighty dilemma by rising above a sea of conflicting testimony and making an act of faith engendered by imagination. Gareth brings to his *rite de passage* a highly self-cultured imagination that enables him to overcome his collusion in deception and to persevere, becoming true Prince, true Knight. Geraint begins with a tawdry self-myth, and his treatment of Enid is so blunt and stupid because his imagination is incapable of anything beyond a low-grade theatricality.

The madness of Elaine, Guinevere, Lancelot, Pelleas, and Balin turns variously upon this central issue. Elaine's case is simple and horrifying. She is the delicate bearer of a fatal either-or imagination—the tender, ingratiating metaphor of an excruciating pathos and of a monotonic, devastating inevitability; and when the two parts of her naked dichotomy between sweet death and sweeter but frozen and unavailable love clash together in her finely tuned but childishly inexperienced imagination, her madness rises momentarily to the shrill, wailing note of a banshee's piercing shriek:

> High with the last line scaled her voice, and this,
> All in a fiery dawning wild with wind
> That shook her tower, the brothers heard, and thought
> With shuddering, "Hark the Phantom of the house
> That ever shrieks before a death," and called
> The father, and all three in hurry and fear
> Ran to her, and lo! the blood-red light of dawn
> Flared on her face, she shrilling, "Let me die!"
>
> *(Lancelot and Elaine,* 1012-1019)

The "action" for which she opts represents her despair of a bardic subtext by which her torn but simplistic psyche can ever be healed. She becomes the victim of an initial self-myth that, being fatal, allows no chance of mythic transformation. Her memory has no resources beyond its current drama, and hence she has nothing but the present to draw upon in the shaping of what might have been an alternative future.

Guinevere's case is so complex and her brush with madness is so lightly sketched that one can hardly speak of her in the present context without a sense of massive disproportion. But the threshold-to-madness moment is there and cannot be ignored. It is recorded in her idyll after Lancelot has discovered Modred spying for hard evidence, and although she is not brought to the depths of madness experienced by the soul in *The Palace of Art,* the parallel is unmistakable:

> Henceforward . . . the powers that tend the soul,
> To help it from the death that cannot die,
> And save it even in extremes, began
> To vex and plague her. Many a time for hours,
> Beside the placid breathings of the King,
> In the dead night, grim faces came and went
> Before her, or a vague spiritual fear—
> Like to some doubtful noise of creaking doors,
> Heard by the watcher in a haunted house,
> That keeps the rust of murder on the walls—
> Held her awake: or if she slept, she dreamed
> An awful dream; for then she seemed to stand
> On some vast plain before a setting sun,
> And from the sun there swiftly made at her
> A ghastly something, and its shadow flew
> Before it, till it touched her, and she turned—
> When lo! her own, that broadening from her feet,
> And blackening, swallowed all the land, and in it
> Far cities burnt, and with a cry she woke.
>
> *(Guinevere,* 64-82)

Guinevere is being traumatized by guilt, of course, but this period occupies a peculiar segment in a complex life-story. Guinevere has become so inured in her alternative fantasy, her self-myth of life as a May-game radiating outward from her, that she cannot conscientiously indict herself at the conscious level for her particular sin. Being fearful of disclosure but not morally self-disclosed, she cannot break out of her self-myth. She can hypothesize action and, when caught *flagrante delicto,* take action of despair, but she has as yet no worthy insight into the real truth. Hence, "the powers that tend the soul" can only "vex and plague her" with a real but uncomprehended distress. Were she not a great lady with imaginative resources numbed but real, she would simply break under the strain and spin off into irremediable madness. But it is her good fortune at the critical hour to reach beyond the memory of the pleasure-myth that began with Lancelot's initial mission and touch a time, obliquely configurated by the little novice, in which her values were shaped and monitored by an exemplary father-king, Leodogran; and out of this self-renewal, this reinitiation into earlier patterns of personality and value, she becomes available to the Arthurian insight and constructs for herself an Arthurian bardic subtext that saves her from suicidal madness. At the final moment, she accepts the Arthurian myth that she has heretofore rejected *(illusion)* and thereby brings her life into a new creative order *(relation)* by which her desperate *confusion* is resolved. She is thus enabled to undertake a simple life-work *(occasion)* that enables her to rise above a chaotic past but lately recognized *(elusion)* and avoid a catastrophic future *(evasion)*.

Lancelot's situation has analogues in those of Elaine and Guinevere. Indeed, it is through a juxtaposition of the images of the two of them, a concentration of the life-experience summed up in his efforts to cope with them both, that he is led to the self-harrowing soliloquy that enables us to understand the basic nature of his dilemma and to believe that he "should die a holy man." Like "Elaine the fair" and Guinevere "the fairest of all flesh on earth," Lancelot is "fair . . . / As a king's son." Schooled in this very special sense of self by the Lady of the Lake, Lancelot mythicizes that self and aspires to be a king. On the one hand, his loyalty to Arthur the King is inviolable; but when Guinevere falls in love

with him, he can yet realize an approximation of his myth, a king-
manqué with a queen who is his, *manqué*. His experience of Elaine
shows him how tender and endearing and fatal mythic self-deception can be; and Guinevere's turbulent rage, casting into the river
the diamond-symbols of his fabricated kingship, shows him what a
fool's paradise he has been living in. And though he has not yet
discovered the myth-based action by which to evade self-destruction (the bardic subtext), he recognizes that life under these circumstances is unsustainable:

> "I needs must break
> These bonds that so defame me: not without
> She wills it: would I, if she willed it? nay
> Who knows? but if I would not, then may God,
> I pray him, send a sudden Angel down
> To seize me by the hair and bear me far,
> And fling me deep in that forgotten mere,
> Among the tumbled fragments of the hills."
> *(Lancelot and Elaine,* 1409-1416)

Lancelot discovers the myth and the action by which to evade self-
destruction through the wild madness of his near-despairing quest
for the Holy Grail, his metaphoric journey into the hell of the
existential self which he just barely survives. It is his vow-within-a-
vow that saves him, the vow to follow on his quest the counsel of
"the one most holy saint." Through all his turbulent, surreal madness, his irreducible minimum of hope enables him to maintain
faith in that counsel and, having faced the rampant lions projected
from his own shield without yielding to doubt, he hears, standing
in the bare, cloistral, tomblike hall of Carbonek, the lark of Hope
singing in the tower toward the rising sun and can believe in his
own eventual resurrection and redemption. Thus his new myth
(illusion) is validated: he is worthy of salvation. His old fabricated
myth, which has self-destructed and almost carried him into chaos,
can now be abandoned because, like Guinevere, his naked existential self has been touched by authentic hope. But this is only a
preliminary part of the bardic subtext; like Guinevere, Lancelot
must yet perform a thousand individual acts of self-renewal and

undergo, with faith but without certainty, countless experiences of jeopardy:

> "up I climbed a thousand steps
> With pain: as in a dream I seemed to climb
> For ever: at last I reached a door,
> A light was in the crannies, and I heard,
> 'Glory and joy and honour to our Lord
> And to the Holy Vessel of the Grail.'
> Then in my madness I essayed the door;
> It gave; and through a stormy glare, a heat
> As from a seventimes-heated furnace, I,
> Blasted and burnt, and blinded as I was,
> With such a fierceness that I swooned away—
> O, yet methought I saw the Holy Grail,
> All palled in crimson samite, and around
> Great angels, awful shapes, and wings and eyes."
>
> *(The Holy Grail,* 832-845)

Thus, Lancelot's story, like Guinevere's, is made both complex and representative by his need to dismantle one deeply interwoven myth and to erect upon the remnant of the authentic self a subtext of salvation.

Set against the austerely muted successes of Guinevere and Lancelot are the gothic failures of Pelleas and Balin. Their madness outruns all expectation of order and implants in *Idylls of the King* intimations as terrifying as those of the Spirit of the Years in Hardy's *The Dynasts:*

> where the roars and plashings of the flames
> Of earth-invisible suns swell noisily,
> And onwards into ghastly gulfs of sky,
> Where hideous presences churn through the dark—
> Monsters of magnitude without a shape,
> Hanging amid deep wells of nothingness.
>
> (After Scene)

Their efforts are, within the limits of their capacities, heroic; but their personal resources are so fragile and the circumstances with which they contend so brutal that their minds are blown in a manner that tumbles all sense even of a tragic order.

Pelleas' madness must be witnessed in the overlapping curve that includes both young Sir Pelleas of the Isles in *Pelleas and Ettarre* and the Red Knight in *The Last Tournament.* For all his simple charm that makes Arthur love him immediately, Sir Pelleas is an ill-fated figure. He comes riding out of his wasteland like a Don Quixote with the hooves of Pan, and he makes a supreme effort that is poignantly sad to live knighthood to the letter and to love. It is a delicate transformation, the conversion of one ontological state into another. Even in the face of the bestial treachery of Gawain and Ettarre, this gentle son of Pan and Arthurian fundamentalist goes by the book; and he rises, in the face of measurable pesonal catastrophe, to genuine tragic stature, indicting the world that has betrayed him, but indicting himself even more. It is Percivale who, inadvertently and ineptly, converts catastrophe into chaos for Sir Pelleas. Tragically bruised by his personal empirical knowledge of infidelity within the knighthood, Sir Pelleas extrapolates Percivale's shabby innuendo concerning Guinevere and Lancelot into global, atheistic, abstract condemnation of the whole Order in which he has been such an exemplary novice-knight. The after-shocks of his fractured literalism leave his world in ruins. He has made of Arthurianism a total myth of self-fulfillment, a textbook way of transforming a barren spiritual wasteland into a magnificent imaginative reality, and when that myth fails him, he is catapulated into despair that reaches an insanely generalized level:

> "No name, no name," he shouted, "a scourge am I
> To lash the treasons of the Table Round."
> "Yea, but thy name?" "I have many names," he cried:
> "I am wrath and shame and hate and evil fame,
> And like a poisonous wind I pass to blast
> And blaze the crime of Lancelot and the Queen."
> *(Pelleas and Ettarre,* 553-558)

With the collapse of Arthurianism, Pelleas' imagination, buoyed up by Arthurianism, collapses too, and the only bardic subtext he can manage is a brutal inversion of Arthurianism with a line-by-line literalness. He founds his "Round Table in the North," and as a maddened rebel against the community that has failed to render him its promised justice, he becomes the center of the " 'flat confusions and brute violences' " of a revenge tragedy in which orderly justice itself is beyond the reach of human expectation. So when the offended community, in the persons of the young men lately knighted, takes its revenge upon the rebel against community, it creates an image which the imagination itself finds almost unendurable. The drunken Pelleas, alias the Red Knight, has fallen headlong into the swamp:

> then the knights, who watched him, roared
> And shouted and leapt down upon the fallen;
> There trampled out his face from being known,
> And sank his head in mire, and slimed themselves:
> Nor heard the King for their own cries, but sprang
> Through open doors, and swording right and left
> Men, women, on their sodden faces, hurled
> The tables over and the wines, and slew
> Till all the rafters rang with woman-yells,
> And all the pavement streamed with massacre:
> Then, echoing yell with yell, they fired the tower. . . .
>   (*The Last Tournament*, 467-477)

Mankind has itself gone mad, and in the "lazy-plunging sea" with which the incident is glossed, we hear "The voice of days of old and days to be," the tidal voice that preceded the coming of man and that will roll "far along the gloomy shores" aeons after his passing (*The Passing of Arthur*, 134-135).

The Pelleas-Red Knight story comes late in *Idylls of the King*. and has reverberations of a chaos more macrocosmic than that seeded in the story of Balin. But *Balin and Balan* brings a different generative quality to *Idylls of the King*. By its explicit use of the doppelgänger formula, it centers the chaos within, and to the degree that that metaphor of inwardness pervades our sense of the total poem, *Balin and Balan* becomes a fundamental imaginative pressure on our full experience of Tennyson's chief poetic accomplishment.

It is not surprising that *Balin and Balan* confirms to an extraordinary degree the relevance of the bardic subtext to Tennyson's

imaginative method as a whole and to his specific treatment of the
theme of madness: the idyll was begun soon after the completion of
Gareth and Lynette, in which Merlin's "Riddling" appears. And although the rich imaginative details with which Tennyson works it
out in this gothic tale of personal devastation can hardly be more-
than hinted at here, its relevance as a monitoring construct can be
briefly suggested.

What happens in *Balin and Balan* is that a young knight, after
being "sent down" by Arthur for three years as a result of his
rageful violation of the code of gentilesse, returns with his model
brother (his "other"), tries vigorously to "move / To music with
[the] Order and the King" (73-74), breaks out again into discord,
and ends in a mad symbolic desecration of the Order and the King
and the violent destruction of himself and his "other." The poetic
process by which this action is worked out in implicit response to
the inevitable question "Why?" suspends the moral issue as not
really relevant and focuses instead on the imaginative authenticity
of that process.

Balin exists in a welter of inner and outer *confusions.* Ever prone
to a self-depreciation so intense that it perpetually hovers around
images of suicide, he can hardly ground the least hint of a slight
from an external source, while at the same time he habitually
treats himself to torrents of self-abuse. After witnessing a moment
of soul-crisis between Guinevere and Lancelot, he translates a disturbing half-realization about them into an intense flagellation of
himself:

> "My father hath begotten me in his wrath.
> I suffer from the things before me, know,
> Learn nothing; am not worthy to be knight;
> A churl, a clown!"
>
> (278-281)

When Vivien hypocritically asks his guidance to Arthur's court, he
defames himself unmercifully:

> "here I dwell
> Savage among the savage woods, here die—

Die: let the wolves' black maws ensepulchre
Their brother beast, whose anger was his lord."
                                            (478-481)

When Balan (the "other") goes in quest of the "demon of the woods," Balin, despairing of even the strictest efforts to "learn what Arthur meant by courtesy, / Manhood, and knighthood," hits upon an *illusion,* the myth that if the Queen will allow him to substitute her crown-royal for the red-tongued beast "toothed with grinning savagery" upon his shield, things will bear a different *relation* to each other and he can avoid *(elusion)* the catastrophic results of his "heats and violences" and "live afresh" (183-196). The favor granted as a harmless humoring of his boyish eagerness but still threatened with raging impulses, Balin, "mad for strange adventure," undertakes an action *(occasion)* in hopes of finding his "other" and escaping *(evasion)* his own self-fulfilling prophecy of doom. It doesn't work, of course; and after a series of gothic episodes—horrible episodes that sap the strength without exhilarating the soul—he is himself taken for the "demon of the woods" by his "other," and they clash in ignorance and die "either locked in either's arm."

Thus, the bardic subtext works very differently from the way it works in *Rizpah,* but the difference is not one of authenticity. Balin fails miserably, but he processes himself through the imaginative formula to his own inevitable, imaginatively just, end; and the aesthetic result is neither pathetic nor tragic, but startlingly and disquietingly gothic. Even the mad act of desecration that triggers his and his "other's" destruction reflects the poet's wholly steady imagination:

        his evil spirit upon him leapt,
    He ground his teeth together, sprang with a yell,
    Tore from the branch, and cast on earth, the shield,
    Drove his mailed heel athwart the royal crown,
    Stampt all into defacement, hurled it from him
    Among the forest weeds, and cursed the tale,
    The told-of, and the teller.
                                            (529-535)

It is the inevitable result of his initiating illusion as his illusion is the inevitable result of his initiating nature; and there is no possibility of any crucial might-have-beens unless one would write quite a different tale of madness and self-destruction. All Balin's memories are of a failed nature: that is the self-myth which he simply cannot dismantle. Thus, the myth that he adopts and the action he undertakes are evasions, not of the confusions of his life or of the catastrophe to which they point, but of the issue itself. All of Balin's inner resources are consumed by self-doubt and brutal anguish, so that he has no capacity for inner transformation. He can only bring his self-doomed destiny to its inevitable term.

Lucretius, the only other major poem of madness in the later Tennyson cannon, also deals with the process of self-mythic metamorphosis. Here the issue is not, as in the cases of Guinevere and Lancelot, the dismantling of a patently false self-myth, but what one does when the perceptual rules are all changed. Lucretius has worked out for himself a wholly conscientious theory of the nature of man and his universe, has created a graceful, poetic rendering of those "truths," and has reached a personal point of "divine Tranquility" (265). That is both his urbane myth of nature and his self-myth. But Lucilia's love-potion changes all that, creating in Lucretius a horrible confusion that must itself be dealt with:

> the wicked broth
> Confused the chemic labor of the blood,
> And tickling the brute brain within the man's
> Made havock among those tender cells, and checked
> His power to shape: he loathed himself. . . .
>
> (19-23)

Lucretius' imagination is whiplashed between his remembered myth of philosophic calm and this new experiential reality for which a new, wholly personal myth must be created and acted upon.

The chief keys to Lucretius' experience of madness and suicide as generically human are the two levels at which his dreams function: the impossibility, intellectually of imaginatively, of being sure that what seems to be a violent aberration is not a true truth; and

his personal unwillingness to live with the latter even if it is only a
genuine possibility. At one level, Lucretius names and claims his
dream (26-46). Although it is an explosive contradiction of his
theory of nature, its images are only perceptual inversions and, as a
student of the mind as well as of the universe, he can easily ground
in the human understanding this playfulness of consciousness. At a
second level, however, in which "colour and life" are added to the
"naked forms" of nature in the aspect of carnal bestiality, he refuses to claim the dream as his own because here there is havoc
rather than correspondence, introducing intolerable possibilities
about the nature of man and Lucretius' own nature as a man. The
fire that shoots out from the standing breasts of Helen scorches
him at a deep inner level that negates the very concept of a
gradually evolvng, ever stabilizing state of human civilization.
Moreover, what appears to be so self-horrifying may in fact be self-
revealing. Although Lucretius does not claim this deeper dream as
his own, he is caught in his own homocentricity and cannot wholly
excuse himself from personal complicity. " 'How should the mind,
except it loved them, clasp / These idols to herself?' " (164-165).
Nature may be self-cleansing, but is man? (173-180). Nor can he be
quite sure that his horror is unmixed with desire: " 'do I wish— /
What?—that the bush were leafless? or to whelm / All of them in
one massacre?" (205-207).

At the beginning of his monologue, Lucretius has not decided to
kill himself (103-104); the process by which he articulates his distress leads him to that resolution and act. And the naked horror of
the experience is not the primary cause. He is led closer to it by the
effects on his mind of the experience: " 'my mind / Stumbles, and
all my faculties are lamed' " (122-123). But it is his long-habitu-
ated mental realism, the ingrained habit of his mind to accept
whatever is, that is decisive. Though this experience is unprece-
dented for him, he does not deny its reality as an experience, and
the acceptance of its horrible truth even at that ungeneralized level
loosens his light if graceful hold on life (219-229).

Lurectius confronts this new and intolerable *confusion* in his life
by creating a new myth *(illusion)* upon which he then founds an
action *(occasion);* and both the myth and the action do have the
effect of enabling him to *elude* an insufferable situation and to *evade*

a progressive degradation. The order *(relation)* which he thereby gives to his existence is necessarily a conjectural one, but it is undertaken without triviality or cowardice. On the premise that a civilized man has the right to a life of civilized dignity, he bases his myth of suicide on very simple and cogent grounds: it is a peculiarly human privilege; there is the very noblest precedent for it; nature can be depended on to recycle him in her own fashion; in the end, all things will return to "atom and void," no longer sensuously apprehensible as man defines sensuousness; and Plato's argument against it is effectively set aside on the grounds that "the Gods are careless . . ." (150). Thus, *Lucretius* follows other models of madness in the Tennyson canon. It is the very refinement of the protagonist's imagination that makes him incapable of coping with a life controlled by this awful collision within the imagination. The reasons he gives for self-destruction are impeccably thoughtful, but that rational train is set in motion by a thundering awareness of intolerable possibilities within the self that he despairs of reconciling.

The Lady of Shalott, The Palace of Art, and The Vision of Sin, all from the earlier Tennyson canon, touch the theme of madness, myth, and action in very different ways. The Lady's moment of madness (109-117) is clearly formulaic according to the basic formula suggested in this essay: she invokes the curse as a result of the imaginative collision brought on in her developed suceptibilities by the peculiar way in which she suddenly perceives Lancelot ("From the bank and from the river / He flashed into the crystal mirror," 105-106) as a magnificent emblem of cosmic reality. And although, being cursed, she does not create either her original self-myth or that myth's transformation, she seems fully reconciled to the fated conclusion. *The Palace of Art* projects a more dynamic process. Here, as in the cases of Guinevere and Lancelot, there is the dismantling of a complexly developed self-myth and the substitution of an alternative myth. But the proportions of the poem make it clear that the poet's primary centers of interest were in the creation of the self-myth (1-212) and the madness that results from the faulted character of that myth (213-288), and *The Palace of Art* is one of the three most extensive dramatizations in the Tennyson cannon of the progress of madness.

First there is confusion, the mind's coordination falling into division. Then follows "dread and loathing of her solitude," which gives birth to self-scorn and the threshold hysteria of scorn of self-scorn: she tries to justify the way she has been acting by finding it rooted in her deepest sense of an authentic self. Next, nightmarish images begin to invade the "dark corners" of her mind, ghastly images of the humanity she has been so proudly aloof from— "white-eyed phantoms weeping tears of blood," hollow shadows with "hearts of flame," standing corpses with their foreheads worm-fretted. She perceives herself in a lonely human backwash, cut off from the rhythms and laws of life. The isolation of which she had been so proud now has a serpent-sting to it, the medium of aesthetic exaltation turns to mud, and instead of being "as God," she is "exilèd from eternal God." The perpetuation motif that she had found in art ("So wrought, they will not fail," l. 148) now mocks her as "dreadful time, dreadful eternity" in which her fearful loneliness takes on the character of a perpetual unrelief, as the palace becomes a tomb, the artifacts no more than the "blackness" of "a solid wall," and the footsteps of humanity in the distance a grand discovery made too late.

It is a complete reversal of the bardic subtext by which the monstrous distortions and dehumanizations of the original myth are laid bare. The false *relation* which her arrogant *illusion* has sought to establish between art and life makes art itself monstrous, and life stripped of art as an authentic ordering principle becomes a mad bedlam of *confusion,* an infinity of incoherence. Such a myth translated into action *(occasion)* induces rather than avoids chaos *(elusion)* and leads inevitably, not to salvation, but to the very self-destruction that art is intended to help men prevent *(evasion).* What enables the "soul" of the poem to reverse the reversed subtext in the brief coda to the main action of the poem (289-296) is the hellish harrowing that she has experienced and the faint memory of "the riddle of the painful earth" which "Flashed through her" (213-214) and never allowed her wholly to forget the "moral instinct" (205). The poem thus reaches backward toward the *persona* in *The Lover's Tale* and forward toward Guinevere.

The Vision of Sin, one of Tennyson's most disquietingly imaginative poems and one of his favorites, fully fits the phrase "the human consciousness in motion." It is a waking nightmare, a "green tea" experience set in the temporal moment between darkness and dawn and in the psychic moment between madness and sanity, a time of monstrous but controlled imaginings. The poem creates a state of being within a state of being, the inner fable telescoping time into a mythic action in which an Epicurean youth passes from overheated pleasure to satiety and then to aged cynicism "affected with the 'curse of nature,' and joining in the Feast of Death." [4] The enveloping consciousness of which this inner fable is a symbolic surfacing is working through such an anxiety-ridden temptation that it seems to be in a threshold-to-madness state. The impingement of J. M. W. Turner's *The Fountain of Fallacy* on the imagery of the poem,[5] together with the encumbered Pegasus (3-4) and the two faces of Dionysus ("Like to Furies, like to Graces," l. 41), suggest that the speaker's anima is compulsively drawn to a palace of sensual art, but he is impeded in the realization of his imperious desires by a terrified conscience that repeatedly emerges in the image of the "awful rose of dawn" (50, 224) which God makes Himself "on the glimmering limit far withdrawn" (223). Thus the fable itself takes an exemplary cautionary turn, but the climactic question at the end—" 'Is there any hope?' "—is a thrust of the speaker's consciousness to which there is no comprehensible answer; and although the narrative opens and closes in the tightly controlled prosodic formalities of the heroic couplet, at its center there is sensual frenzy climaxing in a ballad and dance of death celebrating some very cogent "mockeries of the world" (202). So what we essentially have here is the recurrent imaginative collision (overwhelming desire colliding with a terrifying conscience anchored in remembered beliefs) which takes the form of a mythic action that, is the curve of its narrative, exposes the falseness of the myth without fully exorcising in the narrative consciousness its magnetic attractiveness. It is the bardic subtext (the inner fable) reshaped within a schizophrenic consciousness (the outer fable) incapable of acting out its own uncompromised bardic subtext, but hovering on its threshold.

At the chronological middle of the Tennyson canon is the centerpiece of his poetry of madness, *Maud*. The subject of *Maud is* madness in an all-encompassing way unparalleled elsewhere in

Tennyson except in the superb miniature *Rizpah* and, in a vague and inadequate way, in *The Lover's Tale*. The speaker in *Maud or the Madness* never achieves genuine sanity: whether he is "fantastically merry" (as in Part I, Canto XXII) or suffering from the dark "suspicion that all the world is against him" [6] *(passim)*, his psyche remains even at his best moments "a little shattered." [7] He is "a morbid poetic soul" and "the heir of madness" who strategizes life with only a deeply faulted success. Despite the intensity of his yearnings, his myths collapse all around him, and even those in which he invests the greatest imaginative energy reward him with only a doomed embrace. [8]

Like Tennyson's other supremely distinctive poems *(In Memoriam* and *Idylls of the King), Maud* was allowed to evolve over a very long period of time. Being a consciousness-in-motion poem, it could not be turned upon a thematic perception but had to wait upon such moments of intuitive insight as had the ring of authentic experiential truth to them. Nor could that authenticity be threatened by an externally imposed story-line and structure: it had to be allowed to evolve from within, emerging out of the idiosyncratic inner logic of a protagonist observed unawares, the continuity being only implicit and the white spaces between dramatic moments being either sufficiently imaginable or negligible. Thus madness surfaces and submerges in a poetic text, a linguistic artifact, that is itself a metaphoric awareness rather than an intellectual concept of madness. And the protagonist's madness is a dimension of his Apollo-gift: his capacity for pain is a measure of his capacity for pleasure. The psychic collisions that finally drive him into the asylum are magnified and rarefied by his own imagination (see especially Part II, Canto IV); the asylum lyric itself (Part II, Canto V) orchestrates in the most imaginative way fragments of memory and judgment into an illusion or myth, rather tentatively held, that he lies in an unquiet grave; and it would seem that he regains a shattered sanity by concentrating on and enlarging his imaginative memory of "the one bright thing to save / [His] yet young life in the wilds of Time" (I, 556-557).

From the beginning, the speaker suffers from such a polluted imagination that he stands on the edge of chaos. Visually intense, his memory saturated with vivid horror, terrified that he may go mad, pervaded with an acute sense of his lonely, unloved state, he spasms frantically in search of a myth. Fable-clutching is a defining characteristic of his consciousness: Echo (and Narcissus), Cain, Mammon, Timour, the Devil, Orion, the "monstrous eft . . . of old, the Sultan, the Maker, Isis, Death, Honor, Cleopatra, Viziers, Oreads, the crest of Juno's peacock, the laurel of Pyramus and Thisbe, the cedars of Lebanon, the "Forefathers of the thornless garden," and so on. It is a habit of his mind to translate experience into myth. His sense of chaos is the result of his having been so long without a personal cohering myth, his previous childhood myth having been shattered with his father's plunge into the pit. Thus he has turned his myth-making energy upon his age, and in the piercing confrontal language which is a persistent index both to his imaginative gifts and his psychic imbalance, he pins it like a scorpion to the wall. He also creates for himself a cluster of inadequate mythic actions: he will go away (but won't); he will bury himself in himself (but doesn't); he will become a stoic or "a wiser epicurean," leading a "philosopher's life in the quiet woodland ways" [9] (but can't).

A genuine myth finally becomes available to him, and after some initial and inevitable psychic stalking, he translates it into action. Thus, the bardic subtext becomes fully operative as his way of "climb[ing] nearer out of lonely Hell" (I, 678). The chaotic *confusion* of his life is brought into meaningful *relation* by the myth of romantic love *(illusion);* and by translating that myth into action *(occasion),* he avoids the devastating effects of a life of chaos *(elusion)* and prevents his ultimate self-destruction *(evasion)*. It is not a perfectly idyllic episode because he does not quite succeed in cleansing his psyche of the sense of being, like his Hamlet prototype, "splenetic, personal, base" (I, 362), and thus purging his destiny of the specter of "some dark undercurrent woe" (I, 681); but it is, on the whole, a remarkably successful mythic action.

The protagonist's myth of romantic love explodes in a personal storm that results in the death of Maud's brother and of Maud herself. This places the protagonist once more on the threshold of madness, and he does in fact go mad. Part II of *Maud* is a richly economical revelation of his slide into madness. The extraordinary thing about the speaker in this sequence is that he never contemplates suicide. He asks God to "Strike dead the whole weak race of venomous worms" (II, 46); but he still nurses in his "dark heart / However weary, a spark of will / Not to be trampled out" (II, 103-105), and this enables him, in an exquisite lyric, to identify with "a lovely shell" on the Breton coast that, however "Frail," has had the "force to withstand, / Year upon year, the shock / Of cataract seas . . ." (II, 72-74).

There are two new forces at work in the speaker in Part II that were not present in his threshold-to-madness situation at the beginning of Part I. One is his personal complicity in "the Christless code" (II, 26): he himself is guilty of "the red life spilt for a private blow—" (II, 331). The other is the imaginative knowledge, indelibly lodged in his memory, of

> where a garden grows.
> Fairer than ought in the world beside,
> All made up of the lily and rose
> That blow by night, when the season is good,
> To the sound of dancing music and flutes. . . .
> (II, 310-314)

Deprived of all possibility of mythic restoration at this point, unable, as he says,

> After long grief and pain
> To find the arms of my true love
> Round me once again!
> (II, 142-144)

the protagonist becomes the powerless victim of a mighty collision within his imagination—restorative memories of an almost perfect love and erosive memories of an almost unforgivable sin—and succumbs to madness.

If it is fair to conjecture, as I have, that the protagonist of *Maud* regains a shattered sanity by concentrating on and enlarging his imaginative memory of "the one bright thing to save / [His] yet young life in the wilds of Time" (I, 556-557), and if the bardic subtext upon which the thesis of this essay is largely based has cogency, then one is justified in taking a view of Part III of *Maud* in which war as such and the Crimean War specifically have very little critical relevance. What we have rather is a compulsive myth-maker trying to give some order to his stripped existential state. He gathers into the needs of his fragile sanity old memories and old patterns. The glory that he finally found in Maud is rooted deep in "A martial song like a trumpet's call" (I, 166), and his ingrained habit of giving body to his ever passionate perceptions through exaggerative language is in visible flow again. He combines these two tendencies of his imagination in the adoption of a new myth *(illusion)* that will bring order *(relation)* out of chaos *(confusion)* and make available to him an action *(occasion)* which will free him from the erosive effects of a purposeless life *(elusion)* and save him from a selfish grave *(evasion)*. That there is something of the death-wish in his mythic idealism seems clear enough; but it does provide a singular opportunity, in his mythic consciousness, to be recon-ciled to his fellow man and reunited with his beloved.

In conclusion, then: (1) Madness is one of the most "abysmal deeps of Personality" to which the human psyche is vulnerable, and Tennyson explored its experiential coordinates from youth to old age, *in* youth and *in* old age. (2) In *Maud* there is the hint of hereditary susceptibility to madness, but in *Maud* as elsewhere, Tennyson saw madness and imagination as very closely allied, madness being the result of a mighty collision in the imagination of a gifted *persona* with which the imagination itself could not cope. The madness may be thunderous but "momentary," as in *The Lady of Shalott* and Guinevere; recurrent and of long standing, as in Lancelot; grotesquely inflated, self-enclosed, and static, as in *The Lover's Tale;* tenuously redemptive, as in *The Palace of Art, Maud,* and *Lucretius;* catastrophic beyond even the tragic vision, as in Pel-leas; both penetratingly sad and positively heroic, as in Rizpah. But without exception, sanity is traumatized by a sudden collision of mighty contraries in the consciousness or pulverized by the self-grindings of a dilemma from which there seems to be no escape. (3) The way out of the paralyzing effects of madness is through an *action* that, being rooted deeply in the authentic self, measures that self and provides the *persona* with something to be done beyond the mere endurance of pain. It is the presence of an action that converts the exacerbated consciousness into the moral being, merges *expressiveness* and *mimesis* into a new species of psychological poetry, and draws the terrifyingly intense metaphor of madness into the mainstream of human experience. We are all susceptible to madness; but madness, being imaginative rather than moral, is itself susceptible to every species of moral outcropping. Guinevere and Lancelot discover an action that is self-cleansing and enables them to establish an authentic if muted moral grandeur. Julian, in *The Lover's Tale*, does not: he is the slave of an imperiously arrogant romantic imagination who cannot or will not subject himself to moral imperatives external to the self-inflations of that imagination. Pelleas also fails, but his failure, unlike Julian's, fills us with a near-unmanageable sadness. He is of that penetrating company of Jude Fawley—a young person who embarks upon the Daedalian fabrication of a new self in the labyrinth of life and for whom the issue quickly shifts from *what* he will be to *if* he will be at all. As Elaine, with an almost unendurably excruciating pathos, threatens our capacity to cling to a stabilizing tragic vision, so Pelleas nearly overwhelms our classical sense of justice and challenges tragedy as the ultimate gloss on the truth of human experience. Finally (4), each of Tennyson's poems of madness is an experiment in narrative form and feeling, and each positions madness in a different relationship to story-telling. Tennyson was the first of the modern psychological poets, and he altered the art of narrative poetry by discovering not just *a* way to process action in character, though *Rizpah* is a superb dramatic monologue. *Each* of his poems is a new way of setting the distressed consciousness in motion, and Tennyson never probes the abysmal deeps of personality in quite the same way twice. His narrative structures are as variable as his *personae,* and each of his poems brings both variables into a new and fascinating combination. In Tennyson's poetry, then, madness is a metaphor, not only of the most devastating human distress, but also of the very greatest aesthetic challenge, a challenge which Tennyson successfully met and thereby changed dramatically the course of modern English poetry.

Notes

1. All references to Tennyson's poetry are to *The Poems of Tennyson,* ed. Christopher Ricks (London: Longman, 1969), and quoted lines are identified in parentheses in the text except in note 9. Ascription of dates also follows this edition. The biographical approach to the subject simply leads to a different kind of scholarly endeavor.
2. Wordsworth's Preface (1800), in *The Prose Works of William Wordsworth,* ed. W. J. B. Owen and J. W. Smyser (Oxford: At the Clarendon Press, 1974), I, 128.
3. Parts I-III were written in 1821-1828, Part IV some forty years later, in 1868. See Ricks, pp. 299-301.
4. Tennyson's comment, quoted in Ricks, p. 718.
5. Christopher Ricks, "Tennyson: Three Notes," *Modern Philology,* LXII (November 1964), 140.
6. The phrases are Hallam Tennyson's, *Alfred Tennyson: A Memoir* (New York: The Macmillan Company, 1897), I, 396.
7. Tennyson, as reported by James T. Knowles. See Gordon N. Ray, *Tennyson Reads "Maud"* (Vancouver: Publications Center of the University of British Columbia, 1968), p. 45.
8. This conclusion may at first seem to contradict some of Tennyson's observations on the poem: he is "raised to a pure and holy love which elevates his whole nature"; when he "has recovered his reason, giving himself up to a work for the good of mankind through the unselfishness born of a great passion." *Works,* Eversley Edition (New York: Macmillan, 1908), II, 508. But nobility and selflessness may be wholly compatible with madness, and psychic imbalance is often accompanied by full use of the basic intellectual functions.
9. I, 121-122, 149.

5.

Enlarging the "miniature epic": The Panic Subtext in Tennyson's *Œnone*

Œnone is, line by line, Tennyson's most "antique" poem: it is suffused with the knowledge of and admiration for the Greek and Roman classics with which he began to shape the first major phase of his career as a poet (early version, 1830). Tennyson drew heavily for his subject matter on " Œnone to Paris" in Ovid's *Heroides* (V), and he was deeply affected in the poem's manner by Theocritus, who provided a dual model in the *epyllion* (or "miniature epic") and the *eidyllion* (or "little picture"). Tennyson further enriched the classical texture of the poem, in the allusive and recondite style of Theocritus, by dozens of echoes from other classical writers such as Homer and Virgil, Aeschylus, Lucretius, and Horace.[1] At this stage in his career, Tennyson aligned himself with the "small-scale-and-high-polish school of poetry" of which Theocritus was the luminous ancient model[2] and with whom Tennyson clearly identified. *Œnone* is a "bucolic idyll" at the center of which is Eros and the erotic paradoxes spawned by him, the foci of poetic interest being the interpenetration of man and nature and the drama that takes place within the human psyche. All of these identifying marks of the poem are thoroughly Theocritan.[3]

92

But Theocritus is known for his lack of "ethical disquisition"; [4] and this makes one skeptical of the ethical emphasis which some of the major Tennyson commentators, pointing especially to the speech of Pallas, have given their readings of the poem.[5] Not only does it seem strange that, in a poem so thoroughly saturated with the Theocritan poetic mentality, Tennyson would have abandoned Theocritus' detachment from moralistic involvement that, working within a miniature scale, made his high formal polish, his stunningly economical symbolism, and his persistent psychological concentration possible; but the ethical emphasis also clearly faults the poem in a most crucial way. The poetic faith mandated by the formal procedure of the poem is that everything emerges from, and in the language of, Œnone's consciousness: either the beauty of the imaginative apprehension lies there, or the formal procedure is a gross imaginative error. To give the speeches of the Goddesses, especially that of Pallas, a sermonic importance independent of Œnone's distressed consciousness is to abandon that poetic faith and to forget that *Œnone* is a highly polished, small-scale miniature, not an inflated ethical declamation.[6]

The soundest and most economical way of giving firm anchorage to a new perception of this superb poem is to outline the building process enacted in it and then to comment more generally on the implications contained therein.

Lines

1-14   This is a verbal painting, a picture of full-bodied natural beauty in a state of semi-suspension, with Gargarus, nature's grandest image, and Troy, the classical image of the destruction of man's most privileged estate, facing each other at the extremes. Thus the Edenic world symbolized by the vale of Ida is drawn into the circle of the undercurrent tragic woe associated with Troy.

14-21   This is another verbal painting: the tragic heroine comes forward to sing her fateful aria, the picture becoming an operatic stage. It is the hour sacred to Pan, when the natural world takes on the character of breathless animation—a universal hush, ominous in this context—and it is counterpointed to the forlorn, mournful, half-maddened state of Œnone, nymph and "Everyman" equivalent in the Panic world of nature. The description of her suggests analogues in both Dido and Cassandra.

22-32   Œnone sings, emphasizing the Panic moment and the fact that she is "alone awake," so heartbroken that she is "all aweary" of her life.

33-43   This is a verse "signature" in which Œnone tells who she is (" 'daughter of a River -God' " and hence a child of Pan) and draws all her clan into her audience—Earth, Hills, Caves, mountain brooks. Then, according to poetic convention, she tells why she sings: to " 'build up all / My sorrow with song' "—by analogy to the like building of Troy (" 'A cloud that gathered shape' ")—and perhaps (" 'it may be' ") to get relief from her personal heartbreak. Thus Troy's fate, like Troy's origins, is analogical to rather than identical with Œnone's: they mirror each other, but they are not the same.

44-62   This is a third verbal painting, in which Nature (Œnone) sees Man (Paris) enter her sacred (" 'dewy dark' ") precincts bearing gifts; and although there are signs of warning—the torrent calling out in the distance, the red streaks on the virgin snow—Nature's heart goes out to meet this beautiful creature Man, coming like a star, like a God, like a rainbow.

Reminder: All of this is taking place in Œnone's memory. It is long after the events themselves, and it is a testament to her soul-fidelity that she remembers them so tenderly. It also suggests that the act of telling them (rather than the raw events themselves) initiates the building process that climaxes in her

ultimate awareness of her " 'far-off doubtful purpose' " (247).

63-88   The theme of heavenly discord is introduced, the
          issue being who is fairest and Man (Paris) being
          designated umpire. Paris is ingratiating but full of
          hubris: Œnone is naive, wide-eyed and open-eared.
          Paris stations her in a cave that, unobserved, she
          (Nature) may see and hear all these negotiations
          between Man and the Gods. The cave's mouth thus
          becomes a picture frame for the *chef-d'oeuvre* in this
          poetic gallery of "little pictures."

89-190   The action (the Judgment of Paris) within the ac-
          tion (Œnone's processive poetic building) is again
          pinpointed at the moment sacred to Pan (" 'the
          deep midnoon' "), and it takes the visual form in
          Œnone's simple, startled, apprehensive conscious-
          ness of what we would call a flamboyant High Re-
          naissance mythological painting, grand in its
          fiction, heightened to the utmost in its style, and, in
          the wide-eyed consciousness of Œnone, terrifying.
          But, in this miniature epic, the perspective on the
          action takes aesthetic precedence over the perspec-
          tive of the painting: Œnone (Nature) watches
          Paris (Man) judge of the fairness of the Gods (Com-
          petitive Idealizations). The competitors are neither
          Greek nor Victorian, as some commentators quib-
          ble, but Goddesses, and they conduct their affairs
          like Goddesses, that is, grandly. Herè says all there
          is to be said for Power, Pallas for Wisdom, and
          Aphrodite, with more body-language than words,
          for Love. Paris is moved by Herè, cooled by Pallas,
          and overwhelmed by Aphrodite; Œnone is intimi-
          dated by Herè, reassured by Pallas, and scared
          sightless by Aphrodite. The importance to the po-
          etic fable is not that Paris makes the "wrong"
          choice: that was inevitable, a foregone conclusion, a
          necessity if time is to be moved forward (as Pope

was to say, *"Whatever is, is right"*). The crucial consideration is its effects on Œnone in the process of poetic building that she has undertaken—her crushing loneliness and grief and what they vehiculate in her.

191-202   Our perspective on Œnone is clarified. She is a simple, natural child of Pan, not a latter-day metaphysician, and she deals with the bases of Paris' choice in a simple, natural way: I must be fair since even leopards wanton after me, and if I had you here, I would show you what it means to be a loving wife.

203-215   Though Œnone's sorrow is centered in her broken heart and her romantic frame of reference is purely sensual, she is yet sensitive to the fact that her pastoral world has been ravaged, stripped of a delicate tissue of sights and sounds, no longer intact. What has happened is felt throughout nature—by the eagle and by the panther—and the mist and the moonlight have lost their exquisite picturesque accompaniments. (The pine trees which Œnone specifically laments have close association with Pan, an association giving rise to the myth of Pitys and Echo.)

216-225   The pathos of Œnone's naive, girlish situation is induced: how she would like to give Eris a piece of her mind!

226-240   The moment of gentle pathos converts to heart-rending despair. A rush of happy memories throws her into paroxysms of grief that seem to have no terminus except in the death she prays for.

241-251   Out of the depths of her personal grief, Œnone emerges as an apocalyptic figure:

"I will not die alone, for fiery thoughts
Do shape themselves within me, more and more,
Whereof I catch the issue, as I hear
Dead sounds at night come from the inmost hills,
Like footsteps upon wool. I dimly see
My far-off doubtful purpose, as a mother
Conjectures of the features of her child
Ere it is born. . . ."

Although her "fiery thoughts" are inevitably premonitory in the reader's mind of the funeral pyre upon which Œnone will be consumed with Paris and of the conflagration of the civilized world symbolized in the destruction of Troy, she does not here set herself forward, like Cassandra, as a prophetess. The issue that she " 'catches' " runs much deeper than the ten years' war between the Greeks and Trojans, and she is not its prophet but its emblem: as it is with her, so will it be with her world. What she hears are " 'Dead sounds at night . . . from the inmost hills, / Like footsteps upon wool' ": she hears the drum-taps of Destiny in the womb of her consciousness, and she feels the birth-pains of a new order in nature. She will not " 'die alone,' " this simple child of Pan, because Pan himself and Pan's millennium will die with her.

252-264   Œnone's personal hurt surfaces again in a new flow of pathos, but her identification, by allusion, with Dido reenforces her role as a victim of Destiny; and it is made clear that, though she has a sister feeling toward Cassandra, Cassandra's fire dances and sounds of " 'armèd men' " are different from the monitions of her consciousness. She does not presume to read Cassandra's omens,

"but I know
That, wheresoe'er I am by night and day,
All earth and air seem only burning fire."
                                   (emphasis added)

The reader of Theocritus' idylls will recognize that his symbolism is characteristically underplayed, so that Tennyson's reiterated
identification of Œnone's fable with the hour sacred to Pan must
be called insistent; [7] and once this premise is accepted, the epic
resonances of *Œnone,* though kept within the rubric of a miniature
in the poem's formal process, enlarge in a startling aesthetic way—
like an exquisite bud opening to full flower before our very eyes.
The pastoral lament of a shepherdess for her lost shepherd, centered in the private sensibility of Œnone, features the larger myth
of the Judgment of Paris,[8] which in turn draws and is drawn into
the most encompassing myth of the ancient world, the subject of
Homer's *Iliad.* This grand myth is again enlarged to include the
end of a natural dispensation, the death of Pan and the old pagan
order; and implicit in the death of Pan is the birth of Christ, by
which the new order is defined.

Working within the privileges of th miniature epic, with its
sharply economical and deeply embedded symbolism, Tennyson
was not invoking that synchronization of the death of Pan and the
birth of Christ which early Christian writers, taking their cue from
Plutarch, attempted to exploit.[9] Nor is there any literalness intended in the association of the death of Œnone with the death of
Pan. The "time" involved is a mode of consciousness, and the
symbolic seeding, while it implies fictional connection and sequence, is expansive in character. The Pan-Christ association,
drawing together qualities of the universal shepherd, is a variation
on that made familiar by Milton's *On the Morning of Christ's Nativity:*

> The Shepherds on the Lawn,
> Or ere the point of dawn,
>   Sat simply chatting in a rustic row;
> Full little thought they then,
> That the mighty Pan
>   Was kindly come to live with them below;
> Perhaps their loves, or else their sheep,
> Was all that did their silly thoughts so busy keep.

(85-92)

But within the miniature epic as exemplified by Theocritus and in the tradition of the symbolist poets of whom he was a conspicuous forerunner, Tennyson wished to be inexhaustibly suggestive. Once the Christian myth is released in the reader's imagination as an analogical counterpoint to the poem's fiction, the suggestive correspondences multiply: heavenly discord; the Edenic garden; the pride, temptation, and fall of man; the apple as common denominator between the two myths; the imaginative translation from Pan to Christ, the metamorphosis of God to Man; the hour sacred to Pan, the hour of Christ's crucifixion, both linked to nature's total responsiveness—universal hush, cosmic cataclysm; the modest maiden as child-bearer of Destiny. The personified attributes of the polytheistic Goddesses—Power, Wisdom, and Love—have their counterparts in the monotheistic Judeo-Christian God—Omnipotence, Omniscience, Benevolence—and the Christian fusion counterpoints the pagan contention as an implicit motive for the self-destruction of the old order and the birth of the new.

But now we begin to spill into theme, and *Œnone* is not an apothegmatical poem. It is a highly polished, deftly monitored "miniature epic" filled with little pictures-within-little pictures and stories-within-stories, anchored delicately but firmly in the exacerbated sensibility of the simple " 'daughter of a River-God,' " and designed to excite the sophisticated imagination through the allusive and recondite manner by which it obliquely and unpretentiously releases the very largest mythic awarenesses.

Notes

1. See the notes to the poem in *The Poems of Tennyson,* ed. Christopher Ricks (London: Longman, 1969), pp. 384-396, and the article by Paul Turner, *JEGP,* lxi (1962), 57-72, upon which Ricks freely draws. All citations of the Tennyson text are to this edition, identification being made in parentheses immediately following the citation.
2. See *The Poems of Theocritus,* trans. with introductions by Anna Rist (Chapel Hill: University of North Carolina Press, 1978), p. 11.
3. Rist, pp. 11-16, and headnotes to the individual idylls.
4. Rist, p. 13.
5. Christopher Ricks speaks of "the moral muscularity at the center of "Œnone' " and says that "it badly damages the poem." *Tennyson* (New

York: Macmillan, 1972), p. 85. A Dwight Culler, giving renewed credibility to G. K. Chesterton's haughty rewriting—"Self-reverence, self-knowledge, self-control, / These three alone would make a man a prig"—says that "Pallas is clearly the 'right' choice, not only because she is approved by Œnone but also because her speech is so obviously the 'moral' of the poem—the passage that generations of schoolboys will have to memorize." *The Poetry of Tennyson* (New Haven: Yale University Press, 1977), p. 78.

6. Tennyson polished the poem quite thoroughly in the 1832-1842 revisions, but he did not alter the poetic fiction or the narrative formulation.

7. In Ovid, Faunus, the Roman Pan, is one of those who "come in quest" of Œnone— "with hornèd head girt round with sharp pine needles, where Ida swells in boundless ridges." *The Heroides* (Loeb Classical Library), trans. Grant Showerman (Cambridge, Mass.: Harvard University Press, 1963), p. 67. Also, in two early versions of what are now lines 71-83, Hermes, whose son Pan is reputed to be, brought the apple of discord. Ricks, *Poems,* p. 389n.

8. This device of a story-within-a-story also has association with Pan: in *Metamorphoses,* Book I, Mercury (Hermes), on a mission to dispatch Argos, tells the story of Pan and Syrinx and the invention of the panpipe.

9. See Philip Mayerson, *Classical Mythology in Literature, Art, and Music* (Waltham, Mass.: Xerox College Publishing, 1971), pp. 219-220. See also Patricia Merivale, *Pan the Goat-God: His Myth in Modern Times* (Cambridge, Mass.: Harvard University Press, 1969).

6.

Tennyson's *The Lotos-Eaters:* Emblem of a New Poetry

In this chapter, I shall take a single short poem of Tennyson's, *The Lotos-Eaters,* and attempt to show how Tennyson drew together some of the main currents of English poetry's literary heritage, transformed into a poetic artifact one of the principal contentions in the contemporary poetic dilemma, and created a new poem which is the emblem of a new poetry.

The nineteenth-century poets maintained the vigorous devotion to the Greek and Roman classics which had marked the tradition since the Renaissance, but they largely abandoned the imaginative idiom (satire, the heroic couplet, epigram) of the intermediate, neoclassical phase of that devotion as they moved away from a poetry of statement to a poetry of experience. They returned instead to that original tendency of English literary Classicism embodied in the imaginative labors of what, for convenience, can be called Elizabethanism. The Romantics and Victorians (modern Romantics all) worked their linguistic and structural variations on the examples of Spenser and Shakespeare, not Dryden and Pope, and they went directly to the classical writers themselves—to Homer, Aeschylus, Virgil, Ovid, and so forth. The great exceptions

were Milton and, in a much more minor way, Chaucer. Chaucer
was a recurrent point of reference for nineteenth-century poets, but
he was not a major influence on a major poet, unless one considers
William Morris a major poet or happens to draw firmer than usual
connections between *The Canterbury Tales* and *The Ring and the Book.*
Milton, on the other hand, looms very large indeed: he was the
great epicist, the great mythicist, and the stylist par excellence. As
the nineteenth century abandoned the heroic couplet and sought
to restore blank verse to preeminence, its great model was Milton;
and they found the note of literary "high seriousness" which so
attracted them as conspicuous in Milton as in anyone, as they
found him the great exemplar of literary learning. Still, Shakespeare was the incommensurable touchstone of language marked
by a bold gloriousness, and serious efforts to restore poetic drama
to the English stage (by Browning in the 1840s and by Tennyson in
the 1870s) took their direction from Shakespeare. Spenser, the so-
called poet's poet, offered guidance not to be found even in Shakespeare. He was a poetic inventor, and the stanza he had created for
The Fairie Queene, with its full body, its complex interlacing rhymes,
and its concluding alexandrine, had tonal qualities—slow, weighty,
stately—which many of the Romantic writers found highly attractive. Further, Spenser had made a high festivity of lyric language,
his rich verbal music creating a sense of heightened imaginative
reality while avoiding the caprice of euphuistic falseness and the
dullness of verbal neutrality. And Spenser's learning had yet left
him free from the more imperious demands of strict Renaissance
humanism, Spenser having retained in a singular way among the
major poets a deep feeling for the emblems of inwardness, "the
collective Unconscious," [1] of the Middle Ages.

So when Tennyson filtered an episode from Homer's *Odyssey*
through an assumed Spenserian sensibility in the creation of a
modern poem, he coined a poetic metaphor of considerable historical significance. Tennyson's use of the Spenserian stanza in the
opening narrative of *The Lotos-Eaters* is not a verse imitation in the
manner of Thomson's *The Castle of Indolence,* and he carries Spenserianism a giant step in literary experimentation beyond Keats's
The Eve of St. Agnes. The Eve of St. Agnes may be a "perfect" poetic
artifact, but it lacks the imaginative ambition of *The Lotos-Eaters.*

Both poems accomplish their respective purposes superbly; but they are very different purposes, and Tennyson's reaches far beyond Keats's. The fiction and the manner of the opening narrative of *The Lotos-Eaters* tells us that Homer is the inexhaustible mine of simple, emblematic human actions; that Spenser is the great English seer, the prophet, of how the poet may transform action into language and form in order to fulfill his imaginative duty; [2] and that the modern poet (here Tennyson types himself) can creatively build on both in his serious efforts to explore in depth the exacerbated consciousness of man, his acute, psychological distresses. Having established the Spenserian imprint on the poetic manner in which the matter of Homer is being transformed, he proceeds in the Choric Song to modify the Spenserianism, breaking down into a free-form ode the stanzaic patterning of the opening narrative, while at the same time altering the imaginative center of interest in the Homeric action, thus making both peculiarly his own. In *The Lotos-Eaters*, Tennyson puts the incomparable simplicity of Homer and the incomparable literary artifice of Spenser to existential modern uses, transforming nineteenth-century Classicism and nineteenth-century Elizabethanism into nineteenth-century modernism. It is an extraordinary instance of literary organicism in motion, both the inherited matter and the inherited manner being metamorphosized before our very eyes as a quite new species of poem emerges.

What Tennyson does in the Choric Song is as startling formalistically as Keats's conversion of the sonnet base into his great odes. He transforms narrative poetry (past tense "they") into dramatic poetry (present tense "we") that is so profoundly intensified lyrically that it aspires to the condition of music.[3] He establishes the strict but commodious Spenserian stanza as the threshold prosodic structure through which Odysseus' mariners are initiated—wide-eyed, open-eared, and weary unto death—to the sights, sounds, and enveloping ambience of lotos-land. Then, as they pass beyond the threshold of initiation—as the inward-looking stanza / ambience reaches the crucial point of actual internalization (" 'We will return no more,' " l. 43; " 'we will no longer roam,' " l. 45)—the stricter stanza dissolves, gradually at first and then with increasing freedom, into a sequence of strophes that take widely varying shapes and patterns until they climax in an inventive recapitulation that is liberated from the contributive strictures of its Spenserian origins and opens up into a magnificent rhythmic and vocal network of thirteener and fifteener triplets, the shift from pentameter couplets to fifteener triplets taking place in the fifth line of the eighth strophe. The transformation begins slowly, the first five lines of the first strophe being strictly Spenserian. Then there is a breaking up of the rhyme scheme into a triplet and a quadruplet, and a premature alexandrine is introduced in line 7. The phrasing is abruptly altered in line 8 through a trimeter line, but this remounts, through four-stress and five-stress lines, to a final alexandrine. The attachments to the Spenserian stanza are less closely maintained in the second strophe: it begins with a triplet, and four trimeter phrasings are introduced, but the pentameter line is still dominant, and again it closes with an alexandrine. What is new in this second strophe is an undercurrent tension: trochees pull against iambs, and the rhythm of sense begins to bombard the metrical rhythm.[4] In the third strophe, the prosodic break with the Spenserian stanza is abrupt: the lines are almost all four-stress, with only three pentameter lines and no alexandrine, and couplets dominate the rhyme pattern. On the other hand, the rhythmic tension has entirely subsided, trochees and iambs eliding smoothly into each other and sense seeming notably at ease with meter. The rhythmic tension resurfaces explosively in the fourth strophe, so that this must be called the dramatic center of the Choric Song.[5] The prose thrust of the first line continues almost throughout in conflict with an equally heightened rhythmic insistence so that a highly dramatic counterpoint invades the lines; and this dramatic counterpoint has a correspondence in counterpoint in the formal metrical/musical sense in lines 88, 90, and 93, in which a somewhat violent counter-rhythm is imposed upon the unyielding iambs. The explosion then subsides into the final couplet, with its easy rhythms, verbal repetitions, and closing alexandrine. The fifth, sixth, and seventh strophes generally maintain the restored equanimity, neither aping nor rebutting their Spenserian origins but working out comfortable, inventive variations, each ending in an alexandrine. Indeed, the seventh strophe, which considerably magnifies the perception of lotos-land embodied in the first strophe, climaxes in a triplet and a double alexandrine. One can fairly say that Tennyson, in thus aspiring to bring his Choric Song to the condition of music, has both antiqued and modernized his Spenserian heritage: he has carried it backward by sympathy with the style and character of the Greek chorus, and he has carried it forward by creating out of his Spenserian legacy a new musical instrument in which the dramatic action is fully centered, fusing intense lyricism and a keen existential dramatic process into a new species of psychological poetry.

The character and place of the "action" in *The Lotos-Eaters* require historical perspective. One of the most important aesthetic issues facing the major practitioners in the art of poetry in the first half of the nineteenth century was the relative place of action and feeling. The most inward-looking of post-medieval ages had dawned, and poets on all sides had caught the spirit of accommodation reflected in Shelley's *A Defence of Poetry* [6]: they must modify their literary inheritance in the light of new cultural needs, and while, in degrees, they were the creations of the new age, they must be its creators, too. Different poets interpreted this need for poetic modernization differently. Thus, Wordsworth set the poems contained in *Lyrical Ballads* against "the popular poetry of the day" on this specific criterion: "that the feeling therein developed gives importance to the action and situation, and not the action and situation to the feeling"; [7] and he aligned this subject in importance with the "beauty and dignity" of the human mind and gave witness to the "multitude" of contemporary "causes" combined against it. At mid-century (1853), in a preface second in importance only to Wordsworth's, Matthew Arnold again emphasized as "the eternal objects of Poetry" "actions; human actions; possessing an inherent interest in themselves. . . ." [8] Like Wordsworth, Arnold asserted a fundamental Aristotelian principle: " 'All depends upon the subject; choose a fitting action, penetrate yourself with the feeling of its situations; this done, everything else will follow.' " [9] Concerned broadly, like Wordsworth, with the humanly debilitating pressures of the times, Arnold gave focus specifically to the literary debility embodied in the following false cousel: " 'A true allegory of the state of one's own mind in a representative history . . . is perhaps the highest thing that one can attempt in the way of poetry.' " [10] The reversal of the role of action and feeling has here become internalized and virtually prescriptive.

Tennyson, who had not been born when Wordsworth wrote his preface and was poet laureate when Arnold wrote his, shaped his art among the massive pressures and chaotic counsel current at the time. He recognized that the engendering and purifying of man's imagination was the chief goal of the modern poet, and he was fully aware of the odds against which he worked. He felt the insistent pressure, both from within and from without, to be relevant to the new age, but he knew that the antiquity or contemporaneousness of his subject matter was essentially beside the point. He was, like Arnold, thoroughly steeped in the Greek and Roman poets, but he saw the transformation rather than the imitation of this rich imaginative inheritance as the obligation of a serious modern poet with major ambitions.[11] He accepted the primary place of the myth in the poem, while accepting too the inward-looking character of the times, a character that, he knew, made imperious demands on poetry. He would not have quarreled with Arnold's principle of the subordinate character of expression in narrative-dramatic poetry, but he would have saved for language a more heightened, processive role than Arnold, applying a corrective to the "Elizabethanism" of the Romantic poets, chose to give it; and although he too, except in some of his juvenilia and verse exercises, avoided "personification of abstract ideas" and "poetic diction," he did not deny the value of personification as a poetic resource, and he would not have taken the level of language appropriate to the *Lyrical Ballads* as applicable to all poetic situations.

What Tennyson actually did in *The Lotos-Eaters* was invoke a union of Classicism and Romanticism. He took a myth or action from Homer and expanded it inward. Without in any way abandoning the primary importance of the action, his penetration of himself " 'with the feeling of its situations' " led him to an internal center of interest that we think of as characteristically Romantic. The really severe critical principle involved here, the collapse of which has distorted modern criticism of *The Lotos-Eaters,* is that *how he felt about it* does not invade the poem: it is not an " 'allegory of the state of [his] own mind.' " *How they felt about it* and how their feelings were set in motion, leading to perceptual movement and resolution, is the unyielding focus of the poet's imaginative attention and an inward-moving refinement of the myth or action. So that as soon as the reader makes a full concession to the poem's demands to be perceived as wholly dramatic—as an example of what Wordsworth speaks of as "an entire delusion," the poet confounding and identifying "his own feelings" with those of the "persons whose feelings he describes" [12]—the Classical integrity of the poem, while fully romanticized, is intact. After reaching that critical point, the student of *The Lotos-Eaters* can be entirely comfortable with the comments of an Aristotelian classicist on Homer's *Odyssey* having no conscious reference to Tennyson's poem but wholly germane to it: "the story makes the characters, not the characters the story"; [13] the characters "show the possibilities of human life; by hearing of them, one knows what it is. But as auditors gain touch with guiding reality by tales of great events, so do the characters by living the events"; [14] "the adventures make [the characters]; [they do] not in a subjective sense make the adventures"; [15] "An experience does not become real because a person feels it, rather a person becomes real because he undergoes what exists. The emphasis is on the human condition, not on private consciousness of it." [16] If this point is not held to with simple firmness, *The Lotos-Eaters* loses its clarity as a metaphor of the modern poet's creative salvaging of both an authentic Classicism and an authentic Romanticism and drifts awash in the unrefreshing waters of subjective, sentimental moralism. The poem is admittedly poised at a point of precarious balance, owing to the ultimate refinement of Tennyson's sensibilities; but the balance is preserved, not lost.

The "action" of *The Lotos-Eaters*, it needs to be remembered, is entirely Tennyson's own. What goes on in the *Odyssey* ix 82-104 bears little resemblance to what goes on in *The Lotos-Eaters*. Tennyson took the episode from Homer's public text, but he put it to his own poetic uses, not involving himself in such Homeric ambiguities as to who exactly ate of the lotos-branches [17] and assuming, finally, an autonomy and individual integrity for his own poem. The reader may enrich his own imaginative experience subjectively, drawing as freely on all parts of the *Odyssey* as he will, but he is not free, even in the light of Homer, to rewrite the Tennyson text. He is not free, at least as a responsible critic of this Tennyson poem, to assert that "We know that when the time comes, that hard voice will ring out again and the mariners will troop back to the oars." [18] We know nothing of the sort if we are reading Tennyson, and even in Homer they were "brought back perforce to the ships, weeping." The point is that we must not read Tennyson's text *via* Homer except where Tennyson chose to make them coincide, just as we must not subject Tennyson's *Ulysses* to a passage in Dante's *Inferno.* J. W. Croker, while willfully obtuse about the poem, spoke half a truth: "How they got home you must read in Homer: -Mr. Tennyson—himself, we presume, a dreamy lotos-eater, a delirous lotos-eater—leaves them in full song." [19] Not even Homer tells us how they "got home," since they failed to get home, but one must truly go to Homer for Homer and to Tennyson for Tennyson; and it is quite true and significant that Tennyson "leaves them in full song."

Further, the "action" of *The Lotos-Eaters* is not the same as that of any other Tennyson poem, and it is dangerous critically to let analogies between this poem and other poems in the Tennyson canon, especially thematic analogies, color our vision of the subject that Tennyson is most carefully working out in this poem.[20] And there are two corollaries to this. One is the stereotyping of our availability to the Tennysonian consciousness—a predisposition to disbelieve that certain kinds of awarenesses, especially keenly disturbing awarenesses, were genuine perceptual possibilities for Tennyson. The other is methodological: the imposition of a simple dualistic structure, in this case ethical, on the intricate imaginative processes of the poem and the consequent reduction of its subtle integration of action, character, and language to a simple moral apothegm.

The Lotos-Eaters is a poem of processive choice-making. From the first word to the last—" 'Courage!' .... more"—the mariners, presumably with Odysseus silently watching, are placed in a situation that totally catalyzes everything that they are—their physical, mental, and spiritual condition, all the stages of their most recent, intermediate, and remotest past, their habitual values, their prospective vision, even patternings of their subterranean consciousness—and moves them to a place in which, except in their dreams, they never thought they would be. Thus the action of the poem, in terms of its effects, is the ultimate human action: through this action, the mariners become what they otherwise could never have been. They become what in Homer they never were—namely, heroes [21]—and they are brought by the action that so deeply affects them to a kind and quality of courage that, ironically, the wily Odysseus has not known and is not intended in the moral exemplum—" 'Courage!' "—with which Odysseus opens the poem. Thus *The Lotos-Eaters* effects a perceptual value-reversal that is, in fact, seeded in a reversal of the first and last words: *more Courage.*[22]

The difference between the two parts of the poem—between the introductory narrative and the dramatic ode—is the difference between excited passivity and deliberative activity, the transition being effected in the closing lines of the narrative by means of a low-toned dramatic implant:

> Then some one said, "We will return no more;"
> And all at once they sang, "Our island home
> Is far beyond the wave; we will no longer roam."

> (43-45)

And they arrive at this breaking point through a process of in-depth penetration and enlargement monitored by a need deep within them—the generic human need, especially keen in older men,[23] for stability, fixity, permanence. This is the first need to surface in their response to lotos-land—"a land / in which it *seemèd always* afternoon" (3-4, emphasis added); it is, like the exhortation of Odysseus, one of the fixed points of reference in the poem. Paired with permanence in their center of need is benignity, including both gentleness in their environment and the inner sense of being well-born, favored. These are the two qualities which they have never known in the changing, ravaging world of their experience, and yet these are the central images of their collective Unconscious. So while they quickly but progressively survey the island with their outer eye, like practiced voyagers who have often survived through good fortune and wit quickened by need,[24] their inner eye is taking yet deeper measure of this extraordinary place,

progressively verifying their sudden intuition that this is the lost
paradise, not of their consciousness, since they have never known
anything like it, but of their Unconscious, that buried self that has
retained an inaccessible, imageless intimation of its ultimate origins. It is at that level that the theme of metamorphosis or release
is taking place through a psychological / imaginative process described in a poem roughly contemporaneous, *The Lover's Tale:*

> Alway the inaudible invisible thought,
> Artificer and subject, lord and slave,
> Shaped by the audible and visible,
> Moulded the audible and visible. . . .

$$(II, 101\text{-}104) \; [25]$$

At the center of their being is an undiscovered, unexplored reality
not in itself accessible to "matter-moulded forms of speech" [26]
which is "Shaped" (given body) by stimuli closer to the surface
both inside and outside the individual (whatever is "audible and
visible") and in turn "Mould[s]" those stimuli, so that an indefinable reality and a seemingly definable reality are in a state of
perpetual interpenetration and can never be consciously separated
and independently known. But since that "inaudible invisible" activity ("thought") is fed by specific outer images ("audible and
visible"), when those images change, what it makes of them
("Mould[s]") will also change, and this is the processive imaginative metamorphosis which the mariners, in their excited passivity,
are undergoing in the introductory narrative of *The Lotos-Eaters.*
They are discovering new images by which that reality-defining,
goal-setting inner apparatus is activated and fed, and it in turn is
shaping a new reality and new goals in their consciousness. Their
spiritual movement is through a process monitored by a theory of
the imagination.

"A land of streams!" It is as though they have suddenly swept
the land with sight and taken a quick survey of its chief features, as
one might move out of a mood with a blink and look at a picture
consciously for the first time. The dominant impression is of a land
of streams—not one but many and each both like and different;

and there is a river flowing from the heartland to the sea. Streams and rivers mean life and vegetation and abundance. Three mountain peaks—further images of permanence and stability—are capped with "agèd snow" and hence cannot be volcanic and threatening; and even the snow is "sunset-flushed"—warm, aesthetically pleasing, benign. The copses signify fertility, and the pines, drenched in refreshing dews, are the vegetal correspondents to the mountain peaks, symbols of Pan and a stable, natural antiquity. It is like a mirage on a desert of sand or sea; or like an emblem of the imagination compensating for a life of deprivation; or *like Ithaca transformed* into a bountiful fairy-land, the central image motivating all their past efforts suddenly reached in the form of a more ingratiating equivalent. In this enveloping mood of subliminal realization, they take a still closer look and see depth and perspective in this charmed world—inland dales, a yellow down bordered by palms, valleys, and meadows rich in aromatic sedge, all bespeaking permanence and benevolence and dependability and hospitality: *home.* Then they see, close at hand, their hosts, deities of the lotos-hearth: their pale faces warmed by the "charmèd sunset," the "mild-eyed melancholy" inhabitants of lotos-land are alternative images to the wild-eyed, harried, desperately discouraged men that they have been—are *themselves* (like Ithaca) *transformed.*

In the fourth stanza of the introductory narrative (28-36), the mariners, who up to this point have been a single company, divide into two groups—those who eat the narcotic and those who do not; and this sophisticates (creates a nice ambiguity in) the Choric Song. It may be, at least at some of its acutest pressure points, a dramatic monologue, the drugged mariners rebutting implicit attempts of their undrugged companions to persuade them of the folly of their ways; or it may be throughout a monodrama, the contention being entirely internal. In either case, it is significant that, although their survey of the island has been chiefly visual, the effects of the drug are chiefly auditory, placing them at a distance in space ("the wave") and in existential state ("the grave") and creating an inner music (the "beating heart"). Under the influence of the drug, the mariners sit down in their spacey world ("upon the yellow sand, / Between the sun and moon") and have sweet dreams "of Fatherland, / Of child, and wife, and slave." But the

sense of permanence and benignity that has been gradually enveloping their consciousness—inner subconscious action stimulated
by outer images, taking its character from those images and giving
to them a transformed character—makes the sea *(vita agonistes)* permanently impedimental ("evermore"), and they yield the Odyssean theme of "return"—passively or receptively at first and then
with choric decisiveness—and make an exchange of "homes."

The "deliberative activity" with which the Choric Song was earlier characterized should not be overdrawn. Although there is unmistakable progression in the total curve of the eight strophes,
there is also rise and fall, perhaps by metaphoric analogy with the
rush and subsidence of the narcotic or the flood and recession of
fatigue and restlessness, weariness, and thrashing. Moreover, the
movement is rhythmic and tonal rather than discursive, although
important "arguments" are deposited. And the issue is not how *we
feel* about them, since we may bring very different value-structures
to bear in forming ethical judgments, but *how we perceive their self-
perception,* how they feel about themselves.

The first strophe is the most slumbrous, with the least rhythmic
tension. The rhymes feature sibilants and labials, and the vowels
simulate the threshold sign of rest after strenuous, wearying toil.
The images are all of soft music, falling rose petals, gentle dews,
cool mosses, weeping flowers, hanging poppies. It is a lullaby over a
cradle endlessly rocking. The second strophe is one extended
"Why?" concerning the human condition which has as its implicit
motive "Why not?"—why not "have rest," "fold our wings,"
"harken what the *inner* spirit sings?" (emphasis added). At the
heart of it is a paradox: must the highest be the most distressed?
Do man's Apollo-gifts demand eternal pain (distress, toil, sorrow)?
Is imperial man imperially obligated? The structure of the dramatic monologue/monodrama begins to function: "Why *should* I?"
is an implicit question, dramatic in both senses. The images all
shift from lullaby to restlessness and struggle, as if the mariners are
too tired to sleep. The rhythmic tension mounts to counterpoint in
the broad sweep (II versus I) as well as in individual lines (57, 69),
and the rhythm of sense conflicts with metrical regularity. The
Stoic philosophy (" 'There is no joy but calm,' " l. 68) hovers un-
certainly between Stoic detachment and Epicurean indulgence. In
strophe III, the rhythm returns to a gentle wash between trochees

and iambs, with a few maverick ripples, and the argument is made
from the world of vegetables and fruits that man should subdue his
struggle to the pattern of quotidianal nature, accepting his "allot-
ted length of days" passively. It is an argument with an analogue
in the Sermon on the Mount (Matthew 6:28-29) concerning the
lilies of the field that "toil not, neither do they spin."

Strophe IV reaches a high level of tension *(agitato)*[27] as the
moral issue is explicitly introduced: "What pleasure can we have /
To war with evil?" (93-94). The mariners focus on death as "the
end of life," playing with the complex meaning ("end" versus goal)
in a strategy of simplification. They point to the brevity of Time,
the ravages of change, the harsh restlessness of war—all contradictions to the benign permanence motif of which they have found an
image in lotos-land. They dichotomize life simply as "long rest or
death" and decline, in the light of their own past, an alternative
view. In strophe V, the rhythms return to the lullaby, rocking
between trochees and iambs. The former tension is hardly audible,
though the subjunctive mood ("How sweet it were") implies a
condition contrary to realized fact, and the drift is from "dreamful
ease" to "dark death." Their identification with the natives moves
into clearer focus ("mild-*minded* melancholy," l. 109, emphasis
added), and they express a desire to overleap the intervening years
of adulthood and return to their "infancy," to a sort of preexistent
womb-state in the dust from which they emerged. They want to
"live again in memory," as though their return is to a home before
the home at Ithaca, a home precedent to the death of birth of
which they have, deep in their Unconscious, fragments of remembrance. Thus the permanence theme and the hieratic theme of
ultimate origins and destinies merge in the image of "Two hand-
fuls of white dust, shut in an urn of brass!" (113). But while they
are tired of life as they have previously known it, their psychic
retreat from combat seems to lead them, in an unlettered, non-
metaphysical way, to intimations of, and longings for, home not
unlike those of "Crossing the Bar"—

> such a tide that moving seems asleep,
> Too full for sound and foam,
> When that which drew from out the boundless deep
> Turns again home.

Strophe VI is a late addition to the poem (1842, not 1832) very strategically placed, and it, along with the line "There *is* confusion worse than death" (Tennyson's emphasis), must be considered crucial in any experience of the poem. The most noteworthy thing about the strophe is its lack of rhythmic tension, of psychic turbulence. It begins with a gracious sentiment and then very matter-of-factly, reasonably, and thoroughly describes the probable changes at Ithaca and the distress that their late return would introduce; and it ends on a note of realistic acceptance. They are not Odysseuses and are not possessed of his "strong" will "To strive, to seek, to find, and not to yield." [28] They are old men, their breath "agèd," their hearts "worn out," their eyes "grown dim"; and they are not tragic overreachers. They welcome the "Sunset and evening star"; they want to "go gentle into that good night." Though death is "dark," they are ready to "Turn again home" and rejoin the ancestors remotest to their memories. They are less confounded by death than confused by life. They have done their share, and they decline to step out of their legend ("the minstrel sings / . . . of the ten years' war in Troy") and try again the impossible task of reconciling the Gods. In strophe VII, too, the metrical tension is almost inaudible, and the imagery has taken on a deeper hieratic quality—"a heaven dark and holy," "the long bright river drawing slowly / His waters from the purple hill," the "acanthus-wreath divine!" The amaranth is "the immortal flower of legend," [29] and moly is the sacred herb given to Odysseus by Hermes as a charm against Circe.[30] So there is a new note of joy and sacred excitement among the mariners, no touch of the swine motif being present.

Strophe VIII is the recapitulation or reprise: it gathers into a crescendo the themes and phrasings of the piece as a whole and gives them a final signature. It is clear from the expansiveness of it that the mariners have processed themselves in the course of the song to rather full reconciliation with a very difficult decision upon which their whole past and a resource deep in their Unconscious have had a bearing. They can at last let old energies flow, old rhythmic patterns freely surface, without fear. The opening (145-149) is firm, rounded, confirmatory; the memory of the recent past (150-152) is vigorous and unintimidated; the oath (153-155), which some commentators see as an effort to shore up a weak position, is a hieratic ritual like other post-novitiate vow-takings; the description of the Gods (156-164) is canonical, popular pagan anthropomorphism based on Lucretius, as is the perfectly realistic description of the condition of man and his mortal destiny (165-170). And if all that is true, then "Surely, surely,[31] slumber is more sweet than toil" to old men with "agèd breath," "hearts worn out," and "eyes grown dim."

Tennyson, as Croker said, "leaves them in full song," and that is a fact of some significance. They have been allowed to break out of the mold in which Tennyson found them in Homer, and he does not in the end return them to it. These anonymous men, little more than the faceless fodder of Destiny in the *Odyssey*, become the center of an action in Tennyson's poem that makes them the focus of an alternative human possibility and enables them, as a small representative group, to assume more individuality and stature than they are granted in all twenty-four books of Homer's poem. If they are self-deceived, the deception is certainly no greater than the faith that, by continuing the unequal struggle, they can, in fact, go home again. And the situation which so transforms and enlarges them extends the possibility that the choice which they deliberately make is an act, not of less, but of more courage.

In conclusion: the consciously released poetic resonances of Tennyson's *The Lotos-Eaters* are almost inexhaustible. Written in 1830-1832 [32] and significantly expanded and revised for republication in 1842, the poem takes an incident from Homer and a poetic manner from Spenser and transforms them in the poem's process, expanding Homer's myth inward and converting Spenser's stanza gradually into an intensely lyrical choric ode, returning Spenser, as it were, to a Greek literary context. He converts a narrative poem into a dramatic poem through the gradual registration of an external action on a responsive internal psyche, shifting from narrative movement to dramatic action at the point at which the external movement becomes wholly internalized; and he further intensifies the drama by making the choric ode the center of the dramatic action, not a gloss on it, and by employing the choric devices of tonality and rhythmic expressiveness as internal poetic guides to action and meaning. But he does much more than formalistically resolve the conflict between Classicism and Romanticism so persistent at the time. He shows how the modern poet, the poet of an inward-looking age, can maintain the imaginative purity inherent in giving the dominant place to the action and still give the myth full development at an internal center where spiritual metamorphosis actually happens. But he does even more: he creates a modern poem of self-pleading or case-making rooted deep in a mythic narrative in which the imaginative transformation that gives strength and timber to the special-pleading takes place and suggests by implication a psychology of the imagination in which an internal center absorbs external images and molds in the consciousness what we habitually perceive as external reality.

Notes

1. See C.S. Lewis, "Edmund Spenser, 1552-1599," in *Major British Writers,* Enlarged Edition (New York: Harcourt, Brace & World, 1959), I, 91-103.
2. My reference is not to verbal echoes of *The Fairie Queene,* but to the whole heightening of the imaginative manner exemplified by Spenser. Christopher Ricks says that "Spenser was the major influence on the style and tone" of *The Lotos-Eaters* and cites specifically I, i, st. 41; I, ix, st. 40; II, vi, st. 10; and II, xii, st. 32 of *The Fairie Queene.* See *The Poems of Tennyson,* ed. Christopher Ricks (London: Longman, 1969), p. 429. All quotations from Tennyson in this chapter are from the Ricks edition, passages being identified in parentheses immediately after the citation.
3. F. E. L. Priestley reads the theme of the poem in a way different from my reading of it, and therefore his perception of the total aesthetic procedure is different; but he is fully attuned to the musical sophistication of the poem. The metrical pattern "must function, not logically by the subject matter, but musically or tonally by sound. And if the poem is read aloud with an attentive ear, it is evident that metrical forms do in fact serve musical purposes." He then goes on to speak of the *forte* and *con brio* of the opening lines and of the "slight *rallentandos* and *accelerandos,* and muted *agitato* movements" of the "choruses." *Language and Structure in Tennyson's Poetry* (London: Andre Deutsch, 1973), p. 57.
4. Tennyson and Swinburne shared this technique of sense at war with metrics, with this important difference, I think: whereas Swinburne tended to submerge sense in an importunate rhythm, Tennyson more subtly submerged rhythm in the irresistible demands of sense.
5. Alternative reader perceptions of the dramatic character of this lyric chorus will be explored at a later point in this article.

6. Tennyson, of course, could not have read Shelley's essay until 1840.

7. Preface (1800), in *The Prose Works of William Wordsworth*, ed. W. J. B. Owen and J. W. Smyser (Oxford: At the Clarendon Press, 1974), I, 128.

8. Preface to *Poems* (1853) in *The Complete Prose Works of Matthew Arnold*, ed. R. H. Super (Ann Arbor: University of Michigan Press, 1960, I *(On the Classical Tradition)*, 3.

9. P. 7.

10. P. 8.

11. The functional difference between these two principles of classical usage can be readily seen in a comparison of Arnold's *Sohrab and Rustum,* the poem with which he illustrated the principles of his preface, and *The Lotos-Eaters.*

12. Preface (1802 and later), in *Prose Works,* I, 138.

13. John H. Finley, Jr., *Homer's "Odyssey"* (Cambridge, Mass.: Harvard University Press, 1978), p. 26, and repeated pp. 27, 40-41.

14. Finley, p. 41.

15. Finley, p. 25.

16. Finley, pp. 29-30.

17. Homer has Odysseus send out three men, but it is not clear whether only two of them or others become lotos-eaters.

18. Priestley, p. 56.

19. As quoted in Ricks, *Tennyson* (New York: Macmillan, 1972), p. 92.

20. I am thinking particularly of the "garden of art" theme and the tendency of some critics to draw *The Lotos-Eaters* into a misty circle of aesthetic temptation, "reading" the poem in the light of such poems as *The Hesperides, The Lady of Shalott,* and *The Palace of Art.* One need not contradict the validity of such analogies, kept at an appropriate distance, in suggesting that a prior and separate aesthetic issue is the meticulous demands of making a good autonomous poem.

21. Finley, p. 53, says that Odysseus' companions are not heroic.

22. One's inclination to think that this is too fanciful will be modified, perhaps, by the recollection that in *Maud,* begun in 1833, Tennyson clearly plays the "embrace" of the last line against the "hate" of the first line.

    I am conscious, of course, that this is a startlingly heterodox reading of *The Lotos-Eaters,* and I have chosen to forego point-by-point contention with other commentators, being fully convinced that, however much my own rhetorical inadequacies may leave a particular perception wobbling, this is the extra turning that Tennyson gave to an otherwise traditional moralistic perception and that the imaginative excitement lies in the extra turning. Further, I believe that a startling heterodoxy may be so common in future Tennyson studies that it will establish a new orthodoxy.

23. The theme of battered age, so pervasive in the *Odyssey,* is made a fundamental part of this poetic text in Tennyson's late addition of strophe VI to the Choric Song: there the mariners speak of ther "agèd breath," "hearts worn out," and "eyes grown dim" (131-133).

24. The sailor-habits that lead them to test the air next draw their attention to the moon. It is "Full-faced above the valley," a good weather omen. And the "slender stream" is, unlike the surging sea, almost bodiless and is comforting as chimney-smoke is comforting.

25. This perception is prescient in a precise way of what Pater will do in *Marius and Epicurean.*

26. *In Memoriam,* xcv, 46.

27. See above, n. 3.

28. *Ulysses,* 70.

29. Tennyson, quoted in Ricks, *Poems,* p. 435n.

30. *Odyssey* x 291-317. Hermes was the father of Pan, and it is among Pan's sacred caves that "the dewy echoes" call (139-140).

31. The formula of overprotest that some commentators see in the repetition here is easily undercut by allowing the voice to fall on the second *surely* in the manner of "Ah yes, ah yes"; and so far as forcing the *will* (versus *shall*) in the last line goes, see the "will" of lines 43 and 45, where the accent is even-voiced.

32. Ricks, *Poems,* p. 429.

7.

In Defense of *Locksley Hall*

Despite its universal visibility among the crucial poems of Tennyson (in anthologies, in the growing number of general studies), *Locksley Hall* has never been approached in print as a complex, self-contained, innovative, subtle, and wholly successful poetic process. The most sensitive and original of the modern commentators on Tennyson's language and structures passes it by with a single reference,[1] and another commentator peremptorily dubs it "an unsuccessful poem" and confesses his surprise that critics have been so persistently attentive to it and that anthologists have given it space that could have been used for better poems.[2] More recently, A. Dwight Culler has shown a circumspect critical attitude toward the poem; and although he has neglected to provide a unified view of *Locksley Hall* as an autonomous poetic structure, he has, in passing, pointed to some of the crucial passages upon which such a view must be based.[3]

Genuine criticism of *Locksley Hall* has been impeded from the very beginning by thematic attitudes rooted in autobiographical assumptions about the poem. Tennyson protested repeatedly against those assumptions. " 'Locksley Hall' is thought by many to be an autobiographical sketch; it's nothing of the sort—not a word of my history in it"; [4] it is "a simple invention as to place, incidents, and people"; [5] *"There is not one touch of biography in it from beginning to end"* [6] (Tennyson's emphasis); " 'Locksley Hall' is an imaginary place (tho' the coast is Lincolnshire), and the hero is imaginary. The whole poem represents young life, its good side, its deficiencies, and its yearning." [7] But the autobiographical assumptions have persisted as the controllers of the way most people think about the poem and have, in effect, imprisoned *Locksley Hall* as a reading act. To do direct battle against such strategic undercutting of the poet's credibility, though tempting, is futile: the lines of contention get too rigidly drawn, and the contest takes on a mimic character as if one were attempting to resolve an archetypal issue. The best one can do critically is to try to make a constructive contribution to the side of the issue one favors as a poetry-reader and, in this particular case, to draw strength from the poet's authority taken, not slavishly, but seriously.

Locksley Hall warrants the utmost critical attentiveness both because it is a pivotal poem in the evolving Tennyson canon and because it clearly points to a new direction in English poetry. It is the first example, in English, of an authentic mythic contemporaneousness, a poetic voicing of that brave new world opening up to a representative modern youth—personally chastened, culturally confused, his prospective vision measurably eclipsed, but capable and determined, in a tight-lipped sort of way, to meet the future without a whimper. It is a poem of divestiture / investiture in which the May-idyll of romantic love is laid aside and the sadder wisdom of a fallible adulthood is put on. Hence, it is an initiation poem, centered in a character of twenty, and its sentiments, like its language and structure, are to be judged by their appropriateness to that particular poetic fiction rather then by sterner standards of a maturer wisdom. The fiction captures a moment in a well-defined stage of the speaker's development, and the poetic process gives rich and dynamic imaginative reality to a meticulously individuated personality in a texture of human and historical time, while simultaneously keeping both the personality and the time wholly available for mythic translation—Everyman at all times. Considered from this critical perspective, Tennyson's comment—

"The whole poem represents young life, its good side, its deficiencies, and its yearnings"—is both perfectly apt and most carefully worded.

Locksley Hall is a mondrama placed in a lightly sketched narrative frame (1-2, 145-146, 194).[8] The latter is important because it suggests how "the actual threads" of the larger story "pass out beyond" the "design" of the central poetic process itself: [9] the public socialization of the speaker, his further acculturation as a man of the new age, is implicit in these narrative fragments. The former is the most crucial aspect of the total aesthetic procedure. As the speaker of a monodrama, the central personality of the poem is freed from all external impediments to self-expression: the "different phases of passion" [10] which he experiences are all released into verbal gesture, and in an episode that is metaphorically climactic, he exorcises, not the memory of the past, but the soul-specter which has continued to haunt him and to make his present a passionate malaise. He exchanges a private myth that has self-destructed (romantic love) for a public myth (social and scientific progress) by which, in a spirit of personal rediscovery, he hopes to achieve an authentic degree of self-fulfillment. Further, the monodrama enables the poet to concentrate in the personality of his speaker all of the cultural imperatives of the age, not only such enveloping coordinates as subjectivism, individualism, and relativism, but also the corollaries thereof, the infinitely variable cultural metaphors by which each time-frame of human history gets its particular definition and, considered generically, refracts the variant metaphors of other time-frames. As he gradually assumes substantial *persona*-dimensions in the poem, the speaker becomes much more than a representative spokesman for his age: *he is the age* as that age is moving from one state of being to another; and since, by virtue of the formalistic imperatives of monodrama, *he is also language,* he is "rhetoricising the conspicuous objects" and converting an era into a style.[11] It is an extraordinary imaginative apprehension—the modernization, not of an inherited Classical myth to be rewritten in the spirit of contemporary relevance, but of mythicism itself; and it points to the long-term literary future, to a major course Tennyson will himself take in poems like *In Memoriam* and *Maud* and to the imaginative apprehensions of such later writers as

Pater, Hardy, Yeats, and T. S. Eliot. It is the poet's renewed recognition that he must save literature by doing for his age—however confused, however eclipsed—what Homer and others did for theirs, namely, create it for the imaginative perceiver by seeing it mythically and thereby energize it and make it creatively usable.

Modern practitioners in this line of mythic contemporaneousness have tended to make rather conspicuous use of irony, and the critics' perception of what Tennyson is doing in *Locksley Hall* has been monitored by what they see as an absence of irony in the poem. Ralph Wilson Rader has been one of the most assertive: "No hint of irony, no frame of dramatic objectification qualifies in the least the extravagantly self-centered emotion of the protagonists in these poems [*Locksley Hall* and *Maud*], so that most competent commentators have seen the two as to some extent mouthpieces for Tennyson himself." [12] Hellstrom is also rather absolute in his dismissiveness of the poem: "If . . . the latter part of the poem is not to be taken at face value as profound, or at least straightforward, but is ironic, then generations of readers have misread it as an expression of Tennyson's hope for the future and the irony must be deemed unsuccessful." [13] Jerome H. Buckley is much more balanced and critically stimulating, but he also sees the speaker as "untouched by the comic spirit." [14] Culler pinpoints what, on the issue of irony, seems to have been one aspect of the critical difficulty with the poem: "The modern reader, approaching it as a dramatic monologue and looking for some evidence of ironic intention, finds none and so leaps to the conclusion that the poet is to be identified with the hero and is to be condemned for that character's extravagance." [15]

Though the creation of a new poetic form is always precarious, it is difficult to imagine a practiced reader of poetry reflecting on *Locksley Hall* as if it were, lightly disguised, a solemn pronouncement on the part of the poet of views that, after a deeply wrenching affair of the heart, he had found the sufficient basis for a firm facing of the future. Almost everything about the poem to which commentators have objected is reasonably obvious, and the assumption that they seem to make, namely, that one of the subtlest of poets was not aware of the most obvious dimensions of his own creation, is hard to credit. The poem sends out signal after signal that the deficiencies of this generic personality are a fundamental part of the poetic apprehension being dramatized in *Locksley Hall:* the irrepressible self-consciousness, the melodramatic gesturing, the blatant egotism, the male chauvinism, the apex-of-civilization posturing, the sick fantasizing, the noble savagery, the sentiment-drenched egalitarianism, the repetitive romanticizing of war, and so forth. Indeed, the speaker is suspended in the keenest and most penetrating medium of irony, and to deny the poet this dimension of his creation is like dismissing Hopkins's sprung rhythm because one cannot find counterpoint in it.

Seen in its rawest form, the poem's pervasive irony is classically dramatic: we perceive things about the character that he does not perceive about himself. And we are enabled to view him thus critically through several strategies used by the poet: by the way he overkills with language; by our suspicion, born of his linguistic extravagance and the neurotic fantasies he creates concerning the newlyweds, that he is attempting to externalize blame and that the external reality may bear little resemblance to the fabrications stimulated by a combination of heightened fancifulness and inner distress; and by our further recognition of the discrepancy between the extremely private myth of romantic sexual love and "the crescent promise of [his] spirit" (187), which projects his imaginative energy outward toward a science-based cultural future so intense that he

> rather held it better men should perish one by one,
> Than that earth should stand at gaze like Joshua's moon in
> Ajalon!
>
> (179-180)

and leads him to emit such dedicated Macaulayese as "Better fifty years of Europe than a cycle of Cathay" (184).

But Tennyson has subtilized this raw irony—made it keen and penetrating—by counterpointing these personal "deficiencies," which are the revealed source of our critical ironic perceptions, to the speaker's "good side," making his scandal a dimension of his glory. He thus creates several rarer ironic possibilities. One is that the "love" to which the speaker gives such fanciful delicacy is little more than sexual lust imaginatively costumed. Another, a corollary to the first, is that the importunate rhythms of his personality have been temporarily interrupted by this idyllic moment of romantic equipoise and inevitably reassert themselves. It is not a question of authorial judging: a frank and healthy sexuality in a young man of twenty is one of the joys of living, and one's personal rhythms should "have scope and breathing space" (167). On the other hand, the subtle self-deceptions of a gifted, romantic, high-minded youth are worthy of wry watching; and they take on magnified metaphoric (and ironic) importance if that youth is an emblem of the new age and his personal disguises are translatable to his role as a culture-figure.

There are many hints of a submerged sexuality in the poem, including the particular memory that triggers the speaker's first verbal reprisal ("And our spirits rushed together at the touching of the lips," 38), the sotted sexual alienation that he fancifully imposes upon the husband-wife relationship (47-55, 77-86), and the bawdy humor hidden in the straight-laced line "They to whom my foolish passion were a target for their scorn" (146). But the speaker's sexual longings emerge explosively in the alternative fantasy (153-171) with which he finally ventilates the impacted emotions which, unrecognized and unadmitted, have force-fed his gesturing, posturing, melodramatic extravagance, both perceptual and verbal. Significantly, this passage, with its rapacious, imperious sexual and romantic primitivism, is played against the only other passage in the poem in which the love alternative is celebrated (21-38) and becomes an implicit gloss on it. Thus the line "Fool, again the dream, the fancy! but I *know* my words are wild" (173, Tennyson's emphasis) applies both to the romantic escapism of a lost paradise populated by noble savages of which the speaker becomes the racial root and to the more "cultured" myth of romantic domesticity suggested by his love-idyll with Amy: it is his distanced, disguised, protective way of dealing with it acceptably to himself.[16] Significant, too, is the placement at the center of this lost paradise / noble savage sequence of the following importunately rhythmic couplet:

There methinks would be enjoyment more than in this
    march of mind,
In the steamship, in the railway, in the thoughts that shake
    mankind.

(165-166)

Although the speaker here, in the middle of his alternative fantasy, turns a "jaundiced eye" (132) on some of the primary symbols of the new age, after he has indulged his romantic fallacy in language and named its falseness, he ultimately resolves his crisis of the imagination ("O, I see the crescent promise of my spirit hath not set. / Ancient founts of inspiration well through all my fancy yet," ll. 187-188) through variations on the same secular symbols reasserted with the same rhythmic importunateness:

Mother-Age (for mine I knew not) help me as when life
    begun:
Rift the hills, and roll the waters, flash the lightnings,
                weigh the Sun.

(185-186)

Thus, the implanting of images and the metrical measuring of language are wholly cooperant in *Locksley Hall,* and the oratorical trochaic couplets, with their ambivalent aesthetic effects, are an organic part of characterization, an indispensable dimension of monodramatic self-revelation. Moreover, one can reasonably conjecture that Tennyson preserved this most precarious balance between the good and the deficient, the admirable and the extravagant, as a result of the complex but delicate motive of the poem. He clearly did not want to demolish his protagonist or the new age he embodies (which also has "its good side, its deficiencies, and its yearnings"). Rather, he sought to induce in the reader both a wry detachment from the speaker's overwrought self-deceptions and a recognition that his imaginative self-processing, however rough-and-ready at some points, works for him, providing a genuine alternative to "wither[ing] by despair" (98). It is ironic that he should have to sacrifice to survival some of the most refined and ingratiating poetic sentiments of a visionary youth and the first taste of romantic love (7-16, 17-38); but, as in the cases of *In Memoriam* (CIII) and *Maud* (Part III), entering the mainstream of life as even a fallible adult takes its toll.

The monodrama is an especially appropriate form for treating a fallible hero. A forerunner of stream-of-consciousness, its dramatic dynamism derives from the inner turbulence of the speaker, from collisions and contradictions, false starts and self-deceptions. An implicit premise of the form is that he will confront the crucial problems at the center of his consciousness, and its character as a "Drama of the Soul" [17] distinguishes it from the more usual course of stream-of-consciousness. But it is not an assumption of the form that he will confront his problem successfully, however he personally measures success. He may simply dig the hole deeper; or he may foreshorten success, emerging from an archetyal conflict with what even he recognizes as a compromise—an unromantic but functional settling. Centered in the utmost intimacies of character, the monodrama works within the rule of all literature of character: not that the protagonist (or speaker) behave consistently, but that some imaginatively meaningful configuration of character emerge from his behavior, more particularly in the case of the monodrama, from his verbal behavior.

The protagonist of *Locksley Hall* is a *speaker,* a language-man, and this is the chief imaginative debt the poem owes to the Moâllakát, "the seven Arabic poems . . . hanging up in the temple of Mecca" which "gave the idea of the poem." [18] The speaker is seeking "comfort" ("consolation"), and in general imitation of the first poem of the Moâllakát, that of Amriolkais, he rekindles his imagination by converting the past, both its pleasures and its pains, into a drama of language; and after suffering, in the present, an acute phase of psychic turbulence that surfaces as verbal bluster so violent that it makes him question his sanity, he is able, gradually and with relapses into psychic / verbal sickness, to knit his future to his remoter and more restorative past and to purge, within the limitations of his personality, the disconsolate and paralyzing pressures of the nearer past. Thus, he achieves "more strength of mind" by reversing the "two topicks of consolation" urged upon Amriolkais by his companion: before his calamity he had been supremely happy ("a youth sublime," 11), and although he has had his "full share" of pain, he has the inner resources, he discovers, to face and subdue it.[19] Central to the imaginative apprehension embodied in the poem, therefore, is not rocking-chair musings, but an encounter session that explodes into a linguistic psychodrama. And although he is not a poet in the stricter sense in which one can apply that title to the *persona* of *In Memoriam*, he is, like the speaker in *Maud*, a "poetic soul" [20] and experiences life at a level that is imaginatively intense. Imagination defines his pleasure, his pain, and his recovery.

Like the protagonist in *Maud*, the hero of *Locksley Hall* has kinship with Hamlet; and though this kinship is not insisted upon,[21] Hamlet's famous question ("to suffer / . . . / Or to take arms") is a useful way of measuring the speaker and of seeing the process which he undergoes. Although he is genuinely poetic, he is not possessed of the abnormal sensitivity that is the source in Hamlet of such depths of misery and despair. On the other hand, he has the capacity, as Hamlet does not, to deal forthrightly with his lesser pain and "to take arms" against a devitalizing situation. But even as an echo of Hamlet, the speaker has been placed by the poet in that line of diminished Hamlets which has been recurrent in modern literature and to which Arnold gave classic expression: "we hear . . . the doubt, we witness the discouragement, of Hamlet and of Faust." [22] He is an eclipsed and barometric modern man, and there is a touch of ironic pathos in the way in which he inflates the cultural shrinkage of which, as a thorough-going secularist and futurist, he is wholly unaware.

But what he can do, he does: he submerges the keen anxieties which he feels about himself and his age, some of them rather finely tuned, and creates a culture-myth to live by. As in the case of other myth-makers in the Tennyson canon—Ulysses, for example, and the *persona* in *In Memoriam*, the protagonist in *Maud*, and many of the chief *personae* in *Idylls of the King*—the credibility of the speaker's myth in *Locksley Hall* in anchored in three basic and essential ingredients. One is his predisposition to believe—his wholly secular faith in the future. This is the primary element in his earliest memories of himself, and it surfaces even in this most Hamlet-like moods (e.g., 132-136):

> Yet I doubt not through the ages one increasing purpose
>   runs,
> And the thoughts of men are widened with the process of the
>   suns.
>
>   (137-138)

A second is his "poetic spirit," his imaginative capacity to rise above an infinity of details and to translate his empirical observations into enlarged visionary metaphors. Lines 187-188 have already been cited in support of the perception that the speaker's crisis is essentially a crisis of the imagination; and this quality of the speaker is unmistakably reenforced by the repetition (15-16, 119-120) of the couplet which most specifically asserts it:

> When I dipt into the future far as human eye could see;
> Saw the Vision of the world, and all the wonder that would
>   be.—

Finally, he has personally enjoyed an engendering experience that has given empirical guidance to the character of his mythic apprehension. In the short curve of his individual history, that initial— and ultimately sustaining—experience is summed up in the couplet

> When the centuries behind me like a fruitful land reposed;
> When I clung to all the present for the promise that it closed;
>   (13-14)

and the pleasurable / painful experience of romantic love has been a temporary distraction from that essentially public jubilation, a private myth that collapses and from the jeopardy of which he saves himself throgh a determined, indeed a willful, renewal of that mythic integration of Space and Time that had so charmed his highly favored youth. Something of the original delicacy of perception has perhaps been lost, but the same essential apprehension, asserted with increased vigor, is represented in his final positioning:

Not in vain the distance beacons. Forward, forward let us
    range,
Let the great world spin for ever down the ringing grooves
    of change.

(181-182)

It is a positioning that can be easily faulted, especially from a
humanistic point of view, and the poet, formally withdrawn from
the text, does not applaud it; but it is wholly in character and
hence deserves full critical praise as an imaginative dramatization
of a subtle and complex kind.

Like Tennyson's other myth-makers, the hero of *Locksley Hall* is
largely imprisonsoned in his culture; unlike them, he accepts that
imprisonment with relish. He does not, like the speaker in *Maud*,
kick violently against the cultural traces. He is not an outsider
looking in, alienated and abstractly hostile, but an insider momentarily diverted from his self-defining cultural enthusiasm. As an
embodiment of the spiritual thrust of the age, typical of a class and
the mirror of its cultural assumptions, he is a myth as well as a
myth-maker. His character, like his action, is complexly metaphorical, and both are used by the poet for serious but purely
imaginative purposes. The hero of *Locksley Hall* does not exist outside the poem itself, and this slice of his imaginary life is a fictive
shaping of representative human experience—historically illuminating but not, except at the level of imaginative suggestiveness,
historical. The critical insight his linguistic existence gives us into
threshold Victorianism—"its good side, its deficiencies, and its
yearnings"—is imaginatively exciting, but he is not rigidly Victorian. "The whole poem," as Tennyson tells us, "represents young
life," and the more we "look through the insistent . . . substance at
the thing signified," [23] the more likely we will be to see that,
though the speaker appears to be frozen in metaphors, he is actually caught up in one of the "various forms of enthusiastic activity" [24] to which a capacious "young life" in all ages is inevitably
and imperfectly drawn.

Thus freed from the critical hazards of a narrow autobiographical reading, *Locksley Hall* takes on enlarged mythic resonance.

Employing with great specificity the cultural metaphors of a particular time-frame and concentrating the action in the consciousness of a conspicuously fallible but imaginative speaker, Tennyson
created a mythic myth-maker who reflects the perennial efforts of a
typical class of young persons, vulnerable but sanguine, to rise
above an infinity of present-day details and to build a hopeful
future on the positive forces within their culture.

Notes

1. F. E. L. Priestley, *Language and Structure in Tennyson's Poetry* (London: Andre
   Deutsch, 1973), p. 78.
2. Ward Hellstrom, *On the Poems of Tennyson* (Gainesville: University of Florida
   Press, 1972), pp. 70-72. Professor Hellstorm, though grossly misled in his
   critical judgment, I think, does accurately identify some of the "wrong reasons" adduced by admirers of the poem ("as a spokesman for his age, as a
   prophet, as an autobiographer").
3. *The Poetry of Tennyson* (New Haven: Yale University Press, 1977), pp. 196-199.
4. *Tennyson and His Friends,* ed. Hallam Tennyson (London: Macmillan, 1911),
   pp. 269-270.
5. Hallam Tennyson, *Alfred Lord Tennyson: A Memoir. By His Son* (New York:
   Macmillan, 1897), II, 379.
6. *Memoir,* II, 331.
7. *Memoir,* I, 195.
8. The text used is that of *The Poems of Tennyson,* ed. Christopher Ricks (London:
   Longman, 1969), and lines cited are identified in parentheses immediately
   following the citation.
9. These phrases are from Walter Pater's Conclusion to *The Renaissance.*
10. The phrase was applied by Tennyson specifically to *Maud,* but it has rele-
    vance to *Locksley Hall:* "The peculiarity of this poem . . . is that different
    phrases of passion in one person take the place of different characters."
    Memoir, I, 396.
11. This is Emerson's characterization of Carlyle's *Past and Present.* See *Journals
    and Miscellaneous Notebooks of Ralph Waldo Emerson,* ed. W. H. Gilman and J. E.
    Parsons (Cambridge, Mass.: The Belknap Press of Harvard University Press,
    1970), VIII, 408; and *"Past and Present," Emerson's Complete Works* (London:
    The Waverly Book Co. Ltd., 1893), XII, 247-248.
12. *Tennyson's "Maud": The Biographical Genesis* (Berkeley and Los Angeles: Uni-
    versity of California Press, 1963), p. 38.
13. Hellstrom, p. 71.
14. *Tennyson: The Growth of a Poet* (Cambridge, Mass.: Harvard University Press,
    1960), p. 77.

15. Culler, p. 197. Professor Culler rightly says that *"Locksley Hall* is a true mono-drama. . . ."

16. The connection between the two was confirmed by Tennyson when he noted that "possibly" he had been affected by the following passage from Beaumont's *Philaster* (IV, i): "Oh, that I had been nourished in these woods / . . . and not known / The right of Crowns, *nor the dissembling Trains / Of Women's looks* . . . / And then had taken me some Mountain Girl / . . . and have borne at her big breasts / My large coarse issue. This had been a life / Free from vexation" (emphasis added). Quoted in Ricks, p. 698n.

17. *Memoir,* I, 396-397.

18. *Works* (Eversley Edition), II, 341, as quoted by Ricks, p. 689.

19. I am following Sir William Jones's summary of the poem of Amriolkais as quoted by Ricks, p. 689.

20. *Memoir,* I, 396.

21. Professor Ricks (p. 689) identifies three "Reminiscences of *Hamlet"* in the poem.

22. Preface to *Poems* (1853).

23. Thomas Hardy, Preface to *The Dynasts.*

24. Pater, Conclusion to *The Renaissance.*

8.

Tennyson's Function of Poetry
at the Present Time:
A Parabolic Reading of *The Princess*

The relatively new inclination of students of Tennyson's poetry to look through the substance at the thing signified has begun to reveal what a truly startling poetic experimentalist Tennyson was. In all of his major poems—say, *The Princess, In Memoriam, Maud,* and *Idylls of the King*—he quietly, persistently, and boldly did the totally unexpected. *In Memoriam* is an elegy, certainly; but it is also an epic of the modern soul's transformations. A carefully individuated Everyman-figure is implanted in a densely textured spiritual / cultural / imaginative ambience and enabled over an extended period of time to work his way through a series of inner crises to new foundations of faith—a new spiritual country—for himself and for those pioneering spirits with a capacity for and sympathy with the journey and the goal. *In Memoriam* is a long narrative poem, dramatically conceived and lyrically executed, on the subject of imaginative human renewal. The monodramatic underpinnings of *In Memoriam* are given revolutionary exposure in *Maud,* and the analogue of Tennyson's elegiac epic in Dante's *Divina Commedia* is replaced, in this lyric drama, by Shakespeare's *Hamlet.* Just as Tennyson had worked most inconspicuously by analogy with Dante in

132

In Memoriam, so in *Maud* he divested himself of the external machinery of Shakespeare's drama, foregoing all but a few vestigial remnants of the *Hamlet* plot, and concentrated instead on the generic modernism of the character and his extraordinary gift for language. The speaker in *Maud* is accessible to the reader only through his own language: *he is language;* and since he is his only audience, we watch and listen by imaginative privilege, witnessing even his disingenuousness from an intimately authentic angle of vision. His lyrics are as variable as his highly volatile moods, and what we get to *know* about him is what we come to *believe* he means by what he says in utter unconsciousness of our more or less watchful presence. The "plot" of the poem is wholly implicit, and the poem's artistic unity is dependent on the reader's willingness and capacity to provide supplementary scenes of the imagintion. *Maud's* modernism is perennial, therefore—the imaginative realization, at a level of genuine intimacy, of a highly gifted, deeply faulted man attempting to cope with such universal coordinates as a congenital nature, memories full of love and hate, an uncongenial society, an imperious and threatening sexuality, romantic love, personal catastrophe, madness, religious-romantic idealization, and participation in the quintessential labor of a nation transformed by crisis.

The experimental character of *Idylls of the King* can hardly be summarized briefly and adequately. It is both a universal reading act, rewardingly available to every grade of reader, and a universal writing act, an anthology of literary forms and procedures leading the reader to a new or refreshed awareness of how dependent an understanding of human experience is on the manner in which it is perceived and / or narrated. Again the poet uses a basic monodramatic formulation, each idyll being filtered through a narrative *persona,* either specified or generically anonymous, inviting the reader's utmost attentiveness to the voice, temperament, and circumstances of the perceiving consciousness. Here the analogue is the Classical epic, but its procedures are reversed as the poem moves away from new foundations to the ruination of a grand mythic apprehension, the epic gradually mutating into elegy. The ruin of Arthur's realm turns on "one sin," as Arthurianism consists of one "secret"; but both flame out in an explosion of analogical refractions in which no one thing can be equated with any other thing but in which everything energizes everything else.

The Princess [1] is the first of Tennyson's startling poetic experiments on a major scale to be published, though it appears to have been the last of the four to be conceived, *In Memoriam, Maud,* and *Idylls of the King* all being seeded in specific writing acts in the closing months of 1833. Thus, the reader may well have a disposition to suspect that Tennyson's earliest realization of an ambition to write long poems, coming as *The Princess* does years after the poet's mapping out of the other works upon which his most substantial reputation rests, has more than a topical center of interest composed in the manner of a *tour de force;* and he gets substantial encouragement for at least tentative efforts to explore the validity of that suspicion from the character of Tennyson's other long poems. The three poems that share with *The Princess* this major category put innovative form to such fundamentally serious uses that one is compelled to see poetic manner as an indispensable key to poetic meaning, and the odds at least favor a comparable imaginative ordering and emphasis in *The Princess.* Moreover, Tennyson's very substantial revisions of the poem for the third, fourth, and fifth editions—insertion of the six intercalary songs (1850), addition of the "weird seizures" and the revisions necessary to accommodate them (1851), enlargement of the Prologue (1853)—are primarily formalistic in character, efforts to clarify the poem's meaning through alterations in its manner.

It is significant that every explicit or implicit remark Tennyson is recorded to have made on the poem turns upon poetic linkage or poetic character, not upon subject matter or thematic intent. "the child is the link through the parts as shown in the Songs (inserted 1850), which are the best interpreters of the poem. . . ." "[T]he words 'dream, shadow,' 'were and were not' doubtless refer to the anachronisms and improbabilities of the story"—that is, as perceived by the Prince within the imaginative context established by the first narrator of the story. The Prince has his flaws as well as the Princess, and his "too emotional temperament and susceptibility to cataleptic seizures . . . was probably intended to emphasize [the] point that something other than physical beauty or 'moral brilliance' " made possible the harmonious reconciliation at the end. The heightened poetic manner of the piece can be traced to the effect of the "gallant and heroic chronicle" [sic] on "the poet of the party" and to the fact that he was requested to "dress the tale up poetically." "A parable is perhaps the teacher that can most surely enter in all doors. . . ." "[T]here is scarcely anything in the story which is not prophetically glanced at in the Prologue." "[T]hough truly original, it is, after all, only a medley." "[I]f women ever were to play such freaks, the burlesque and the tragic might go hand in hand." Several of these comments have an independent importance that will be developed later in this essay, but seeing them as a cluster underscores their emphasis on poetic manner rather than topical subject matter. But even more significant than the absence of comments on the poem's manifest subject matter—women's education and the equality of the sexes—is the fact that Tennyson's elaborate efforts to get the public to "see the drift" of the poem leave that subject matter virtually untouched; and this suggests that the poet's primary concern (his "drift") is centered elsewhere. In this chapter, I shall argue that such is in fact the case—that for all the undeniable relevance of the woman question to his age and to his poem, Tennyson's real focus in *The Princess* is on the function of poetry at the present time. The topicality of the phrase "at the present time," obviously drawn from Arnold's "The Function of Criticism at the Present Time," is used in an Arnoldian sense—not as topically limited, but as topically urgent. The "Condition of Woman" question, like the "condition of England" question in Carlyle's *Past and Present,* was the topical metaphor—large, contentious, and crucial—by which Tennyson, like Carlyle, chose to demonstrate the relevance of modern letters to modern life. Being an age-old question, it had an authentic archetypal character to it, persons of substance dividing on the issue perennially; being an increasingly acute contemporary question, it challenged those who preferred justice to fruitless confrontation and conflict to explore new, imaginative ways of perceiving the issue in the hope that some generative model of perceptual behavior might emerge among those, at least, who might be expected to contribute an enlightened leadership to the present and the future. This, Tennyson apparently concluded, was poetry's way; and, as Emerson had said of Carlyle with particular reference to

Past and Present, Tennyson attempted to domesticate "the modern system, with its infinity of details, into style. . . ." [2]

One becomes increasingly careful about assigning influences to Tennyson's work, his imagination having a very special way of transmuting the materials upon which he drew and acculturating them entirely into a Tennysonian context; and he examined his own awarenesses so simultaneously with his study of both life and the old masters that it is usually impossible to say what was the source, what the confirmation, what the unconscious parallel. But there does seem to have been a very substantial imaginative sympathy between Tennyson and Carlyle. They were very different personalities, of course, and they imprinted language with very different literary idioms, Tennyson being exquisitely finished as Carlyle was magnificently burly. Still, Tennyson, who did for his age through poetry what Carlyle did through prose, was especially attentive to Carlyle's work and was probably encouraged by it to be steady in his own individual perceptions and bold in his literary formulations. *The Princess,* for example, was begun before *Past and Present* was conceived of, but the two share a fundamental and barometric imaginative concern—namely, the indispensability of modern letters to the quality of modern life. Jocelin's Chronicle in *Past and Present,* the literary text that enabled Carlyle to see both the past and the present through Jocelin's eyes, has its counterpart in "the gallant glorious chronicle" of *The Princess,* the literary text which fuels the imagination of the "poet of the party" and determines to a considerable degree the character of *his* tale of the past and present. Further, the fairy-tale mode of *The Princess* has far deeper rooting in the imaginative sensibility embodied in the Kunstmärchen of the German Romantics as transplanted into English literature through Carlyle's *Sartor Resartus* than in the storylines of the *Persian Tales* and the *Arabian Nights:* it is a fully developed aesthetic reorientation, as Carlyle had shown in his critical work on the German Romantics, suspending habitual patterns of discursive thought and functioning obliquely by a kind of imaginative osmosis, the affective result being an organic transformation of the perceptual apparatus rather than a confrontation between intellect and intellect or between the intellect and the imagination. So when Tennyson says that "A parable is perhaps the teacher that

can most surely enter in at all doors," his reference is to an imaginative mode that is so distanced from contemporary debate formulae that it gives to the reading experience a new-old character
that touches the controversy only indirectly by affecting the sensibility. It anchors the issue in the imaginative affections and
becomes a model, not of contention, but of an imaginatively satisfying resolution. It is, implicitly, an assertion that although literature must deal with life—even harshest contemporary life—it must
do so in literature's way, "by the framework and the chord." The
very concept of a literary "medley" has the fullest exemplification
in Carlyle, especially in *Sartor Resartus,* in which varieties of narration, language, argument, biography, fiction, character, metaphor,
style, fairy-tale, satire, and seriousness are blended into a heightened celebration of the mythic imagination. Even the symbol of
Ygdrasil which is lightly sketched in the blank-verse lyric "Our
enemies have fallen, have fallen" and the pervasive Time-metaphor are most conspicuously identified with Carlyle's use of them.
So while one might not want to assert the specific influence of
Carlyle on *The Princess* or to use the several analogies and parallels
cited here as arguments for the specific literary character of the
poem, he can legitimately see *The Princess* as having a firm aesthetic orientation for which there was ample precedent in Carlyle.

Setting aside for the moment Tennyson's major alterations of
the poem, all of which need to be looked at in detail, we can see in
the forging (shaping, counterfeiting) of the "sevenfold story" itself
a fundamentally aesthetic act in which one must look through the
substance at the thing signified. The "poet of the party" has had a
profound influence on the ultimate literary product. He has
brought to it the imaginative excitement generated by "the gallant
glorious chronicle" (Prologue, 49), which he has then passed on to
the group by reading to them some pages from it, especially those
concerning the " 'miracle of noble womanhood!" (Prologue, 48,
120-124). He has then gone on to create the first part of their
spontaneous tale, firmly establishing its imaginative character—its
genre, its fiction, its chief *dramatis personae,* its motives, its basic
conflict, and its comedic/tragic potentialities. Finally, he has
"drest it up poetically," so that it has a reasonably finished look
while yet retaining the marks of its origin in oral community com-

position. Thus, what we have is a single written poetic composition which is an amalgamation of seven oral contributions to a parabolic tale, the source of whose stimulation and shape is an inherited literary document—in short, the metaphoric evolution of a canonical text.

At an early stage in the composition of *The Princess,* Tennyson had made the noncanonical remnants of the oral origins of the poem more conspicuous than they are in the final text, designating by name or by character-type a representative group of collegian story-tellers.[3] This strategy had aesthetic interest as making more emphatic the dynamic evolutionary character of a poetic text of the kind symbolized by *The Princess* and as introducing the monodramatic motif to be found in varying degrees in Tennyson's other major poems. But it was in conflict with the idea of a fully canonical poetic text, and Tennyson finally decided in favor of the latter interest. Thus, except for the reminder in the interlude between Parts IV and V, the reader of the *story* is allowed to "forget" the narrative assumption by which the oral tale emerged. But the reader of the *poem* is not allowed to forget: he is expected, through a finely tuned aesthetic note-catching rather than through obvious guideposts, to hear the difference between one poetic voice and another, not as indispensable to an intelligent and appreciative reading of the poem, but as an ultimate aesthetic refinement of the poetic experience. It is a development of the utmost importance to Tennyson's chief narrative poems. Though experimentally developed in *The Princess,* in which it may not be considered entirely crucial, it becomes indispensable in the reading of *In Memoriam, Maud,* and *Idylls of the King,* where the "other voices" of a complex character or of different characters must be heard if the poems are to be read with any genuine aesthetic sophistication. The voice that we hear in Part I is the canonical voice, a personative voice that sets the ground-tone, neither mocking nor solemn, but creatively seeding the tone and theme against which the other voices will play. The voice of Part II is more attitudinal, undercutting through language in a conscious way ("harangue," "fulmined," "daffodilly") and inflating the narrative with ironically staged melodramatic theatricality. The inscription, which is his—"LET NO MAN ENTER IN ON PAIN OF DEATH"—draws Dante's *Inferno* in as an absurdly exaggerated literary analogue. Part III projects a voice of worldly cynicism. The speaker's language is less persistently inflated, though "inosculated" flounders through the texture; but his images are more intensely psychosexual, his incidents more strategic, his characterizations both precarious and profound. He introduces the first of the "weird seizures" and thus moves the tale toward an underlying implicit level. The organic implications of the compositional method become more apparent in Part IV. The poetic voice becomes at once more resonant and more delicate, and the serious probings introduced by the third voice are pursued at an ever deepening level, the exposure of the intruders leading to heightened role-playing and self-justification on all sides. The mock-heroic is sustained through personal gesture, epiclike posturings, and rhetorical declamations; but the profound and potentially tragic nature of the perceptual disclocations of the principals begins a full and deeply threatening flow. The May-game is over, and all future negotiations must be seen in the harsh light of entirely possible disaster. Thus the interlude (between IV and V) is very strategically placed: Lilia sings a tenderly tragic ballad that both reflects the crucial *literary* point to which the tale has come and, through the very act of singing, processes herself and the others toward a "warbling fury." Thus the psychic appetite, in fear that the promised imaginative feast will not in fact be delivered, sets up a calculated clatter—*"feigning* pique at *what she called* / The raillery, or grotesque, or false sublime" (emphasis added)—in implicit confirmation that the movement has in fact already turned toward a sublime crescendo and that the aesthetic anxiety is lest it falter in fulfilment.

The speaker of Part V has a martial voice and a soldier's sense of humor, and his is perhaps the most precarious of the poetic tasks of the piece. He has to tidy up the campy elements in the earlier story and move it gradually toward a half-real / half-false epic quality. He disposes of the former with a broad-wink humor and manages the latter by creating a war of words between Ida and the Prince's father, by placing the genial ruffian Arac, a parody of stalwart bravura, at the center of the negotiations, and by filtering the metaphoric (rather than mock) battle through the Prince's strange, extended dream-state, thus making it both real and surreal. The voice in Part VI reflects the keenest sense of the ambiguities of a now fully serious situation. He places the Prince (his imaginary self) in a "mystic middle state" of psychic / imaginative suspension between life and death, where he is an observer-listener while his own destiny is in the balance, a central actor who does not act. The critical movement of the part is the transformation of Ida, whose frozen heart, already touched by the child, is gradually warmed by gratitude, sorrow, love, and the bombardment of tender far-off memories until she can finally overleap the stratifications of the more recent decade of doctrinaire idealism and become again a young girl wanting forgiveness. She is resocialized, opening once more to the vulnerabilities of humanness. The least remnants of bantering remain, and the psychosexuality that has been a permeating presence in the poem surfaces abruptly in a stunning image: "the doors gave way / Groaning, and in the Vestal entry shrieked / The virgin marble under iron heels . . ." (VI, 329-331). Part VII is sustained by an epic voice with fully audible lyrical resonances, moving the conflict into strong but gentle resolution having grand but simple metaphoric outreaches. Everything that has been learned in the process of poetic voicings comes to a vigorous but delicate equipoise.

The symbolic reverberations or parabolic implications of the simple, unpretentious narrative device used in *The Princess* are rich and far-reaching. In the first place, it implies that literature is made of literature, that there is an organic continuity from imaginative act to imaginative act, that "Our echoes roll from soul to soul, / And grow for ever and for every" ("The splendour falls on castle walls," following III, 347). Second, in Shelleyan terms, the poet is both the creator and the creation of his age: he attempts to find a modern expression for a modern outlook, and in so doing, he must be responsive to the spiritual needs of his particular time and place, altering inherited literary structures to accommodate a contemporary sense of literary relevance, but using his art to induce in his contemporaries a magnified imaginative awareness of the generic nature of their cultural metaphors. Third, by bringing his readers (listeners) within the circle of his own imagination, the poet of the piece enables them, according to their individual characters and capacities, to be poets too, providing them with a structure in which to function creatively. Thus, through the rubric of this "sevenfold story," the reading act and the writing act are merged in a thoroughly dynamic way, each reader (or listener) being compelled by the "mouth-to-mouth" rules of the game to give a writer's attentiveness to the reading act. Fourth, the fairy-tale which the community of writers / readers creates is, like the "hoard of tales" of the chronicle at Vivian-place, itself "Half-legend, half-historic," embellishing with all the heightening resources of the aesthetic imagination a crucial contemporary topic and removing it, through the legendlike capacities of the fairy-tale, from a literal contemporaneousness to an imaginary time of historic perenniality. Finally, the pattern by which the story moves to its canonical status suggests classic analogues in such prototypical literary texts as the *Iliad* and the *Beowulf*—namely, canonical texts that emerged from oral traditions sustained by diverse hands and kept alive by the well-practiced habit of men in all ages, modern as well as ancient, to kill the tyrant Time by telling and listening to stories.

The *form* of the fairy-tale as deployed in the *total* literary experience of *The Princess* has even richer aesthetic implications. We look upon the fairy-tale as the freest form of the literary imagination to which people of all age groups are most wholly available: we all love fairy-tales in at least the half-belief that we can all write fairy-tales. Thus, it is the form in which the reading act and the writing act seem to merge in the human imagination; and this suggests that it is as nearly innate to the way human creativity works as a literary form can be. But the historic fact is that the early nineteenth century rediscovered the fairy-tale and invented ways to put it to sophisticated literary uses, just as the early nineteenth century discovered the literary usability of the child. Tennyson combines these two literary discoveries of his century in *The Princess*, a fairy-tale with a child at the center of its awarenesses; and the issue in which the two imaginatively merge is a truly generative creativity. The fairy-tale, like the child, is a gentilizing influence, returning sophisticated and contentious adults, at least in the poem's parable, to a state of unwarlike imaginative love that makes ideal generation possible—sexual, intellectual, social, artistic. So the conflict over the character the completed tale should take—"mock-heroic,

gigantesque" or "true-heroic—true-sublime," male-"mockers" versus female-"realists"—which the canonical poet attempts to reconcile by moving "in a strange diagonal" (Conclusion, 10-28) has
several levels of genuine significance. The subject of women's
equality itself, generative of so much emotional intensity of both
the derisive and the fanatical kinds, requires, if its serious implications are to have any chance of surfacing, an oblique literary approach. The males, even if they are not chauvinistic barbarians of
the Prince's father's ilk, have almost necessarily to be the mockers,
since they are operating from a position of entrenched strength and
have, they think, nothing to gain and everything to lose; and the
females, suffering from historical disenfranchisement in many aspects of life, must realistically take the matter with deep seriousness, even if they are not grand deluded monists like Ida. But the
poet of the piece does not impose the "solemn close": it evolves
organically out of the infectious fairy-tale process itself in the total
literary experience embodied in the poem, including the choric
ballads that the women sing and the "silent influence" they have
as an audience of Maiden Justice figures.

The six intercalary songs were Tennyson's first major addition to
The Princess after its initial publication (third edition, 1850). He
added them, he says, because "the public did not see the drift" of
the poem; and he comments further: "The child is the link through
the parts, as shown in the Songs . . . , which are the best interpreters of the poem. . . ." They obviously require, in the poet's judgment, very careful reading if we are to get at his genuine "drift."

The songs are child-centered in a rather oblique way—at the
domestic level or at the symbolic level of continuity or at the heart-
ache level of absence or at the implicit level of personal redaction.
They are, above all else, *songs*—lyrical awarenesses rather than
arguments, not directly dependent on the story-line, though functioning at an organic level as aesthetically distanced inner codas-
introductions to the movements of the fable. As brief lyrics, they
emphasize the importance of identifying with the feelings expressed rather than with the arguments anchored in various char-
acter-types or with the mechanisms of the plot. They have an
independent monodramatic lyrical integrity that parallels the
movement of the larger fable, as "O that 'twere possible" has a

degree of autonomy independent of *Maud*. They are analogous, at an even more obscure level of wholly implicit plot, to Wordsworth's Lucy-poems and Arnold's *Switzerland*-poems—lyrical ballads moving along a continuum of feeling and leaving the peculiarities of plot in a field of white spaces. Implicit in that movement is the perception that the redemption of men and women in conflict depends on the resurgence of feelings of love and gentleness rather than on success in interpersonal or cultural competition. The child thus becomes the primary resuscitator of a lost past, a lost paradise, the symbol of renewal through memory of moments of incomparable quality in our lives when love was fullest, gentlest, most authentically pleasurable, quintessentially co-creative.

"As through the land at eve we went," spoken by the male, describes with utmost economy a critical moment in the love relationship between a man and a woman when, in the late summer / early autumn of their lives, through dullness, boredom, inattention, they fall out of love. Memory of their lost child, released by the "little grave," induces a suffusing tenderness—love renewed through shared sorrow—that enables them to reach back through the intervening years of alienation and recapture the superb moment of their lives. It is a metaphor, embedded in sorrow, of the finding of the child, and thus of themselves, in contrast to the losing of the child that Ida preaches. "Sweet and low, sweet and low," both a lullaby and a prayer, perspects married love from the female point of view. The mother's role as protector and nurturer of the child in the father's absence is at the center of the dramatic lyric tableau, and she is enveloped, through the fulfillment of this duty, with serene faith, expectancy, and love. Tenderness toward the child is tenderness toward the husband and the love relationship, and its effects on her radiate outward to her pictorial image of a world benign and luminous. It is a "nesting" song, and the sounds are those of "the moan of doves in immemorial elms." "The splendour falls on castle walls" is an intensely lyrical dramatic monologue, like Matthew Arnold's "Philomela"; and like Arnold's poem, it celebrates the surprise of a sudden aesthetic revelation. A magnificent picturesque panorama, part natural, part man-made, is abruptly raised to a level of sublimity by a burst of sunset light, and the aesthetic experience is expanded and reenforced by the sounds of a bugle that seem to find their counterparts among the austere beauties of "cliff and scar." Something indestructible seems to be added to the universe of man and nature that simply was not there before. Sounds, like satellites, are released into the cosmos, close at hand and getting fainter but clearer in the distance, impressing on the mind's eye exquisite forms of sight and sound and inducing thoughts that lie deep in the awakened consciousness. *What we are* at a level of spiritual imaginativeness takes on a confirmed reality and a credible perpetuity, this being the quality that we engender in the universe and thereby knit the remotest past to the eternal future, our brightness becoming a dimension of its brightness, our music of its music.

"The voice is heard through rolling drums" is a war lyric and has a deeply ironic cutting edge to it. It expresses a psychological truth, the mind through memory reaching, in the face of danger, into a golden time and being ennobled by the values memory sees in a family portrait. But the rolling drums are also suggestive of drum-taps, and the trumpets awaken thoughts of farewell to the fallen hero, so that the simple lyric introduces a note of the most penetrating ambiguity: the "him" in "strikes him dead" has a high degree of ambivalence about it; and regardless of who is killed, the family portrait created by memory may belong equally to the killer and the killed. "Home they brought the warrior dead" is another psychological dramatic lyric in which the release into fluidity of frozen emotions traumatized by sudden grief (the *rigor mortis* of the living) is examined. The eulogy does not give relief; the starkest acknowledgment of death fails too. The oldest and wisest know that love's labor does work: the child of their best love enables the widow to yield her life in the service of that love's fruit and reminder. "Ask me no more: the moon may draw the sea" is the most thematically oblique and precariously balanced of the songs. Depending on the reader's perspective, it may be read as a lyric monologue, a dramatic monologue, or a monodrama, the audience being generic, personal and individual, or internal. As a monodrama, the implicit dialogue is a dialogue of the mind with itself, and the detachment being effected in the poem is not from sexually romantic love but from romantic perception—a critical moment of withdrawal from a collapsed dedication and reentry into the more domestic mainstream of life. The speaker could be the shepherdess of "Come down, O maid" and the speech a recognition of the failure of a lonely quest on the severe heights. The "love" addressed would then be the companionable vocation, dearly loved yet but a "wandering fire" that the speaker, while recognizing its genuine attractiveness, must now relinquish.

There is about the lyrics as a whole a movement toward solemnity, an awakened recognition and a real but reluctant decisiveness—from domestic alienation redressed to the social alien restored to natural, quotidian rhythms, the solitary wanderer come home again to society. But while the songs have conspicuous relevance to the subject matter of *The Princess,* their relevance is larger than that subject matter, touching lyrically the process of imaginative restoration in man and woman which is germane to all the metaphors of stress and conflict which they may encounter in life.

The "weird seizures," Tennyson's second major addition to the published poem (fourth edition, 1851), show that if this or any other human conflict is ever to be resolved, it must be resolved at the perceptual level and that the affections are the precarious center of both our delusions and our truest realities. The poem turns on the discovery of an authentic spiritual love, and behind the quest lies a persuasion like that expressed by Wordsworth: "This spiritual love acts not nor can exist / Without Imagination . . ." (*The Prelude,* XIV, 188-189).

The very first thing we are told about the Prince's temperament is that he is "amorous" (I, 2). He is a May-figure who, like Guinevere in *Idylls of the King,* must work his way toward a realization that the "highest" can be the "most human too"—the grandest act of imaginative perception made possible through the gradual cultivation of a truly imaginative love; otherwise, like Gawain, another May-figure in the *Idylls,* he may become, if he lives, shabbily dissolute. From the beginning, he is caught between confrontal forces—the reverent mildness, graciousness, tact, and tenderness of his saintly mother and the secular, brusque, pedantic, judgmental harshness of his father, a connubial conflict of qualities which have symbolic relevance to the two Idas with which it is his destiny to come to terms or fail of fulfillment. But there are subtler divisions centered in his own nature, sketchily suggested by his two companions—the somewhat ribald Cyril and the gentle virginal Florian. Further, he suffers from the prophetic fate (or "weird") of his blood that he will "come to fight with shadows and to fall" (I, 10), while at the same time his peculiar nature is such as to resist that fatality:

> for spite of doubts
> And sudden ghostly shadowings I was one
> To whom the touch of all mischance but came
> As night to him that sitting on a hill
> Sees the midsummer, midnight, Norway sun
> Set into sunrise. . . .
>
> (IV, 548-553)

Thus, the Prince is very much like the rest of us who play parts in the Human Comedy: amorous, caught between appearances of reality, confused about our imperious sexuality, fated to fight with shadows and to fall, and yet resilient, hope springing eternal in our very human hearts.

Like the Prince, too, we generally begin our initial journey into adulthood with certain apparent guarantees (expectations) that get confused and equivocated or even positively betrayed; and being short on experience as well as imagination, we try to maneuver life with a somewhat saucy fancifulness ("pranks of saucy boyhood," VII, 323). Being young, sanguine, self-confident, and in love with love (a pictured face, a luxuriant tress), we seek out our quiet bowers, dote upon our fixed images, hear even in the woodland breezes duets in Paradise that are, like love, bitter-sweet ("the songs, the whispers, and the shrieks," I, 97), and tell ourselves, as if it were a voice from heaven, that we cannot lose (" 'Follow, follow, thou shalt win,' " I, 99). Being blithely callow, we see life as a May-game and play by May-game rules. This is the spirit in which the Prince and his companions play the charade-in-drag; and although it sustains serious undercurrent motifs—androgyny, youth's confusions over sexuality, the hermaphroditic character of the artistic imagination—it is essentially a comedic measure of the grossly immature imaginative perception—on the part of both the boys who participate in the charade and the girls who fail to see through it. As a literary device reminiscent of the masque, it has both an artistic and an attitudinal quality: highly stylized humor is aesthetic in character; and the psychosexual notion that boys play-acting as girls somehow preserves the delicate integrity of girls is rather bizarrely ironic.

The Prince's first "strange seizure" within the time-frame of the parable itself comes in III, 167-174, and the language in which it is narrated anchors it securely in an imaginative / perceptual frame of significance. It is suddenly induced by the sight ("I gazed") of Ida, with all her Amazonian qualities, in a frozen image, an artistic tableau, and it has a double reference—both to the thing seen and to the seer. The elements of the picture become "a hollow show," "a painted fantasy," "empty masks"; the observer of the picture becomes "the shadow of a dream, / For all things were and were not," but fueled with the intensest kinds of potentially aesthetic feelings ("My heart beat thick with passion and with awe"). This suggests a double exposure of dislocated imaginative truth, in the thing seen and in the seeing eye, but it suggests, too, that an adjustment is possible, both of the eye-lens and of the tableau, though the perfect picture will necessarily be difficult to achieve. He is the "shadow of a dream" in that his dream of life is false and he the dreamer is twice removed from truth; Ida, on the other hand, though her "show" is "hollow," is at the center of a distorted reality worthy of passion and awe by virtue of the very grandeur implicit in its false magnificence. Thus, the education of the Prince in authentic imaginative truth under the tutelage of the Princess has real but faulted plausibility, and the education of Ida at the hands of a transformed Prince becomes one of the imaginative possibilities of the piece.

In his second "weird seizure" (IV, 537-544), the Prince is no longer "the shadow of a dream," though reality and perception are still out of focus for him:

> I seemed to move among a world of ghosts;
> The Princess with her monstrous woman-guard,
> The jest and earnest working side by side,
> The cataract and the tumult and the kings
> Were shadows; and the long fantastic night
> With all its doings had and had not been,
> And all things were and were not.

His false, boyish dream—like his costume and his falsetto voice—
has ceased to function, but the truth of the world with which he
will have to cope is still beyond his imaginative grasp. He is in a
chaos of metaphors (an infinity of details) which he has not yet
found the imaginative style to master, and sound is added to sight
in a discordant jumble that must rise to genuine fluid harmony if
the world is ever to become coherent and creative for him. But art
and life do seem to have moved a degree closer together in that his
language is less theatrically oriented and stresses concepts common
to both art and life: ghosts, monsters, jest and earnestness, shadows, fantasy.

The third "weird affection" (V, 466-470) is the most complexly
induced of the three and brings the Prince to the brink of hopelessness. It has been decided that the matter of the contract will be
settled through violence, and the Prince knows, with Carlyle, that
even justice wrought through violence is unjust. But there is a
certain old-fashioned honor in it, too. He has read Ida's grand
oration (V, 364-413), and although she is "inexorable—no tenderness—/ Too hard, too cruel" (V, 504-505), there is an undeniable
degree of justice in her position; and in the postscript, at least, she
does express concern for his safety and tenderness toward the child.
He has heard his father's declamation (V, 428-456), and, mixed
with the intransigent chauvinism, there is a degree of raw admiration for Ida's rebellious grandeur. But it is near the hour when his
fate will be determined, and his mind goes on a memory-voyage,
recollecting both the morning when he decided to " 'Follow, follow' " a destiny that he was so sure that he would " 'win' " and the
"sorcerer's curse / That one should fight with shadows and should
fall" (V, 464-465). As a result, his mind is stripped almost bare of
aesthetic referents, and he slips into a state that is largely pre-
conscious—a "forgotten," "memorial" past in which even being
"the shadow of a dream" is a "dream." This is the prelude to the
battle in which he will in fact "fall," his imagination in despair of
coping unless there is a transformation in the thing seen as well as
in the seer.

The Prince's wound in the battle is metaphoric. He suffers from
a brain fever that takes him to a Life-in-death state "Deeper than
those weird doubts" can reach (VII, 36), a state like that of "in-

fants in their sleep" (VII, 39). As he begins to move again toward consciousness, he is caught in the whiplash of delirium, a semi-conscious symbolic surfacing of the deep conflicts within him pared down to a very narrow focus—namely, the worthiness of his affection for Ida. He recovers consciousness sane, but weak and disoriented, not at all sure that he will live. Ida, in the meantime, has moved complexly and organically into a state of love for him, and in a most delicate moment of precariousness between reality and dream, they consummate their first kiss:

> "If you be, what I think you, some sweet dream,
> I would but ask you to fulfill yourself:
> But if you be that Ida whom I knew,
> I ask you nothing: only, if a dream,
> Sweet dream, be perfect. I shall die tonight.
> Stoop down and seem to kiss me ere I die."
>
> (VII, 130-135)

It is a moment of perfect imaginative equipoise—not strong, but true. He accepts the difference between appearance and reality and rejects the old appearance parading itself as reality; and if he must die without the fulfillment to which he aspired in delusion, he would leave life with at least a perfected metaphor on his lips, a truth unadulteratedly imaginary.

But she is *not* the old Ida whom he knew, and his old confused self *does* die that night, so that when he gains strength, they can self themselves differently and work through, in a spirit of imaginative love, the residual problems that require only the language of generative faith to resolve them. The truth born thereof purges the old sorcerer's curse from his blood: " 'my doubts are dead, / My hunting sense of hollow shows: the change, / This truthful change in thee has killed it' " (VII, 372-329). Thus, the "weird seizures," like the intercalary songs, while they are clearly relevant to the metaphors of the particular subject matter of *The Princess*, have a quite independent relevance. Both the Prince and the Princess suffer from the ordinary faults of immaturity, both being simplistic in their strategies for realizing their goals and both brought, from different but analogous starting points, into the mainstream of human life. Their problems are problems of perception. The Prince lives too much in the sentiment of the past; the Princess rejects the past and its sentiments and is a doctrinaire futurist. The Prince has an inadequate sense of self and lacks personal solidity; the Princess has an overweening sense of self and is solid to the point of hardness. As they move toward each other in the parable, they release a new sense of the relevance of all Time to the human solution of human problems and of the need for significant form rather than frozen images, for fluid structures rather than immutable blueprints. But neither one of them, however imaginative, is capable of correcting a socially sterile situation alone: both must change if either is to find fulfillment.

An enlarged Prologue was the last major revision Tennyson gave *The Princess* (fifth edition, 1853), and he commented on that revised Prologue as follows: "there is scarcely anything in the story which is not prophetically glanced at in the Prologue."

The most curious aspects of the Prologue, with its 239 lines, are how few lines are devoted to the subject of women's rights, how many lines turn on the question of style, and how central to the consideration of style is the issue of contemporaneity. The tone is, from beginning to end, decidedly upbeat, as "The nineteenth century gambols on the grass" (third edition, 1850, 232). The time seems benign, progressive, and ameliorative, a period of civilized benevolence and goodwill. But not creative, heroic, or grand. Even the most barometric sign of the times—the scientific toys of the Mechanics' Institute—is gimmicky, a sportive recreation on a par with cricket and a country dance to the accompaniment of a "twangling violin" (85); and it quickly leads to satiety, not to a "quickened, multiplied consciousness." [4] There is nothing in the "angry models" of the steam engine or the "petty railway" or the "mimic stations" of the telegraph to compare with the stylish elegance of the "Grecian house" or the imaginative excitement of the "Gothic ruin" ("high-arched and ivy-claspt, / Of finest Gothic lighter than a fire," ll. 91-92) or the authentic nobility of "the gallant glorious chronicle" (49). Even the anthropological artifacts "Jumbled together" on the tables, miscellaneous souvenirs of a dilettantish collector, have a seriousness and a distinctive character lacking in the conventional technological products of the time. So the climactic passage of the Prologue has about it a keen ironic edge:

> "Then follow me, the Prince,"
> I answered, "each be hero in his turn!
> Seven and yet one, like shadows in a dream.—
> Heroic seems our Princess as required—
> But something made to suit with Time and place,
> A Gothic ruin and a Grecian house,
> A talk of college and of ladies' rights,
> A feudal knight in silken masquerade,
> And, yonder, shrieks and strange experiments
> For which the good Sir Ralph had burnt them all—
> This *were* a medley! we should have him back
> Who told the 'Winter's tale' to do it for us.
> No matter: we will say whatever comes."
>
> (220-232)

Indeed, the irony threatens to spill into positive sarcasm. That they should need a "summer's tale" to relieve their boredom in this most privileged of moments in this most congenial of seasons in this most enlightened of centuries is one key to it. Another is the very special phrasing used to describe their narrative roles—" 'each be hero in his turn! / Seven and yet one, like shadows in a dream.—" The allusion, of course, is to the Prince's "weird seizures," and the "poet of the party" thus places the company of narrators under the sorcerer's curse—that "none of all our blood should know / The shadow from the substance" (I, 8-9)—a suggestion that this is a curse from which people generally suffer but that it is especially virulent at the present time.

The further allusion to the unities—of "Time and place" and action—seems to be a wry reversal-through-inflation of the pressure on the poet to deal with contemporary problems. The "Time" called the present can never be isolated and autonomous, as the

Gothic ruin, the Grecian house, the "gallant glorious chronicle," even the jumble of anthropological artifacts, all show; literal "place," however neat and commodious, is the source of present boredom, and it is the object of the poet's imagination to transport the reader to a metaphoric space, an emblematic place, what Carlyle referred to as a mode of consciousness; and unity of action can never be inherent in an infinity of present details, which give an imperious impression of multitudinousness rather than unity, but must be imposed by the poet, who sees even current objects and episodes generically, *sub specie aeternitatis.* So the exclamation "This *were* a medley!" has to it a cutting ironic edge, as the emphasis suggests, the more literally contemporaneous, the more totally chaotic; and this irony seems still to reverberate in Tennyson's remark about *The Princess,* reported by Frederick Locker-Lampson in 1869, that "though truly original, it is, after all, only a medley." Tennyson may have felt, more than twenty years after the original publication of *The Princess,* that it was a fine poem of limited ambition; or he may have yielded, with a touch of bitterness, to the persistent diminution of his poetic effort, the critics having missed the fine edge of irony with which he had attempted to draw them toward his latent and more imaginative meaning.

Two other allusions in this climactic passage are double-edged. The "good Sir Ralph," presiding deity of the place, may have "burnt them all" because of a benighted medieval attitude toward scientific experiments as the work of the devil; but the gallant partner of Richard I's victory over the Saracens at Ascalon in 1192 may also have wanted to singe his descendants for the condition of exceedingly low emprise to which they have deteriorated. And Shakespeare may be invoked honorifically; or the sad state of poetic apprehension among the "gambols" of "the nineteenth century" may indeed require the best efforts of the greatest of English poets if, at the present time, poetry can hope to rise above such a diminished level as "only a medley."

The "talk of college" in the Prologue is certainly not such as to make one sanguine about Ida's choice of an instrumentality for " 'plant[ing] a solid foot into the Time' " (V, 405). It is mostly a tale of truancy and Proctor-baiting, sycophancy and sanctimoniousness.

They boated and they cricketed; they talked
At wine, in clubs, of art, of politics;
They lost their weeks; they vext the souls of deans;
They rode; they betted; made a hundred friends,
And caught the blossom of the flying terms. . . .
                                                    (1959-163)

Even when they "stayed at Christmas up to read," they were always on the move or at the wassail bowl or killing time with
"Charades and riddles" and story-telling. This is all very different,
of course, from the sectarian solemnity of Ida's university; and
although it is probably offered as a fair portrait of the way a representative set of young males comported themselves at the English
universities in the first half of the nineteenth century, it is not a
paradigm. Rather, it gives institutional anchorage to the un-
natural and unequal and unimaginative division of the sexes and
shows how inimical to the culture one of its own cultural assumptions can be. And although the idea of an enlightened modern
university might be drawn from a balanced merger of the two
models, the Arnoldian concept of true culture as a knowledge of
the best that has been thought and known in the world's history is
not a concern of *The Princess*. In fact, a monistic emphasis on
knowledge emerges as morally defective and practically coun-
terproductive. Poetry's business is not the inculcation of intellective knowledge, but the engendering of imagination by touching
the primary affections at the most primary level, so that our basic
human arrangements, which later inevitably get frozen into rigid
institutional structures, may be rooted in imaginative affection.

There is another model for the parable in the Prologue—that of
Lilia. Still "Half child half woman" (l. 101), Lilia appears to occupy some middle ground between the imperial Princess and the
young girl of eight from whose head the mother snipped the sacred
tress. She is very different from Ida, good-naturedly play-acting in
her mortal expostulations that draw the mask of tragedy to Walter's face (208-209) and lead him to imagine her as " 'six feet
high, / Grand, epic, homicidal . . .' " (218-219). She has not been
under the influence of a man-hating Lady Blanche, but the pattern

of social frustration, anger, and simplistic, black-and-white solution has already begun to form in her psyche, so that the poetic imagination has firm justification in her relatively "real" metaphoric representation for building the grand, monolithic symbol that Ida represents in the fairy-tale itself. Thus *The Princess* is not a myth-poem, an entirely fictive configuration of representative human experience, but a legend-poem: like the "gallant glorious chronicle," it is "Half-legend, half-historic" (30) and hence a firmly designed aesthetic exemplification of what the contemporary poet can most fruitfully do in dealing with the subject matter of his own or of any time.

The blank-verse lyrics which were an important part of *The Princess* from its first publication in 1847 all center around Ida and, through their individual character and her reaction or relationship to them, figure as indispensable aesthetic measurers of her imaginative transformation. "Tears, idle tears" (IV, 21-40) is perhaps the most exquisitely sad lyric lament in English, the tear that it evokes from the maiden harpist who sings it having a genuine aesthetic reality. Perfectly attuned to the harp, it is penetrating as vibrant musical sound is penetrating, setting in motion depths of feeling that are as distinctive as the taste of alum and as inexplicable as the unmet future. Gentle words accumulate to give it an undefined definition—"Fresh," "Sad," "strange," "Dear," "deep," "wild"—and its primary, universal, and cyclic stimulus is named— the picture of "the happy Autumn-fields." It is an all-suffusing sentiment, rising out of man's mysterious analogues in nature— fulfillment and decay, expectation and loss, birth and death, love known as overture but missed as crescendo. The memory in which it is rooted is mysterious too: racial as well as personal, it makes the past more all-enveloping and penetrating than the present, the young feeling that they are the result of everything that ever was (fulfillment) and that the best has already been, that they came belatedly to a heritage already strangely archaic (loss). But the way this superb lyric is deployed in *The Princess* becomes a primary illustration of the function of poetry at the present time. Ida, the universal director-reformer, chairman of the board, has called for the singing with a rather unctuous, sterotyped right-mindedness: " 'Let some one sing to us: lightlier move / The minutes fledged with music' " (IV, 18-19); but she is grossly unavailable to the imaginative affection of the song itself. It is a deceiving Siren-song against which " 'we should cram our ears with wool' " (IV, 47); all our sentiments about it should be dismantled, and all its aesthetic artifacts of imaginative aspiration be allowed to go to rack and ruin! Who needs a harp when he can have a trumpet? What is the past to one who has the future by the forelock? What is a half-awakened nightingale to a "poising eagle" (IV, 64)? Thus, Ida takes on the character of all those rugged individualists who are disdainful of everything they seem to have got along so well without, a grand Captain of Ideological Industry with a vest pocket full of clichés about culture. Her head is stocked with historical images selected by a thesis-ridden mind, and her college is "furnished" with artifacts whose significance is reduced to her crusading purposes. Her industry happens to be women's rights through education; but she is an inadequate woman and an inadequate educationist, as she is an inadequate aesthetician. She has never been "a maid," leaping from young girl to Amazonian crusader. Hence, the sentiments expressed in "Tears, idle tears" are no part of her experience, are instead an index to her personal emotional deprivation. And the system with which she wants to alter the world is the very system by which her own youth has been victimized. Lady Blanche has played to her the role of a Sir Austin Feverel: she has evolved a frighteningly plausible system of education rooted in hurt and hatred of her husband extrapolated to include all males and has used it, in a spirit of rigid, self-righteous high-mindedness, to pollute the adolescence of a tender, talented, privileged, dedicated, egocentric girl. And Ida's excruciating difficulties in ultimately reknitting herself to a healthier personal past derive from the fact that it is a past of which she has been deprived. So "Tears, idle tears" becomes a poetic touchstone by which the pathetic fool's gold of Ida's fabricated self is exposed.

"O Swallow, Swallow" (IV, 75-98), though very different, is placed as a complement to "Tears, idle tears." It is introduced by a request from Ida that has deep ironic reverberations:

> "Not such as moans about the retrospect,
> But deals with the other distance and the hues
> Of promise; not a death's-head at the wine."
>
> (IV, 67-69)

The poetic implications of her language are very different from her discursive intent: the "moans" of the near personal future are engendered; the "other distance" is almost upon her, and the "hues / Of promise" are very dark indeed; a "death's-head at the wine" of love is almost the Prince's destiny, as the darkest night of the soul is hers. But "the other distance and the hues / Of promise" also has reference to aspects of youthful experience other than the " 'groanings which cannot be uttered' " of St. Paul—namely, love and hope, experiences of deep personal sentiment of which Ida has also been deprived by the system that has shaped her. The Prince is both the singer and the composer of the song, and hence it also measures him in relationship to her. It is a love lyric and a nesting song, both erotic and connubial. It contrasts the fertility of the North (the Prince's country) with the wantonness of the South (Ida's terrain) and thus names the " 'bright and fierce and fickle' " adventure upon which she has embarked. It reverses the pursuer-pursued roles of Venus and Adonis, while it sustains the coupling motif, and it echoes lightly the sentiments of "To the Virgins to Make Much of Time." Its music and pictorial imagery fully render its sensuous amorous intent—the swallow-flights, the swallow-sounds (" 'pipe and trill / And cheep and twitter' "), the swallow-body in the white rhythmic cleavage. Ida's response is one of haughtiness to levity: " 'A mere love-poem!' " is the predatory male's way of enslaving the female and can be deadly, as she knows from the case of one she loved. She herself has written poetry, but always with grand thematic purpose;

> "Valkyrian hymns, or into rhythm have dashed
> The passion of the prophetess; for song
> Is duer unto freedom, force and growth
> Of spirit than to junketing and love."
>
> (IV, 121-124)

The Prince's song may be too private, too purposeless and self-indulgent; but though it may neglect the larger cultural needs of the world, it is not intellectually monistic, like Ida, who tries to freeze Time (" 'laid up like winter bats,' " l. 126) until her singular purposes are all accomplished. And this attitude of Ida's perhaps motivates and justifies the unsung song of the piece, Cyril's "care-less, careless tavern-catch / Of Moll and Meg, and strange experi-ences / Unmeet for ladies" (IV, 139-141). The reader is left to fill in this white space for himself, but clearly it is ribaldry's trolling rebuttal to the sterile, inflated, doctrinaire, unrealistic abstractions being promulgated so dogmatically by Ida.

Ida's song—"Our enemies have fallen, have fallen"—is, presum-ably, one of her own "Valkyrian hymns." She assumes the role of one of the maidens of Odin, atop her own Valhalla, and in a voice that rolls funeral drums, she celebrates the victory of Destiny over her enemies through the symbol of Ygdrasil, the great ash tree of Norse mythology whose roots and branches hold together the uni-verse. In his love song, the Prince had compared her to the late-leafing "tender ash," and now in her cosmic prophecy she has bloomed with a vengeance. But her efforts to play the Valkyrian role—to conduct the souls of "heroes" slain in battle to Valhalla and attend them there—are frustrated by events. She finds herself entirely isolated in her godlike role, as mankind's values turn uni-versally against her; she has irrefragable debts to pay even to her "enemies," and so the neatly packaged Destiny which she has just celebrated in a grand Wagnerian aria begins to unravel all around her. It is one of the great universal truths that tragic poetry teaches us: at the moment it reaches climactic fulfillment, the overweening ego crumbles to a fall. At her epic apogee, Ida does not have a friend left: even the words of her dead mother—" 'Our Ida has a heart' " (VI, 218)—are hurled into her teeth by the mildest of fa-thers. Her assumed godlike grandeur is given a few simple, human tests—the return of the child to its mother, Psyche's plea, " 'yet speak to me, / Say one soft word and let me part forgiven' " (VI, 201-202), the opening up of the Palace-hospital to all the injured males; and although she finally yields to each in turn, her sense of self is left in total shambles. Such profound moral, psychological, experiential, formalistic revelations have always been the function of poetry, and they are the function of poetry at the present time.

The final two songs of *The Princess* are read from a book ("A volume of the Poets," VII, 159), and thus the poem ends where it began—with literature. They are both read by Ida "to herself" "Deep in the night (VII, 158) as she watches over the precariously ailing Prince. She has already given him a gesture of her love—a kiss—and has begun to emerge as true woman, suggesting to the brain of the Prince, "drowsy with weakness," [5] Aphrodite rising from the sea (VII, 148-154). What Ida must do now is fully and frankly acknowledge the exact character of her fault and establish new foundations of faith—in her simple but magnified humanness and in the simple but creative human way. She must accept her fall fearlessly and perceive it as fortunate.

"Now sleeps the crimson petal, now the white" (VII, 161-174) is an adaptation of the Persian ghazal or love-ode, a poem using highly conventional prosody and imagery, somewhat analogous as used here to the English love-sonnet. It captures, in the most delicate psychosexual suggestiveness, that moment of physical and spiritual union when two persons totally blend into one. It is impossible to distinguish the speaker as male or female, and thus the metaphor of androgyny that has been pervasive throughout the poem is brought to poise in a resolution of the most seductive fulfillment and illumination. There is no sexual contest, and the intellect is quite irrelevant. Time is at last one with all spirits who have achieved this epiphanic moment of serene imaginative love.

"Come down, O maid" (VII, 177-207) is touched with "the Greek Idyllic feeling" traditionally identified with the Alexandrian poet Theocritus. Again, as in the Prince's song, the roles of Venus and Adonis are reversed: Adonis pleads for the return of Aphrodite, not from hell but from the "mountain heights," and the adaptation is consistent with the parable of *The Princess,* since the traditional male-female roles have themselves been reversed. The chief images are obliquely suggestive of the ritual of the festival of Adonis, the Adonia: "the sacred marriage *(hieros gamos),* the symbols of fertility, the death and disappearance of the youthful lover, and the plea for his return." [6] But the mythic subtext, though aesthetically enriching, is not the primary source of the song's affectiveness. The voice itself, simple and musically ingratiating, is full of love and *joie de vivre,* idyllic domesticity and generous providence. It is the shepherd's plaint for his lost shepherdess; what he offers is the richest harvest of the fertile heart's abundant goodness, and what he asks is a faithful act of faith.

Ida's recognition of the true truth (VII, 212-227) is enabled by
these two poems. She admits her lack of humility, that it was really
"power in knowledge" rather than truth that she sought. She accepts the fault as within herself, "something wild within her
breast," though she knows, too, that she had received "ill counsel."
The girlhood that she had cast aside is now claimed as her full
measure, and she indicts herself bitterly but truthfully: " 'Ah fool,
and made myself a queen of farce!' " (VII, 228). Her dark journey
into "all the faultful Past" is finally broken by her ability to identify with one of the gentlest of nature's creatures, a little brood-
bird eager to fulfill her duty of love:

> Till notice of a change in the dark world
> Was lispt about the acacias, and a bird,
> That early woke to feed her little ones,
> Sent from a dewy breast a cry for light:
> She moved, and at her feet the volume fell.
>   (VII, 234-238)

In the final dialogue-duet (VII, 239-345), in which the Prince,
because of Ida's shattered self-confidence, takes the role of good
counselor, some of the chief metaphors and motifs of *The Princess*
are clarified and reenforced. Ygdrasil is brought out of Ida's sexual
isolation and made cohabitant with man:

> "For she that out of Lethe scales with man
> The shining steps of Nature, shares with man
> His nights, his days, moves with him to one goal,
> Stays all the fair young planet in her hands—
> If she be small, slight-natured, miserable,
> How shall men grow?"
>   (VII, 245-250)

The androgyny metaphor is stripped of any hermaphroditic implications, the fusion of strength and gentleness being preserved,
but sexual love fully implanted:

"For woman is not undevelopt man,
But diverse: could we make her as the man,
Sweet love were slain: his dearest bond is this,
Not like to like, but like in difference."
                                    (VII, 259-262)

The motif of the "losing of the child," which had been a central
trope of Ida's crusade, is placed in perspective. Child-nurture must
always be a conspicuous dimension of motherhood and is not a
contradiction to the development of a woman's full capacities as a
distinct person: as she cannot be man, so she must not cease to be
woman, since from this counterpoint comes the music of life (VII,
267-270). Ida's aggressive futurism, which led to her contempt of
the past and a rewriting of history, is dissolved into a metaphor of
recovery, in which, once the sexual contest which began with the
fall and made such horrid shows is ended, the future becomes the
Edenic past:

"And so these twain, upon the skirts of Time,
Sit side by side, full-summed in all their powers,
Dispensing harvest, sowing the To-be,
Self-reverent each and reverencing each,
Distinct in individualities,
But like each other even as those who love.
Then comes the statelier Eden back to man. . . ."
                                    (VII, 271-277)

But this can never be achieved through contentious abstractions of
Ida's recent kind. It must actually start somewhere: " 'Dear, but let
us type them now in our own lives . . .' " (VII, 281-282).

The Prince's intense mother-reverence is then brought into critical focus: Can a man who has taken his mother as his ideal of
womanhood and based his "faith in womankind" on her model
ever really love another woman in a very different way? The
Prince's answer, though conscientious and complex, is unequivocal
and is the chief metaphor of his own process of maturation in the
poem. His love for Ida has had a long period of gestation, too; and
the "strange doubts" from which he has suffered have had their

source in the discrepancies between reality and appearance, including that between his mother as model of womanhood and her and between the woman in her and the iron mask she wore. But now two things have happened: she, like his mother, has given him birth (" 'Given back to life, to life indeed, through thee,' " VII, 324); and she, like his mother, has become authentic, killing his doubts and " 'haunting sense of hollow shows' " (VII, 328). The Grace of Brightness now shines on him: as the child Aglaïa first began to dispel Ida's mists, so Ida has now dispelled his. The past has not been lost, but it has melted into the present and, like man and woman reconciled in imaginative love, cooperant but different, promises a fair future:

> "all the past
> Melts mist-like into this bright hour, and this
> Is more to more, and all the rich to-come
> Reels, as the golden Autumn woodland reels
> Athwart the smoke of burning weeds."
> (VII, 333-337)

Then, in the closing lines, *The Princess* reveals the central perception with which it began: poetry, too, is organic and " 'Melts mist-like into this bright hour.' " As the poem had been initiated through the imaginative fertilization of "the gallant glorious chronicle," so it finds its climactic imaginative analogue in *Paradise Lost*:

> "O we will walk this world,
> Yoked in all exercise of noble end,
> And so through those dark gates across the wild
> That no man knows."
> (VII, 339-342)

In conclusion, then, Tennyson's *The Princess* is, in a primary sense, a poem about poetry. Written during the period when he had shaped for himself his poetic role, it reflects an authentic responsiveness to the pressure on the poet of the genuine needs of his times and of contemporary literary commentators to make poetry relevant to those times. This presented no abstract problem: poetry had always aspired to create "an image of the mighty world" and therefore had always had contemporary relevance, Homer, Dante, Shakespeare, and Milton being imaginatively contemporaneous with all ages. But the acutest external pressure on Tennyson—and on letters generally—was to be topical, to use topical subject matter. This did present a practical problem. A major poet with major aspirations, while he was the creation of his age, had to be its creator too; and though he certainly needed to be true to his age, he also needed to be true to himself as a poet and to the poetic tradition which made it possible for him to be a poet. So Tennyson experimented in *The Princess* with a poetic fusion of these obligations: he dealt with a crucial topical subject—the condition of women—in poetry's metaphoric way. But in doing so, in treating a topical subject poetically, he chose what was for him as a poet a more fundamental subject having acuter topical relevance even than the condition of women—namely, the function of poetry at the present (or any) time. Like Wordsworth, Tennyson knew that no significant issue of archetypal as well as topical human contention could be resolved without spiritual love; and he knew, also like Wordsworth, that "This spiritual love acts not nor can exist / Without Imagination . . ." (*The Prelude*, XIV, 188-189).

Imagination was, of course, the poet's primary business: only the poet, including the degree of poet in each of us, can bring illumination and order to the infinity of problems and attitudes that hector even conscientious men in every age. In the working out of this primary topic of the indispensability of the poetic imagination to creative human perception, Tennyson put especial emphasis on form. He suspended the parable in which one topic evolves (the condition of women) in another parable in which a different but inextricably related topic evolves (significant or imaginative form), suggesting that it is only through imaginative form that the prior topic can even begin to be fruitfully looked at. Thus the whole literary procedure is set in motion by an imaginative reading act; the genial but uninspired miscellaneousness of the times is emphasized; and the central topic of the current condition of women is subjected to an imaginative metamorphosis in which the poet of the party creates a circle of the imagination into which all parties to the narrative are drawn. The poem creates, not only a fairy-tale distance at which the topic of the condition of women is placed, but also a fairy-tale process in which the reading act and the writing act are fully and dynamically fused, all parties—men and women, young and old, past and present—having a creative role in the shape and movement of the imaginative literary experience. It begins lightly and ends solemnly because the imaginative process itself gradually draws the participants into an awareness that the topic is as serious, properly perceived, as creative human survival itself—that the future cannot be bright unless peace between the sexes is achieved since marriage and generation are themselves at issue. The principals in the fable suffer from faulted imaginations, and poetry itself—the intercalary songs, the blank-verse lyrics, the poetic fable—becomes the chief instrument of interpretation, measurement, and movement, as the final anchorage of the fable's language and perception is in a literary text of incomparable poetic quality, *Paradise Lost*. Thus, the function of poetry is shown to be what it has always been—man's chief instrument of perception and renewal; and its function at the present time, a function of conspicuous urgency, is to show that a literal contemporaneousness is not man's *need* but his *problem* and that poetry's function is to induce in him—through brightness, joy, and bloom—an imaginative ability to see his problems *sub specie aeternitatis* and thus to strengthen in him both the instinct and the capacity to survive.

Notes

1. The text referred to throughout is that in *The Poems of Tennyson,* ed. Christopher Ricks (London: Longman, 1969), and passages are identified in parentheses as appropriate after individual citations. The editorial apparatus of this edition is also heavily drawn on in the commentary, especially quotations from Tennyson or quotations from others that are known to have had Tennyson's approval. Materials from the headnote (Ricks, pp. 741-743) are used with standard quotation marks, but without footnotes; materials drawn from more out-of-the-way places are duly noted.
2. *"Past and Present." Emerson's Complete Works* (London: The Waverley Book Co. Ltd., 1893), XII, 247-248.
3. Ricks, Appendix A. pp. 1768-1769.
4. Walter Pater, Conclusion to *The Renaissance.*
5. Tennyson's own comment, in Ricks, p. 834n.
6. See Philip Mayerson, *Classical Mythology in Literature, Art, and Music* (Waltham, Mass.: Xerox College Publishing, 1971), p. 191.

9.

In Memoriam in Aesthetic Context

The new critical awarenesses presumed to be dominant in Tennyson studies for the last twenty years (since, say, 1960) have done less for *In Memoriam* than for any other crucial Tennyson text. *In Memoriam* has never been a neglected poem in the sense that *Maud* and *Idylls of the King* were neglected, but criticism of it has become flat, repetitious, and circular. The overall approach to the poem has not much improved upon the work of the nineteenth century itself—upon such perceptive and familiar pieces as those by Charles Kingsley (1850), R. H. Hutton (1888), and A. C. Bradley (1901). The extraordinary exception is T. S. Eliot's essay on *In Memoriam* (1936),[1] one of the great modern meditations on the poem. Eliot's essay is most remarkable, like *In Memoriam* itself, for its Unthought [2]—for the field of thinking into which it induces the reader rather than for individual thoughts it formalizes. Again like *In Memoriam*, there is a subterranean awareness flowing in Eliot's essay, as if he were gazing at the subconscious Tennyson subconsciously. A number of his insights and theoretical expectations strike a false note—his influential characterization of *In Memoriam*'s "unity and continuity," his assertion that *Ulysses* does not tell a

164

story, his dissatisfaction with the lyrical-dramatic fusion in *Maud* and with the failure of the poem to deliver Tennyson's "profound and tumultuous feelings"; but the essay moves the mind and sensibilities of the reader into new fields of response. The sundry quibbles Eliot provokes are compensated for when such highly suggestive observations as the following emerge: "It happens now and then that a poet by some strange accident expresses the mood of his generation, at the same time that he is expressing a mood of his own which is quite remote from that of his generation. This is not a question of insincerity: there is an amalgam of yielding and opposition below the surface of consciousness." [3] The comment gets so close to the internal center both of *In Memoriam* and of the Tennysonian experience in poetry that it is explosively significant. Tennyson suddenly seems to exist in a new medium of illumination, not crisply and brightly, but profoundly. Our understanding of the deftness with which he made his poetic decisions and took his poetic chances, combined with the sudden sensitivity to the penetrating psychic pain that his precarious poetic poise cost him, makes us available at quite a new apprehensive level to the Tennysonian space in poetry, an imaginative space that almost filled the 1830s, '40s, and '50s and made every other poet of those literary decades a "contemporary of Tennyson," subordinate even if, like Browning, major. Eliot is inexhaustibly provocative, too, in what he calls the "religious" character of *In Memoriam:* "It is not religious because of the quality of its faith, but because of the quality of its doubt. Its faith is a poor thing, but its doubt is a very intense experience. *In Memoriam* is a poem of despair, but of despair of a religious kind." [4] The legitimate reasons for being uncomfortable with these sentences do not negate the recognition that Eliot has touched the center of the poem's formal experience and has thus compelled the reader, and given him the confidence, to explore afresh and from the perspective of zero spiritual budgeting the true dimension of the "dark undercurrent woe" [5] with which the speaker of *In Memoriam* undertakes to cope. The notion that religious despair cohabitates with epithalamic joyousness in the poem pushes us toward the possibility that it is more crucially dramatic than is usually perceived and shifts, at least experimentally, the focus of our search for the poem's affective center. We become collaborative with the author (reading act with writing act) in the exploration, not of what Tennyson thought, but of *how* a stand-in for the human race (Tennyson in the context of ourselves) might have moved from one state of being to another state of being.

The mainline modern view is compended by Jerome Hamilton Buckley in *Tennyson: The Growth of a Poet* (1960) and by Christopher Ricks in *Tennyson* (1972). F. E. L. Priestley, in *Language and Structure in Tennyson's Poetry* (1973), though he devotes only a scant six pages to the poem, reveals a finely tuned literary sensibility and whets the reader's appetite for a great many more of his perceptions of the poem's method, its place in the classical / modern literary tradition, and its individual poetic excellences; but unless he gives us a full-length study of *In Memoriam,* Professor Priestley can hardly hope to redirect its critical history. Paul Turner's *Tennyson* (1976) enriches our awareness of the dense fabric of literary indebtedness in the poem and turns our attention in a new way to the role of the speaker and of the speaker's sense of self. In *The Poetry of Tennyson* (1977), A. Dwight Culler says a good many usable things—for example, "It is a poem of process, not of product" and "We feel the weird potency of language to realize itself"—but his chief new contribution is to the formalistic and ideological models and analogies lying in the English background of the poem, a contribution of exemplary erudition. Both Turner and Culler provide substantial new evidence supportive of the thesis (which neither of them articulates) that *In Memoriam,* at least in one of its major coordinates, is literature made of literature. And yet, except for such differences of emphasis and of individual critical talent, no one of the major Tennyson commentators distinguishes himself from any other in his treatment of *In Memoriam*—not by his distinctive critical methodology and not by any demonstrated capacity or desire to perceive the poem in a fundamentally different way.

One general observation that makes this state of affairs seem curious is that the very substantial input that Tennyson has himself made into our understanding of the poem's intention, structural and perceptual, is clearly and consciously corrective of the autobiographical / ideological emphases of the traditional criticism of *In Memoriam.*[6] But Tennyson's comments have, judged by the critical record, achieved very little of their corrective intent. Tennyson's aesthetic formalism, nondoctrinaire but consciously monitorial, has been so consistently ignored by the biographical critics and the ideologists that it seems almost futile to recur to its main elements: "that this is a poem, *not* an actual biography"; that it "was meant to be a kind of *Divina Commedia,* ending with happiness"; that "the different moods of sorrow as in a drama are dramatically given"; that the " 'I' is not always the author speaking of himself, but the voice of the human race speaking through him"; that "the divisions of the poem are made by the First Xmas Eve (Section XXVIII), Second Xmas (LXXVIII), Third Xmas Eve (CIV and CV etc.)." [7] There is, in these familiar authorial glosses on *In Memoriam,* more encouragement to approach the poem formalistically than we have on 90 percent of the major poems in English. And Tennyson gives the matter a subtler and even more pressing tone in his remarks to James Knowles on the two occasions of his reading *In Memoriam* aloud in 1870 and 1871:

> It is rather the cry of the whole human race than mine. In the poem altogether private grief swells out into thought of, and hope for, the whole world. It begins with a funeral and ends with a marriage—begins with death and ends in promise of a new life—a sort of Divine Comedy, cheerful at the close. It is a very impersonal poem as well as personal. There is more about myself in *Ulysses,* which was written under the sense of loss and that all had gone by, but that still life must be fought out to the end. It was more written with the feeling of his loss upon me than many poems in *In Memoriam* . . . [*sic*]. It's too hopeful, this poem, more than I am myself. . . . [*sic*]. The general way of its being written was so queer that if there were a blank space I would put in a poem . . . [*sic*]. I think of adding another to it, a speculative one, bringing out the thoughts of *The Higher Pantheism,* and showing that all the arguments are about as good on one side as the other, and throw man back more on the primitive impulses and feelings.[8]

Tennyson has reached a most delicate place in his sense of his poem. It is clearly his chief inclination to declare the poem's autonomy, but with that steady conscientiousness that is one of his most dependable personal qualities and which makes him appear to waffle on crucial issues, he "saves" the realizations that, as a member of the "whole human race," he too is involved in the poem's "cry" and that the poem is "personal" in two ways—as written and partially motivated "under the sense of loss and that all had gone by" and as cast, however generically, in a formalistically confessional mode. Still, Tennyson has a clear sense of the poem as quite distinct from himself, a sense that, although he was the instrument of its actual composition, it took on a mind and character of its own, coming out at a perceptual / affirmational place ("too hopeful") to which he cannot himself subscribe. If he added another poem that would neutralize this "too hopeful" hope of *In Memoriam*,[9] he would have as its purpose to "throw man back more on the primitive impulses and feelings." The phrase has a startling significance, reminiscent surely of Rousseau (who, according to Professor Dwight Culler, had invented the form that Tennyson would use for his next poem, *Maud*) [10] and prophetic of the anthropological theories of modernists like Levi-Strauss. Without in any way undercutting the integrity with which *in Memoriam* works, Tennyson suggests that it is an apex-of-civilization poem, shaped not by "the primitive impulses and feelings" primarily but by the thoughts and expectations, the intellectual needs and psychological structures, the dilemmas and fideistic deprivations of a highly advanced culture—right, perhaps, but culturally specialized.[11] Like the speakers in *Locksley Hall* and *Maud*, the speaker in *In Memoriam* is a man of his age in a closely conceived way, embodying both its strengths and its limitations; and since, in the poem itself, this is worked out formalistically, the language-man who speaks in *In Memoriam* becomes himself a mythic representative of the age and is to a degree imprisoned in it. He is thus a mythic myth-maker and configurates, for mankind at large, a process of self-saving within a specified cluster of cultural metaphors, the process being universal, the cultural metaphors being infinitely variable.[12]

Tennyson's use of two poems referentially in speaking of *In Memoriam* deserves more serious and elaborate attention than the commentators have traditionally given it. Like the *Divina Commedia*, *In Memoriam* is an imaginative configuration of the "way of the soul";

by distant analogy to Dante's poem, it is divided into three parts, according to the Christmas sections; and it has its levels—"nine natural groupings" marking the stages of the *persona's* grief and thought. The *persona* of *In Memoriam* is, like the *persona* of the *Divina Commedia,* a poet; and the *persona* in each case has a poet-guide—in the *Divina Commedia,* it is the symbolic Virgil, and in *In Memoriam,* true to the poem's internalized form, it is the poet-in-himself, the imaginative dimension of Everyman. The famous parting between Dante and Virgil as the pilgrim enters the Paradiso has its counterpart in *In Memoriam,* Canto CIII. This is the second "climax" of the poem, a highly stylized dream-vision "Which left my after-morn content." A parable of the decisive moment in the pilgrimage of the *persona,* the dream-vision employs imagery which echoes from the early aesthetic canon of Tennyson's poetry: the hall (a sort of poetic sanctuary or hospice), the maiden Muses, the fountains of imaginative inspiration ("distant hills / From hidden summits fed with rills / A river sliding by the wall"), a private world full of the sound of music ("The hall will harp and carol rang"), creativity dedicated to noble purposes and an instrument of suprasensuous perception. But that, though good in itself, is not enough: life is for action, for commitment. So "then flew in a dove / And brought a summons from the sea" (in *The Hesperides,* "the outer sea"; in *The Lotos-Eaters,* "the deep mid-ocean"). It is not easy: aesthetic withdrawal, especially of the most refined kind, is as attractive as the womb ("And when they learnt that I must go, / They wept and wailed"); but, though painful, it is essential, and its compensation is development, growth, magnification of both art and the individual. But what then? What happens to poetry (imagination, artistic apprehension) after it has enabled man to reach reconciliation with life and reunion with a lost dimension:

"We served thee here," they said, "so long,
And wilt thou leave us now behhind?"

So rapt I was, they could not win
    An answer from my lips, but he
    Replying, "Enter likewise ye
And go with us:" they entered in.

Thus, the pilgrim in *In Memoriam* is not required to part from his Virgil: in the evolving dispensation, his "pagan," his natural, human poet-guide, is indispensable.

And this brings us to the most fruitful context in which to think of *In Memoriam* in terms of the *Divina Commedia*—namely, the analogue-of-opposites. Dante's poem is generally considered the quintessential Christian poem, culminating in the Nirvana-New Jerusalem of the Beatific Vision, the Rosa Mystica. Written by a supremely religious poet at the beginning of the fourteenth century, the *Divina Commedia* orchestrates the philosophy, theology, mysticism, science, history, ethics, and aesthetics of the Christian Middle Ages into a crescendo of superb imaginative affirmation. But *In Memoriam*, while it orchestrates in a minor key the science, history, philosophy, ethics, aesthetics, and fragmented theology of the post-Christian Modern Ages, was written by an authentically skeptical poet who was deeply aware that the fabric of belief available to Dante was simply not available to modern man, that not only had the superb integrity of medieval Christianity been lost, but that Christianity had itself been lost, that for him, his contemporaries, and the men of centuries to come, Christianity might retain its value as a moving metaphor and analogue but that it could never again be a singular creed. For him and his kind, if they would have a myth (and he thought they would), they must make their own (and he thought they could).[13]

Ulysses, Tennyson's second referential poem, is integral to this view of the analogy between *In Memoriam* and the *Divina Commedia.* Ulysses is an impersonal / personal stand-in for all those alienated, disconsolate souls for whom the world has lost a past integrity and who must "rise on stepping-stones / Of their dead selves to higher things" *(In Memoriam*, I, 3-4). The speaker of *In Memoriam* is of an unidentified youthful age, while Ulysses is an old man; but the two poems meet at a point of perception and in a processive structure that is independent of age. Both speakers, the ancient Ithacan and the younger European, have an overwhelming sense of loss: they are face to face with death, the one perhaps immediate and prospective (his own), the other immediate and retrospective (his beloved friend's); but they converge on a question of living rather than of dying (on what terms is life worth sustaining, worth "willing"?) and on a process by which global dreariness, a universal metaphor of death-in-life, is transferred into an epiphany both personal and impersonal. Ulysses is the prototypical mythic mythmaker of whom the speaker in *In Memoriam* is the latter-day heir; and the specialized character of his fiction in its many versions should not deflect us from uninhibited scrutiny of the ritual of renewal which he enacts in the Tennyson text and from the realization that, despite the distancing diagonal of age (both personal and cultural), temperament, and an incomparably rich literary resonance (Western man's oldest and most perennially used story of individual man's life-struggle), *Ulysses* is a little *In Memoriam.* Like the speaker in *In Memoriam,* Ulysses' acutest need is for spiritual refreshment, for a revitalized faith in his ability to convert deep personal stress and soul-sterility into the energy that will enable him to renew himself and voyage into new spiritual spaces. The ritual of language which constitutes his monodrama [14] is climactic in that it is the result of an extended period of self-erosion and takes on a now-or-never urgency, differing in this from *In Memoriam,* in which the whole time-consuming process moves from point-zero to climactic affirmation and where the movement of a representative poetic spirit through a peculiar time-frame is a dimension of the poetic character of the piece. But in both poems the rich lode which the speaker mines is the self-lode: their identity or sense of self is what is essentially threatened, and their identity, magnified and enlarged by the struggle resulting from their fortunate fall into the jeopardized self, is what is ultimately restored. It is a complex process because the self is both highly individual and social, and the social self often loses sight of the individual self, absorbing it into its fabric. Thus, in Ulysses' first sentence both the "I" and the "race" can serve as the subject of "know not me." Indeed, his initial peevishness, not creditably but credibly lashing out at all the nearest images of his distress, is the result of his sense that his individual self is being de-created by his socialized situation; and in lines 6-32 he undertakes an urgent ego-strengthening, the touch of hubris undercut by the intensity of his need to put himself together again, to define himself anew through a remembrance of things past, to reconstitute an identity *capable* of sailing "beyond the sunset, and the baths / Of all the western stars . . .

(60-61). Read in this context, the much-maligned passage on Tele-machus (33-43) represents a moment of serene balance and forth-rightness: having reasserted his own sense of self, Ulysses is capable of yielding a discrete and admirable identity to another, even to his son, for whose prowess in public affairs he, as a conscientious king, must be very grateful since that is what makes it possible for him to seek his own private fulfillment. The admirable verse-paragraph with which the poem reaches its climax is, like the last "natural grouping" of *In Memoriam,* a jubilation of the rediscovered and reaffirmed self and of the unequivocal recognition that space and time are not impediments to the spirit's true odyssey. The "I" of *In Memoriam* and the "I" of *Ulysses* are very different personalities functioning in very different fictions, but their motivation and their self-processing give the poems which embody them a strong sense of imaginative community.

This sense of imaginative community is reenforced by the influ-ence on the character of both poems of a strong symbolist presence. It is well recognized by students of modern poetry that what later became known on the Continent as the symbolist movement or manner in poetry (Verlaine, Mallarmé, Maeterlinck) [15] had emerged as an unmistakable poetic presence in Tennyson's work almost two generations earlier. (Mallarmé, the oldest of the French group, was not born until 1842.) Two of Tennyson's poems have been especially cited as representatively symbolist, *Mariana* (1830) and *Mariana in the South* (1832), and it is certainly fair to say that in these poems, Tennyson, like the symbolists, is representing percep-tions and emotions by indirect suggestion rather than by direct expression and that such "meaning" as the poems have is rendered symbolically through particular objects, words, and sounds. The two temperaments and the divergent cultural settings embodied in the two poems are sustained by markedly different symbolic imag-ery; and *Mariana in the South* hints at psychological complexities— the self-enshrined lady, the self-depreciated lady in a rather heated medium of psychosexuality—not present in like degree in *Mariana.* But it should also be noted that, although the *Mariana*-poems are firmly recognizable examples of a symbolist presence in Tennyson's early poetry, that presence can be generalized far beyond these two poems and seen as one of the defining characteristics of his poetry.

It can be seen especially in the cluster of female delineations—for example, *Claribel, Madeline, Adeline*—in which, through a highly stylized lyrical insistence, mysterious depths of personality are explored, inconclusively and for their own sake. And it can be seen also in such dramatic lyrics as *The Lady of Shalott, OEnone, The Hesperides, The Lotos-Eaters, Ulysses, The Vision of Sin*, and *Tithonus*. These poems may at first seem far more susceptible to placement in a network of thematic interpretation external to themselves as individual poems—for example, the "garden of art" theme; but that thematic network has proved ultimately inconclusive, and it has often been woven at the expense of the poet's primary fascination with strange states of being.

For example, one need not deny the possible relevance of *The Hesperides* to the theme of the artist in difficulty to perceive a primary emphasis other than the expresssly thematic. *The Hesperides* presents two quite distinct apprehending states of consciousness—that of Zidonian Hanno and that of the daughters of the Evening Star; and the structure of the poem, a free-verse choric ode framed in by a blank-verse narrative, dictates that first consideration be given to the witnessing (the enveloping) consciousness, namely, Hanno's. We are told nothing really conclusive about Hanno's witnessing, but we are told enough to set in motion curiously haunting speculations—his relationship, by analogy, with both Hercules and Ulysses, the intrepid laborer and the fabulous voyager, the man of public conscience, action, and discovery; the essential strangeness to him of the experience, negatively defined by what it was *not* like—"the warbling of the nightingale," the "melody of the Libyan lotus flute," metaphors of alternative life-styles having more public currency and thus more available to him; the normative level at which he responds—"voices, like voices in a dream, continuous," real / unreal, heard but hardly believed. The incantatory choric song, embodiment of the other consciousness, is deeply permeated with anxiety, recessiveness, irreconciliation ("Hesper hateth Phosphor, evening hateth morn"). It projects a cabalistic psyche whose mysteries are occult, only vaguely conceptual (e.g., the numerology), primitivistic—full of weariness, simplistic morality, "drunkenness," and an irresistible awareness of ensuing death. That is all the poem is, all the poem "means." Like symbolist poetry generally, with its music, lyric drama, dense texture of imagery, impersonative tonality, inexhaustible suggestiveness, *The Hesperides* is generative in that it moves the reader's awareness into a new psychological space, brings him alive from an internal center outward, his and the poem's.

Another poem that explores symbolistically a fascinating psychic landscape is *The Vision of Sin*.[16] Like so many of Tennyson's poems, *The Vision of Sin* is wholly monitored by the confessional "I," and the primary question that it raises relates to the nature of the narrating *persona*. (*In Memoriam*, though a a very different poem, is in this context essentially comparable.) It is a psychological poem in which the speaker reveals his deepest inner tensions by letting them surface in the form of a surrealistic dream-vision at the center of which (Canto IV) is a ballad of death rendering a dance of death. The poles of the speaker's tension are implicit: a terrifying sense of something called "God" (the "awful rose of dawn") counterpointed by a compulsive fascination with sin, death, and the ultimate meaninglessness of life. True to the poem's character as a dream, hovering between pleasurable identifications and nightmare, the speaker employs disjointed narrative and submerged symbols, pressing upon the reader the primacy of the experiential rather than the conceptual as the poem's affective center; and since the experience wells up from the unconscious, it yields to interpretive speculation rather than to interpretive reduction. The threshold symbol of the encumbered Pegasus ("a horse with wings, that would have flown / But that his heavy rider kept him down," ll. 3-4) suggests the special terms on which the troubled psyche will evolve, terms which are consistently expanded by the symbol of the child as ostler in the palace of sin (which, in these special terms, is also a kind of palace of art). This movement is considerably reenforced in Canto II: musical addicts responding frentically to a "nerve-dissolving melody" (44), a Dionysian or Bacchanalian revel employing the two marks of Dionysus in line 42: "Like to Furies, like to Graces," the benevolent inspirer of music and poetry and the patron of orgiastic revelry (perhaps the "luxurious agony" of line 43).

Canto III is the pivotal recitative of the poem, followed by the aria of Canto IV. In Canto III, after the exhaustion of the Bacchic revel, and before the ballad of death in which the Bacchic theme ("Fill the cup and fill the can") is given a grotesque (both comic and terrifying) rerendering, the alternative of a "God" first emerges, a strangely ambiguous symbol, a vast nature-image suggestive principally of Aurora riding in her rose-colored chariot and accompanied by "heavy, hueless, formless, cold" vapors (53) and promising, at most, an inevitable naturalistic cyclic rebirth. In Canto III, too, the narrative becomes least coherent: the "madman" of line 56 defies firm identification; the warning he would have given if he could is unidentified; the phrase "within my head" (59) seems to refine the essential locus from which Canto IV is then apprehended, a clue perhaps to the singularly argumentative character of Canto IV. The speaker in Canto IV dramatically enlarges Tennyson's gallery of geriatric consciousnesses (Ulysses, Tithonus, Merlin, Tiresias, the Ancient Sage, and so forth); and although it is filtered through the "I" of *The Vision of Sin,* his cynical world-view (his "mockeries of the world") is not without a high degree of cogency, so that in Canto V the "I" of the poem, amid images of universal decay, imagines / dreams the voices of four commentators interpreting this nadir-gloss on human value-myths, climaxing in the cry, "Is there any hope?" (220). The answer, though heard, is unintelligible, and the ambiguous "God" again makes "Himself an awful rose of dawn." *The Vision of Sin,* then, though very different from *The Hesperides* in terms of the peculiar psychic landscape that it explores and the narrative structure that is uses, is, *as an aesthetic procedure,* genuinely comparable: it is a lyric drama employing an impersonative tonality and functioning through a dense texture of idiosyncratic imagery to set in motion in the reader a new and strange cluster of imaginative awarenesses that, in their endless suggestiveness, resist traditional modes of closure.

To focus, then, on the character of the symbolist manner that had so pervasive a presence in the poetry of Tennyson, we should remind ourselves that it was a major manifestation of that broader current of "aesthetic poetry" that became the dominant innovation of nineteenth- and twentieth-century art and that Arthur Hallam saw [17] as the result of the artist's determination not to suffer his mind "to be occupied, during its periods of creation, by any other predominant motive than the desire of beauty. . . ." It depended for its sustenance, not upon ideas as such, but upon carefully controlled imaginative "luxuriance"; not upon self-revelation, but upon the embodiment of the self in the moods of "ideal characters." Drawing from the visual arts, it emphasized a "vivid, picturesque delineation of objects"—a dense texture of images; drawing from music, it employed a great "variety of . . . lyrical measures, and exquisite modulation of harmonious words and cadences to the swell and fall of the feelings expressed." It turned, not upon thoughts, but upon "elevated habits of thought" and sought to impart a carefully judged tonality as a means of "communicat[ing] the love of beauty to the heart." [18] The symbolist "never asserts; he suggests," said Swinburne; [19] he does not deal in conceptual correspondences but in structures. Having as his goal the engendering of imaginative apprehension in others, he attempts to make the reader participatory in his creation, assuming a relationship to it analogous to that of a reader. He aspires, like aesthetic poets generally, to "the condition of music" in his poems, and music is his special instrument because, as Baudelaire said, "true music suggests analogous ideas to different minds." [20] He works toward his goal of the inexhaustible stimulation of beauty through "evocation, allusion, suggestion" [21] and attempts to give language itself the primary creative role: "If the poem is to be pure, the poet's voice must be stilled and the initiative taken by the words themselves. . . . And in an exchange of gleams they will flame out . . . and thus replace the author's breathing in lyric poetry of old— replace the poet's own personal and passionate control of verse." [22]

This is where Tennyson's aesthetic perceptions were centered in the fall of 1833 when he first drafted *Ulysses* and wrote the earliest-known cantos of *In Memoriam.* Under the influence of a strong symbolist flow, he devoted himself to poetic constructs that were lyric / dramatic in a retrospectively climactic way, poetic moments in which the whole history of a person or a people comes to poise, the poems inducing awarenesses of infinite white spaces for each reader to fill in according to his inclination and ability. *Ulysses,* for example, induces thoughts of three thousand years of fable, setting up a narrative rhythm between Homer, Dante, and Tennyson. All of our educated assumptions about this crafty, courageous, noble archetypal man are given a sudden jolt by the peevish wearisome voice with which he begins his speech, and our attention is riveted in part by an imaginative anxiety about an issue largely literary— what has happened to Ulysses? As he restores himself to heroic proportions, he restores us, too; and this makes us imaginatively available to the very different self-proportioning which Tennyson's Ulysses, as distinct from Homer's and Dante's, undergoes. It is a poem of progressive self-cleansing and of stronger and abler voic- ings: the disconsolate weariness of lines 1-5 is flushed by the nostal- gic self-restoration of lines 6-32; this makes possible the dignified equilibrium and fair play of lines 33-43, which in turn frees the spirit, in a scale-running of varied tonalities—discovery, gratitude, rumination, gleeful expectation, speculation, acceptance, and he- roic resolution—to expand organically into a metaphor of mega- phonic magnificence (44-70). Besides this "initiative taken by the words themselves" in the self-processing of Ulysses, the poem leaves irresolute and endlessly suggestive crucial aspects of both the form and the fable. Is it a soliloquy, dramatic monologue, public address, monodrama, or some combination thereof? To what de- gree is the speaker a hero as distinct from a tragic overreacher; to what degree is the poem merely psychologically exploratory, mor- ally aware rather than morally conclusive? Who are these "mari- ners" to whom Ulysses refers when in fact he returned, in Homer, the solitary survivor of his homeward journey? Is it intended that we adopt the myth of Ulysses' second and fatal voyage, or is this spiritual venting a sufficient end of and for itself? The very special terms in which Tennyson speaks of Ulysses—that it "was written under the sense of loss and that all had gone by, but that still life must be fought out to the end" –suggest that the poem functions in a keen experiential medium, even its protagonist's conceptualiza- tions being essentially experiential dimensions of character, and that, like the "true music" of which Baudelaire speaks, it is meant to evoke "analogous ideas in different minds."

The Morte d'Arthur, like Ulysses an example of literature made of literature, is deeply penetrated by a symbolist aesthetic. The ban- tering frame in which it was eventually set ("The Epic") dimin- ishes any tendency to read the poem conceptually and draws attention to its tonality ("hollow oes and aes, / Deep-chested mu-

sic") and to its capacity to induce a dream-vision (287-302) having
its own analogous imaginative reality. Its operatic effects are given
a very firm visual setting, so that the uncertainty of its imaginative
implications is in no way traceable to vagueness of story or im-
precision of image. The two consciousnesses that are counterpointed in the poem's procedures (Arthur versus Bedivere) open up
the value-questions to the nth degree, as the aesthetic issue had
been posed in the opening frame. The rituals of the throwing away
of Excalibur and of Arthur's departure (like a dying swan in a
dream) have a rich connotative suggestiveness which is more beautiful than any translation into conceptual meaning could be because it releases language to function at a suprarational level that,
despite his doubt, enables Arthur to visualize his island-valley
"Deep-meadowed, happy, fair with orchard-lawns / And bowery
hollows crowned with summer sea. . . ." The death of Arthur (if
there was a death) implies a birth (if there was a birth), and the
reader's imagination is engendered with curiosity about that
"goodliest fellowship of famous knights" and the "one good custom" that was the source of such "delight."

The most lyrically dramatic of the late 1833 poems is *Oh! that
'twere possible,* the seed-lyric of *Maud* and a near-companion-piece to
In Memoriam. That its place in poetic / psychological time was
retrospectively climactic we know from the place Tennyson gives it
in *Maud* (Part II, Canto IV) and from the history of *Maud*'s composition—that it "was written, as it were, *backwards.*"[23] Without
the full context of *Maud* as a guide to its dramatic coordinates, *Oh!
that 'twere possible* is one of the most oblique poetic experiences for
the reader of the Tennyson canon, and it is symbolist in as unadulterated a form as the *Mariana*-poems. From the *cri de coeur* with
which it begins to the near-desperate, willful, shattered epiphany
with which it ends, the poem projects a terrible beauty through
"evocation, allusion, suggestion," unfolding before us the exacerbated modern psyche of a *persona* on whose "heavy eyelids" the
"anguish hangs like shame." There is some promise of ultimate
recuperation in the images of solace available to his memory, but it
seems inevitable that the "juggle of the brain" and its "dull mechanic ghost," his total isolation from human fellowship, the sur-

real character of visual and auditory surroundings will tear yet deeper his unquiet mind and heart and drive him to at least temporary insanity. That the speaker has a highly poetic sensibility is clear enough even in this isolated monodrama. The love that he had felt for his "bride" had been both passionately sexual and lyrically imaginative, and he has now to deal with both "sisters" of his psyche. The former, generated by doubt, guilt, and self-indictment, haunts him as a ghastly specter and surfaces "With the moving of the blood, / That is moved not of the will" (96-97). The latter, his true soul-mate, resides half-hidden in his only bright memory; and by an act of willful imagination, he "paint[s] the beauteous face / . . . In [his] inner eyes again," "shadow[ing] forth [his] bride / . . . In the silence of his life—" (78-84). Moving along the exposed nerves of the speaker, the poem has an overall tonality of acute psychic pain, but the rapid progress of the monodrama through abrupt changes of awareness and collisions of awareness releases, stanza by stanza, a great variety of subtonalities—passionate imprecation, soft sensuous nostalgia, ghastly reality, tormented loneliness, self-doubt, lamentation, acceptance of death as the only gateway to reunion, and so forth. Thus in a fully symbolist poem nurtured in the same time-womb as *In Memoriam* and a near-companion to it, Tennyson gave lyric / dramatic voice of a thoroughly authentic kind to an impersonative fiction that read the basic motive of *In Memoriam* (death and the human strategies of coping) in a very different way from that of the elegy.

There is, I suggest, in the aesthetic context developed here reasonable justification for taking a view of *In Memoriam* significantly different from the traditional view. On some matters, such as the poem's autonomy, it will encourage us to be a bit bolder and firmer in drawing our conclusions. It will enable us to develop new perspectives on the specialized character of the poem's spiritual stresses and resolutions, on the aesthetic process around which the poem coheres, and on the relationship between poetry and truth (*Dichtung und Wahrheit*) which the poem explores. On a somewhat more fragmented scale, it will justify reopening briefly such questions as the poem's peculiar compositional history and the nature of the poem's unity.

The death of Arthur Hallam did not make Tennyson a great poet; but a great poet received word on October 1, 1833, that his dearest friend, an Apollo-like figure who had brought sunlight to his days and magnification to his imagination, who had stirred both his blood and his spirit, had died suddenly of apoplexy in Vienna two weeks earlier. His personal grief, we have reason to believe, was deep and genuine, but not devastating. Tennyson was a poet, and Hallam had been the especial friend of his muse, so that from the very first Tennyson's response to this richly emblematic event—a young man of truly extraordinary promise wasted "in the wilds of Time"—must have had a substantial imaginative component. Inevitably, he would use poetry to celebrate, even to hyperbolize, this "miracle" of personal experience who had nurtured in him a poetic capacity, who had even perhaps taught him that nurturing the poet in Everyman is the modern poet's imaginative imperative. But Tennyson was especially a poet-practitioner in the highly psyched nineteenth-century tradition of aesthetic poetry, a tradition that held, in the words of Hallam himself, that "Whenever the mind of the artist suffers itself to be occupied, during its periods of creation, by any other predominant motive than the desire of beauty, the result is false in art." [24] Thus, it seems unlikely that Tennyson would have been seriously tempted to celebrate the memory of his friend through an outright violation of the basic poetic principle that he and that particular friend shared. Tennyson, moreover, must at this time have understood as keenly as Matthew Arnold would, twenty years later, assert, that "A true allegory of the state of one's own mind in a representative history . . ." [25] is not the highest one can hope for in poetry. On the contrary, he would certainly have agreed with Arnold that the "eternal objects" of poetry are human actions "which most powerfully appeal to the great primary human affections: to those elementary feelings which persist permanently in the race, and which are independent of time." [26] We have reason to think, further, that Tennyson's imagination was, during the months immediately following Hallam's death, more generically, more metaphorically, more mythically alive than at any other period of his life. At that time, he actually began to write all three of the long poems upon which his most substantial reputation rests: *In Memoriam* (Cantos

IX, XVII, XVIII, XXVIII, XXX, XXXI, XXXII, LXXXV), *Maud* ("Oh! that 'twere possible"), and *Idylls of the King* ("Morte d'Arthur"). So it seems likely that, at a time when he was most resolutely determined to take charge of his career and shape the writing acts of his life, he would have taken a sharply aesthetic view of the character of the works he was then projecting, and this likelihood is strengthened by the ultimate character of those works and by the fact that he took so long to complete them, *In Memoriam* being the one he brought to term most quickly. Finally, the poetic background to 1833—the poetic history implicit in the writing acts of the immediately preceding years—shows clearly the following well-defined tendencies and fascinations: a fascination with strange psychic states; a strong symbolist flow; habitual use of a counterpoint of perceptions, "the dialogue of the mind with itself"; the confessional mode as a formalistic device, combined with the impersonative mode, so many imaginary persons not himself; a habit of combining the lyrical with the dramatic, of seeing lyrics dramatically and drama lyrically; a tendency to employ brief poetic structures, to write relatively short poems; a disposition to experiment boldly with inherited genres and subject matter. All of these tendencies and fascinations are so conspicuously relevant to *In Memoriam* and are so coherent with what Tennyson has told us about his view of the poem that they should enable us to describe *In Memoriam* rather more forthrightly than is usual. *In Memoriam* is a boldly experimental species of elegiac narrative fusing into harmonious balance strong lyrical and dramatic flows and employing as a formalistic device the confessional mode; the poem, as both a psychological and reflective process, is vehiculated through an imaginary poet-*persona* whose subtly varied and complex psychic states, often spilling into or in collision with each other, surface through a dense fabric of images, tonalities, and emblematic narratives in a long sequence of short lyric / dramatic cantos which contribute incrementally as well as organically to a representative modern soul's spiritual / aesthetic recuperation.

All sympathetic students of Tennyson will recognize that, from the very first, he had both a most delicate poetic problem and the necessary temperamental and aesthetic resources to deal with it successfully. He had an imperious need to elegize his friend, but his letter to Hallam's father—"I attempted to draw up a memoir of his life and character, but I failed to do him justice. I failed even to please myself" [27]—suggests how difficult he would find it to do so; and he could hardly have been insensitive to the sort of reservation expressed by his friend Edward FitzGerald, "Don't you think the world wants other notes than elegiac now?" [28] The fact that his grief was a personal and private affair did not present the most challenging problem: he was well practiced in the use of impersonative structures through which a soul's deepest inner anguish could be empathetically released, and he had been brought to a pervasive symbolist manner in his writing acts by his recognition that "If the poem is to be pure, the poet's voice must be stilled and the initiative taken by the words themselves. . . ." [29] A poetry of "evocation, allusion, suggestion" was fully available to Tennyson in 1833. Therefore, how *not* to do it can hardly have presented much serious difficulty. Even the writing act itself was fully manageable by a poet with so much practiced mastery of his craft, so much aesthetic refinement and energy, and such apostolic zeal as Tennyson clearly had at this time.

The crucial challenges which Tennyson faced were how to achieve poetic sincerity and poetic conscientiousness. Although the elegy would surely be impersonative ("impersonal"), it would have to be so in a very "personal" way. Not only was Tennyson's intimate relationship with Hallam public knowledge among a limited but substantial number of people who would expect that intimacy to be reflected with genuine fidelity in any elegy from his pen; but death and coping with death were generically personal events to a readership that had begun to reach far beyond college walls. Hence a classical elegy with a simulated personal quality, however perfect a poem Tennyson might make of it, would satisfy neither the poet nor the public. It must be contemporary and, with the requisite "suspension of disbelief," true. Only then could the poet escape the charges of insincerity and irrelevance.[30] The issue of poetic sincerity made subtle formalistic demands on the poet: how he used his subject matter to achieve a high degree of verisimilitude.

The issue of poetic conscientiousness draws us deep into the poet's fundamental purposes. His first obligation was to himself as an aesthetic poet: he must maintain throughout as his "predominant motive . . . the desire of beauty"—above loyalty, gratitude, indebtedness, wisdom, love—not because beauty is better than truth, but because it is truth's engenderer. To make beauty genuinely available to others was the only thing that he as a poet was dependably good at. His second obligation was to Hallam, his great and gifted friend: he must lend Hallam out, let others know how infinitely significant—generically, metaphorically, mythically—this miracle of human experience had been for him and could be for them. Arthur Hallam, emblematically perceived, enabled one to return to their bases in individual and generic human experience the myths that inflated one's imagination—myths like that of the fabulous King Arthur and of the fabulous Christ, enabled one to touch truth both sensuously and spiritually. That truth must be anchored in personal experience, and hence the myth must be historicized—must have a "life of Arthur"-component rooted in the synoptic testimony of one who could bear witness to his exquisitely giften humanness and, through the outreaches of a purely human imagination, project into myth his divinity. Therefore, the poem contains numerous historical episodes out of the "life of Arthur" as the poet knew him. But the poet's obligation to Hallam did not include the essentially nonpoetic recall of literal biography or the revelation of literally personal responses; and it certainly had no place, poetically, for personally erotic love-letters to the dead.[31] Only by being severely poetic in his treatment of Arthur could Tennyson fulfill his obligation to his dead friend and enable that aspect of his poetic conscientiousness to cohere with other components of it. Hallam was obviously one of the great enablers of *In Memoriam*, helped to make the poem possible; but he did not pull against its poetry.

Tennyson's third and all-enveloping obligation was to his readers—the writing act's obligation to the reading act. Like Carlyle, Tennyson was, throughout his lifetime but especially during the period of writing *In Memoriam*, anxious about the growing disregard for the central relevance of imaginative letters; like Carlyle, too, and the generation of writers imaginatively fueled by Carlyle, Tennyson believed that keeping the social affections and the imagination alive and finely tuned among modern men was increasingly one of the primary duties of the modern man of letters. Imaginative awareness thus became one of the writer's shaping concerns. The elegy, especially, turned upon one of the universal events—the death of a dear one—by which the affections were severely tried, most particularly in an age in which traditional religious supports had become and were every day becoming less available. A truly modern elegy thus offered the poet an opportunity to deal with one of the desolate hollows in human life and to relate it to the avalanches of despondency from which almost everyone at some time suffers. Moreover, death and disbelief had become so cognate in the minds of people increasingly disinclined to believe in the miracle of personal immortality that a modern elegy would inevitably open itself up to the thorny questions of belief and the believing mind. But Tennyson knew that his personal voice was not the voice of the human race and that any traditional creed that he might personally articulate had "many a purer priest, / And many an abler voice' . . ." (XXXVII, 3-4). The world was not short of creeds, it was short of believers; and the time's "purer priests" tended to be locked into particular beliefs. What modern man—and hence Tennyson's readers—needed was not particular beliefs or exchanges of particular beliefs, but an imaginative apparatus of self-processing that would enable them, through a keener sense of self and of the spiritual rhythms of their fellow-man, to achieve a refreshed recognition that man's myths—the attachments of his spiritual/imaginative nature—are rooted deep in his humanness and in "miracles" fully available to his personal experience. For such a modification of man's perceptions Tennyson, along with Carlyle, was especially qualified: it would enable him to employ everything that he had become and was becoming as a poet to one of the central issues of man's life in this world and to use his imagination both apostolically and poetically.

The apostolic dimension of *In Memoriam,* its urgent perceptual communication to the reader, would, Tennyson as a master-poet knew, clothe itself in language and structure in due course. He was not posting theses on the church door at Canterbury, and hence the poem could not organize itself (or be organized) ideologically. His subject matter, the ritual of occasion, and everything he had become as a poet dictated that he keep his poem in solution for as

long as necessary by maintaining a most delicate (even a precarious) balance between the poem as writing act and the poem as
reading act, between the need to communicate and the need to
defer meaning until creation and access to creation had reached an
imaginatively acceptable balance. "I did not write them," he tells
us with customary understatement, "with any view of weaving
them into a whole, or for publication, until I found that I had
written so many." [32] Kept in perspective, it is a most helpful
revelation: Tennyson, although he worked steadily at the writing
act itself over a period of years, avoided poetic closure until the
meaning—the reading act—had revealed itself by emerging out of
the writing act. Through poetic faith (an *authorial* suspension of
disbelief) and poetic technique (its "queer way" of "being written"), Tennyson enabled *In Memoriam* to come into being.

It was an act of high imaginative courage, but there was no
touch in it of floundering around: he clearly knew what he was
doing from the very beginning. The stanza he created, after some
initial experimentation, strongly suggests that he was counterpointing, prosodically, the quatrains of Gray's *Elegy* [33] and was
perhaps competing for Gray's broad popular audience. By reducing the stately (heroic, oratorical, public) pentameters by one foot
and by shifting the rhymes so that they could no longer ring out
and draw attention to themselves, he stripped artifice of artificial-
ity, internalized the poetic experience, converted argument to
meditation, totally altered the elegiac tonality.[34] The earliest cantos that he wrote ("Fair ship," IX; "Thou comest, much wept for,"
XVII; " 'Tis well; 'tis something," XVIII; "When Lazarus left his
charnel-cave," "Her eyes are homes of silent prayer," XXXI-
XXXII; "This truth came born with bier and pall," LXXXV; and
so forth) reveal in broad but unmistakable strokes the imaginative
tendency of the poet: a strong symbolist flow; a mood of gentle but
firm acceptance; a suggestion that, although the ultimate confirming revelation is denied one, the emblematic narratives of human
experience show that human "loves in higher love endure." Canto
LXXXV, especially, by its early composition and crucial placement in the completed poem, shows that the central aesthetic perception of *In Memoriam,* one of the chief components of the poem,
had, even in 1833-1834, already fully surfaced. Indeed, it is fair to

describe Canto LXXXV as an "inner" *In Memoriam.* The exemplum of the piece is there—(" 'T is better to have loved and lost, / Than never to have loved at all—")—as is a suggestion of the larger poem's ultimate narrative curve:

> My heart, though widowed,[35] may not rest
> >   Quite in the love of what is gone,
> >   But seeks to beat in time with one
> That warms another breast.

There are imaginary tableaus—the dead one received into heaven; imaginary dialogues in which spiritual communion is affirmed, physical communion denied; lyrical imprecations; mythic magnifications of the deceased— "All-comprehensive tenderness, / All-subtilizing intellect"; recognition that nature's every aspect and motion ("every pulse of wind and wave") animates in the classical memory of the living a persistent presence of the dead. But most important of all, in terms of the poem's total coherences, there is an unequivocal suggestion of just how the speaker's recuperation is dependent on the "strong imagination," of how his grief may "with symbols play" and his "pining life be fancy-fed":

> Likewise the imaginative woe,
> >   That loved to handle spiritual strife,
> >   Diffused the shock through all my life,
> But in the present broke the blow.
>
> My pulses *therefore* beat again. . . .
> >   (emphasis added)

As Wordsworth had said in *The Prelude* (XIV, 188-189), "This spiritual love acts not nor can exist / Without Imagination. . . ." Thus, however many false starts Tennyson may have made in the composition of discarded cantos, he clearly had, almost from the start, a fruitful imaginative grasp on the general drift of *In Memoriam.* Some important elements—for example, the character of the speaker-*persona* who would narrate the piece—still needed firmer imaginative definition, and hundreds of experiential cantos bodying forth the soul's stresses and renewals still had to be written. Moreover, the choice of a way "of weaving them into a whole" apparently came late in the compositional process—the result, one may conjecture, of the character assumed by the accumulating cantos. But the poetic manner (stanza form, confessional mode, the use of individual lyric/dramatic cantos, tonality) is clearly visible even in the very earliest writing acts.

It was suggested above that the poet-speaker of *In Memoriam* "is a man of his age in a closely conceived way" and that, as a mythic representative of that age, he processes a mythic apprehension having particular, though not exclusive, relevance to that age. Thus, like the Ulysses of Tennyson's poem, he becomes a latter-day mythic myth-maker. That he is carefully individuated as a speaker-protagonist in a soul-drama is a further dimension of the imaginative firmness and precision of the author if that very individuation has visible generic lineaments.

In Memoriam is obviously projected against a cultural ambience in which various degrees of skepticism ("The faithless coldness of the times," CVI, 18) seem imperious—a cultural condition, the poem suggests, engendered by a complex of causes: a positive cult of doubt, which only the few can successfully manage and for the many is disastrous (XXXIII); the tendency of a moribund Christianity not to rerelease its life-force or human/divine secret, but to tinker with its externals (CXXVIII, 10-22); the "passionate intensity" with which those caught up in the fervor of moral outrage would subsume every other consideration to an attack on the "system":

> "Is this an hour
> For private sorrow's barren song,
> When more and more the people throng
> The chairs and thrones of civil power?"
> (XXI, 13-16)

This is in turn blended with a psychic devotion to scientific discovery for its own sake, regardless of its implications for other life-values or life-illusions:

"A time to sicken and to swoon,
    When Science reaches forth her arms
    To feel from world to world, and charms
Her secret from the latest moon?"
                                    (XXI, 17-20);

a cynical incredulity regarding such magnified human potentialities as nobility, wisdom, beauty, truth *(passim);* a bullish distrust
of and impatience with the private imperatives of poetic apprehension (XXI, 7-12, and *passim*).

The speaker-protagonist, though estranged from such a cultural
ambience, is to a degree imprisoned in it: doubt lies heavy on his
heart, and he must find a way of reconciling doubt with faith;
science, particularly, is at war with faith, knowledge with love, and
unless he can find grounds for a harmonious acceptance of both
their imperatives, he will lack the will to live; orthodox Christianity as a spiritual dissolvent of the distresses of his secular state
has ceased to function, and he must discover new bases for the
inner spiritual force that will free him from the impediments of
time and space that ring him in; he realizes that one of the effects
of the trauma from which he suffers has been to alienate him from
his kind, but until he comes to terms with his private self, a public,
socialized self is simply not available to him; and being himself a
poet, he must depend on poetry's imaginative uses, but exactly
what they are and how they function is one of the primary lessons
which *In Memoriam*'s self-processings must teach him.

Thus the speaker-protagonist is fully complicit in the poem's
cultural broad-strokes. But he is a poetic *persona,* not a cultural
mannikin; he has personality definitions that make it especially
difficult for him to yield to the value-transfers requisite for his
recovery, though the strengths which are his weakness in the short
term make his ultimate conversion all the more reliable. For example, he has a strong disposition to believe, but to believe as he has
always believed, even as his forefathers believed. He is, habitually,
a man of active, resolute will only too capable of toughing it out, of
enduring pain as if the endurance were itself a virtue. His mind
tends to work within either-or structures, contentiously and dogmatically. His acute "irrepressible self-consciousness" is a source of

both his scandal and his glory: thrown back upon himself in this startling way, he is a bundle of exposed nerve ends, but it is in that same sanctuarial self that he will find reconciliation and contentment. He has a strong devotion to the deities of the hearth, strong domestic ties and a reverence for "Use and Wont"; and although this devotion imprisons him for a time in his discomfort, these deities of the hearth will be a major source of personal steadiness and of a serene affirmation of the rhythms of human love and generation. His rural background near the sea has provided for his psyche patterns of expectation—of tidal flows and predictable seasons; and after he has weathered this cataclysmic eruption and risen to a higher level of expectation, those rhythmic patterns will reemerge and again be a part of his sense of himself and of his universe. He has been to the university and participated in all the intellectual flamboyance (the "spiritual strife") associated with that youthful experience; but the subliminal guilt which is now, in his soul-disease, fueled by memories of that behavior will pass as he gains a wholesome recognition of the legitimate place of the intellect in a mature man's spiritual beliefs. He tends to equate knowing with normalcy, becoming anxiety-ridden lest his perceptions are themselves so deranged that he is not even thinking what he thinks he is thinking; and it will take time and growth for him to recognize that, at some indispensable levels of human awareness, knowing is not only impossible but impedimental.

But the most delicate and indispensable dimension of the speaker-protagonist's individuation is the very special character of his passion. That he is intense in his passion, few appreciative readers of *In Memoriam* will deny; the very sincerity of a poem that depends above all else on sincerity is ineradicably rooted in the authenticity of the *persona*'s passionate responses. Without that belief (or suspension of disbelief) on the reader's part, the poem collapses into distastefulness. Sorrow, of course, is the all-absorbing passion upon which *In Memoriam* turns: it is his profound personal sorrow that makes his life so turbulent in the present, and it is out of sorrow that he builds a bridge to the future. But the poem, as Tennyson tells us and as we see, is dramatically conceived: "The different moods of sorrow as in a drama are dramatically given . . .",[36] and it seems unlikely that Tennyson, with his strong dramatic sense, would have equated thematic evolution with drama or ignored the indispensability of complex motivation to a genuinely dramatic apprehension. Dramatically speaking, the implicit and inevitable questions are these: Why does he take it so hard? and why does his grief surface in such erotically oriented images? The explanation of homosexuality offered by some critics simply will not do: it suffers from an astuteness syndrome characteristic of biographical criticism and is grossly reductive. It assumes that Tennyson was either explicitly inducing a homosexual theme into *In Memoriam* or that, unlike the critics, he did not know what he was doing. The first assumption implies a literal transfer of an unsupported conjectural relationship between Hallam and Tennyson to the poem and ignores the poem's impersonative dimension; the second assumption ignores the pervasive presence in Tennyson's poetry of a most delicately handled psychosexual awareness, a sound basis for concluding that, in the matter under discussion, he would have known exactly what he was doing.

And yet, sexuality does appear to have a substantial place in the speaker-protagonist's passionate turbulence and thus appears to be a conscious aspect of his character-definition. Recognition that *In Memoriam* is basically concerned with the process of maturation—maturation of "religious" view, of personality, of poetry—gives us perspective on this subject. The speaker-protagonist, like his counterparts in *Locksley Hall, The Princess,* and *Maud,* is a young man at a certain stage in his development, beyond adolescence but before manhood. Reared in a domestic rural culture, except for a few years at the university, he has been (the poem seems to suggest) heretofore untouched by those revolutionary experiences of life through which manhood is hurried along—such experiences as being entirely responsible for, and accountable to, oneself in a strange environment, going to war, losing touch with the old continuities and verities, achieving sexual fulfillment and learning thereby what it means to be a new and entirely separate whole. He is still, in these respects, a "child" with a child's "language." He feels the imperious demands of an unnamed sexual longing, and he yearns in an ill-defined way for "worldliness." At this juncture in his personal myth, a beautiful young prince comes into his life, treating him royally and filling his soul with all the metaphors of the true, the good, and the beautiful. That magnificent world becomes his world as they think and feel as one with an elective affinity that transforms his staid though imaginative domesticity into a thousand and one equivalents of the *Arabian Nights,* redolent of Tuscan poets and Argive philosophy and all the splendor of a glorious past and future. They travel in foreign lands, the young prince falls in love with his sister, and all the idyllic present seems an assured permanence. He is a budding poet, translating all this graciousness and universal harmony with naive but personally authentic magnification, reaching microcosmically into the inner heart and macrocosmically into the deep heavens. It is all very expansive and sensuous and sexually sublimated and doomed—two virgins youths singing a duet in paradise. Even the catastrophe has a fablelike quality: the young prince dies suddenly while traveling in a foreign land, a story-book city to the east. The speaker-protagonist is thereby thrown into a chaos of emotions, *and hence a chaos of metaphors,* when "On the bald street breaks the blank day" of reality. All the ritual of sublimation—of the world, of the future, of the truth, of himself and his sexuality—suddenly evaporates, and he is face to face with suicide or with personal metamorphosis. It is from his earlier life—from the old, habitual, resolute, and rhythmic domestic continuities—that he draws the irreducible minimum of strength to live; it is from what he had been combined with what he has become that he draws both the energy and the perception for the remaking of himself. In the meantime, he flounders around among metaphors and analogies trying to bring his two worlds together and to authenticate a love that was sublimated to a fairy-tale level but must be described in the language of domestic realism. He does so with the precariousness that we all recognize, and it surely testifies to Tennyson's steady boldness that he undertook such a delicate poetic office with, we may assume, full consciousness of its dangers.

To return, then, to the broader strokes of the mythic representativeness of the speaker-protagonist of *In Memoriam.* The motif of rootedness / maturation which is an aspect of character-definition has broad cultural implications: it is an aspect of the *Bildungs*-theme that is pervasive in the literature of the nineteenth and twentieth centuries. It has a short narrative curve in the dramatic structure of *In Memoriam,* but the control of the boy over the emergent man in the poem is highly suggestive of the child as "father of the man" perception with which the literary century was launched. Representative, too, of the century's larger workings is the speaker-protagonist's resistance to change. Caught up in a maelstrom of emotional turbulence—the Baphometic fire-baptism of which Carlyle speaks—he resists investing himself with the symbolic clothes of modernism and seeks solace in dogmatic retrenchment, lockings-in lest he cease to exist. He holds out, especially in the sequence of cantos between the first and second Christmases, against the rational implications of the new science because of the awful specter, *to him,* of disbelief, clinging, like the age, to an *ancien régime* in religion lest all the values that make life orderly and beautiful be lost in a world gone to chaos. Without a religious tradition there cannot be a moral tradition, and even love becomes mere bestiality. Like the age, he has great difficulty releasing his hold upon "forms" even though "the spirit breathes no more" (CV) through them. Finally, the representativeness of the speaker-protagonist of a poem on the subject of spiritual renewal challenges the reader to relate his self-processings to the two great religious movements that flowed deep into the century—Evangelicalism and Tractarianism. The poem shares with them a clear sense of urgency—the death of Arthur (with his Christ-analogues) being not too fancifully translatable as the death of Christianity itself. Evangelicalism as a publicly behavioral impetus fueled the more moralistic tendencies of the age and incited more raw religious emotion; and in both of these respects it touches Tennyson's *persona.* Its two basic tenets—literal interpretation of the Bible and every man his own interpreter—are also relevant: the speaker must learn not to make even of Christianity a magical talisman, but he must do it in his own way, finding the fountains of spiritual flow in his innermost self. And it is perhaps more than curious, in thinking of mythic representation, to note that the years in which *In Memoriam* was basically composed coincide almost exactly with the freshest and most coherent years of the Oxford Movement (say, 1833-1841), so that as Newman and his associates were attempting to renew a living Church of England in a grand effort to deal with an almost universally felt need of the times, Tennyson was independently exploring ways in which the individual could renew his own life out of the resources of his humanness and his human experience; and Tractarianism shared with Tennyson's poem a deep commitment to the aesthetic values of life.

If, then, the speaker-protagonist of *In Memoriam* can be said to be a carefully individuated mythic representative of his age (and, with a change of metaphors, of all ages), the age and the individual mirroring each other back and forth, it remains to be shown what kind of myth he makes to justify calling him, by analogy with the Ulysses of Tennyson's poem, a latter-day mythic myth-maker. The myth-making process enacted in *In Memoriam* turns upon two basic recognitions: the need to find a spiritual alternative to traditional Christianity and a faith in the indispensability of the poetic imagination as a way of renewing spiritual truth.

In Memoriam is not anti-Christian, certainly; but it not essentially Christian either, is "Christian" only by analogy. The opening prayer—prologue, invocation—is addressed to a "Strong Son of God, immortal Love"; and although the stock response of a reader brought up in a so-called Christian culture is to equate Christ with Love, he is by no means compelled to do so exclusively in this poem. The myth of a Love-Divinity negotiating between or mediating Omnipotence / Omniscience and human need / frailty is not exclusively Christian, as even the pervasive Prometheus legend reminds us. That the poet-speaker is not following a traditional Christian theology is made clear enough in the next two stanzas, in which the "Son of God" is given the attributes of a classical Universal Progenitor; and the answer, in stanza 4, to the implicit question "What art thou?" centers the issue, not in God, but in man:

> Thou seemest human and divine,
>   The highest, holiest manhood, thou.
>   Our wills are ours, we know not how;
> Our wills are ours, to make them thine.

This is no more Christian per se than comparable postulations to be found in Shelley or Plato and hence not essentially Christian at all. Further, the Christmas sections are most noteworthy, not for their expression of genuine Christian sentiments, but for their lack of such expression. Rather, they rehearse stock responses to social rituals, secular habits rooted in childhood; so that the third Christmas is not celebrated at all. Instead, the Christmas metaphor is returned to its originating context, man's universal expectation of rebirth:

> But let no footstep beat the floor,
>   Nor bowl of wassail mantle warm;
>   For who would keep an ancient form
> Through which the spirit breathes no more?
>
> Be neither song, nor game, nor feast;
>   Nor harp be touched, nor flute be blown;
>   No dance, no motion, save alone
> What lightens in the lucid East
>
> Of rising worlds by yonder wood.
>   Long sleeps the summer in the seed;
>   Run out your measured arcs, and lead
> The closing cycle rich in good.
>   (CV, 17-28)

Finally, the "bell song" of Canto CVI jubilates, not the Christ that was, but "the Christ that is to be"; and whether or not one identifies the "slowly dying cause" of line 13 specifically with Christianity, at least the Christ-myth-in-the-making is elaborated as a religion of humanity rather than as a religion of divinity. What the speaker slowly and painfully learns is that Christianity no longer works as a cluster of external rituals, revelations, and tenets, but must be returned to its creative source—man's deep sense of his authentic self—and must flow outward from the inner fountains of imaginative love and thence flood his universe with a mysterious celestial light:

> And *what I am* beheld again
>   *What is,* and no man understands;
>   And out of darkness came the hands
> That reach through nature, moulding men.
>   (CXXIV, 21-24, emphasis added)

What needs to be renewed, then, is not the churches or the universe, but the self; and for this, man's one indispensable resource is the imagination.

The rebellion against death, the passionate uprising against a cataclysm of the heart, is the central fictive metaphor of *In Memoriam* as sorrow is its chief emotional outcropping. But the central agony lies much deeper: it is an elemental struggle with the self, a struggle as archetypal as that of the ancient hermit in his desert cave, and it results from the inevitable turning upon the self of the implicit question of the Prologue, "What art thou?" It is Ulysses' question, it is Everyman's question. How can you know what you believe except as you know who you are? And with what "keen and delicate instruments" is one to undertake so irreducible and urgent and difficult a task? Not, *In Memoriam* seems to suggest, with human knowledge and human reason, but with human affection and human imagination. There must be a deeply felt human need; there must be time; there must be a capacity, however raw, for human love, a capacity to see in the record of purely human experience degrees of magnificence; there must be a genuine desire for self-renewal; and there must be guidance. Everyman must have his Virgil because, again to quote Wordsworth, "This spiritual love acts not nor can exist / Without Imagination . . ." (*The Prelude,* XIV, 188-189).

That the *persona* of *In Memoriam* is a poet (that is, is in touch with his Virgil) is signaled everywhere—in single lines, in cantos and combinations of cantos, from first to last. At the beginning, he is somewhat defensive about practicing his craft: it is a "sad mechanic exercise" for dulling pain (V); it is a bulwark against madness (XV); it is simply his nature to do so:

> I do but sing because I must,
> And pipe but as the linnets sing. . . .
> (XXI, 23-24)

But gradually, in his anxiety to affirm an alternative to man-as-satyr "bask[ing] and batten[ing] in the woods" (XXXV, 24), the poet-speaker begins to overstep himself. This introduces the first of three poetic sequences (XXXVI-XXXVII, XLVII-XLIX, LIV-

LVIII) in which the organic use of the poetic imagination in the poem's process can be clearly seen.

In Canto XXXVI, the poet-speaker, desperate in his torturous efforts to affirm the reality of life eternal and haunted with the fear that there is no "hope in dust," turns aside from his personal quest and gives voice to a resolution borrowed from the Christian revelation:

> Though truths in manhood darkly join,
>   Deep-seated in our mystic frame,
>   We yield all blessing to the name
> Of Him that made them current coin;
>
> For Wisdom dealt with mortal powers,
>   Where truth in closest words shall fail,
>   When truth embodied in a tale
> Shall enter in at lowly doors.
>
> And so the Word had breath, and wrought
>   With human hands the creed of creeds
>   In loveliness of perfect deeds,
> More strong than all poetic thought. . . .
>   (XXXVI, 1-12)

At this, Urania rebukes him, accusing him of "prating"; and his Melpomene accepts as just the rebuke, extenuating it only in relation to his passionate yearning for closure and thus his temptation to equate "truth" with the "Word" of the gospel revelation:

> "But brooding on the dear one dead,
>   And all he said of things divine,
>   (And dear to me as sacred wine
> To dying lips is all he said),
>
> "I murmured, as I came along,
>   Of comfort clasped in truth revealed,
>   And loitered in the master's field,
> And darkened sanctities with song."
>   (XXXVII, 17-24)

It is a crucial turning because the poet-speaker is in danger of foreshortening his personal quest, of yielding to his pain, by substituting the good for the best and thus not breaking through to a fully authentic renewal of the self. The associations that he induces are high-minded enough—the reverent recognition of Christ's "divine message to the poor," the sacramental ritual to the deceased, unqualified acceptance of Christ as a master in the art of imaginative love—but it is also, in essence, an action of despair both of discovering for oneself the "truths" that "in manhood darkly join" and of the strength for that quest of "poetic thought." As Urania tells him, he is not yet pure enough either as prophet-priest or as poet-priest to adopt such easy solutions, however admirable their faith may itself be:

> "Go down beside thy native rill,
>   On thy Parnassus set thy feet,
>   And hear thy laurel whisper sweet
> About the ledges of the hill."
>   (XXXVII, 5-8)

In short, go be yourself—a poet—close to nature and wait patiently to see what you yourself can learn in that way.

A comparable overstepping and redaction—a retreat into authentic perspective—takes place in the second sequence (XLVII-XLIX), though here the speaker brings himself up short. In XLVII, he gets carried into the subtleties of scholastic philosophy, adjudicating "Eternal form" to accommodate his yearning for at least a moment of humanized reunion. In fact, he loses touch with reality in his fanciful self-inflation and becomes a bit absurd:

> And we shall sit at endless feast,
>   Enjoying each the other's good:
>   What vaster dream can hit the mood
> Of Love on earth?
>   (XLVII, 9-12)

Quickly, though, in a mood of subdued reaction, he disclaims the philosopher's role altogether:

If these brief lays, of Sorrow born,
   Were taken to be such as closed
   Grave doubts and answers here proposed,
Then these were such as men might scorn:

Her care is not to part and prove;
   She takes, when harsher moods remit,
   What slender shade of doubt may flit,
And makes it vassal unto love:

And hence, indeed, she sports with words,
   But better serves a wholesome law,
   And holds it sin and shame to draw
The deepest measure from the chords:

Nor dare she trust a larger lay,
   But rather loosens from the lip
   Short swallow-flights of song, that dip
Their wings in tears, and skim away.

                (XLVIII)

In the veiled allusion to Urania, the speaker accepts both the implicit rebuke for what he has just been doing and the justness of the instructions that she had given him, celebrating fully the virtues of his lower but self-restorative poetic range. But in conjunction with his disclaimer of the heights of thought (a role as philosopher-poet), he disclaims, too, the depths of feeling (the poet-tragedian). Rather, he "sports with words" in the sense that he does not put them to their extreme, self-devastating uses, and he "better serves a wholesome law" in that he chooses deliberately to function in that middle ground where thought, feeling, and expression meet and interact "To make the sullen surface crisp" (XLIX, 8). Nor is his grief now so privately imprisoning as it was, locking him into either-or constructs: "From art, from nature, from the schools, / Let random influences glance . . . (XLIX); and thus, though from time to time still "the sorrow deepens down," there is a clear recognition on his part that imaginative fancy is in fact working and that his inner self is no longer where it recently had been.

The whole process of *In Memoriam* turns, in a sense, upon the crucial stanzas of the third sequence (LIV-LVIII). Realization of the awful truth—of the fundamental unresolved conflict between our *knowledge* of Nature and our *faith* about God—is given full, desperate exposure, including the admission that we *know* nothing about God and cannot resolve, intellectually, the knowledge / faith dilemma. The poet-speaker swings emotionally from the weeping child and prostrate suppliant to the willful denouncer of a monstrous discord of mythic magnificence—"Dragons of the prime / That tare each other in the slime" (LVI, 22-23). It is the poet's Melpomene, his "earthly Muse," who now panics in despair, and the poet himself, now grown stronger, tries to soothe her, while admitting, with a "terribly pathetic" allusion to Catullus,[37] that he "shall pass; [his] work will fail" (LVII, 8). It is Urania who in turn soothes him, reminding him of his delicate responsibilities as a poet and of the higher courage required for recuperation:

> The high Muse answered: "Wherefore grieve
>   Thy brethren with a fruitless tear?
>   Abide a little longer here,
> And thou shalt take a nobler leave."
>
> (LVIII, 9-12)

Thus, all things have a lower and a higher: even poetry can lead one into a puling melancholy, a Byronic defiance, or, with time and poetic perspective, enable him, even among truly tragic circumstances, to "take a nobler leave." It is not a matter of logic, and the archetypal ideological contention is certainly not resolved. At the center is the human psyche, and its choice is not one of argument but of response: it chooses the destiny, not of the cosmos, but of the self because in the self, at least, love and knowledge merge and give the self a radiant center out of which to build its own understanding—its own myth—of Nature and God.

The processing of the imaginative self is very gradual in *In Memoriam*, the time-metaphor being indispensable to its credible workings. The speaker begins to understand that his "wealth" will be "gathered in, / When Time hath sundered shell from pearl" (LII, 15-16); he begins to believe that, *in time*, he will " 'take a

nobler leave'" (LVIII, 12). Out of "painful phrases wrought /
There flutters up a happy thought" (LXV, 6-7); to the bemused
modernist who looks negligently "On songs, and deeds, and lives,
that lie / Foreshortened in the tract of time," he replies with re-
juvenated firmness:

> But what of that? My darkened ways
>   Shall ring with music all the same;
>   To breathe my loss is more than fame,
> To utter love more sweet than praise.
>   (LXXVII, 3-4, 13-16)

He recognizes that "fancy" has fed his "pining life" back to health
(LXXXV, 96) and that it is "the imaginative woe" that "Diffused
the shock through all my life, / But in the present broke the blow"
(LXXXV, 53, 55-56). It is "fancy" that flies

> From belt to belt of crimson seas
>   On leagues of odour streaming far,
>   To where in yonder orient star
> A hundred spirits whisper "Peace."
>   (LXXXVI, 12, 13-16)

Having gradually, through a process that can fairly be dubbed
"technique as discovery;" fully affirmed the indispensability of
imaginative apprehension to the way of the modern soul, the poet-
speaker is prepared for the first of the two climaxes of the poem—
XCV. This is a mystical experience psychologically induced. But if
we assume, as the structure and progress of the poem suggest, that
such a reunion was possible only after the full affirmation of the
dependability of imaginative apprehension, then we can expect
that the aesthetic dimension of the mystical experience and belief
will be again articulated. This in fact is what happens in the
poem's second climax—CIII—and it is essential to note that the
mystical reunion of Canto XCV, though an entirely credible result
of memory and yearning and near-tactility (the "noble letters")
and an index to the epiphanic moment to which he has become
fully susceptible, is not what sustains him: that "trance / Was can-

celled, stricken through with doubt" (XCV, 43-44). It is the dream-vision, to which the Muses are integral, that leaves his "after-morn content."

The final "natural grouping" of the poem is made up of all that follows from the dream-vision, and it is here that the myth-making becomes fully and imaginatively dynamic; it is here that the one who died—that extraordinary and supremely gifted man—is translated into a metaphor of cosmic reconciliation—"an eye / Where God and Nature met in light . . . (CXI, 19-20). He is no longer simply a secular man—a young life wasted "in the wilds of Time" *(Maud,* I, 557), but a mythic Man-God whose lineaments or attributes can be perceived, however faintly, in the noblest types visible in each cycle of the race. He has imaginative clarity of vision, "seraphic intellect and force," "impassioned logic," high purpose without asceticism, physical passion with purity, strength wedded to gentleness (CIV). The principle of cosmic order and the life-force of creative change radiate outward in a grand mythic metaphor from the poetic imagination:

> Large elements in order brought,
>   And tracts of calm from tempest made,
>   And world-wide fluctuation swayed
> In vassal tides that followed thought.
>   (CXII, 12-15)

>   A lever to uplift the earth
> And roll it in another course,

> With thousand shocks that come and go,
>   With agonies, with energies,
>   With overthrowings, and with cries,
> And undulations to and fro.
>   (CXIII, 15-20)

The poet-speaker who was, at the poem's beginning, near-undone by a cataclysm of the private heart can now accept with serenity the turbulent violence of cosmic cataclysmic change because the heart has found its "reasons that the reason knows not of," has found in the self's authenticity and spiritual / aesthetic illumination wrought of harshest personal experience a mirror of a universe that can, he believes, move onward through both continuous growth and violent rupture, under star and storm, toward "one far-off divine event" (Epilogue, 143).

In Memoriam, then, is a way of the soul in the deepest and most complex sense. Its ultimate subject is truth and truth's availability to a distressed and confused modern man. Like the Carlyle of *Sartor Resartus,* Tennyson seems to have perceived that modern man stands at a Byronic-Goethean crossroads: he can conclude, with Byron, that "Sorrow is Knowledge: they who know the most / Must mourn the deepest o'er the fatal truth" *(Manfred,* I, 10-11); or he can hold, with Goethe, that, although sorrow is indeed knowledge, "men may rise on stepping-stones / Of their dead selves to higher things" *(In Memoriam,* I, 3-4). Like Carlyle, then, Tennyson closed his Byron and opened his Goethe; and like Goethe and Browning, he recognized the difference between "dead truth" and "live truth" as a difference of the spirit awakened through the engendering imagination with which truth is apprehended. Like the Browning of *The Ring and the Book,* Tennyson also recognized that art was the "one way possible / Of speaking truth, to mouths like [his] at least" since "Art may tell a truth / Obliquely, do the thing shall breed the thought, / Nor wrong the thought, missing the mediate word" *(The Ring and the Book,* XII, 843-844, 859-861). So he took the facts, the "pure gold" of personal historical experience, blended with them the alloy of his genericizing imagination, shaped them into a ring of poesy, and then disappeared, letting the poem become "all in all." Like Browning, Tennyson realized that what he, Alfred Tennyson, might perceive *in propria persona,* in and of himself, was only one of an infinity of details with which a harassed modern man must deal; but that what modern man might come to perceive through imaginative participation in the contest, the agony, of a surrogate-self would become organic in the self through an irreversible imaginative metamorphosis. It was the difference between life as prose and life as poetry, between a "diary" and a poem, between "An allegory of the state of one's own mind in a representative history" and a typological action enabled to exist as it exists and always has existed in nature—Everyman discovering that the "Kingdom of Heaven" is within him. Through a personal crucifixion that initiates a journey into the Hell that is within him too, he finds in the irreducible will to live a universal metaphor of reality. It is a dependable foundation upon which to station the existential self and from which to climb "nearer out of lonely Hell" (Maud, I, 678); and the difference, for Everyman, between mere stunted endurance and ever widening apprehensions of correspondence and of harmonies innumerable moving outward in time is the degree of "poet" that Everyman can nurture in himself. Tennyson became then, like Browning, not an irreverent Faust, but a conscientious Elijah:

> Ah yet, even yet, if this might be,
>   I, falling on his faithful heart,
>   Would breathing through his lips impart
> The life that almost dies in me. . . .
>   (XVIII, 13-16)

This early (and early written) cri de coeur of the speaker reflects both the desperate longing and the diminished spiritual state that, as a result of the poet's imaginative attentiveness, will convert themselves into jubilant affirmation and a full sense of spiritual well-being. But organically, from the inside out, from the innermost resources of the persona in the innermost depths of the poem. The bold external experimentalism of In Memoriam as an elegy has an even bolder experimental center: it pursues, at the poetic distance of generic representation, pursues with the utmost delicacy and unyielding relentlessness, answers to man's most indispensable and resistant questions—who (or what) am I? what (or who) is truth? It pushes its persona almost without parallel—approximated perhaps by such poems as Swinburne's On the Cliffs and A Nympholept and by the inner stanzas (Part II, stanzas 25-28) of Hopkins's The Wreck of the Deutschland. The speaker-protagonist, though allowed to back and fill, is not allowed to sidestep the real realities, is not allowed, even in passionate extremes, to give mere grace to his melancholy, traditional unction to his soul; instead, he is forced, with epical inevitability, to face and yield to the answers. Hence, *In Memoriam* does not have a classical architectonic unity, is not subdued to genre-structures. It has the unity of a credible human patterning, the unity of a poetry that takes its shape from the rises and falls, the retreats and attacks, the chafings and railings and yieldings and jubilations of a human psyche that endures and learns from an almost insufferable distress of spirit. Even the expansive "ninth grouping" has the authentic versimilitude of jubilee: after weathering the fire-storm, the speaker dilates the good news.

It is not surprising, then, that Tennyson took so long in the composition of *In Memoriam*. He had discovered the precision that, as a craftsman, he was capable of, and he was in touch with the profoundest spiritual realities of his time. But he had, as he also certainly knew, a symbolist sensibility that dealt in awarenesses, not arguments, worked through organically induced suggestion rather than theme. It would have made a rhetorically superficial shambles of his finely tuned aesthetic apprehensiveness had he attempted to arbitrate directly the ideological cross-currents of his age. He recognized fully the usefulness of debate as a formal structure of ideological contention, but he moved the debate-formula inward, anchored it in imaginary personality, and thus signaled his perception that the character of a proposition is altered by the will to believe it and the quality of the believing mind. He knew that imaginative letters, to be truly relevant to a modern reader, must bring that reader within the circle of the imagination itself, must make him participatory in the imaginative enterprise. Institutionalized dogma had failed man, and the era of the poet-as-dogmatist (the poet as teacher, the poem as statement) was over; the era of the poet-as-witness and creator of witnesses had been invoked. So throughout the 1830s and '40s and '50s, Tennyson played the role of the poet-as-witness by creating a great gallery of representative witnesses to man's efforts, in all ages, to deal with his problems, especially with the problems of identity and belief, existence and coherence. He did not, like Browning, try to oversimplify the issue; and he did not, like Arnold in his poetry, hedge it. He knew that, to the degree that he created a truly generic *persona* with a truly generic concern, he was as a human being complicit in the creation. Moreover, Tennyson, as the record shows, had an ear finely tuned to the poetry-reading public: he judged better than any of his contemporaries their poetic expectations. Tennyson did not pander to that public. On the contrary, he understood both what they needed and what they wanted, and his apostolic zeal as a poet was so intense that he wanted to produce a poetry that in fact worked for those for whom it was intended, as it worked also for him. Therefore, Tennyson, with rare exceptions, did not, like Browning, set up barriers of access to his poetry: he was not a coterie-poet or a poet of the ivory tower. And yet, as this essay on *In Memoriam* has tried to suggest, Tennyson was one of the profoundest of modern poets and one of the most innovative: *In Memoriam* is the boldest elegy in English as *Maud* may be the boldest poem. So Tennyson, perhaps because it was his imaginatively enveloping nature to do so, took a well judged middle ground between the market place and the ivory tower, between impersonality and personality, between ideas and raw experience because he knew, perhaps, that that is where most of us are and that that is what most of us need. But working courageously and authentically in that middle ground, he produced a poetic canon that radiates outward toward both those who read on the run and those happy few for whom poetry embodies the profoundest awareness rendered by a master-craftsman, not confrontally but, in the long run, irresistibly.

Notes

1. T. S. Eliot, *Essays Ancient and Modern* (New York: Harcourt, Brace & Co., 1936), pp. 186-203.
2. The term is Martin Heidegger's in a paragraph translated by Jonathan Culler as follows: "The greater the thought of an author—which has nothing to do with the extent and number of his writings—the richer is the Unthought of his intellectual work: that is to say, what emerges first and only through his thought as Not-yet-thought." See *Structuralist Poetics* (Ithaca: Cornell University Press, 1975), p. x.
3. P. 196.
4. Pp. 200-201.
5. The phrase is from *Maud,* I, 681. The text of Tennyson used throughout is *The Poems of Tennyson,* ed. Christopher Ricks (London: Longman, 1969). Wherever appropriate, identification of passages is given in the text in parentheses immediately following the passage quoted.

6. An excellent representation of Tennyson's comments on the poem is provided in the headnote to *In Memoriam* in the Ricks edition, pp. 853-861.

7. Hallam Lord Tennyson, *Alfred Lord Tennyson: A Memoir,* 2 vols. (London: Macmillan, 1897), 1, 304-305; hereafter referred to as *Memoir.* There is no attempt to editorialize this selection of comments but to select passages with strict formalistic implications.

8. James Knowles, "Aspects of Tennyson: A Personal Reminiscence," *The Nineteenth Century,* XXXIII (1893), 182 (also quoted in Ricks, pp. 859-860).

9. Tennyson, of course, wrote numerous countervailing poetic structures.

10. *The Poetry of Tennyson* (New Haven: Yale University Press, 1977), p. 194.

11. This apex-of-civilization syndrome is pervasive in the nineteenth century, visible in Macaulay's *Bacon,* in Mill's *On Liberty,* and (negatively) in Newman's *The Idea of a University,* gaining climactic relevance in Goncharov's *Oblomov* and Conrad's *Victory.*

12. Walter Pater works out a comparable processive formulation in *Marius the Epicurean.*

13. Christianity, of course, is and promises to be magnificently mythic; but for the time being, at least, cultural tendencies toward a dogmatic literalness led the poet to use the Christian revelation in a carefully dislocated way—referentially rather than credentially, as an illuminating analogue rather than an accessible body of belief.

14. Not quite dramatic monologue, more than soliloquy.

15. Blake in England and Baudelaire in France also bear the marks of an incipient symbolist aesthetic, the latter especially having a substantial and direct influence on later symbolist formulations.

16. Tennyson commented on the poem as follows: "This describes the soul of a youth who has given himself up to pleasure and Epicureanism. He at length is worn out and wrapt in the mists of satiety. Afterwards he grows into a cynical old man affected with the 'curse of nature,' and joining in the Feast of Death. Then we see the landscape which symbolizes God, Law, and the future life" (quoted in Ricks, p. 718).

17. "On Some of the Characteristics of Modern Poetry, and on the Lyrical Poems of Alfred Tennyson," a review (1831) of Tennyson's *Poems, Chiefly Lyrical,* reprinted in *The Writings of Arthur Hallam,* ed. T. H. Vail Motter (New York: Modern Language Association, 1943), p. 184.

18. I have here deployed Hallam's summary of the "five distinctive excellencies" of Tennyson's poetry, *ibid.,* pp. 191-192.

19. *William Blake,* in *The Complete Works of Algernon Charles Swinburne,* ed. Gosse and Wise (London: William Heinemann, 1926), XVI, 149. *(Prose Works,* IV).

20. "Richard Wagner and Tannhäuser in Paris," in *Baudelaire as a Literary Critic,* trans. with an introduction by Lois Boe and Francis E. Hyslop, Jr. (University Park: Pennsylvania State University Press, 1964), p. 199.

21. *Five Letters from Stéphane Mallarmé to Algernon Charles Swinburne* (privately printed, 1922), pp. 13-14.

22. Mallarmé, in "Crisis in Poetry," *Mallarmé: Selected Prose Poems, Essays, and Letters,* trans. with an introduction by Bradford Cook (Baltimore: Johns Hopkins University Press, 1956), pp. 40-41. I am indebted for aspects of the foregoing summary to Jerome J. McGann, *Swinburne: An Experiment in Criticism* (Chicago: University of Chicago Press, 1972), pp. 57-60.

23. *Memoir,* I, 379.

24. See note 16 above.

25. Preface to *Poems* (1853), *The Complete Prose Works of Matthew Arnold,* ed. R. H. Super, 11 vols. (Ann Arbor: University of Michigan Press, 1960-1977), I, 8.

26. Preface to *Poems* (1853), p. 4.

27. Letter of 14 February 1834, printed in the Eversley Edition of *The Works of Tennyson,* ed. Hallam Tennyson, 9 vols. (London: Macmillan, 1908), III, 258.

28. Letter to W. B. Donne of 29 January 1845 in *The Letters and Literary Remains of Edward FitzGerald,* 3 vols. (London: Macmillan, 1889), I, 149.

29. Mallarmé. See note 21 above.

30. Although Tennyson would have agreed with Arnold's view, as expressed in "On the Modern Element in Literature," that what is most relevant is most modern, he was clearly fascinated with the poetic relevance of topical contemporary subject matter.

31. The suggestion, based entirely on a reading of *In Memoriam,* that the relationship between Hallam and Tennyson may have been homosexual has become widespread, vulgar, and antipoetic. Nowhere outside the poem do we have any testimony from their numerous intimates during the years they were closely associated—youthful years not known for life-long discretion—that their relationship was sexual, nor has any one of the critics revealed his credentials, personal or professional, for trustworthy acuteness on the issue. The commentary has been sloppy, critically unprofessional, and too tedious to be prurient.

32. *Memoir,* I, 304-305.

33. Ricks, *Poems,* p. 859, tells us that "Early fragments of *In Memoriam* use the *abab* stanza."

34. For a different but provocative emphasis on this matter, see Christopher Ricks, *Tennyson* (London: Macmillan, 1972), pp. 228-229.

35. This much-celebrated and misinterpreted metaphor of the "widowed" state of the speaker appears three times in these earliest compositions (see also IX and XVII), twice describing his "race" and once his "heart." It is useful to remember that the metaphor is also used by Arthur *(Morte d'Arthur,* 11. 122-123) speaking of himself as "laid widowed of the power in his eye / That bowed the will. . . ." This explicating companion-context suggests that the speaker of *In Memoriam* means that he was bereft of a support that kept his mind keen, his heart tender, and his will resolute.

36. See note 30 above.

37. Tennyson's phrase, in Ricks, *Poems,* p. 913n.

10.

Tennyson's *Maud:*
New Critical Perspectives

Although Tennyson's *Maud* has, during the past twenty years, been receiving more and better critical attention and critics with the most modernist interests have shown an awareness of the poem's conspicuous relevance to several main coordinates of twentieth-century poetry, relatively little attention has been given to the poem's aesthetic procedures and aesthetic awarenesses. This chapter will concentrate almost exclusively on those aspects of the poem.

At the heart of *Maud* is a centralization of what, in "The Palace of Art," Tennyson called the "abysmal deeps of Personality": everything that happens in the poem's procedures is a surfacing *de profundis* of that personality through language. The protagonist is language: he knows where he is at any given moment on the spectrum of experience by the language he uses; and he recognizes through the cogent symbolism of language the next experiential phase available to him. Thus he moves along, processes himself through, language; and one of the exciting questions inherent in *Maud* is where language will ultimately lead the protagonist—to genuine freedom or to enclosure merely sublimated? But the place of the reader may or may not be the place of the speaker. The reader, being an exacerbated modern person himself, may totally identify with the speaker and accept him as a guide to the resolution of problems with which the reader has been personally unable to cope, seeing the speaker's self-processing as preferable to anything he himself has been able to achieve. Or he may suspect that the speaker, even like himself, is caught inside an imprisoning circle and, if empathetically watched, may provide a clue, not to the speaker's liberation, but to the reader's. If either of these reader-identifications becomes an authentic possibility, *Maud* has moved the practice of letters to a new vantage of relevance, inducing the reader to participate in this lyrically vehiculated drama at a metaphorically self-redemptive level.

The issue of literary relevance enfolds the poem in another significant way—the relationship of the times to the poem's procedures. If one regards *Maud* as a metaphor of the times— not only as a narrative configuration of a *persona*-protagonist but also as a representation of an imperious socio-ethical network having a clear topical as well as a mythic frame of reference—then it is necessary to estimate the extent of the effect of the socio-ethical network on the *persona*-protagonist. One possibility is that this network functions as a real truth but is used essentially as a backdrop to the action and that the protagonist moves away from a crippling psychological estimate of his world as he gains the energy of new / renewed love. Another possibility is that, from the poem alone, we have no way of judging this cultural ambience objectively since it emerges entirely out of the protagonist, the only thing we really know being that this is how he says he sees it.[1] A third possibility is that Tennyson in *Maud,* in the spirit of Carlyle in *Past and Present* and of Ruskin in *The Stones of Venice,* is treating this socio-ethical network and this *persona*-protagonist organically, is suggesting the systemic nature of modern man's malaise, exploring the notion that modern man has so internalized the system that to some very visible degree he has become the system. Thus, when we speak of a sick society, we are speaking of sick people who have a chicken / egg relationship to the sickness; and when we speak of a renewal of that society, we must recognize that such renewal is ultimately and genuinely dependent upon the renewal of the individual, without which there is no hope. To the degree that one sees validity in what can be called the systemic consciousness of *Maud,* he can legitimately approach the several coordinates of the poem in a new way.

The protagonist has been, for perhaps as long as a decade before the poem begins, locked into a certain perception of his socio-ethical world. He has felt it with great intensity, and it has colored vividly his whole sense of available alternatives. His intensity has probably given a melodramatic coloration to that world, but the high coloring does not negate the possibility that what is so intensely true to him is true independent of his perceptual peculiarities. Indeed, the organic process of the poem suggests that it is true at a level of reality beyond the solipsistic. The speaker does in fact find his miracle of experience—he finds Maud and the reciprocal love that has as its *"proper function . . . the ennobling and energizing of the human soul."* [2] The poem builds beyond the suggested consummation of this love (Canto XVIII) to the exultant jubilee of Canto XXII ("Come into the garden, Maud"), a Victorian polka [3] and a Dionysian revel replete with the two faces of Dionysus, highly poetic, highly orgasmic. But on the very brink of success, his self-renewal fails him. At a moment of intense sexual expectation and consequent vulnerability, he succumbs to the "Christless code" of his socio-ethical situation and murders a man whom he has broadly indicted but who in the crisis demonstrates remarkable generosity of spirit (" 'The fault was mine, the fault was mine,' " II, 1).[4] In short, that private, personal, self-centered myth fails him, and he cannot break out of the imprisoning circle of his world's socio-ethical system.

The protagonist's selfish myth having failed in the end to liberate him—having turned love to death consistent with the foreboding of Canto XVIII—he has to find a way of dealing with his self-harrowing memories and impulses, and this he does by sublimating, by idealizing, his death-wish. In Part II, he plays with death, praying to God in the first canto to eradicate the race:

> Arise, my God, and strike, for we hold Thee just,
> Strike dead the whole weak race of venomous worms,
> That sting each other here in the dust;
> We are not worthy to live.

(45-48)

In Canto V, he prays to be buried deeper:

> I will cry to the steps above my head
> And somebody, surely, some kind heart will come
> To bury me, bury me
> Deeper, ever so little deeper.
>
> (339-342)

But he is not a suicide. During the ten years of self-mastication preceding the action of the poem, there is no indication that literal self-destruction was his inclination; and throughout this crucial Part II, he is heroic in the courage with which he appraises the "miracle of design" by which his life, like the shell's, has, despite its fragility, withstood "the shock / Of cataract seas . . ." (73-74). His doom is near, he seems to know, but it will be more than just death:

> Courage, poor heart of stone!
> I will not ask thee why
> Thou canst not understand
> That thou art left forever alone:
> Courage, poor stupid heart of stone.—
> Or if I ask thee why,
> Care not thou to reply:
> She is but dead, and the time is at hand
> When thou shalt more than die.
>
> (II, 132-140)

What the speaker does to make the death he wishes for acceptable is to add to its nakedness a robe of public myth. By bringing the exaltation of service to his fellow-man to his death-wish, he can give it a religio-ethical significance that makes it more than mere death and gives it a distant Christ-analogue. He can thus free himself of the "ghastly Wraith" that has haunted him throughout Part II, identify Maud as the blessed dream-figure (the Beatrice) of Part III, and "embrace the purpose of God, and the doom assigned" (III, 59).

There is a slight alteration in the prosody between the first and last cantos of the poem, from hexameters to pentameters, and that slight alteration seems to suggest the limited movement the speaker has ultimately been capable of. He is no longer a dog in the manger snarling at his kind, but neither has he escaped the imprisoning circle. His consciousness has taken on but a slight degree of change. He perceives that "It is better to fight for the good than to rail at the ill," but he has not broken out of the system. The noble inflations with which he has magnified death simply make it more tolerable to die within the system. The narrative curve is from one kind of burial to another kind of burial— from burying himself in himself to burying himself in a cause that will result in his being buried at sea or in foreign soil.

That the system is still intact, even in the psyche of the speaker, is clear from the last canto of Part II:

> Prophet, curse me the blabbing lip,
> And curse me the British vermin, the rat;
> I know not whether he came in the Hanover ship,
> But I know that he lies and listens mute
> In an ancient mansion's crannies and holes.
> Arsenic, arsenic, sure, would do it,
> Except that now we poison our babes, poor souls!
> It is all used up for that.
>
> (295-302)

Hence, one can say that the crushing reality of a socio-ethical system has not been blinked at or sentimentalized. The speaker has, despite his eccentricity and the resistance implicit in his abstract hostility, to a degree taken "the print / Of the golden age . . ." (I, 29-30). And what has happened to the speaker is generic only in a limited specialized way, cognate with his mock-hysteria: the war is his private metaphor of a self-exorcism to which he has given public inflations as a way of adorning his own death-wish.[5] What is generic in the broadest public sense is the poet's implicit realization that the imprisoning circle of the dominant socio-ethical system is almost impossible to break out of even by a highly imaginative *persona* anointed with a miracle of blessed personal experience.[6]

The notion that there is a close integration of the method of the poem with its social, psychological, and aesthetic awarenesses is irresistible. The monodramatic form and the imprisoning circle have suggestive *prima facie* correspondences; and if one will simply avoid rigidities, he will see that the monodramatic form is aesthetic in a far-reaching sense. In *Maud,* it is a total method. Unlike the soliloquy as used in the traditional drama, it is not counterpointed against set dramatic scenes of character socialization and negotiation and plot propulsion; it does not provide a moment of specialized revelation within a predominant context that releases its perceptions by a conspicuously different method. In *Maud,* it is all we have: it is to the dramatic soliloquy what Hopkins's sprung rhythm is to counterpoint—a whole new set of aesthetic rules and aesthetic expectations. Spiritual movement takes priority over dramatic structure as the defining characteristic of the piece, and that movement is propelled by lyric energy. Moreover, this spiritual movement is centered entirely in character, and it is imperative that the reader watch very carefully what monodrama does to character.

By making the speaker his only audience, monodrama internalizes all tests of authenticity. The speaker is language: language is our only key to him as it is his only key to himself. Only language enables him to move from one point to another, to deceive or to restore himself. As the exclusive form within which he has to function, monodrama is both a forced patterning and a released patterning, a literary procedure that allows him to have his say symbolically *in extenso* but forces him to say credibly what is on his mind. The monodramatic form in the particular case of *Maud* is another condition of the speaker's imprisonment. He cannot escape the form, and his perceptual / behavioral adjustments have to take place within the severe limitations imposed by his nature (the poet's imagining), by the formal requirements through which that nature takes on the appearance of language (the poet's imagining too), and, as has been suggested, by a socio-ethical network that has become systemic (the poet's imaginative realization of a man absorbed by time and converted into a metaphor of itself). The consciousness alteration that is an explicit and central revelation of the way *Maud* works is complicated, of course, by the startling experimentalism of the poem. Although it was organically prepared for by the writing acts of more than thirty years, there is no model or paradigm of it in the works of Tennyson [7] or of any other English poet. It is ultimately the result, not of infinite shadings, but, after much practice, of a leap into a distinctively new form. Such literary boldness requires adjustment by both poet and reader, since the consciousness of everyone involved in the enterprise must be altered to some degree, and it is not the poet's assumption that, as initiator of an imaginative process, he has any dogmatic role in the poem's functioning. Language, the poem's ultimate subject, is capable of deceiving the poet and his imaginary *persona* and his unknown reader; so after he has enabled the created consciousness to emerge in both his own and his co-creator's (or reader's) consciousness, the poet's work is done except insofar as he chooses to play the role of reader with exclusive rights of textual revision.

The poet's own key to the poem's procedures is direct enough: "The peculiarity of this poem . . . is that different phases of passion in one person take the place of different characters." [8] And perhaps Hallam Tennyson's next few sentences, in which he attempts to recapture the emotive effect of his father's follow-up to this key remark, give us the most dependable clue for applying that remark to the way the poem works:

> The passion in the first Canto was given by my father in a sort of rushing recitative through the long sweeping lines of satire and invective against the greed for money, and of horror at the consequences of the war of the hearth.
>
> Then comes the first sight of Maud, and "visions of the night," and in Canto iv. a longing for calm, the reaction after a mood of bitterness, and yearning for
>
> A philosopher's life in the quiet woodland ways.
>
> But the clarion call of the "voice by the cedar tree" singing
>
> A passionate ballad gallant and gay,
>
> awakens a love in the heart which revolutionizes and inspires the whole life.[9]

The clue would seem to be that each canto embodies a different phase of passion, even that the cantos emerge in response to distinguishable "phases of passion." Thus, the poem evolves out of the sensibilities of the protagonist, taking its shape from the natural *movement* of his emotions through their various stages, reaching an emotional apogee before inevitably collapsing and forcing the protagonist to a different order of emotional resource and reconciliation. Expanded and contracted movement seems to be a more appropriate phrase to describe the poem's procedures than architectonic structure; and the reader is drawn to the question of just how, poetically, the protagonist moves from passionate phase to passionate phase.[10]

Language is clearly the crucial processive device. Each canto has a different emotional center, ranging from a complex concatenation of currents of feeling (e.g., Cantos I, IV, VI, X, and XVIII of Part I, Cantos IV and V of Part II) to relatively simple or austerely poised emotional moments (e.g., Cantos III, VII, XI, XII, XXI of Part I, Cantos III or Part Two and VI of Part III).[11] But complex or simple, the cantos move to a different or a deepened state of apprehension as language surfaces and signals the consciousness of the speaker to the next shading of the issue—opens gradually the next perceptual door, inducing the successive phases of feeling through the illumination that language casts into the next dark space. Language is the speaker's Virgil, as Maud is his Beatrice.

In Canto III of Part I, for example, in which all of the jubilant and ominous outreaches of the poem are briefly set in turbulent motion, the speaker records a night in which his sleep was interrupted by a threshold state between dreaming and remembering and image-processing that became so intolerable that he got up and walked out into the late spring night. The experience has been prepared for, both psychically and linguistically, by a preceding event. The speaker has had his first glimpse of Maud *rediviva*, and he has attempted to freeze her in language that will keep him heart-free: "Faultily faultless, icily regular, splendidly null, / Dead perfection, no more" (I, 82-83). This "immortal diamond" satisfies his imaginative associations (e.g., the *Arabian Nights)*, his sense of fairness (seems to do her justice), and his revulsion against materialism (as a precious stone she does not threaten his emotional vulnerability). It is a loincloth strategy that fails, of course, and both Maud and language have their revenge upon the speaker. She invades his subconscious, "taking revenge too deep for a transient wrong / Done but in thought to your beauty" (I, 92-93), a beauty that he will come to see as "the one bright thing to save / My yet young life in the wilds of Time" (I, 556-557); and even now she is "star-sweet on a gloom profound" (I, 91).

Language takes a more furious revenge:

> all by myself in my own dark garden ground,
> Listening now to the tide in its broad-flung ship-wrecking
> roar,
> Now to the scream of a maddened beach dragged down by
> the wave,
> Walked in a wintry wind by a ghastly glimmer, and found
> The shining daffodil dead, and Orion low in his grave.
>
>   (I, 97-101)

The experience itself, however stressful, now has an existence in tropes: language has translated it into its permanent, referential state. The speaker had tried to be language of one sort, positioning himself in relationship to Maud called "Cold and clear-cut" (I, 79, 88). But it won't hold. Language explodes in recriminatory images of shipwreck and sexual ravage and "a wintry wind by a ghastly glimmer" and death and the grave.

Canto IV then begins compensatorily. The thunderous emotional turbulence of Canto III is replaced by a new atmosphere and physical prospect and by a very different effort at linguistic positioning. From the grove where he sits, he sees three worlds: the emerald, ruby, sapphire world of a gay, bountiful season reaching out toward a soft azure seascape; the world of the village "with gossip, scandal, and spite"; and Maud's world "up in the high Hall-garden" where he can "see her pass like a light." He renders a private perspective on each of these worlds—nature, civilization, the individual—tagging them, packaging them in language, pinning them to the bulletin board of life with a phrase. The village becomes a "hubbub of lies," the habitat of a "little breed" "Where each man walks with his head in a cloud of poisonous flies." Nature, despite its bland and bountiful aspect, is "one with rapine":

The Mayfly is torn by the swallow, the sparrow speared
                              by the shrike,
And the whole little wood where I sit is a world of
                              plunder and prey.

With Maud, however, the speaker is a good deal more circumspect. In a deeply ironic foreshadowing, he spells out one phase of his doom: "But sorrow seize me if ever that light be my leading star!" On the other hand, he tries to build around himself a linguistic sanctuary in which he can take refuge, an imaginatively fabricated medium in which he can walk more comfortably than "the sultan of old in a garden of spice." [12] He sees himself as "a stoic" or a "wiser epicurean," and he rejects the role of both scientist and poet in favor of the "passionless peace" of "a philosopher's life in the quiet woodland ways. . . ." But the reader knows that the protagonist would have to unself himself, would have to divest himself of his characteristic language, to be passionless. Thus, his Lucretian desire to "flee from the cruel madness of love" promises a somewhat Lucretian result; and the images with which he invests Maud—a "milk-white fawn" who has "but fed on the roses and lain in the lilies of life"—have a poignantly reflexive quality. He charges her with a lack of life-experience that he himself has not had and that, at a level of primary significance, she will enable him to have.

The speaker's very acute susceptibility to the powerful resonances of language—his volatile availability to language—turns him, in Canto V, out of one sanctuary into another. He hears Maud singing "A passionate ballad gallant and bay, / A martial song like a trumpet's call!" and the lily maid of the preceding canto becomes the Saint Joan of this. Indeed, his availability to language with its magnetic rhythms and lyric burdens moves him away from the "long sweeping" hexameters that have dominated the first four cantos into a free-verse lyric dominated by a "wild voice pealing" the trimeters and tetrameters of the old ballad line that, by its verve and chivalric sentiments, indicts the satire and invective and personal horror that have been the essential substance of those hexameters. But despite the recognition thus enforced that he is "languid and base" compared with the men of whom she sings—

men that in battle array,
Ready in heart and ready in hand,
March with banner and bugle and fife
To the death, for their natire land

—he still insists upon positioning himself linguistically at a fabricated distance from her so that he can both "adore" and remain heart-free:

Silence, beautiful voice!
Be still, for you only trouble the mind
With a joy in which I cannot rejoice,
A glory I shall not find.
Still! I will hear you no more,
For your sweetness hardly leaves me a choice
But to move to the meadow and fall before
Her feet on the meadow grass, and adore,
Not her, who is neither courtly nor kind,
Not her, not her, but a voice.

The transparent self-deception, underscored through linguistic reiteration, with which, through a strategy of language, he attempts to deal with his growing love for Maud confirms the central strategic place of language in his monodramatic formulations. It is part of his psychic extravagance, and it repeatedly surfaces as a device for protecting his flanks. This he does in a most self-conscious manner in the following canto in dealing with Maud's brother:

What if that dandy-despot, he,
That jewelled mass of millinery,
That oiled and curled Assyrian bull
Smelling of musk and of insolence,
Her brother, from whom I keep aloof. . . .
                    (I, 231-235)

If he is to have any success in his aloofness, it would seem, then he must create a linguistic icon of a thoroughly distasteful sort. He must solidify his contempt in a language capable of giving stability to his psychic and emotional fluctuations.

Since it does not seem either judicious or necessary to discuss all of the cantos of *Maud* even from the perspective of this crucial issue, it should be enough to relate to it the three cantos that, according to the poet's son, Tennyson "liked best": "I have led her home" (XVIII), "Courage, poor heart of stone!" (Canto III, Part II), and "O that 'twere possible" (Canto IV, Part II, the seed-lyric of the whole poem).[13]

In Canto XVIII ("I have led her home, my love, my only friend"), the poem reaches its supreme moment of serene equipoise, its lyric apogee. The language of the preceding canto, with its cosmic sunburst of passion and its rampant sexual energy, suggests that in the white space between it and Canto XVIII one can reasonably write *consummation,* a speculation confirmed in a degree in the eighth division of Canto XVIII:

Is that enchanted moan only the swell
Of the long waves that roll in yonder bay?
And hark the clock within, the silver knell
Of twelve sweet hours that past in bridal white,
And died to live, long as my pulses play. . . .
                         (1, 600-664)

The Elizabethan sexual imagery here and elsewhere in the lyric and in the surrounding lyrics suggests fulfillment. As a result, all of the warring elements in the speaker find reconciliation in as nearly redemptive a state of being as his primitive myth of personal erotic love can achieve for him. The language is no longer ferocious or willful or mock-hysterical, but simple, authentic, calm, and in fullest flow. Its deep satisfying harmonies draw strength and substance from many sources: the *hieratic* (the "gates of heaven," "a perfumed altar-flame"); the *mythic* ("thy great / Forefathers in the thornless garden"—the first paradise); the *cosmic* ("the boundless plan," the "soft splendours" of "happy stars" as well as the "tyrants in [their] iron skies"); the *literary* ("The dusky strand of Death inwoven here / With dear Love's tie, makes Love himself more dear");[14] the *pastoral* (the "honeyed rain and delicate air," the delightful darkness, the "enchanted moan," "the noiseless music of the night"). Even his tortured past is now a source of reassurance ("*I have climbed nearer out of lonely Hell*" [author's emphasis]), and in his simple happiness, he hears and sees with a new acuteness ("A livelier emerald," "A purer sapphire"), and his imagination releases the most delicate fancies:

> But now by this my love has closed her sight
> And given false death her hand, and stolen away
> To dreamful wastes where footless fancies dwell
> Among the fragments of the golden day.
>
> (I, 665-668)

Despite the full flow of this language of a satisfied and happy love, however, there is a counterpointing undercurrent of anxiety that mints itself on the language of the canto regardless of the speaker's determination that "it shall not be so." It finally names itself as "some dark undercurrent woe," and the reader immediately connects this with the "sad astrology" passage with its language of "Innumerable, pitiless, passionless eyes, / Cold fires, yet with power to burn and brand / His nothingness into man" and with the speaker's anxiety over the Love / Death relationship:

> O, why should Love, like men in drinking-songs,
> Spice his fair banquet with the dust of death?

We hear in these lines, as elsewhere in the poem, the vocal stresses of *personae* as divided in time as Hamlet and J. Alfred Prufrock; and this, along with the more explicit language of anxiety cited above, leads to the conclusion that the divided self who is the protagonist of *Maud* is, even in his supreme moment of serene equipoise, divided still. And when, in addition, we note the reiterative formula at the beginning of the canto—"There is none like her, none" (600), "None like her, none" (605), "There is none like her, none" (611)—we realize that the "dark undercurrent woe" that finally surfaces in the language at the end has been present throughout and has shaped even the language of affirmation that dominates the canto. Thus, the speaker again attempts to be language according to his needs and preferences.[15]

The mind-heart dialogue of "Courage, poor heart of stone!" (Part II, Canto III) stands between the shell-lyric (Canto II) and the seed-lyric (Canto IV) and represents a truly heroic effort of the protagonist to stave off madness and to survive. At the end of the preceding canto, he had equated "passionate love" with "harmful love" and had, in a fresh rush of generosity, put Maud's "holy and high" comfort ahead even of his life. But she is the one who has died (the fifth death in a series of wastings), and the speaker is faced with a potentially disastrous crisis that he sees as, in large part, a crisis of language. Thus, he uses language strategically, perhaps gorgonizing his own heart, certainly attempting through language to avoid a lavalike eruption of language that would destroy him: "I will not ask thee why," he says, and, implicitly, if I should make some egregious blunder and "ask thee why, / Care not thou to reply. . . ." Like the speaker in *In Memoriam*, he uses one order of language to avoid a more destructive order of language ("The deepest measure from the chords," XLVIII, 12), attempting to diffuse "the shock through all [his] life / But in the present [break] the blow" (LXXXV, 55-56).

Some indefinite period of time has perhaps elapsed between Cantos III and IV, so that "O that 'twere possible," for all its imprecatory lyric grief and forecast of madness, represents a stage beyond the volcanic, eruptive madness that, linguistically, the speaker was attempting to avert in Canto III. Much of the language in the seed-lyric is recapitulative, sustaining fragmentary memory-voyages into the imagery of the past. The tension of the canto derives from the speaker's sense of two different Mauds, her of "the realms of light and song" and a shadow-Maud, projection of "the blot upon the brain," who mixes "memory with doubt." But the language is recuperative, too, striking a dream-tone or doze-tone that, despite the fact that he is slipping inevitably toward madness, will save him from completely self-destructing. He is not ultimately a Prufrock, but he finds a Prufrockian vocabulary and voice in which to take some wounded rest:

> But the broad light glares and beats,
> And the shadow flits and fleets
> And will not let me be;
> And I loathe the squares and streets,
> And the faces that one meets,
> Hearts with no love for me.
>
> (II, 229-234)

The near-flaccid weariness made emphatic by the last phrase of each line and the wail carried by the vowels at a subliminally affective level add to the modern voice of the speaker a penetrating psychic pain.

It is surely fair, then, to say that part of the experimental brilliance of *Maud* is that Tennyson enabled the drama of this "morbid poetic soul" to take its organic movement from language. And in the varieties of his protagonist's lyric-dramatic articulations, he orchestrates voices that we readily recognize as, among others, voices from the poetry of Shakespeare, Donne, Marvell, and, prophetically, T. S. Eliot.

The ease with which one can get close to the creative center of *Maud*—its human awarenesses, its poetic procedures—without becoming ideological would seem to suggest that "ideas" in the controversial sense have far less to do with the basic concerns of the poem than is often assumed. *Maud* would seem rather to be a lyrical-dramatic artifact in which there is centered a tremendously gifted and exacerbated *persona* who has so suffered the traumatic thumpings of circumstance that his "pulses closed their gates with a shock" on his heart and froze him in mid-adolescence in each of his vibrancies—sexual, aesthetic, socio-ethical, and so forth. Like Narcissus,[16] he has long companioned himself and become self-fixated. Indeed, the "dreadful hollow" which he hates so intensely at the beginning of the poem may have a correspondence in the clear woodland pool of Narcissus: an open mouth with bloody lips and ribs of the gums and hard palate that has gorged itself on his father's body, dinting and tearing it with its teeth.[17] And it is a clear dimension of the speaker's character at the beginning (and indeed at the end, though with less intensity, less monomania) that he is a raging ideologue. But it is equally clear that his thoughts are a dimension of his sense of self, of his experience of life, as it is clear to the reader that they are another metaphor for his self-enclosure, of the self-righteousness that is an aspect of his self-fixation. Implanted in his character, they are not simply objective ways of looking at the world; they are exaggeratedly intense, almost monomaniacal ways of looking at the world and are thereby translated to outcroppings of character rather than ideas *per se*. This intensity, this monomania, this narcissism sends out other complex signals as well: that his redemption is seeded there and that to some degree it will be a faulted redemption. He clearly has the energy for self-renewal if he is fortunate enough to find someone to love and thus discover a way of breaking out of his self-enclosure at the level of deep personal sharing; but unless he is grossly romanticized, unless his fiction is constructed of fairy-tale parts, his glory must also be his scandal, and he will not rise totally above his negativism and imbalance.

We have seen his residual negativism at work in the "dark undercurrent woe" of "I have led her home, my love, my only friend" (Part I, Canto XVIII). Perhaps his imbalance reveals itself with some precision in the most famous canto of the poem, "Come into the garden, Maud" (Part I, Canto XXII). It is a marvelous lyric, like the centerpiece of a full-dress modern musical. Its rhythms and rhymes are as importunate as a tom-tom, and it revels in its polkalike physicality with an exuberant psychosexuality that is near-climactic. The whole world is orchestrated to the rhythms of his sexual expectancy, so that what we have is not so much an extreme exploitation of the pathetic fallacy [18] as it is a simulated symphony in which the speaker as director is bringing on the various voices of his orchestra of flowers as the bandleader inside the ballroom is directing the "flute, violin, bassoon":

> There has fallen a splendid tear
>   From the passion-flower at the gate.
> She is coming, my dove, my dear;
>   She is coming, my life, my fate.
> The red rose cries, "She is near, she is near;"
>   And the white rose weeps, "She is late;"
> The larkspur listens, "I hear, I hear;"
>   And the lily whispers, "I wait."

One is reluctant to be critical of such an exuberant orchestral jubilee; but surely the speaker is as "fantastically merry" here as anywhere else in the poem, and we have Hallam Tennyson's authority that, in his father's conception of his protagonist, this is the other side of the same coin as "his suspicion that all the world is against him." [19]

The coupling is of the very first importance: socio-ethical nega-tivism and fantastical merriment are equivalent metaphors in the author's conception of his character. To the degree that one can accept this, *Maud* moves away from ideological poetry of thematic statement in the direction of symbolist poetry of inexhaustible sug-gestion; and to that degree ideological theme-hunting is demoted as a dependable critical strategy for opening up this central poem in the Tennyson canon, and ideas take their place as dimensions of character. Thus, we are moved closer to the recognition that Ten-nyson, like Wordsworth and Hardy, put the highest premium on awareness; that he had a quite extraordinary ability to gain entry to the self-enclosures into which complex characters sometimes withdraw; and that he was one of the great originals of modern poetic experience, using the discipline of his individual talent and the mastery of his inherited literary tradition to create unique structures through which to penetrate and release the most reso-nant perceptions of some of the chief coordinates of modern man's efforts to cope.

Notes

1. This is F. E. L. Priestley's position in *Language and Structure in Tennyson's Poetry* (London: Andre Deutsch, 1973), pp. 107-108.
2. R. J. Mann, *Tennyson's "Maud" Vindicated: An Explanatory Essay* (London, 1856), as reprinted, in part, in J. D. Jump, ed., *Tennyson: The Critical Heritage* (London: Routledge & Kegan Paul, 1967), p. 209.
3. John Killham reports Harold Nicholson's strange "revulsion" (*Tennyson*, p. 233) at the discovery that Canto XXII "opened to the rhythms of a Vic-torian polka" and suggests that that was the dance being danced inside. See "Tennyson's *Maud*" in *Critical Essays on the Poetry of Tennyson*, ed. Killham (London: Routledge & Kegan Paul, 1960), p. 225.
4. The text of Tennyson cited is *The Poems of Tennyson*, ed. Christopher Ricks (London: Longman, 1969). *Maud* is in three parts, and lines are numbered by part, not by canto and not consecutively throughout; hence, line references, given in parentheses at appropriate places in the text, are to part and line.
5. The war issue has begun to fade somewhat in criticism of *Maud*, and the charge of war-mongering is seldom made any more. But there is still the tendency to translate this private character-metaphor into a Tennysonian overview. For example, A. Dwight Culler, in *The Poetry of Tennyson* (New Haven: Yale University Press, 1977), p. 204, says that "what Tennyson's drama seems to mean is that the evils of the age are so great that they cannot

be assuaged by the holy power of love but only catastrophically by the holy power of war." There may be some harsh truth in the concept itself, but it can hardly be said that that is what Tennyson's drama means when one remembers that the character, though no longer institutionalized, is still "shattered."

6. This view of *Maud* as a metaphor of the times in one of its fundamental aspects gives a new perspective to the frequent judgment that Tennyson, in part at least, succumbed to his age. " 'He mastered circumstances,' his dear friend Jowett said of him, 'but he was also partly mastered by them'; to the extent that he was mastered by circumstances, much of his poetry, despite its lyrical brilliance and technical finish, is necessarily prevented from being poetry of the very first rank." (Ralph Wilson Rader, *Tennyson's "Maud": The Biographical Genesis* [Berkeley and Los Angeles: University of California Press, 1963], pp. 119-120.) This crucial turning in the criticism of Tennyson has often taken *Maud* as its confirming text; and having read the poem biographically, commentators have taken the protagonist's problems with his age as Tennyson's own problems. But it should be noted that Tennyson, like Carlyle, had to *see* his age quite uninhibitedly in order to translate it mythically: only the authoritative eye could discover perennial patterns in topical circumstances. He may have become, as Shelley in *A Defence of Poetry* says the poet must become, both the creation and the creator of his age—may have been washed by its infinity of details in an indelible way. But so far from being the impediment that is sometimes suggested, Tennyson's detached responsiveness to the characterizing coordinates of his age enabled him to convert that age into style, as modern poetry has ever increasingly attempted to do.

7. *Locksley Hall,* though a true monodrama, comes later than the seed-lyric out of which *Maud* grew.

8. Hallam Tennyson, *Alfred Tennyson: A Memoir. By His Son* (New York: The Macmillan Company, 1897), I, 396.

9. *Memoir,* I, 396-397.

10. The theory of the poem's processes being developed here is in conscious distinction to Christopher Ricks's effort to give "some sense of the shape of *Maud . . .* by selecting the seven sections which most strongly distill its phases." See *Tennyson* (New York: Macmillan, 1972), pp. 256-261. My emphasis is on total organic movement.

11. There is no need to press all of the cantos into such a dichotomy between the complex and simple, and of course if a simultaneity of awarenesses has taken place in the reader's imagination, all cantos are at once simple and complex. Canto VI of Part III is called relatively simple because, although the exposition and narrative are elaborate, the emotion itself is essentially singular—idealized acceptance. Cantos XVII and XXII of Part I, the sunburst lyric and the celebration of a jubilant sexuality, are emotionally simple, imagistically explosive and complex.

12. Killham, pp. 226-227, draws attention to the several references to the Ara-

bian Nights with particular attention to their "justific
tion into the poem of "a device employed by the P
Ghazel, or Ode. . . ." It would seem, too, that the
speaker's traumatically stunted growth. For a man of
disposed to fit his ideas to the settings of the Arabia
done playfully as it is later in the poem, suggests botl
and imaginative immaturity.

13. *Memoir,* I, 398.

14. The manner of these lines is clearly that of the coupl
sonnet or of the tag in the plays.

15. R. J. Mann discusses this canto extensively, though
emphasis. See Jump, pp. 201-209.

16. The myth of Narcissus and Echo, with variations, is
Maud, as the fiction suggests and as the fourth line ("And Echo there, whatever is asked her, answers 'Death' ") and the adoration of the "beautiful
voice" in Canto V signal. Tiresias' prophecy, Ovid's *Metamorphoses* III, is
germane: when asked whether the boy would live to a ripe old age, the
ancient seer replied, "Yes, if he does not come to know himself." Indeed,
"metamorphosis" is a central concept on which the poem turns. What has
been said about the imprisoning circles of the protagonist's situation—his
nature, his socio-ethical ambience, the aesthetic form in which he functions—
suggests that "narcissim" is a metaphor having significant interpretive relevance to *Maud.* And it may have been to keep his subtext from surfacing too
obviously that Tennyson twice changed "sweet Narcissus" to "shining
daffodil" (trial edition, I, 101, and III, 6, in Ricks, *Poems,* pp. 1048n., 1091n.).

17. Ricks, *Tennyson,* p. 253, sees an analogy in "a bleeding woman." Some Freud-
ians would combine the two images.

18. Jerome H. Buckley, *Tennyson: The Growth of a Poet* (Cambridge, Mass.: Harvard University Press, 1960), p. 145.

19. *Memoir,* I, 396. This reminds us that Tennyson originally entitled the poem
Maud or the Madness, that he characterized his speaker as "the heir of madness" *(Memoir,* I, 396, 402), and that he was pleased with the professional
recognition that he received concerning the authenticity of his handling of
the asylum sequence. The prominence that madness held in Tennyson's
thoughts about the poem invites us to think of the many ways in which the
notion is relevant: congenital madness, the systemic madness that is a dimension of his linguistic and metaphoric magnifications and intensities, the
whiplash madness of events and self-realizations that pushes him over the
brink into the asylum, the shattered sanity (a serene, sublimated, Christ-like
madness) with which he can finally "embrace the purpose of God, and the
doom assigned."

11.

The Poetry of Swinburne:
An Essay in Critical Reenforcement

It has taken a century for Swinburne's reputation as an indispensable man of letters to pass beyond the polemical stage: he has finally become a part of the warp and woof of modern thinking about modern letters. Critics have become shy of denying that Swinburne was one of the imperious shapers of the language, structures, consciousness, and aesthetics with which the twentieth century began its career in poetry and criticism. His conspicuous faults are still intact as are his extraordinary strengths, and the debate over the "essential" character and value of his poetry will continue as long as it is read. But our freedom from the critical monism that laced our sensibilities at mid-century and our new willingness to admit that an exciting literary realization is what makes a day of literary study worthwhile have moved us off-center and made us critically available to new literary recognitions and experiences. It has not been an extreme alteration: most people's methodologies, like Swinburne's conspicuous faults, are still intact; and *pluralism* and *impressionism*, while obviously relevant terms, are too vague or too heavily weighted to be precisely usable. Nor was an extreme alteration needed: the polemical century in Swinburne

227

criticism (say, 1866-1966) could not have been sustained had there not been good poetry-readers on both sides of the issue. Moreover, we should not overgeneralize our critical availability to Swinburne: the group of critics and students of modern aesthetic continuities who do not feel threatened by Swinburne's sexual sensibility, ideological consciousness, linguistic explosiveness, and subject matter derring-do is still relatively small, and it is most unlikely that the undergraduates of the 1980s will march around the quadrangles chanting *Dolores.* What *is* likely is that the process of literary placement, now in visible flow, will continue uninterrupted and that Swinburne's part in moving literary matters forward when they threatened to stagnate in the acknowledged successes of Tennyson and Browning will gain firmer and crisper, if not universal, recognition and acknowledgment.

Swinburne's part in moving literary matters forward was itself very literary, resulting in that superb bookishness so ably and ardently defended in the "Dedicatory Epistle" to the collected *Poems* (1904). For Swinburne, great books were major spiritual events in human history, quintessentially alive and usable; great artists were the tutors, the singing-masters of men. With Shelley, Swinburne believed that "A poet is the combined product of such internal powers as modify the nature of others; and of such external influences as excite and sustain those powers; he is not one, but both. Every man's mind is, in this respect, modified by all the objects of nature and art; by every word and every suggestion which he ever admitted to act upon his consciousness; it is the mirror upon which all forms are reflected, and in which they compose one form." [1] Swinburne had a deep, liturgical reverence for the writers, texts, myths which formed his literary inheritance, and he celebrated, in both poetry and prose, his keen sense of gratitude for what writers had given him (along with his penetrating awarenesses of the distinctive qualities of their imaginative labors) more broadly, more graciously, and more profoundly than any other English poet has ever done. The "external influences" that excited and sustained his "internal powers" were primarily literary: he had, from schoolboy days, a truly remarkable availability to the literary imagination, and he yielded without trepidation to its transforming influences, so that by the time he went up to Oxford, he was estranged from his own generation by the specialized character of his imaginative experience.

Thus, it is no petulant challenge to the ultimate stature of Tennyson, Browning, and Arnold to say that Swinburne's first volume of dramatic lyrics, *Poems and Ballads* (1866), is more accomplished than *Poems, Chiefly Lyrical* (1830), *Pauline* (1833), and *The Strayed Reveller, and Other Poems* (1849) on the basis, not of a single criterion, but of a whole cluster of criteria: the firmness of its language, the precision of its imagery, the boldness of its experiential probings, the dramatic redirection it attempts to give to poetic purpose (creative awareness rather than moral judgment, perception *is* meaning), the far-reaching character of its experiments with form, the breadth and originality of its literary frame of reference. Swinburne might possibly top out early, but he came on initially with extraordinary imaginative zest and technical finish.

Special note should be taken of Swinburne's conscientious craftsmanship, one of the most experimental and varied of the nineteenth century. He was fascinated with all species of genre, with poetic forms as means of rendering perception, and the formal constructs to which he turned his hand were very numerous indeed: sonnets and sonnet sequences, odes, choriambics, sestinas and double sestinas, elegies, sapphics, ballads and double ballads, triads, nocturnes, epitaphs, poetic drama in the Greek mode, poetic drama in the Elizabethan mode, masques, dramatic narratives, threnodies, dirges, epicedes, rondels, roundels, rondeaux, dialogues, monologues, soliloquies, litanies, monotones, epilogues, verse translations, verse adaptations, and so forth. The implications of such a catalogue, however incomplete, thoroughly contradict easy statements about the "lawlessness" of Swinburne's poetry. He was deeply devoted to the rubrics of poetry in a large variety of manifestations; and although he was impatient of imitation gone sterile and wooden in its effects—imitation that had lost its soul, as he said of Arnold's Greek imitation *Merope*, Swinburne's desire to give "fuller scope and freer play of wing to the musical expression" should not be interpreted as licentiousness. "Law, not lawlessness, is the natural condition of the poetic life," he wrote in the "Didicatory Epistle"; "but the law must be itself poetic and not pedantic, natural and not conventional." [2]

Besides being a brilliant amateur in Greek and Roman literature, Swinburne had so full and firm a grasp of the new poetry of the nineteenth century in Europe that some of the most distinctive poets and characteristic movements seem to coverge upon him and his work. He was a close student of Blake, Byron, and Shelley, feeling the full force and unsability of their varied Romanticism; he was dedicated in a special way to Hugo, Baudelaire, and Mallarmé, earning a high reputation among the French for an exceptional understanding of their literature; he wrote incisively on such contemporary English authors as Rossetti, Morris, Arnold, Meredith, Charlotte Brontë, Tennyson, and Dickens, maintaining currency with the literary nuances through which the spiritual ambience of his own time could be intuited. His interest in the literature and art of the Middle Ages was reenforced by his close association with the Pre-Raphaelites, as was his modified aestheticism; and he was a shaping practitioner in the Symbolist and Impressionist movements. Finally, Swinburne was perhaps the period's most accomplished critical student of Elizabethan and Jacobean drama. Thus, he brought balance and brilliance to almost every important aspect of the nineteenth-century literary enterprise. He was as austerely literary as Sappho and Aeschylus, as psychically free as Blake, as urgently engaged as Shelley, and as "modern" as Whitman, Hopkins, and Hardy.

Shelley had spoken of powers that "modify the nature of others": thus, to the poet as the *creation* of his age, as Swinburne in many ways was, Shelley added the poet as *creator* of his age, as Swinburne in many ways tried to be. Like his great predecessors in the poetic art, Swinburne tried to induce illumination through beauty, to lend his talent out, to show others how soul-serviceable letters could be; like his contemporaries, he employed as his most characteristic method a dramatic conception energized by an importunate lyricism. As is true also of Tennyson and Browning, both qualities must be yielded to Swinburne if one would give his poetry a chance to work. By denying him the former, by refusing to acknowledge that Swinburne's poetry is "dramatic, many-faced, multifarious," [3] one essentially denies him his birthrights as a modern poet—such rights as poetic access to the historical imagination; the ability to gain entry into the self-enclosures of strange but representative imaginary *personae* (metaphor, myth); the indispensable recognition that modern poetry, the creation of an age of collapsed structures, is increasingly a poetry of the missed mediate word in which the author's primary concern is with the truth (fidelity, affectiveness) of his representation rather than with ideological conveyance. Such far-reaching denials would threaten the viability of any modern poet—of Tennyson, for example, and Browning and Arnold; and they threaten the viability of Swinburne by reducing his poetry to the verbal diffuseness that T. S. Eliot called "one of his glories," [4] but that ultimately strips Swinburne of the peculiar creative center—the generative apprehension peculiarly Swinburne's own—from which his special language strategies organically emerge. Swinburne claimed that his poetry was "dramatic, many-faced, multifarious," and the critic who chooses to deny the claim accomplishes nothing but the impoverishment, in a significant degree, of modern English poetry.[5]

Just how Swinburne sought to "modify the nature of others" is the chief concern of the serious critic of his poetry: it enables one to see better the dramatic principle by which his poems are structured, and it redefines what is meant by the content of his poetry. Poetry itself became the subject of much nineteenth-century literary endeavor when writers began to realize that the imagination was itself in the profoundest difficulty as secular man floundered about in an infinity of secular details. This is one of the central awarenesses that Tennyson and his contemporaries had inherited from the earlier Romantics: science and fable were at war with each other over the consciousness of man; and Matthew Arnold, who repeatedly drew attention to the hazards of multitudinousness, reiterated the faith that poetry would survive religion in recognition that the counterproposition was arguable too. Swinburne and his generation inherited an acute version of this anxiety: it was perhaps the chief motive behind both the go-for-broke, no-compromises extravagance of the art-for-art's-sake movement and the stabilizing effect of that movement on the literary endeavors of that same generation. Like Wellington in his use of squares at the Battle of Waterloo, they needed a technique for closing ranks against the onslaughts of a positivistic, materialistic mentality (natural science, sociology, political economy, religious literalness and dogmatism), and the technique they adopted was aesthetic and attitudinal: they declared that the integrity of art depended upon the autonomy of art. As a guide to the proper motive in the actual writing act, such an aesthetic attitude is beyond criticism: it is a practical technique for keeping the pen from pandering to both the pulpit and the proletariat; but as guide to the appropriate subject matter of art, it is simply inadequate. Swinburne pointed to this distinction in his review of Victor Hugo's *L'Année terrible:* "In a word, the doctrine of art for art is true in the positive sense, false in the negative; sound as an affirmation, unsound as a prohibition . . . while we refuse to any artist on any plea the license to infringe in the least article the letter of the law [of autonomy], to overlook or overpass it in the pursuit of any foreign purpose, we do not refuse to him the liberty of bringing within the range of it any subject that under these conditions [the integrity of the work of art] may be so brought and included within his proper scope of work."[6] Thus, even after he had freed himself from the more simplistic and dogmatic forms of art for art's sake,[7] Swinburne still maintained, in the broader tradition of aesthetic poetry, that for an artist in the act of composition to prefer any object over artistic beauty would inevitably by false in art.[8] This is, perhaps, the closest one can serviceably draw the aesthetic toga around Swinburne: he was certainly devoted throughout his career to high imaginative principle and to imaginative purity of literary execution; the question of how much of a purist he was in art-for-art's-sake doctrines at a given moment in his career, though legitimate as a subject of aesthetic discourse, is surely impedimental (and may even be false) to a discussion of his special poetic achievement.

We begin, then, with a useful cluster of critical inclinations toward Swinburne's poetic canon: that he was especially responsive to the literary (particularly the poetic) experience of the whole Western tradition, being unusually attentive to the literary structures that his predecessors and contemporaries had found imaginatively useful; that he was explicitly devoted to the dramatic (or impersonative) principle, even in lyric poetry and even when the *structure* used was not specifically dramatic;[9] that the energy of his poetry has a lyric source, not just an importunate lyricism of technique, but also what one of his earliest critics called a "terrible earnestness"[10] fueling that technique; that he functioned in the highly developed nineteenth-century tradition of aesthetic poetry, with its customary emphasis on imaginative principle and careful workmanship; and that his primary object as a poet, the object to which he devoted all of his resources as a poet, was to "modify the nature of others."

One of the most deceiving aspects of Swinburne's poetry has been his importunate lyricism—that rapidly moving rhythmic persistence that he himself parodied in *Nephelidia*. More than any other single and conspicuous element, this quality gives the aesthetic fingerprints to Swinburne's poetry, defines its idiosyncrasy. And yet, for all its incomparable and seemingly inexhaustible virtuosity, the "swift and splendid roundabout" [11] of Swinburne's verse has frequently diminished the reader's ability to get at his meaning or to perceive his deeply woven thought-patterns. But it should be noted that there is in all of Swinburne's serious poems a fundamental and fully functional tension between unreined rhythm, so to speak, and austerely reined sense—a pervasive counterpoint between superficially licentious rhythm and the corrective rhythm of meaning, so that, although Swinburne formulated no metrical invention comparable to Hopkins's theory and practice of sprung rhythm, the more one "fetches" the meaning out of Swinburne's poems through oral projection, the more one is caught in that suspension between the powers of prose and the powers of poetry that Hopkins sought to achieve through sprung rhythm. Take, for example, the first stanza of *Hertha*. The poem as a whole moves anapaestically, the chief variable, as in anapaestic verse generally, being frequent iambs. But it would be licentious to read the first (or any) stanza as if anapaests were the primary guide to projection (or oral understanding): be it a reader vice or a reader dullness, it is poetically reductive. Rather, properly read, this opening stanza is in fact quite analogous metrically to the opening stanza of Hopkins's *The Wreck of the Deutschland:*

Thou mastering me
God!
Í am thát whích begán;

Giver of breath and bread;
Oút ŏf mé thĕ yéars róll;

World's strand, sway of the sea;
Oút ŏf mḗ Gód ánd mán;

Lord of living and dead;
Ḯ ám ḗquăl ańd whóle;

Thou hast bound bones and veins in me, fastened me
      flesh . . .
Gŏ́d chángĕs, ańd mán, ańd thĕ fórm ŏf thĕ́m bŏ́dĭlў;

Ḯ ám thĕ soúl.[12]

The poems are not identical, certainly; and Swinburne is not using
an uncodified species of sprung rhythm. But "fetch of meaning" is
as essential to a right reading of Swinburne's poetry as it is to
Hopkins's, and once one gives full value to this genuine dimension,
a very different poet from that of the parodists begins dramatically
to emerge.

The Second Chorus of *Atalanta in Calydon* ("Before the beginning
of years") illustrates another sort of diminution of meaning resulting from the rhythmic gallop into which Swinburne tempts his
reader, ironically drawing him off from the sense to the aesthetic
physicality of the gallop itself. But the fact remains that this chorus
is a musical composition celebrating, in a wholly serious fashion,
genesis and the creation of man. Before order as perceived by man
("the beginning of years"), there were forces which, if they did not
absolutely need him, went into the multimating that generated
him: Time, Grief, Pleasure, Summer, Remembrance, Madness,
Strength, Love, Night, and Life. But even in their primal state
("before the beginning of years"), these forces were not isolated,
self-contained, and self-sufficient. Time had need of grief as relief
from its own heartlessness, and Grief was tolerable to itself only if
it had hope of an end: hence, grief had also need of time. Pleasure
needed pain for self-definition, as Summer needed nakedness, de-
flowering, to call itself summer. Memory and madness were cosmic
bedfellows in a rhythm of fall and rise because, even "before the
beginning of years," Memory had lost its paradise, and fear had
intuited doom; Strength was impotent; Love was mutable; Night
and Life shared a horizontal "shadow," call it light, call it death.

Man comes, therefore, *not* "trailing clouds of glory," and Swinburne is, intuitively, the least Wordsworthian of poets; *Man Is,* existing between a sleep of pre-existence and a sleep of post-existence. He did not believe himself into being or think himself into being or hope himself into being, and he is not the beloved child of Jehovah called God. He is not the product of some empirically calculable evolutionary process, and "nature red in tooth and claw" provides no instrument adequate for his measure. He is the reality of a whole welter of cosmological forces, no one of which is adequate in itself; and while there is an imperious dimension of despair in his existence, despair does not define him—nor does hope. "Let there be light" did not eradicate darkness; and "I am the Word" implies "I am the Silence" too.

There is no need to "agree" with the choric explanation of man's creation rendered here: *Atalanta in Calydon* is not an instrument of ideological conveyance but a dramatic representation, and the Chorus appropriately takes its place in the medium of lyrical drama. But there is so clear a pull between lyric rush and conceptual reflection that one is forced to wonder why. The explanations that seem most relevant probably function as a cluster rather than singly. Swinburne could have learned from Bryon the ironic technique of undercutting his own seriousness: running it through with negligent rapidity takes any stress of a pompous solemnity out of it. As one of Hopkins's contemporaries, Swinburne would have understood the aesthetic desirability of an explosion of meaning: although he took the chance of being misread by readers on the run, there would be the compensation of a magnified aesthetic excitement for those readers for whom the recognition of poetic device and strategy added immeasurably to the pleasure of reading poetry. And of course one can generalize this technical tension of contraries into a perception of pattern in Swinburne's consciousness and accept it as a primary index to the dynamic center of a poetry devoted to the modification of internally nonconfrontal habits of thought among some classes of readers: Swinburne had begun his career of imaginative processing, not only of his readers' perceptions, but of their very modes of perceiving.

The tone and substance of the Second Chorus from *Atalanta in Calydon* lead very naturally to thoughts of *Hertha.*

Swinburne said of *Hertha,* "Of all that I have done, I rate *Hertha* highest as a single piece, finding in it the most of lyric force and music combined with the most condensed and clarified thought." [13] This remark does not say all that Swinburne might have said about the poem, but it must be taken seriously. In the first place, he isolates the poem—"as a single piece." This is important because Swinburne tended to see his poem-clusters, at least loosely, under the rubric of "monodrame" or monodrama, no one piece quite independent but all, taken together, articulate of variations on the voice and "internal center" of man.[14] Second, Swinburne speaks of the poem's "lyric force and music"; and he seems to be talking, not about a single quality, but about two interrelated qualities—mutually supportive but not necessarily mutually inclusive. On the one hand, there is the vocalization, the personal, resonant voice of the symbolic speaker; but more than that, there is complex rhythmic tension, verbal dissonance, carefully monitored phrasing, scale-running through very severe control of open and closed vowels, all ending, after much suspension, in a harmonized resolution. In short, "lyric force" alone is not quite adequate to describe the poem's aspiration to the "condition of music."

Swinburne speaks of *Hertha* as "combining" with this "lyric force and music" "the most condensed and clarified thought": this combination of combinations is the poem's imaginative center. We know that Swinburne was much troubled in the execution of the poem's thought-structures. He began the poem in October 1869 and completed "seventy lines or so." For the next two months, he fretted over the central question as to "why the symbolic goddess, from whom 'all evil not less than all good proceeds and acts, should prefer liberty to bondage. . . .' " Having broken out of this dilemma, he wrote lines 71-95 and 166-200 at the end of 1869 and the beginning of 1870. Sometime later he added the long section (96-115) on Ygdrasil and completed the poem's continuity.[15] We know, too, that in thinking through the subject at the heart of the poem, Swinburne moved away from both Hellenic and Judeo-Christian resolvents; but apparently, too, although he mythologized his primitive ontology through the Germanic goddess Hertha, he was susceptible in his contemplations to thoughts he found in Emerson's "Brahma" and in Hippolyte Fauche's ten-volume translation of *Le MahaBharata,* about which he became deeply enthusiastic.[16] In *Hertha,* he attempted to give dramatic exposure to deeply perspected thought about the nature of the universe and man's place in nature (a highly telescoped *De Rerum Natura* and *Essay on Man*), concentrating Hertha's complex ontology into a 200-line dramatic lyric, a most remarkable poetic concentration. This condensation, cognate with the poem's procedures, is made possible by the dramatic situation implicit in the poem: Hertha addresses a representative type of man—"children of banishment, / Souls overcast" (87-88) suffering the keenest distress of spiritual blindness as the lights they have walked by are one by one going out—and what she says is what, at this crux in time, this particular audience needs to hear and is capable of hearing. Further, according to the ontological imperatives that Hertha jubilates, she has equal need of man, and this reenforces (in the willing suspension of disbelief required by the poem) her motive for responding to man's particularly characterized need. Thus, the poem emerges out of a double intensity equally shared by speaker and audience, and the solemnity of her tonal projection, oracular in a long literary / hieratic tradition, is wholly appropriate to its dramaturgical movement.[17] The metaphor of the poem's action is a crucial conjunction in universal interdependence, homocentricity and theocentricity equally shared in a passionate equipoise out of which emerges the voice of the all-encompassing reality principle, the universal AM, with a singular existential revelation: "I bid you but be" (156).

To be free in Hertha's sense is certainly a very naked experience—naked of illusions about death, about the "shadow" called God, about human limitations, about millennial notions of consummate human experience, about things turning out for the best—"the (to me) most hateful charge of optimism, a creed which I despise as much as ever did Voltaire." [18] The *lux fiat* of this new testament of universal God-Man is this: "To be man with thy might / To grow straight in the strength of thy spirit, and live out thy life as the light" (74-75). Why, asks Hertha of man, do you impose a hierarchy upon the universe, diminishing yourself through a God-Myth in a puling diminution like this:

"I am I, thou art thou,
I am low, thou art high"?
(33-34)

What do you know about your origins, how you came to be? Who has "given" or "sold" you such "knowledge"? The wilderness? the sea? night? the winds? self-generated insight? "Have ye spoken as brethren together, the sun and the mountains and thou?" (60). What have you learned about the present *or* the past from prophets or poets or religious oracles or rulers or spirit even or flesh even? In the mystery of AM, Time is only one of the myriad manifestations of totality, like life and death, war and peace, light and shadow, "all reigns and all ruins" (135), which "drop through me as sands." Your God, which "I . . . set . . . / In your skies" (91-93)—which means *you* set him there since "thou art I," since *we* are inseparable, reciprocal reality—this "strange fruit . . . / Of faiths ye espouse" (161-162) is stricken, trembling, full of anguish, which means that *you (we)* are stricken, trembling, full of anguish, because *you (we)* created him, *you (we)* fed him, and now *you (we)* are passing through the awful, identity-blowing, soul-chilling act of de-creating him. Let him go; stop exhausting your love on him; slay this child of your (our) thought; abandon this shadow game of teleological futilities—of origins and destinies and transient dispensations—*and be!* Hertha (and man), therefore, ministers to the birth-pangs of a renewed man (and a renewed Hertha): "I have need of you free" (158) means equally "You have need of you free"; "You have need of me free"; "We have need of us free." Man's "growth" like Hertha's has "no guerdon / But only to grow . . ." (138-139); but in order to grow, man, like Hertha, must first simply and nakedly *be.*

In *Hertha,* then, Swinburne emerged as the singing-master of the reality principle. Written in the full sweep of his entry into his majority as a poet, *Hertha* casts eminently usable light on the whole canon of Swinburne's work. By creating a mythic moment in the history of man's spiritual perceptions, he induces the reader to immerse himself in an imaginative experience through which his sense of his place in the universe of time and space can be briefly re-processed and, according to his individual susceptibilities, modified. But even if his perceptions are not altered by the experience, the imaginative re-processing itself will, if frequently enough repeated, have a liberating and restorative effect upon the reader's imaginative nature.

Poems and Ballads (1866) is not centered in subject matter, though the sexual sensibility projected by many of the poems—a libidinous magnetism ritualistically heightened and counterpointed to an exhausted supernaturalism divested of all attractions of the naturally beautiful—is urgent. Rather, the book consists of poems of process, critical turnings in the history of the development of souls, very much in the manner of Rossetti's *The Blessed Damozel,* Morris's *The Defense of Guenevere,* and Browning's art-ring and religion-ring poems in *Men and Women* and *Dramatis Personae.*[19] For example, the superb dramatic lyric *Itylus* takes both its lyric rush and its clash of perceptual responses to the tragic vision from Philomela's efforts, as the nightingale, to ground in her own nature the conflicting appearance of her sister Procne's detached freedom from the woeful memory of the "small slain body, the flower-like face" of her slain child. The lyric turbulence of the poem emerges from the contrasting voices of the nightingale feeding "the heart of the night with fire" out of a "heart [that] . . . is a molten ember" and the rapid, fleeting, twittering swallow. But Philomela works her way through the awful truth to a new level of woeful realization:

> O sister, sister, thy first-begotten!
> The hands that cling and the feet that follow,
> The voice of the child's blood crying yet
> *Who hath remembered me? who hath forgotten?*
> Thou has forgotten, O summer swallow,
> But the world shall end when I forget.
>
> (55-60)

This is her Apollo-gift—to suffer the "Eternal passion! / Eternal pain!" that endeared her to the Romantic sensibility—but in the poem's process, she resists acceptance of a hardly credible realization until her availability to tragic truth forces her to yield. And although *The Leper* gets much of its macabre, terrifying, madhouse effect from the simple balladlike stanza and the matter-of-fact childlike language so strongly reminiscent of *Porphyria's Lover,* a curiously energized mind in motion, working through its tale of voyeurism, necrophilia, and even perhaps homosexuality at a strange remove of heterosexual ritual,[20] to its stressful stalking of

God, is the poem's imaginative center. There is a tantalizing uncertainty about the exact nature of the speaker's quarrel with God (hate? defiance? faith?), but the anxiety-ridden inversions of his character suggest that ultimately he depends on God to satisfy the longings of his nature for eternal punishment, that his underlying lust is for immortal degradation and pain. Thus, it is a poem of spiritual movement, dependent on the aesthetic power of shock, challenging the reader's imaginative persistence and the outer limits of his empathy.

The mythohistoricism implicit in *The Leper* is the structuring device of the *Hymn to Proserpine*. Called by Swinburne "the death-song of spiritual decadence" (as contrasted with the *Hymn of Man*, which he called "the birthsong of spiritual renascence"),[21] the *Hymn to Proserpine* was intended as a dramatically conceived lyrical utterance of the "last pagan," the swan song of an imperial patrician simply revolted by this new cult of death and ugliness. The term "spiritual decadence" is both historical (paganism is exhausted) and personal (the speaker is spiritually exhausted, too). He addresses his hymn primarily to Proserpine as the goddess of the lower world, of death, dormancy, and sleep. But on a secondary level at least, he also addresses her as the goddess of change, of cyclic alterations, and in this there is a significant degree of irony: the hymn of a man to the goddess of change who will die rather than change; instead, he will don the mask of Roman fortitude and make no truce with this barbaric cult. Ironically too, his death-wish turns upon his persuasion "that love hath an end"—that is, he cannot make the transfer from his habitual imperial concept of love as symbolized by Venus-Aphrodite, mother of Rome, source of color and light and pomp and a splendid sensuousness, to a concept of love ragged down to these beggarly *prolétaires!* Thus, Swinburne's *Hymn to Proserpine* is legitimatized through a rather fully apprehended historical-symbolic character, and a high degree of inflexible haughtiness is a predominant dimension of that character; but he is also nobly conceived, a worthy poet and scholar who is loyal to his personal past as well as to his sense of a cosmic past that runs deep into the nature of reality, "the wave of the world," out of which Venus inevitably arose and will, after rest, arise again. In Swinburne's poem, Julian the Apostate becomes an archetypal figure, a supremely imperial man whom time abandons and who, with a fascinating haughty nobility, stands tall and unyielding, loyal and doomed: he processes before our eyes a representative and imaginatively compelling way of perceiving.[22]

Imaginative self-processing is the cohering denominator of Swinburne's poetry, drawing together his private and public myths, his early and late phases. It is the central index to his recognition that serious literature is a transformational, a conversional, mode through which one's consciousness attempts to modify the consciousness of others. This imaginative self-processing is at the heart, both spiritually and structurally, of three of Swinburne's indispensable later poems: *Thalassius, On the Cliffs,* and *A Nympholept.*

Thalassius has always been considered a key poem in the Swinburne canon by serious students of his life and works; it is also a useful poetic document by which the student relatively fresh to Swinburne's idiosyncratic perceptions and linguistic devices can test the degree to which he has become comfortable with the Swinburne poetic idiom, can see if he understands it line by line and as a whole. *Thalassius* is a poem which, despite its perceptual promise / threat to elude one, is processive in a very controlled way and renders its informing myth(s) coherently.

The autobiographical relevance of *Thalassius* is almost always referred to, and it is sometimes called an "autobiographical poem." That the poem has autobiographical relevance seems clear; but it might be more critically just to say, rather than that it is an autobiographical poem, that one of the analogues of the poem is to be found in the life of Swinburne. At that perfectly legitimate but severely limited level, one can say that the poem treats of the supreme influence with which Swinburne credits Walter Savage Landor as having had on his poetic / psychic / moral life; of the period of profligacy / apostasy (psychic dislocation, sensual abandonment, imaginative distortion) represented by the period of the *Poems and Ballads, First Series;* and, finally, of his recovery of the promise of his "youth sublime." And even if one shifts and enlarges the field of the autobiographical analogue—for example, seeing the poem as a reflection of a recurrent tendency in Swinburne, especially but not exclusively in the late 1870s when he was threatened with physical, psychological, and imaginative bankruptcy, to research himself, his personal history as well as his poetic canon, and to establish new foundations, metaphoric or real, for his poetic future—even so, the autobiographical analogue is incommensurate with what actually happens in the poem. The reader may fairly be reminded of Wordsworth's *The Prelude,* but there the autobiographical analogue is far more commensurate with the poem than is the case with *Thalassius.*[23]

Despite variants on the autobiographical analogue, *Thalassius* is conspicuously a mythic poem concerned with health, sickness, and recovery. Its "I" is generic—highly idiosyncratic but representative at least of the happy few for whom the Hellenic values it celebrates are or become accessible through the poetic process itself—the process of this poem and of others. Those values—of natural, heroic, idealized, and unadulterated man—are engendered by Apollo (bright, fiery, musical-poetic) and Cymothoe (mysterious, free, regenerative) and are inculcated by a sort of Chiron-figure (wise and beneficent centaur, teacher of such diverse heroes as Achilles and Asclepius, patron of medicine) through poetic renderings ("song for wine") of the wisdom of the past ("food of deep memorial days long sped"). The poetic catechism is rather extensive: not to prize life overmuch, certainly not to prefer life to justice; to perceive Liberty, or Freedom, as indispensable even to a valid conception of the existence of God and thus to see slavery as a denial of God; to reconcile the old antagonism of life and death and to see them as a blended continuum of nature; to nurture "the soul within the sense" (the activated imagination) and thus put to flight darkness and sleep (animal torpor) and move man toward the godlike; to learn love as an order of value beyond self and sense, by which it dies, and to reach through "word or deed" to service visible beyond self, by which it lives; to learn hatred of all forms of slavery—of body and of spirit—and to labor "Inexorably, to faint not or forget" until the world has been wholly freed of kingcraft; to cultivate the mystical, prophetic quality of hope—the suprasensuous instrument of the soul by which it "sees the days of man, the birth / Of good and death of evil things on earth / Inevitable and infinite, and sure / As present pain is, or herself is pure" (193-196); to recognize one's limitations as a mortal and to learn to fear lest one thus gifted fail to be fearless.

The turbulent inner sequence of the poem is magnificently orchestrated: Love is stripped of all its Apollonian qualities and reflects instead the darkest side of Dionysus, in which joy becomes sorrow, life becomes death, cosmic order becomes cosmic chaos, discordant, "hot with ravenous rapture," "shrill [with] blithe mockeries":

> Even at the breathless blast as of a breeze
> Fulfilled with clamour and clangour and storms of psalms;
> Red hands rent up the roots of old-world trees,
> Thick flames of torches tossed as tumbling seas
> Made mad the moonless and infuriate air
> That, ravening, revelled in the riotous hair
> And raiment of the furred Bassarides.
>
> (364-370)

The motive for this turbulent aberration is given as inescapable ("ineluctable"): the protagonist, being human, can hardly bear ("half distraught with strong delight") the pure "great light" and the pure "great sound" and respond to the "heaven of revel"—"as if all the fires of the earth and air / Had laid strong hold upon his flesh, and stung / The soul behind it as with serpent's tongue . . ." (228-230). Nor did some *deus ex machina* rescue him: he simply rode "the red waves of the revel through" and then "on some winter's dawn of some dim year" went back "to the grey sea-banks" and fell into a long recuperative sleep and, "in sharp rapture of recovering tears," restored his passion for the truly spiritualized past.[24]

The autobiographical analogue is one way of glossing this inner movement of the poem, but it is reasonable to generalize that personal motif to the growth or stages of human development in the broad: the stage of passionate chaos—"where strife / Of thought and flesh made mock of death and life"—of the passage from youth to fully integrated maturity (what Wordsworth called the stage of the "Grand and Simple Reason"). And the peculiar imagery with which the poem develops suggests a larger and more compelling myth as the poem's central formulation, a cultural-historical myth dividing Western civilization into three broad phases of health, sickness, and potential recovery—the golden age of Olympian Hellenism; the chaotic, perverse world of physical and psychic violence institutionalized at Rome and transmuted, through Judeo-Christianity, into an all-blanketing cult of frenzied priestcraft and religio-psychotic barbarism; the post-Christian era, when "the red ways of the [Roman-Christian] revel" have been ridden through and imaginative man at last has some opportunity to remember "deep memorial days long sped" and thus recover the "freshness of the early world."

It is not to be expected that in such a redaction as *Thalassius* on one level probably is—a reorientation of the poet's response to the life-perceptions embodied in *Poems and Ballads, First Series*—that Swinburne would make unmistakable an interpretation of the "Galilean" era so distasteful to his readership as that originally poetized in poems like *Hymn to Proserpine* and *Dolores* had been; but it is also unlikely that he would have reread his interpretation of the effects of that era on spiritual and socio-political man as an essentially perverse interpretation. So as he gave the autobiographical analogue developmental perspective, he gave the cultural analogue perspective too by moving his Apollonian god of love forward in time and adapting his myth—as indeed Christianity adapted it—to an inverted value-system that prized mildness, meekness, pity, sweetness, with a god whose "voice / Speaks death, and bids rejoice":

> "I am he that was thy lord before thy birth,
> I am he that is thy lord till thou turn earth:
> I make the night more dark, and all the morrow
> Dark as the night whose darkness was my breath:
> O fool, my name is sorrow;
> Thou fool, my name is death."
>
> (298-303) [35]

Not as it in itself necessarily was, but as the child of Apollo and Cymothoe, tutored by "A warrior grey with glories more than years," must inevitably see it.

On the Cliffs is a moment-of-truth / transformation poem in which the Greek poetess Sappho is the controlling symbol / catalyst: like Sappho, the speaker stands on the cliffs; the "meaning" of Sappho, if he can discover it, will provide the illumination by which he will act. Only Sappho, proto-voice of lyric poetry, priestess / priest, gynandrous devotée of Aphrodite / daughter of Apollo, can utter the "word" that will make the difference between clinging and hurling.

The setting and tone of the poem's opening lines are both firm and crucial: he stands, not as Sappho must have stood on the Leucadian heights filled finally with tragic illumination and exaltation; he stands, rather, at a middle height "Between the climbing inland cliffs above / And these beneath that breast and break the bay" (24-25): below him "the gaunt woods" "cling" "Fiercely" "to the grim soil"; above him the "flowerless hawthorn" "Hold fast" to "steep green sterile fields." The speaker broods, like the symbolic landscape, at the inertia-point between night and day, hate and love, spiritual life and spiritual death; a wintry summer, a twilight zone, with only the barren consciousness—"Too dim for green and luminous for grey" (23)—holding the speaker rooted to this "tortive, serpent-shapen" life.

And yet, even the speaker's spiritual dryness, his "inward night" (31) is "mined with a motion" [26] of alternative possibility, Sappho's possibility:

> may be
> A man's live heart might beat
> Wherein a God's with mortal blood should meet
> And fill the pulse too full to bear the strain
> With fear or love or pleasure's twin-born, pain.
>
> (4-8)

And this alternative possibility with which the speaker's spirit is roped—"roped with, always, all the way down from the tall / Fells or flanks of the voel" ("a pressure, a principle, [Apollo's] gift") [27]— is indispensable to the process-of-spirit enacted in the poem: it is not the sentimental creation, but the credible resurrection, of this submerged spirit that the poem pursues.

First he addresses "the wind that walk'st the sea" (28-35): but the sea-wind, like Hopkins's lost souls, is worse off than he is: "wing-broken," "spirit-broken," wailing "in outer darkness." *These he is not:* however presently inert, his spirit has other touchstones. He rejects the puling sea-wind and hears, through the tragic voice of Philomela, the turbulent, storm-tossed, lightning-rent confrontation of passion and justice as immortalized in the *Oresteia* of Aeschylus, how he "With an anvil-ding / And with fire in him forge[d] [the divine] will." [28] But Night, "the core" of whose "all-maternal heart" was thus "rent apart" (44-45), is "dumb" to him, "makes answer none" (64-69).

Having rejected the one and been ignored by the other, the speaker then addresses the votive of night, the nightingale: "God, if thou be God,—bird, if bird thou be . . ." (70). From this point forward, a ritual of purifying perception is enacted. At first (72-89), he offers, as token of his worthiness, recollected pain—the memory of "the fruitless years of youth dead long ago," when the "same sea's word unchangeable" left him with

> Strength scarce enough to grieve
> In the sick heavy spirit, unmanned with strife
> Of waves that beat at the tired lips of life.
>
> (87-89)

But such offer fails in the very process of offering: sadness is but "a dream [man] weaves him as for shadow of [the nightingale]," whose Apollo-gift is quite other:

> This gift, this doom, to bear till time's wing tire—
> Life everlasting of eternal fire.
>
> (102-103; *passim* 90-103)

Then he offers a more inward, more distinctive identity (104-127)— "a sleepless hidden thing," a heart of fire—unquenchable and insatiable—which, at its best, has not sought "The joys, the loves, the labours" which, while they bring men comfort, "stay the secret soul with sleep" (113).

At line 128—in what appears to be a rather thorough-going transfiguration of a similar line in Keats ("Thou wast not born for death, immortal Bird!" ➤ "We were not marked for sorrow, thou nor I")—the speaker takes heart of his identification with the nightingale and celebrates, like her, his Apollo-gift:

> We were not marked for sorrow, thou nor I,
> For joy nor sorrow, sister, were we made,
> To take delight and grief to live and die,
> Assuaged by pleasures or by pains affrayed
> That melt men's hearts and alter; we retain
> A memory mastering pleasure and all pain,
> A spirit within the sense of ear and eye,
> A soul behind the soul, that seeks and sings
> And makes our life move only with its wings
> And feed but from its lips, that in return
> Feed of our hearts wherein the old fires that burn
> Have strength not to consume
> Nor glory enough to exalt us past our doom.
>
> (128-140)

The word *doom,* like Keats's *forlorn* but with very different results, turns the speaker's thoughts again to the *Oresteia,* to the terrifying case of Cassandra, who tried to have the Apollo-gift without paying the Apollo-price and who, faced with her own doom, saw clearly the preferable fate of Philomela—ravished and tongueless, but immortal songstress.

Having arrived at this point of identification and validation, the poet-speaker (161 ff.) begins to explore the divine mystery, the sacred mythology, of song. The nightingale was servant in the house of Sappho—constant singer and inconstant lover; and the gods, with their "strange grace," gave the nightingale Sappho's immortality: to "burn and bleed" inwardly, "errant on dark ways diverse," and to sing eternally: "the grace to die not, but to live / And lose nor change one pulse of song, one tone / Of all that were thy lady's and thine own" (183-185). The speaker, having passed the threshold of the mystery, then sings a "Hymn to the Nightingale" (192-214): "Love's priestess . . . Song's priestess," a hymn of praise for one beyond praise; a hymn of pity, dreams, and love for one whom pity, dreams, and love can only wrong. Moving then to the ritual of naming (231), he importunes Sappho for a yet more personal and direct answer than the air or earth or sea can give, claiming *knowledge* of her, *fidelity* to her, *kinship* with her, utter *responsiveness* to her "first Lesbian word," and exultant *participation* in her festivals as the basis for the boon he asks (215-257). But these are preparatory and do not generate the "voice," the "words," the answer that the religious *devotée* seeks: the speaker's "word," though ardent and genuinely imprecatory, is not yet pure enough and penetrating enough to release "the word" of Sappho. That evocative awareness emerges in lines 267-292, in which, with imaginative understanding unalloyed by self-pleading, the speaker chants his apprehension of the august singularity of Sappho:

> What have our gods then given us? Ah, to thee,
> Sister, much more, much happier than to me,
> Much happier things they have given, and more of grace
> Than falls to man's light race;
> For lighter are we, all our love and pain
> Lighter than thine, who knowest of time or place
> Thus much, that place nor time
> Can heal or hurt or lull or change again
> The singing soul that makes his soul sublime
> Who hears the far fall of its fire-fledged rhyme
> Fill darkness as with bright and burning rain
> Till all the live gloom inly glows, and light
> Seems with the sound to cleave the core of night.
>
> The singing soul that moves thee, and that moved
> When thou wast woman, and their songs divine
> Who mixed for Grecian mouths heaven's lyric wine
> Fell dumb, fell down reproved
> Before one sovereign Lesbian song of thine.
> That soul, though love and life had fain held fast,
> Wind-winged with fiery music, rose and past
> Through the indrawn hollow of earth and heaven and hell,
> As through some straight sea-shell
> The wide sea's immemorial song,—the sea
> That sings and breathes in strange men's ears of thee
> How in her barren bride-bed, void and vast,
> Even thy soul sang itself to sleep at last.

Sappho's Lesbianism is seen as a defining metaphor, gynandrous woman telescoping in herself the outreaches of human passion and perception denied to ordinary "man's light race"; ultimately, like the "tall nun" in Hopkins's ode, she had one "fetch" in her—namely,

> that place nor time
> Can heal or hurt or lull or change again
> The singing soul that makes his soul sublime. . . .
> (273-275)

The "singing soul" which was her *primum mobile* uttered its "sovereign Lesbian song," and song itself was hushed in awe before it, and the inner recesses of the universe were penetrated by it ("earth and heaven and hell"): like the *lux fiat* or the initiating *Word* or the *"It is ended"* of other world-rites and mythologies. And she, too, like other mythic prototypes, underwent her death-resurrection ritual: in her Apollonian ecstasy, she dove into the sea ("her barren bride-bed, void and vast") and fructified the world of severe imagination and song.

Then and only then, the mysterious reality having been apprehended at its inner heartbeat, is the voice of Sappho released. Atthis, to whom it was addressed, did not hear it; and it was / is not heard here in the northland because it is a "song of life" too fearful:

> the song that made
> Love fearful, even the heart of love afraid,
> With the great anguish of its great delight.
> (318-320)

In place of its terrifying reality, the northland has filled its ears with swan songs, love ditties, dirges that take the reality out of death and hymns of peace that pull the teeth a ravin and ruin—has used poetry as a way of protecting the spirit from the awful truth. But Aeschylus heard, and I hear; and

all time
Hears all that all the ravin of his years
Hath cast not wholly out of all men's ears
And dulled to death with deep dense funeral chime
Of their reiterate rhyme.

(343-347)

—that is, to the degree that man has not, in all ages, heard only the drum-taps of destiny and dulled his senses with funereal opiates, he has heard Sappho's "song of life."

Against this mortality syndrome, the speaker sets a cosmic counterpoint of life: a religion of light and life and song with its "treble-natured mystery" (Apollo-Sappho-the nightingale), in which are included the analogical mirrors of God-Mankind-Nature, and its testament of song through which man, born into life, can know at a great but excruciating level *love* and *change* and *wrath* and *wrong*.

On the Cliffs, then, is one of the most intensely religious poems in English and one of the most original. It foregoes the traditional referents of reconciliation—both the mediating wounds of Christ and the warm womb of "nature's holy plan." It turns aside, too, "from all hearts else on quest" *(Thalassius,* 440-441) and communes with its own heart, recognizing that only in his heart and in his heart's correspondences can man find reality confirmed. It rejects nature spirit-broken as an adequate measure; and it rejects world-sadness (an equivalent to Wertherian *Weltschmerz*) as incommensurate with world-reality as perceived even by the self. The song of the nightingale is *not a song of sorrow,* however audible sorrow may be in the ground-tone of reality; and mutability, like ravin and ruin, though real enough and predominant as the controlling apprehension of English poetry, is a death-note, not a life-note. The heart knows and the song of the nightingale confirms that, along with world-change and world-wrong, there is world-love and world-wrath. And without presuming to explain the mysterious mixture called life, the heart finds its correspondences, not in the spilt religion of a puling modern melancholy and not in the humanly erosive half-solutions of modern Christianity, but in the authentic voice of Aeschylus and in the authentic voice and act of Sappho. They are the fit singing-masters of the soul of man; theirs is the awesome awareness worthy of the liberated spirit of man. They at least, to adopt Walter Pater's language, "represent men and women in [their] bewildering toils so as to give the spirit at least an equivalent for the sense of freedom." And though their combinations are inevitably fatal, they at least "work out for themselves a supreme dénouement." [29]

A Nympholept, like *On the Cliffs,* is a difficult, dynamic poem: it employs an ancient concept or metaphor—panic or nympholepsy—but the "I" of the poem is the reader's guide into the psychological anxieties and reconciling perceptions which evolve only as the lines and stanzas themselves evolve. Here is Hertha's naked man and free and, if he can overcome fear, creatively susceptible to a transforming experience so fundamental to the realities of self and its access to the universe—to naked, secular, but imaginative man's correspondences in nature—that, *the speaker fears,* as he moves inward to the experience, "if any there be that hath sense of them none can say" (28):

> For if any there be that hath sight of them, sense,
> > or trust
> Made strong by the might of a vision, the strength
> > of a dream,
> His lips shall straiten and close as a dead man's must,
> His heart shall be sealed as the mouth of a frost-
> > bound stream.
> > (29-32)

The phrase "the speaker fears" becomes necessary since some critics observe that the existence of the poem stands in open contradiction to such assertions on the part of the speaker.[30] Perhaps not. Presumably the speaker, when he utters these lines, has not yet had the experience that lies at the heart of the poem. Therefore, he speaks of it as a "vision" with essentially supernatural ingredients; and a dimension of his fear is that, if he looks upon divinity unclothed, he will be frozen mute, is afraid "lest he see what of old men saw / And withered" (146-147). So extraordinary is the experience as he approaches it, so inaccessible except to "the soul in my sense" (225), "the spirit within the sense" (1), "sense more subtle than senses that hear and see" (161), so essentially spiritual, that until he has in fact undergone it, he can characterize it only in god-charged, fearful concepts ("Shall a man's faith say what it is? or a man's guess deem?," 1. 35).

In the ritual of deepening consciousness which the poem gradu-ally unfolds, the participant (speaker) must transmute fear and pain into hope and love. Otherwise, man remains victim of real but lower perceptions and is denied the renovating, transforming perception:

> Sleep, change, and death are less than a spell-struck
> > dream,
> And fear than the fall of a leaf on a starlit
> > stream.
> And yet, if the hope that hath said it absorb not fear,
> > What helps it man that the stars and waters gleam?
>
> What helps it man, that the noon be indeed intense,
> > The night be indeed worth worship? Fear and pain
> Were lord and masters yet of the secret sense. . . .
> > > (186-192)

It is in his approach to this perception of the indispensability of *hope* and *love* that the speaker-protagonist deals with basic issues of man and nature in a way that again inevitably draws one's thoughts toward Hopkins. Indeed, the stanza made up of lines 127-133 celebrates the "divine contraries" very much in the manner of the spirited apprehension of *The Wreck of the Deutschland*:

> Smiling and singing, wailing and wringing of hands,
> > Laughing and weeping, watching and sleeping, still
> Proclaim but and prove but thee, as the shifted sands
> > Speak forth and show but the strength of the sea's
> > > wild will
> > That sifts and grinds them as grain in the storm-
> > > wind's mill.
> In thee is the doom that falls and the doom that stands:
> > The tempests utter thy word, and the stars fulfil.
> > > (127-133)

And the resolutions of the two poets are remarkably similar:

Hopkins:

> Not out of his bliss
> Springs the stress felt
> Nor first from heaven (and few know this)
> Swings the stroke dealt-
> Stroke and a stress that stars and storms deliver. . . .
> *(The Wreck of the Deutschland,* 41-45)

Swinburne:

> In thee is the doom that falls and the doom that stands:
> The tempests utter thy word, and the stars fulfil.

The speaker in Hopkins's poem, magnified by terror, flings his "heart to the heart of the Host"; [31] the speaker-participant in *A Nympholept* has available to him only his naked humanness, yet he finds there adequate sanctuary. When the stars mock his efforts to find place with the "Lord God of ravin and ruin and all things dim" (148-149),[32] he asserts, not the nature of Christ, but the nature of men: "Whose souls have strength to conceive and perceive thee, Pan, / With sense more subtle than senses that hear and see" (160-161). Indeed, the process pursued in *A Nympholept* is the burnishing to new brightness that quality of man (spiritual, imaginative) which will enable him to cope with a higher degree of joy.

Finally, Hopkins's excrutiating cry in some of the sonnets of terror—for example, "O the mind, mind has mountains; cliffs of fall / Frightful, sheer, no-man-fathomed" *(No Worst, There Is None)*—has its muted counterpart in *A Nympholept* with this difference (besides differences of created tone, true voice of anguished spirit): the speaker in Hopkins's sonnets has known his God with some fullness, has even made Him and eaten Him, and is crying out against a momentary alienation from Him; the speaker-protagonist in Swinburne's poem has never known his at all, is humbly trying to find him:

What heart is this, what spirit alive or blind,
   That moves thee: only we know that the ways we trod
   We tread, with hands unguided, with feet unshod,
With eyes unlightened; and yet, if with steadfast mind,
   Perchance may we find thee and know thee at last for
     God.

                            (164-168)

This is not to overstructure comparisons between Hopkins and Swinburne but to demonstrate by analogy that *A Nympholept* is a basically religious poem and that it is religious both in its procedures and in the substantative questions with which it attempts, experientially, to deal.

The climactic revelation of *A Nympholept* is that its speaker-protagonist is not dependent on supernatural agencies external to himself for his epiphany or quintessential illumination: he is earth-born ("An earth-born dreamer, constrained by the bonds of birth," 1. 232); and so is the nymph: "Earth-born, or mine eye were withered that sees, mine ear / That hears were stricken to death by the sense divine, / Earth-born I know thee, but heaven is about me here" (264-266). Whether it is his spirit or hers, breath of her life or his, his sense is filled "with a rapture that casts out fear" (260-261). "Terror" is suspended, as are "doubt," the sense of "wrath" and of "imminent ill"—or, as Hopkins put it, "That guilt is hushed by, hearts are flushed by and melt—"; [33] and the speaker-participant is totally and magnificently reconciled to himself and to his universe: "fulfilled of the joys of earth" (237); "the goal of delight and life is one" (248); "Heaven is as earth, and as heaven to me / Earth" (271-272).

In short, Hertha's "guerdon of growth"—the reward, the recompense, of free, secular, naked, *imaginative* man—is confirmed.

The Lake of Gaube, though fully independent and discrete as a poetic / experiential structure, can be considered as a jubilation of the state of being resultant from the more exploratory, ritualistic religious probing of *A Nympholept. The Lake of Gaube* is a wildly exhilarating poem, exulting in opposites, the "divine contraries"—the heights and the depths. It turns upon the world of Ceres—bright, warm, fertile and familiar—and the world of Proser-

pine—"girdled about with the darkness and coldness and strangeness of death" (40); it moves from Panic noon to Plutonian night.
And yet, between them there is no dissevering dilemma: the mountain peak at noontide is "one / Glad glory, thrilled with sense of
unison / In strong compulsive silence of the sun" (6-8); as the
swimmer plunges downward into the unfathomed water, "It clasps
and encompasses body and soul with delight to be living and
free: / Free utterly now, though the freedom endure but the space
of a perilous breath . . ." (38-39).

In the poem's "tag" (55-70), the speaker is led to raise life-death
questions of which the two experiences recounted are images or
symbols. But he offers, like Hardy, no answer: "We wonder, ever
wonder" but "No answer I" *(Nature's Questioning):* "Deep silence
answers" (63). Only fear itself could have crippled him and made
his exhilarating revel, his excited testing of the horizontal, impossible; because fear is the great kill-joy, making life hateful and horrible. More than that, the speaker does not presume to know or say.

Swinburne's poetry lay too long in an inadequately marked
grave. He suffered the sentence of a magnificently gifted poet who
refused to massage the sentiments, to add grace to the melancholy,
of self-harrowing modern man. Instead, he removed, relentlessly
and one by one, the sacrosanct vestments by which man dressed up
and disguised reality and allowed his priests and kings to suborn
the testimony of consciousness. The most thoroughly homocentric
of English poets, Swinburne saw man, not by the measure of
thought or creed or moral habit, not as derivatively social or political: philosophy and religion, ethics and socio-political institutions
either diminished man or positively enslaved him. Swinburne was
the poet of consciousness and of the instrument of consciousness,
language; and his poetry is an exultant, freely but severely structured revel of language, not for its own sake, but as a jubilant
celebration of consciousness. This, in turn, leads to two defining
characteristics of his work: its almost exclusive dependence upon
literature itself—the quintessential language—for its referents; and
its almost exclusive emphasis on the apprehending awareness
rather than the apprehended object. Swinburne thus found his
validating models, not in the conceptualizing proclivities of an
enlightened neoclassicism nor in the sensuous precision and con-

creteness of touch, taste, and smell of Wordsworthian-Keatsian Romanticism. Schooled in Blake and Shelley and Baudelaire, he turned more and more to the literature of tragic apprehension—to the Elizabethan and Jacobean dramatists and to the Greek tragedians—as he more deeply perceived that the consciousness of man finds its most ennobling stature in the complexities of tragic awareness.

If, as Ruskin said, Swinburne was "plague-struck," it put him into the company of Turner and Byron, Blake and Shelley, and brought into the contemporary consciousness awarenesses "wonderful and beautiful," "dreadful" and "deadly." Like them, Swinburne was in touch with ancient perceptual realities about to break forth in a star-shower of stunning fright. The Judeo-Christian game was played out, certainly, but so was the Graeco-Roman Renaissance. The old order and the new / old reality were moving into a state of re-mix so turbulent and so alien to the habits and expectations of the overwhelming majority that cries of shame, chaos, and despair were likely to be the groundtone of the cultural future. The nineteenth century had managed, as Hardy was to show in *The Dynasts,* to put down the attack on the *ancien régime* that had surfaced with local violence at the end of the eighteenth century, but at an awful price: it had simply put anachronism in place again and ignored the imperious future. Swinburne was plague-struck by his devastating perception of the discrepancy, the chasmic gulf, between the cosmic, historical, and personal truth of things and the painted shell that civilization, especially as monitored by statecraft and priestcraft, pretended to be the truth. This cult of civilization had become a substitute religion and hence must draw on itself all the fire of the future.

Swinburne's attack upon the high-Parnassian torpor of the 1860s tightened the sphincters of those in charge—like a firebrand hurled into a costume ball of papier-mâché; and in retrospect it seems brilliantly strategic. His appeal was to readers of avant-garde poetry—sophisticates with highly refined sensibilities, likely themselves to be disaffected with cultural centrism. Moreover, the illusion of a monolithic cultural coherence that church, state, and a conservative press might like to sustain was in fact deeply faulted—Darwin, Marx, Mill, and the Ruskin of *Unto This Last* were abroad in the land; and so a furor of public outrage might go hand in hand with more than a flurry of private relish. To that degree, Swinburne was actually running with a subterranean current. To those who had become bored with Tennyson and Browning must be added those who relished a heightened verbal style and who felt that they had been poetless since the death of Shelley. There is, too, Swinburne's startling poetic manner, projecting in a geuinely ambivalent way blasphemy-in-beauty / beauty-in-blasphemy, saying shocking things breathtakingly, memorable even without a conscious act of memorizing. And beyond all this there is that flow running strong and true in Swinburne's poetry that displaces the behavioral clichés of his culture (and ours) and demonstrates that the reader must simply come alive and begin to sort matters out for himself if he is to be a competent reader of the signs of the times and of the poetry of the future.

Notes

1. Preface to *Prometheus Unbound, The Complete Poetical Works of Percy Bysshe Shelly* (Boston: Houghton Mifflin, 1901), p. 164.
2. *The Poems of Algernon Charles Swinburne* (London: Chatto & Windus, 1904), p. xvi. This is the text used throughout this chapter with line numbers given in parentheses immediately after the quotation.
3. *Notes on Poems and Reviews,* in *Swinburne Replies,* ed. Clyde K. Hyder (Syracuse: Syracuse University Press, 1966), p. 18.
4. "Swinburne as Poet," in *The Sacred Wood* (New York: Alfred A. Knopf, 1921), pp. 131-136.
5. Though the denial is habitual, in whole or in part, in the criticism of Swinburne, it is conspicuously arbitrary: besides Swinburne's own statements and the pervasive presence of the impersonative mode in the poetry of the period, we must note that Swinburne began his literary career as a dramatist, completed at least ten plays, and wrote four volumes of criticism on one of his persistent literary fascinations, Elizabethan and Jacobean drama.
6. Review (1872) of Victor Hugo's *L'Année terrible,* in *The Complete Works of Algernon Charles Swinburne* (London: William Heinemann, 1926), XIII, 244.
7. He tells us that during this period he was under the particular influence of Rossetti.
8. This is the context established for "aesthetic poetry" by Arthur Henry Hallam in his review of Tennyson's *Poems, Chiefly Lyrical* in 1831. See T. H. Motter, ed., *The Writings of Arthur Hallam* (New York: Modern Language Association, 1943).

9. Swinburne's emphasis, in *Notes on Poems and Reviews,* on phases of passion as dramatically relevant justifies this extension of the dramatic principle.

10. Henry Morley, review in the *Examiner,* September 22, 1866, pp. 597-599, as reprinted, in part, in *Swinburne: The Critical Heritage,* ed. Clyde K. Hyder (New York: Barnes and Noble, 1970), pp. 42-48.

11. The phrase is I. A. Richards's.

12. The text of Hopkins used is *The Poems of Gerard Manley Hopkins,* 4th ed. by W. H. Gardner and N. H. Mackenzie (London: Oxford University Press, 1967).

13. *The Swinburne Letters* (1959-1962), ed. Cecil Y. Lang (New Haven: Yale University Press), III, 15.

14. This dramatic principle, however one weights it, must surely be kept in mind as a corrective when one is inclined to debauch George Meredith's almost pre-Swinburnian comment that Swinburne lacked an "internal center."

15. See *Letters,* II, 45, 79-80, and Fanny E. Ratchford, "The First Draft of Swinburne's *Hertha,*" *MLN,* 39 (1924), 22-26. See also Jerome J. McGann, *Swinburne: An Experiment in Criticism* (Chicago: University of Chicago Press, 1972), p. 250.

16. See *Letters,* I, 227, n. 2.

17. This is analogous to the dramatic coordinates in Hopkins's ode: the *persona* who undergoes the harrowing spiritual stresses of the poem's central experience is a soul habituated to learning spiritual lessons through the "stroke dealt": he gets what he needs.

18. *Letters,* II, 80.

19. Much can be discerned about Browning's central concerns in these poems by fitting them roughly into the "rings" designated and reading them as representative of different points or perspectives on the same or a comparable issue—thus using *The Ring and the Book* as Browning's model aesthetic structure.

20. There is a suggestion at least that he uses her abandoned body as a way of "touching" the "golden hair" and "mouth" of the knight with whom "Her fervent body leapt or lay" (66).

21. As quoted in Georges Lafourcade, *Swinburne: A Literary Biography* (London: Bell, 1932).

22. The spirit of Sappho is processed in *Anactoria,* a poem of adaptation and expansion in which what Sappho has to say of herself is greatly inflated by what the poet *would have her say.* She passes through an intense and desperate human love to a sistership with Venus, to the severest criticism of god, to a final sense of her own great immortality—greater than that of god or goddess—through the gift of poetry. Thus the singing soul realizes that, despite its almost intolerable pain, it has a compensatory ecstasy that its nature will not yield as long as it lives.

23. The elaborate developmental section of *Thalassius* can be partially identified as the "Growth of a Poet's Mind," what happens there resonating to some degree to Wordsworth's lines "Fair seed-time had my soul, and I grew up /

Fostered alike by beauty and by fear" *(Prelude,* I, 301-302); and the process of recovery has quite distinct Wordsworthian echoes:

> Thence in his heart the great same joy began,
> Of child that made him man:
> And turned again from all hearts else on quest,
> He communed with his own heart, and had rest.
> And like sea-winds upon loud waters ran
> His days and dreams together, till the joy
> Burned in him of the boy.
>
> (437-443)

24. Two Arnold poems may be echoed here: *The Strayed Reveller* and *Memorial Verses,* the former for the Apollonian-Dionysian contrast and the revel, the latter for the recuperative concept and language: "He spoke, and loosed our hearts in tears. / He laid us as we lay at birth / On the cool flowery lap of earth; / Smiles broke from us, and we had ease . . ." (47-50). The Arnold text used is *The Poetical Works of Matthew Arnold,* ed. C. B. Tinker and H. F. Lowry (London: Oxford University Press, 1950).

25. "Thou hast conquered, O pale Galilean; the world has grown grey from thy breath; / We have drunken of things Lethean, and fed on the fulness of death." *Hymn to Proserpine,* ll. 35-36.

26. *The Wreck of the Deutschland,* l. 26. The cross-references are meant to suggest a central commonality between the two poets.

27. *The Wreck of the Deutschland,* ll. 30-32.

28. *The Wreck of the Deutschland,* ll. 73-74.

29. The concluding paragraph of the "Winckelmann" essay in *The Renaissance.*

30. See McGann, p. 188.

31. *The Wreck of the Deutschland,* l. 21.

32. The Hopkinsian ring of the language and language-structure is notable.

33. *The Wreck of the Deutschland,* l. 46.

12

Marius the Epicurean:
Beyond Victorianism

One mark of the genuine classic in Walter Pater's *Marius the Epicurean* is the imaginative fidelity with which the author presses the motivating question behind the work through its many necessary stages to its own, its peculiar, idiosyncratic solution. How would a well-defined imaginary *persona* ("Himself—his sensations and ideas"), placed within a deeply textured fabric of imaginary cultural time, work out his individual destiny? To the degree that the *persona,* however distinctive, is typical of a class and the fabric of time is genuinely refractive, the book is mythic in character; and this is another mark of the genuine classic in *Marius.* But, although Marius' meticulously defined temperament is perennial and the death-rebirth, scatter-cluster metaphor of time ("New-old, and shadowing Sense at war with Soul") is cyclical, the muted importunities of the protagonist's situation (his character, his era) give the book a ground-tone similar to that described by Arnold speaking of the ambience of Empedocles: "The calm, the cheerfulness, the disinterested objectivity have disappeared: the dialogue of the mind with itself has commenced; modern problems have presented themselves; we hear already the doubts, we witness the discouragement, of Hamlet and of Faust." [1] In that special sense, *Marius the Epicurean* is a modern mythic classic of superb imaginative fidelity. Like other apex-documents of the century— *The Prelude, Sartor Resartus, Idylls of the King, The Ring and the Book, Middlemarch, Jude the Obscure*—it is *sui generis,* drawing its sustenance from everywhere but ultimately one of a kind. Like Arnold and Newman, Pater knew that the truly essential questions are archetypal: the book is shaped by this awareness. Again like Arnold and Newman, he knew that the nineteenth century had become the arena of a ferocious contention of archetypal ideas. But Pater had been more deeply attentive than either Arnold or Newman to the efforts of nineteenth-century art to deal with nineteenth-century ideas, had heard more clearly, had meditated more deeply the voices that were new. Amid the welter of conflicting apprehensions—Epicurean materialism versus Platonic idealism, Lockean empiricism *(sentio)* versus Cartesian rationalism *(cogito)*—he had heard Goethe's question *(But is it true, is it true for me?)* at a personally functional level, and he had instructed Wordsworth—had carried analysis beyond perception to absorption. Arnold and Newman clearly recognized the omnipresence in their time of such forces as individualism, subjectivism, relativism; Pater yielded to them.

That he yielded to them so thoroughly is a principal source of the creative energy sustaining *Marius.* The work continues to exercise a magical influence over an increasing readership, not because of its equivocally seen but authentic "Christianization" of Marius, but because of its relentless secularization of him. In this respect, Pater had much in common with Thomas Hardy, the contemporary who shares with him a conspicuous critical revival: both may be fairly characterized by the term *homo religiosus* as Erik Erikson uses it in *Young Man Luther;* [2] neither personally found a satisfactory basis for a religious faith in the usual sense; both looked with detached but acute sympathy upon men's perennial religious maneuverings and aspirations but did not blink at the naked truths of modern epistemological reality; each in his fashion had a genuine faith in the ability of art to keep man's myths from hardening into fact and to free him, at least equivalently, from a wholly mechanical view of his universe.

Pater's persistent effort was to place character—the artist, the mystic, the cynic, "the children of this world"—firmly within a secular context and to explore attentively the negotiation of the individual temperament with his highly particularized cultural moment. Both the individual and his moment are in states of motion, of death and resurrection, of *being* only through *becoming;* hence, the very act of writing about them is a presumptuous act, an imaginary approximation of a process in which three variables (writer, character, culture) are made to appear to have a significant relationship to each other, the variables being symbolic of variables to the nth degree and the writer knowing full well that he only imagines he is doing what he appears to be doing. It was inevitable, then, that Pater's characters should be elusive, threatening to evaporate before our very eyes; that many of his narrators' comments should have a quality of improvisation about them, insights suddenly born; that his sentences should often abandon an ideal of neoclassical shapeliness in their feel for perceptual fitness; *but also,* that his design should be very firm and his empiricism thoroughgoing.

John Locke's presence in the nineteenth century, like Francis Bacon's, was so generalized, organic, and, so to speak, mythic that one must be cautious in assigning a direct and primary influence of "the father of modern epistemology" on a writer so late as Pater. Locke had so dyed the waters in which writers in the Romantic tradition swam that, despite the repeated references to "the tablet of the mind white and smooth" in *Marius* and the crucial manner in which Pater orchestrates Lockean sensation in the "Conclusion" to *The Renaissance,*[3] no claims need be made here for the direct and primary, as distinct from the derivative and pervasive, influence of Locke on Pater. But the Lockean presence, however received, is diffused throughout Pater: like the positive side of the Heraclitean doctrine, Locke's empiricism makes it possible for life to have significant meaning within the severest circumscription.

Marius, like all of Pater's fictions, has a crisp epistemological center. Like them, it is a study in the formation of consciousness—a subtle, painstaking exploration of the sources, limitations, affectiveness, and conditions of knowledge and its usability. Its distinctiveness—its firmness of design—depends, not just on its being a study in a strange temperament, but on its exploration, through that temperament, of experientially conditioned and evolving stages of awareness. By combining serious examination of the knowable with carefully delineated personality, Pater created a new and prescient form of epistemological and psychological fiction. Like Locke, Pater abandoned the field of futile speculative disputes and accepted man as fated to a great ignorance.[4] Like Locke, he turned away from cosmology as a center of fruitful interest and satisfied himself with exploring the understanding, the mind of the perceiver, cognitive knowledge. Like Locke, he abandoned the doctrine of innate ideas, abandoned as fruitless the quest for essences, accepted as an imperative fact that "Knowledge is of things we see" *(In Memoriam,* "Prologue"), that the mind at birth is a *tabula rasa,* that the basic content filters in through sense experience, and that all ideas are merely complexes of the basic, simple ideas thereby acquired. Thus, the visual intensity and verbal tactility of Pater are firmly rooted in a carefully considered view of man, his resources and his limitations. Further, his apprehension of the inescapable subjectivity of knowledge leads to other conspicuous aspects of Pater's fictions: the essential *societal* isolation of the individual—the more isolated the more conscientious his quest for genuine experience / knowledge; the *psychological* impenetrability of one person by another as a result of the oneness of his personality and the rings of experience that are therefore peculiar to him—the less penetrable the less habitual and stereotyped. For man thus limited, experience takes on a heightened urgency because man, like his experience, is in a perpetual state of unbecoming; and from the uneasiness thus induced he takes the energy for movement. Like Locke, Pater turned away from the hypotheses of the rationalists and substituted for a Cartesian first principle *(Cogito ergo sum)* a Paterian-Lockean first principle *(Sentio ergo sum).* Pater's epistemology, like Locke's, is an experiential epistemology founded on "the integrity and saving power of the simple sensation" (Tuveson, p. 24), upon which are built complex ideas, reflection, memory, imagination, the elusive vagaries of association, the dissolution of the ego as a hard-core identity, and the reorientation of the personality to an ongoing process—or, as Proust was to say, "The disintegration of the self is a continuous death" (Tuveson, p. 30). Finally, Pater's experiential epistemology, like Locke's, leaves "religion and virtue secure" (Tuveson, p. 16)—that is, untouched—and suggests as a goal for *homo sentiens* a continual multiplication of continuously refined experiences and a caution lest the mind set up "a barrier between reality and consciousness" (Tuveson, p. 24). It is within this specifically defined epistemological context, clearly Lockean, that Pater's language and ideas take on serious and resonant significance; that it can be meaningfully said that the "Conclusion" to *The Renaissance* mediates between the analytical-critical and the critical-creative centers of his canon; and that we have the principal antidote to a chaotically impressionistic response to his exquisitely refined perceptions and firmly designed prose pieces.

The organic character of *Marius the Epicurean* can be initially perceived through attentive scrutiny of Chapter 2, "White-Nights," in which the major motifs or "themes" of the book are unmistakably sounded. The shape and substance of Marius' adolescent consciousness are delicately woven by patterns induced from his hereditary and cultural experience and are translated by the telling into psychic forms or structures. "White-Nights" itself is the first of the "curious houses" through which he will journey and the one to which he will return symbolically when the haunting curse of his incompleteness has been removed: "So, that beautiful dwelling-place lent the reality of concrete outline to a peculiar ideal of home, which throughout the rest of his life he seemed, amid many distractions of spirit, to be ever seeking to regain." [5] His reverence for the memory of his father and the supportive traditions he has inherited from him is somewhat severe, love distanced to awe, conditioning his relationship to other men and requiring a delicate transformation. The hieratic dimensions of his personality distinguish Marius sharply from his ancestor Marcellus; but beneath his somber conscientiousness, he retains the debonair grace, the love of "beauty and order in the conduct of life," the moral-aesthetic authority of the eye which characterized Marcellus and which, transformed, make the nonpuritan phase of the early flowering of Christianity so magnificently attractive to him. His early associations with his mother—reverence for the dead, maternity, spiritual delicacy, the house as *sacellum* or sanctuary—get their ultimate fulfillment in Cecilia and the radiance of Cecilia's house. His negative conscientiousness ("a certain vague fear of evil, constitutional in him") is dramatically symbolized in the copulating snakes; and the pity and fear that he feels toward these emblems of "a humanity, dusty and sordid and as if far gone in corruption" become, again on the negative side, the motive forces for his quest for perfection, the springs of an uneasiness that requires action. His susceptibility to mysticism is repeatedly suggested, most specifically in connection with augury:

> And if you can imagine how, once in a way, an impressible boy might have an *inkling*, an inward mystic intimation, of the meaning and consequences of all that, what was implied in it becoming explicit for him, you conceive aright the mind of Marius. (Chap. 2, p. 16)

It is, of course, this susceptibility that enables him to transcend, occasionally, the ramparts or horizons of the world and to touch, fleetingly and imaginatively, a supersensual order of reality. One such moment, the most dramatic in the book, occurs in Chapter 19 ("The Will as Vision"), prior to his introduction to Christianity as a peculiarly energizing ritual of experience. It is his preternatural awareness of a "divine companion" by which his conscience is transformed from negative fear to positive gratitude and he acquires "a definitely ascertained measure of his moral or intellectual need, of the demand his soul must make upon the powers, whatsoever they might be, which had brought him, as he was, into the world at all" (Chap. 19, pp. 71-72). This crucial motif-within-a-motif is seeded at the very beginning of "White-Nights" in the quotation from "a quaint German mystic" concerning " 'the mystery of so-called *white* things,' as being 'ever an after-thought—the doubles, or seconds, of real things, and themselves but half-real, half-material' " (Chap. 2, p. 13). Finally—and most importantly of all—the "anima naturaliter Christiana" is fetal in "White-Nights":

> And from habit, this feeling of a responsibility towards the world of men and things, towards a claim for due sentiment concerning them on his side, came to be *a part of his nature not to be put off.* It kept him serious and dignified amid the Epicurean speculations which in after years much engrossed him, and

when he had learned to think of all religions as indifferent, serious amid many fopperies and through many languid days, and *made him anticipate all his life long as a thing towards which he must carefully train himself, some great occasion of self-devotion,* such as really came, that should consecrate his life, and, it might be, its memory with others, as the early Christian looked forward to martyrdom at the end of his course, as a seal of worth upon it. (Chap. 2, p. 18; emphasis added)

Marius is organic, then, in the firmest and most specific formal sense of that term: it grows outward like a plant.

The work is organic, too, in its use of literary materials. A large part of Pater's purpose is to create a unity, a perenniality, out of the value-quest of Western man. The inner process through which Marius goes is Europeanized, refracted in Greece, Germany, France, England, and in a sort of perpetual, emblematic Italy. In "White-Nights," for example, his religion of the hearth has its English counterpart; his relish for landscape is for "the grave, subdued, northern notes . . . the French or English notes"; the narrator glosses his experiences by drawing upon Euripides, Saint Augustine, and "a quaint [nineteenth-century] German mystic." This in turn is relevant to the narrative method of *Marius:* the dual omniscience of the narrative voice, both intimate with every nuance of Marius' sensations and the ideas that emerge out of them, on the one hand, and, on the other, nimbly moving, like the *Zeitgeist* itself, up and down the physiognomy of Western Europe as a sort of spiritual ecologist noting with controlled animation the mutations and analogies that characterize this cultural climax forest, this organic unity in diversity. From this culturally enveloping perspective, Epicurus is a contemporary of John Stuart Mill; Heraclitus and John Locke are spiritual brothers; Dante and Saint Francis are recoverers of the debonair grace lost with the edict of Constantine; the liberation of spirit felt by Marius at school in Pisa is analogous to "the *Neu-zeit* of the German enthusiasts at the beginning of our own century" (Chap. 4, p. 48); and Plato can easily be imagined walking the Cumnor Hills. The most obvious alternatives to this narrative method—highly imaginative critical history after the manner of Burkhardt or *Meditations / Conversations* after the manner of Marcus Aurelius himself—would obviously have restricted, obscured, and essentially destroyed Pater's purposes in the novel. The fragment of a diary that Marius keeps in imitation of Marcus Aurelius ("Sunt Lacrimae Rerum," Chap. 25) even suggests that Pater considered and rejected the Aurelian model on literary as well as moral grounds, seeing the literary strategy as enclosing and limiting in a manner analogous to the philosophical apprehension.

The "transformation" through which Apuleius' story of Cupid and Psyche goes ("The Golden Book," Chap. 5) is an excellent example of Pater's organic use of literary materials.[6] He puts Apuleius' *Metamorphoses* through yet another metamorphosis, letting it radiate through the first full stage of Marius' development. It is presented as one of those "truant" books by which youth perennially rises above the *"débris"* of daily living and perceives its ideals in "emphatically sensuous" metaphors. No apology is made for the personal transformation; indeed, the narrator asserts that Marius "saw in it doubtless far more than was really there for any other reader" (Chap. 6, pp. 93-94). That it moves Apuleius far in the direction of Dante—from coarseness to earnest idealization, from boyish petulance to " 'Lord, of terrible aspect' "—is its central imaginative revelation. It functions in the manner of an elaborate but crystalline dream[7] in character not unlike that experienced by the poet-speaker in lyric CIII of *In Memoriam*.[8] In the dream-myth Marius' most pressing anxieties and aspirations work themselves out in idealized fashion—his consciousness of his unusual gifts, his longing for companionship and for an imaginatively perfect domicile or art palace, his petulance toward his mother, his distance from his father, his fear of psychic violation under the pressure of a maturing physicality, his faith in his ultimate ability, though after prolonged struggle, to solemnize a private marriage of body and soul. He is, in his dream-myth, both Cupid and Psyche, androgynous; and the warning he gets is of the dangers, not of "most sweet [sexual] usage," but of rash curiosity. His negative conscience surfaces in the reptile image, upon which the harpies of his soul play; and he suffers acute anxiety lest he face death alone and unreconciled. The subconscious role Flavian plays as a prompter of his dream-myth is perhaps hinted in the figure of Pan, and there is little reason to blink at the notion that the dream is in part homoerotically induced. Marius is in the stage of adolescent hero-worship, and he plays a distinctly feminine role to Flavian's greater age, physical maturity, masculine beauty and prowess ("corruption"), brilliance, strange origins, and ambition. Moreover, this homoerotic motif is carried through the rest of Part I—in the refrain of Flavian's *Pervigilium Veneris* (*"Cras amet qui nunquam amavit, / Quique amavit cras amet"*), in Marius' sharing of his body heat with the dying Flavian, and in the tag with which Part I ends:

> *Quis desiderio sit pudor aut modus*
> *Tam cari capitis?—*

What thought of others' thoughts about one could there be with the regret for "so dear a head" fresh at one's heart? (Chap. 7, p. 120)

The critic, then, need not so much carp at Pater's strippings from the original (salty realism, broad humor) as marvel at the appositeness of his mythic discovery and the organic way in which he evolved literature from literature.

The weaning of Marius from his past which had created the conflicts that surfaced in his dream-myth is completed by the death of Flavian. In a willful act, he "piously stamp[s] on his memory the death-scene of a brother wrongfully condemned to die" (Chap. 7, p. 119) as a way of shutting out the passage into his wounded consciousness of emblems of happiness out of childhood, cutting off both the religion and the poetry of that earlier time. Rejecting, too, the theatrical blandishments of a Romantic mysticism, he undertakes a year of rigorous intellectual endeavor to discover grounds of trustworthiness in himself and his world. He attempts

> to determine his bearings, as by compass, in the world of thought—to get that precise acquaintance with *the creative intelligence itself, its structure and capacities, its relation to other parts of himself and to other things,* without which, certainly, no poetry can be masterly. (Chap. 8, p. 126; emphasis added)

An innate blend of temperamental qualities that reach toward epicurean materialism and religious idealism save him from perishing in the turbulent cross-currents of philosophical speculation (rash curiosity) and enable him to find genuine, if necessarily temporary, footing as a neo-Cyrenaic. For Marius, this anchorage is as much psychological as philosophical and serves a cautionary purpose in the novel: though he clearly suspends for the moment important integers of the self, he avoids the ravages of both a flamboyant transcendentalism and a hypothesis-ridden rationalism by making secular sacraments of the Me and the Now:

> The peculiar strength of Marius was, to have apprehended this weakness on the threshold of human knowledge, in the whole range of its consequences. Our knowledge is limited to what we feel, he reflected: we need no proof that we feel. (Chap. 8, p. 138)

Though the world may be an illusion, sensation is real to the sensor; and although it does not enable Marius to transcend "the flaming ramparts of the world," it does save him from "bewildering [himself] methodically" (Chap. 8, p. 140, a quotation from Michelet), free him from propositions whose only validity is as "a fixity of language," and enable him to gain perspective over the maelstrom of abstruse philosophies:

> Abstract theory was to be valued only just so far as it might serve to clear the tablet of the mind from suppositions no more than half realisable, or wholly visionary, leaving it in flawless evenness of surface to the impressions of an experience, concrete and direct. (Chap. 8., p. 141)

It is this epistemological empiricism that saves Marius in his first major crisis and enables him to go through a prolonged period of what Samuel Butler would call "crossing"—getting himself out of himself and something else into him. Through almost all of Part II of the novel, the past goes unremembered and the future unprojected. Accepting *"Life as the end of life,"* Marius devoted himself to study and observation in an effort to refine "all the instruments of inward and outward intuition," to make his "whole nature" "one complex medium of reception, towards the vision—the 'beatific vision,' if we really cared to make it such—of our actual experience in the world" (Chap. 8, p. 143). To this effort he brings a well-developed tendency toward ethical idealism so that his *hedonism,* so called, though fully experiential, has no touch of the grosser forms of self-indulgence:

> Not pleasure, but fulness of life, and "insight" as conducting to that fulness—energy, variety, and choice of experience, including noble pain and sorrow even, loves such as those in the exquisite old story of Apuleius, sincere and strenuous forms of the moral life, such as Seneca and Epictetus—whatever form of human life, in short, might be heroic, impassioned, ideal: from these the "new Cyrenaicism" of Marius took its criterion of values. (Chap. 9, pp. 151-152) [9]

A complete education—culture in the broad humanistic sense espoused by the Greeks, the Renaissance, and the European nineteenth century—is Marius' goal.

The final pathetic efforts of Flavian to give poetic voice to his imaginative sense of things, his rich latter-day pagan sadness, had introduced a strain of medieval note-catching; and throughout Part II, that medieval prophecy begins to swell, magnified gradually through Marius' attentive curiosity about and response to four stimuli, "concrete and direct"—landscape, Cornelius, Lucius Verus and pagan entertainment, and Marcus Aurelius.[10]

The splendor of Augustan Rome and its environs has already begun to mutate into the ruined picturesqueness of the medieval and modern periods. The Empire has lost its stability on the perimeter, the residue of wealth at the center is depleted by futile if heroic efforts to stave off the barbarians and the future, the plague has left whole districts untouched by human industry, subject to organic vegetal encroachment. Washed in golden sunshine and bathed in liquid air, the visual effects are incomparably pleasing aesthetically, but the inevitable insight they bear is of mutability and the vanity of human wishes. It is within this symbolic topography of an obsolescent past that Marius meets Cornelius.[11]

That the relationship between Marius and Cornelius is shadowy is, in part, the result of the narrative method of the novel (analogically distanced) and of its center of interest (sensations and ideas); but there is also Marius' assumption, formed during his adoption of neo-Cyrenaicism, of the essential isolation of the individual: not only that "no one of us is 'like another, all in all'" (Chap. 8, p. 143), but that "we are never to get beyond the walls of the closely shut cell of one's own personality" (Chap. 9, p. 146). Hence, there is no dramatic or physical "touching" between Marius and Cornelius (the homoerotic element in Marius' relationship with Flavian is entirely absent). The mysterious magnetism that the young Christian has over the detached pagan, though sensuously delineated (soul mirrored in personal style), is spiritual, intimations of a secret experiential knowledge unknown to himself, hints, according to Marius' inverted *déjà vu* prescience,[12] that Cornelius is the finest essence of the future. Quite unmistakably, Cornelius is the flower of the dawning Middle Ages, the Christian knight, *miles gloriosus Christianus,* the perfection of pagan cultivation transformed into chivalry by the magic touch of a delicate mysticism. That there is a mysterious potency about Cornelius, Marius knows empirically: "It was as if his bodily eyes had been indeed mystically washed, renewed, strengthened" (Chap. 14, p. 235), but the exact nature of the secret is hidden from him:

> But of what possible intellectual formula could this mystic Cornelius be the sensible exponent; seeming, as he did, to live ever in close relationship with, and recognition of, a mental view, a source of discernment, a light upon his way, which had certainly not yet sprung up for Marius? (Chap. 14, p. 234)

Lucius Verus, on the other hand, is paganism on its degenerate side. Cruel, vulgar, ostentatious, totally lacking in *humanitas,* he has become the "patron or protégé" of the dark Diana—not the virgin protectress of regeneration, but the "Deity of Slaughter—the Taurian goddess who demands the sacrifice of the shipwrecked sailors thrown on her coasts—the cruel, moonstruck huntress, who brings not only sudden death, but *rabies,* among the wild creatures" (Chap. 14, p. 238). The games celebrating the religious rites of his marriage to the Emperor's daughter include piercing the bellies of animals in foal so that their young will spill out on the white sand and the dexterous cutting of a criminal's skin from his leg "as neatly as if it were a stocking" in ritualistic reenactment of the punishment of Marsyas after his failure in the musical contest with Apollo.

Between these symbols of aspirant chivalry and jaded, sterile bestiality stands the gracious, benumbed, unhappy figure of Marcus Aurelius—refined Stoic, delicate and generous friend, patrician priest, persecutor of Christians, and silent partner in the "manly amusements." [13] Marius might have found the Emperior affective in a very different way had his initiation into the strange celestial courtliness of Cornelius not already begun. After all, Marcus Aurelius' reputation for philosophic rectitude, for detached poise, for severe self-scrutiny are legendary in his time and find resonance in Marius. But he fails the young provincial on two essential grounds: Marius has in fact begun his experience of Cornelius; and Marius' experiential empiricism has put an ontological gulf between him and Marcus Aurelius. Not only does the Emperor's philosophy fail him in his efforts to transcend death; he is himself the victim of a death apprehension. As Cornelius promises the debonair, graceful, energetic, supremely hopeful side of the Middle Ages, Marcus Aurelius promises its dark, ascetic, hardened, official, public side—its Inquisitional side.[14]

The ontological difference between Marius and Marcus Aurelius is worth stressing. Whereas Marius' "soil of human nature" engenders life, warmth, intensity, Marcus Aurelius' soil, with "the ascetic pride which lurks under all Platonism" (Chap. 12, p. 200), engenders *contemptus mundi,* death, grayness, enervation prophetic of the decay of Rome visually and "the hermit of the middle age" spiritually (Chap. 12, p. 201). At the gladiatorial games, he tolerates tawdry theatrical cruelty because he does not *see*—that is, he practices visual and hence moral detachment so that his very tolerance becomes a vice. Marcus Aurelius suffers from a benumbed imagination: by the very regimen of his Stoicism, essentially theoretic or abstract, he has closed his eyes to the sensible world, has ceased to correlate his consciousness with reality, and hence has allowed his genuine imagination to wither at the source. Having long since ceased to look on nature as a tactile, sensuous reality and having depended, rather, on "the imaginative influence of the philosophic reason," when he seeks access to the "Celestial City" of Plato, he can only divine, "by a kind of generosity of spirit, the void place, which another experience than his must fill" (Chap. 17, p. 40).[15] Marius recognizes the delicate soul of Marcus Aurelius—"a soul for which conversation with itself was a necessity of existence"—but sees in his tolerance of patent evil, in his *Tristia* or melancholy, in his contempt for the body, in his attitude toward suicide, in the inadequacy of his philosophy in the face of personal grief, in the "hard contempt" for pain that enables him to execute his prisoners and persecute the Christians, the manifestations of a thoroughly unhappy spirit ultimately inaccessible to common sense, practical reason, and even self-evident justice. Marcus Aurelius, then, is the man who has closed his options: by virtue of his temperament and his particular philosophical response to his culture, he has clouded the "receptivity of [his] soul" and settled for a "mechanical and disheartening theory of [humanity] and its conditions" (Chap. 28, pp. 220-221).[16]

By the end of Part II, Marius' memory, long suspended, begins to revive, and in the third sequence a process of organic integration—of enlargement and renewal—is initiated. Under the influence of the eloquent and urbane Cornelius Fronto (master rhetorician whose discourse on the *Nature of Morals* is remarkably suggestive of Newman's definition of the quintessential secular gentleman), he is drawn, not to the adoption of a beautifully humanistic Stoicism, but to a recognition of the severely limited character of his own neo-Cyrenaicism. It, too, is monistic, exclusive; it has served him well, but it has been too peremptory in its attitude toward the cumulative moral traditions of the race, and it has isolated him against a now-emergent need for community. He is beginning, as it were, to look homeward, imagining a "visible locality and abiding-place, the walls and towers of which, so to speak, he might really trace and tell, according to his own old, natural habit of mind" (Chap. 15, p. 11). At this point, he has not found the secret of Cornelius, but he feels the pressing need of some secret for the conversion of desire into conduct. He, like Aurelius, is touched with longing for the Celestial City; and despite the coordinates of his alienation from Aurelius, he finds in the "conversations with himself" the suggestion of two possibilities of inestimable attraction: "the divine companion, whose tabernacle was in the intelligence of men" and the thought that " 'Tis in thy power . . . to think as thou wilt' " (Chap. 18, pp. 48-49).

Out of this cluster of importunate elements—streamings of reminiscence, an uneasy shift off-center from an old anchorage, brotherhood with Cornelius of the secret apprehension, proximity to the acute sufferings of Marcus Aurelius, spiritual echoes of Plato, inner longings—Marius, in visual surroundings poised and expectant, experiences an epiphanic dream-vision that, although it does not leave his "after-morn content" *(In Memoriam,* CIII), yet projects and in part determines his destiny: "The experience of that fortunate hour, seeming to gather into one central act of vision all the deeper impressions his mind had ever received, did not leave him quite as he had been" (Chap. 20, p. 75). As the final chapter of the third part, "The Will as Vision" is obviously placed with great care: the climactic spiritual experience of Marius' life occurs *before* he undergoes the close experience of Christianity.

What happens to Marius in "that fortunate hour" is wholly natural, the imaginative orchestration of all the sensations and ideas that have lain uncoordinated in his consciousness, a momentary harmonious inflation of all of the metaphors of desired possibility:

> Through one reflection upon another, he passed from such instinctive divinations ["of a living and companionable spirit at work in all things"], to the thoughts which give them logical consistency, formulating at last, as the necessary exponent of our own and the world's life, that reasonable Ideal to which the Old Testament gives the name of *Creator,* which for the philosophers of Greece is the *Eternal Reason,* and in the New Testament the *Father of Men*—even as one builds up from act and word and expression of the friend actually visible at one's side; an ideal of the spirit within him. (Chap. 19, p. 68)

Marius "willed" his vision in a holistic sense: it was an organic and integrated, a fully expressive mythic realization of his knowledge and need; and it attuned him to his future. It enabled him to overreach the cell of self, to remember loving instead of being loved, to feel conscientious gratitude instead of conscientious fear, and to rise, analogically but intensely, to a brotherhood beyond Flavian or even Cornelius, to a "divine companion"

> to whose boundless power of memory he could commit his own most fortunate moments, his admiration, his love, Ay! the very sorrows of which he could not bear quite to lose the sense:—one strong to retain them even though he forgot, in whose more vigorous consciousness they might subsist for ever, beyond that mere quickening of capacity which was all that remained of them in himself. (Chap. 19, pp. 70-71)

The terms are crucial: "memory," "admiration," "love," "sorrow," "consciousness," "permanence." They are not qualities peculiarly Christian, though the mythic realization of them will be configurated most visibly for Marius in the symbols, rituals, and *personae* of the incipient Christian expectancy. Nor do they require supernatural inducement: they flow, inevitably for a temperament like Marius', by a flawless imaginative leap from the Self to the Self-not-Self like that of Browning's David: "See the Christ stand!" ("Saul," 1. 312); or, "the Christ," like America, is here and now or nowhere; or, "the Christ" is within me, I am "the Christ."

Several years elapse between Marius' epiphanic moment and the dénouement of the novel; and the panels of experience to which we are made privy reveal, through a series of measurings, not his *conversion* in the religious sense, but his *transformation* in the Apuleian sense. The chapters entitled "Two Curious Houses" (20 and 21) contrast his adolescent fervor, under the homoerotic influence of Flavian, over "The Golden Book" of Apuleius with the gently ironic fantasticality of Apuleius himself—Platonism ritualized into a theatrical life-style; and the direction and distance he might have traveled from "home" had he followed the Flavian-Apuleian way are given sharp definition by the juxtaposition to the house "at Tusculum" of Cecilia's *sacellum,* the house as maternal sanctuary, in which the "hieratic refinement" of the "boy-priest," so long striven against, is freed and waxes strong as Marius begins to recognize that his prolonged and strenuous efforts to unself that original self "had made his life certainly like one long 'disease of the spirit' " (Chapt. 21, p. 107). Led on by the excitement of his initial experience and driven by "a deep sense of vacuity in life" (Chap. 23, p. 128), Marius "informed himself with much pains concerning the church in Cecilia's house" (Chap. 22, p. 109), and what he discovered was a magical moment in the history of man's self-renewals.

In the chapter entitled " 'The Minor Peace of the Church,' " the dual omniscience of Pater's narrative method is strained to the utmost. In it, he relates Marius' private experience and perception of Christianity at a historical juncture when

> the church was true for a moment, truer perhaps than she would ever be again, to that element of profound serenity in the soul of her Founder, which reflected the eternal goodwill of God to man, "in whom," according to the oldest version of the angelic message, "He is well-pleased" (Chap. 22, p. 117)

to the perennial efforts of Western man to renew himself. In order to create this formal illusion, the narrator stresses the organic evolution of this moment out of the past—the promise of the New Testament, the "Peace" of the Antonines, the adoption by Christianity of "many of the graces of pagan feeling and pagan custom" (p. 125), the movement from Greek to Latin, from Greek liturgy to Latin liturgy, the adaptive growth of ritual "by the same law of development which prevails everywhere else, in the moral as in the physical world" (p. 126), the "spirit of life itself, organising [a refreshed] soul and body" out of "the dust of outworn religious usage" (p. 126). To this organicism, he adds that peculiar aptitude of Marius', not actually to foresee the future—to descend, "by *foresight,* upon a later age than his own" (p. 117)—but so particularly to sense an original tendency of human "genius" as to be in touch with its future as with its past. The voice of the cultural historian then translates this aptitude into specific historical analogues of "that regenerate type of humanity"—Gregory the Great, St. Francis of Assisi, Dante, Giotto, Raphael, Montaigne, Bunyan, Rousseau—in which "a certain debonair grace, and a certain mystic attractiveness" (p. 111) achieve dominance over puritanism and asceticism, which inevitably have their dominance over persons and periods too. In particular—here and in the following chapter ("Divine Service")—Marius witnesses "a veritable regeneration of the earth and the body" in the "naturalness," "comely order," "elegance of sanctity," "cheerful temper," and "aesthetic charm" of Christianity's most privileged hour sensuously rendered and received.

All this is, in turn, set over against the brilliantly arid dialogue between Lucian and Hermotimus in "A Conversation Not Imaginary" (Chap. 24), in which Marius witnesses both an oblique exaggeration of his former self (his naivete, egotism, and essential isolation) and a gentle deflation of Lucian's Socratic method as a means of grace, its brilliance and elegance leading, at best, to refined capacities rather than to imaginative fulfillment. "Sunt Lacrimae Rerum" (Chapt. 25), modeled after Marcus Aurelius' "conversations with himself," again distances Marius from the Emperor by the particularity with which his perceptions of pain and sorrow are individualized;[17] and in "The Martyrs" (Chap. 26), stories of personal heroism in the face of outrageous persecution of Christians are contrasted to "the hard contempt of one's own or other's pain, of death, of glory even, in those discourses of Aurelius!" (Chap. 26, p. 187). "The Triumph of Marcus Aurelius" (Chap. 27) is an ironically counterpointed narrative in which Marius bids farewell in spirit to that *"anima infelicissima"* and turns home to the reverent task of burying his ancestors and to the acceptance of himself as *"the last of his race!"*

The near-universal critical dissatisfaction with Pater's resolution of the fictive career of Marius is troublesome. Since there is no lack of clarity in what actually happens in the final chapter, one would expect that dissatisfaction to be argued on grounds of imaginative infidelity on the author's part. In general, such is not the case: the critics tend to crucify *Marius* on factitious dilemmas and to impose upon the novel their personal dissatisfaction with the outcome. A notable exception is Harold Bloom, who clearly identifies issues that are genuinely critical:

> What can be urged against Pater, fairly, is that he evaded the novel's ultimate problem by killing off Marius before the young man grasps the theological and moral exclusiveness of

Christianity. Marius could not remain Marius and renounce; forced to make the Yeatsian choice between perfection of the life and perfection of the work he would have suffered from a conflict that would have destroyed the fine balance of his nature. Whether Pater earns the structural irony of the novel's concluding pages, as a still-pagan Marius dies a sanctified Christian death, is quite legitimately questionable.[18]

Here, at least, are two genuine critical challenges to Pater's imaginative fidelity: evading the novel's "ultimate problem" and failing to "earn" the final "structural irony" of his work.

A reader can legitimately come down squarely on the side of Pater on both issues so long as he sees *Marius* as a novel of *transformations*, not *conversions;* and so long as he recognizes in Pater's central awareness a concept of perennial types, human metaphors of shifting dominances in the organic evolution of man. As has been argued above, Marcus Aurelius represents the type, softened somewhat by individual differences, that, in a later, official Christianity promulgated by Constantine, will embody, among other things, "theological and moral exclusiveness." Hence, Marius' close understanding of and detailed self-distancing from the Aurelian apprehension and life-style are, without a wrenching anachronism, equivalent to a critique of the stern puritanism that would dominate the Christian Church for a thousand years. Marius is not a Cornelius, as Marcus Aurelius is not a Lucius Verus: both look forward very tentatively to the new age, groping toward it without a resounding revelation and faith, each bearing a different temperamental strain that will determine its essential mix. So, although renunciation would be too severe a term, Marius does look face to face and without illusion at his stern medieval cohabitant.

In deciding the second issue, one must make a careful distinction between *ambiguity* and *irony* and then judge cautiously the ironic reverberations of the final chapter. There is nothing ambiguous about Marius' end: he is not a hero or a Christian member or a martyr. Through a mild impulsive act of generosity, he arranges the liberty of Cornelius, the beloved brother and Christian, and undergoes the harshnesses of a five-day journey on foot in rough weather through rugged terrain. He is abandoned by the soldiers in the care of a group of provincial Christians when it is clear that he will not survive the rest of the journey; and after several days of sinking and rallying, consciousness and delirium, experiencing wide swings of emotion, he dies, having received unsolicited the final rites of the Church, and is buried under the mistaken notion on the part of his nurses that he is a martyr to the Faith. He knows—as do the narrator and the reader—that he is not a formal Christian or a martyr (he does not die "a sanctified Christian"); and so the ironies are the traditional irony of fate and the dramatic irony of our awareness of the peasants' misunderstanding.

The principal illumination of Marius' final hours is not that he is miscast, but that he is precisely cast:

> At this moment, his unclouded receptivity of soul, grown so steadily through all those years, from experience to experience, was at its height; the house ready for the possible guest; the tablet of the mind white and smooth, for whatsoever divine fingers might choose to write there. (Chap. 28, p. 220)

It is in this and this alone that Marius' essential integrity resides; and in this he can freely resonate to the ultimate significance, *for him,* of the Christian renaissance-of-spirit: "There had been a permanent protest established in the world, a plea, a perpetual afterthought, which humanity henceforth would ever possess in reserve, against any wholly mechanical and disheartening theory of itself and its conditions" (Chap. 28, p. 221). "Natural Christianity," as it evolves in *Marius,* is not a theology or any other form of hardened fact; it is a magnificent, organic, cyclical, inevitable, and wholly natural emblem of the regenerative genius of man; and it is, so seen, conspicuously available to individualistic, subjective, relativist modern man if he is true to himself, keeping his spirit conscientious and his options open. It is the most visible and elaborately developed "art" of religious worship known to Western man, the flower of his Jewish, Greek, and Latin, his European, ritualistic inheritance; and it is known, if it is known at all, to the degree that the individual can reestablish contact with this manifestation of an "original tendency" in the "genius" of his culture.

Marius the Epicurean is a truly extraordinary literary text, the focal document for a study of the transformation of the creative spirit of the nineteenth century into the creative spirit of the twentieth.[19] In a broad but particularly meaningful sense, it traces the organic evolution, the periods of rise and fall, of an "original tendency" of the "genius" of cultural Western man; and in that broad sense *Marius* is the most accomplished product in English of the nineteenth century's highly developed "science of origins." Pater excels even Arnold in creating a satisfying illusion that one has been in touch with a nimbly moving *Zeitgeist,* that the pulses have been actually felt, and that even what has been omitted is implicit in what has been said.

But it is in a narrower sense that it can be said that Pater, specifically in *Marius the Epicurean,* brought nineteenth-century turbulence, its urgent advocacies, to a point of poise and channeled its flow into the twentieth century. The case of Matthew Arnold is again relevant. There was no quarrel between Pater and Arnold, and efforts to create one by the critics have been critically wasteful. Pater owed to Arnold a conspicuous debt which he made no effort to disguise: it is consistent with Pater's view of the organic evolution of insight that he should have recognized that the role Arnold had played helped to define his own role. But the difference between them is also conspicuous. Arnold, too, was a student of origins and an accomplished interpreter of the chief literary and spiritual texts of Western man; but Arnold had not kept an attentive eye on the artistic experiments of his contemporaries (Tennyson, Browning, Ruskin, Rossetti, Morris, Swinburne, Pater); and, with the possible exception of Wordsworth and Byron, his look at the Romantics had been a rather broad sweep-through. The close critical care which he began to give to Wordsworth's earlier and later contemporaries came at an advanced stage in Arnold's life and literary career and can hardly be called formational.[20] Pater, on the other hand, recognized very early that, of the centuries that had gone into the making of him, his own was the most imperious; and he studied the Romantics and their successors from Blake to Swinburne with meticulous and self-regarding care. More like Newman than Arnold, Pater was also curious about the ways in which gigantic philosophical personalities—Spinoza and Locke, for example, Bacon and Kant—had conditioned the *sensibilities* of his nineteenth-century contemporaries and the degree to which currents of perception and belief had infiltrated life-style. So while Arnold resisted or ignored many of the private, subterranean spiritual currents of his own century, Pater felt their flow and yielded to their wash. Pater was not more or less concerned than Arnold about ethical questions; he was concerned differently. Arnold asked the individual to measure himself by the touchstone; Pater measured the touchstone by its functional relevance to the individual. Like Newman, Pater recognized that Leo and Augustine did not change, but that their affective influence over the individual could change from moment to moment so long as he was alive. So, while Arnold's generic cultural observations have a brilliant metaphoric luminosity, Pater's, despite their aptness and their richness, do not, because Pater has distanced thought to *the experience of thought.* Whether the voice we hear is that of an imaginary character or of an imaginary narrator or, as is most usual, an interpenetration of the two, it is the confessional voice of an inquiring spirit in a carefully shaded state of spiritual experience.

Pater accepted, then, as Arnold and his Victorian contemporaries did not, a precariously solipsistic anchorage: he found it ultimately inescapable. Not having been, like Carlyle, a drafter of what Michael Timko calls the "charter" or "style" of Victorianism,[21] he was not bound by its articles. Blake and Wordsworth and Keats are as organic in Pater as are Tennyson and Browning, and Locke monitored his apprehensions as thoroughly as did Darwin. In the Arnoldian quarrel with the Romantic aesthetic, Pater would have been as much on the side of the Romantics as on the side of Arnold; and if *culture* meant "inward development" to the Romantics and civilized ethical and social living to the Victorians (Timko, pp. 619-621), it meant both to Pater. Finally, Pater could abandon Romantic metaphysics without abandoning the Romantic effort "to convert [knowledge] into an energy finer than intellectual." [22] He accepted all the implications of the "subjectivity of knowledge," for himself and for others; and then he went on a most meticulous and far-ranging quest for knowledge, not to find a talisman, but as an available strategy for transforming a confessed solipsism into a quintessential barometer of his cultural legacy. Paradoxically, Pater's position is more analogous to Newman's than to that of any other Victorian: the least dogmatic to the most dogmatic. Newman's ritual of personal fulfillment was worked out through divine revelation and the sacramental Church, Pater's through human revelation and the sacrament of the climactic Here and Now; but both were moved by the same conscientious aspiration—that the light within them be not darkness—and both were trying to save their souls.

What Pater did for the twentieth century—in which he energized, until very recently, few major critics and several major poets—was to channel a full-bodied intellectual, spiritual, and aesthetic inheritance into a temperament, a portrait, of the artist, broadly conceived, "perfecting" a life in a work of art called *Marius the Epicurean.* The result is an artifact in which the artist (say, Yeats) can watch the artist-in-form (say, Pater) watching the artist-in-life (say, Marius). It is a formulation, an aesthetic structure, by which two crucial burdens can be eased: the burden of the past (what one does with so rich an inheritance) and the burden of the present (how one relates art to life). Moreover, Pater evolves his aesthetic structure, his regenerative artifact, in a manner especially congenial to the twentieth century: the authority of its learning is beyond question and the modesty of its tone is beyond reproach. Even the eclectic form of *Marius*—philosophical romance, historical novel, *journal intime,* prose poem, culture epic, critical essay turned inward and personal—is a dimension of its revelation, and the clarity and narrowness of its resolution are aspects of its acceptability. The fact that it was a prototype of the "new novel" of Joyce, Mann, and Hesse could go unheralded because *Marius the Epicurean* was obviously so much more than an experimental novel: it was an examination of touchable possibilities for the self-renewal of a certain type of distressed modern man.

Pater's remove from the refreshment of Saint Francis of Assisi is almost exactly equidistant in time to Marius' remove from the refreshment of Socrates. As the Greek dispensation had hardened into anarchy of mind and distress of spirit by the time of Marius, so had the Renaissance dispensation, initiated by Saint Francis, hardened into anarchy of mind and distress of spirit by the time of Pater. Marius had found his renaissance-of-spirit in a rediscovery, through the cultural affectiveness of the metaphor of the Incarnation, that mankind need not succumb to "any wholly mechanical and disheartening theory of itself and its conditions," a discovery made possible by his prolonged and disciplined effort to develop "his unclouded receptivity of soul." The equation completes itself: the old Renaissance has run the course of its usefulness as human refreshment, and the anarchy of mind and distress of spirit which characterize the times are both inevitable and prophetic. Man is self-regenerative, and the massive machinery of modern life will ultimately drive him, not to succumb, but to discover an alternative theory of man and his conditions. But his chief hope of discovering this, of reestablishing contact with an "original tendency" of his "genius," is by making "the house ready for the possible guest; the tablet of the mind white and smooth, for whatever divine fingers might choose to write there."

Notes

1. Preface to *Poems* (1853).
2. (New York: Norton, 1962), as indexed. On page 261, Erikson characterizes the "integrity crisis" of the *homo religiosus* as a precocious concern with "questions of how to escape corruption in living and how in death to give meaning to life."
3. See especially the second paragraph of the "Conclusion."
4. Throughout this paragraph, I am indebted to Ernest Lee Tuveson, *The Imagination as a Means of Grace* (Berkeley: University of California Press, 1960), pp. 16-24.
5. *Marius the Epicurean: His Sensations and Ideas,* 2 vols., Library Edition (London: Macmillan 1910), Chap. 2, p. 22. Since the chapters are numbered consecutively throughout, reference to volume number is unnecessary. Subsequent references to *Marius,* given in the text, are to this edition.
6. Critics have tended to praise or chide Pater for his translation of Apuleius, but their remarks, with the partial exception of Knoepflmacher, are mostly beside the point. See Eugene J. Brzenk, "Pater and Apuleius," *CL,* 10 (1958), 55-60; Paul Turner, "Pater and Apuleius," *VS,* 3 (1960), 290-296; U. C. Knoepflmacher, letter to the editor, *VS,* 4 (1961), 411-412.
7. The serious import of dreams has been suggested in Chapter 3 ("Change of Air"), including Aesculapius' faith in dreams.
8. The reader of *Marius* may repeatedly be reminded of Tennyson's concerns and procedures: his fascination with psychic states, his repeated implication that all myth is culturally organic, his creation of *persona*-poems in which perception rather than thematic judgment is the controlling focus. The illuminating analogies between *In Memoriam* and *Marius* would be a fit subject

for a separate essay. The two works deploy very different *personae,* and their narrative curves are different, but several authorial assumptions about how mythic procedures are made credible are common to the two: the protagonists' predisposition to believe; their highly tuned imaginative apparatus, by which they are able to transform one order of reality into a quite different order of reality; and the "miracle of experience" by which the transformation is catalyzed.

Another of several Victorian poems inviting comparison with *Marius* is Browning's *Sordello,* but this too would require a separate essay. The product of a welter of ambitious inexperience, *Sordello* is Browning's effort to write his *Marius:* the focus of Browning's attention is Sordello's "sensations and ideas": Sordello's dilemma is to a considerable degree induced by his Epicurean dimension—the conspicuous attraction of a life of aloofness, detached from action and indulgent in the imaginative pleasures of a privileged observer; Sordello's cultural moment is analogous to Marius'—the age of the troubadours, when the chaotic struggle between Emperor and Pope is at its height, the Renaissance is in the making, the investiture of modern man is at issue, and the emergence of the poet as secular seer is a cultural possibility.

9. The reiterated critical complaint about Marius' *passivity* seems a bit negligent of Pater's *locus:* Marius is not a picaro of the high road, but of the sanctuarial consciousness, and within this particular preserve, he is in a state of constant activity.

10. The Empress Faustina is an early prophecy of *la belle dame.*

11. Cornelius is not "another Flavian," as some commentators suggest (e.g., Richmond Crinkley, *Walter Pater: Humanist* [Lexington: University of Kentucky Press, 1970], p. 154). Indeed, Flavian is pointedly normed downward by the measure of Cornelius. At the marriage games ("Manly Amusement," Chap. 14), from which Cornelius simply and solitarily withdraws, the narrator comments: "And how eagerly, with what a light heart, would Flavian have taken his place in the amphitheatre, among the youth of his own age! with what an appetite for every detail of the entertainment, and its various accessories" (p. 235).

12. "The impression thus forced upon Marius connected itself with a feeling, the exact inverse of that, known to everyone, which seems to say, *You have been just here, just thus, before!*—a feeling, in his case, not reminiscent but prescient of the future, which passed over him afterwards many times, as he came across certain places and people" (Chap. 7, p. 114).

13. The tendency of even the best critics of Pater and his novel to see the critique of Marcus Aurelius turning simply on the abstract nature of his "love of humanity" and "his helpless grief at the death of his child" is clearly reductive of Pater's complex apprehension. See, as an example of this tendency on the part of one of the best critics, Iain Fletcher, *Walter Pater* (London: Longmans, Green, 1959), p. 25.

14. This prescient metaphoric contrast between Cornelius and Marcus Aurelius is made unmistakable in Part III, Chapter 18, " 'The Ceremony of the

Dart.' " Of Marcus Aurelius, pp. 50-51: "Marius, a sympathetic witness of all this, might almost seem to have had a foresight of monasticism itself in the prophetic future. With this mystic companion he [Marcus Aurelius] had gone a step onward out of the merely objective pagan existence. Here was already a master in that craft of self-direction, which was about to play so large a part in the forming of human mind, under the sanction of the Christian Church." Marius notes the contrast between Aurelius' "monastic" *Tristia* and Cornelius' indomitable hope in the full face of evil: "With Cornelius, in fact, it was nothing less than the joy which Dante apprehended in the blessed spirits of the perfect, the outward semblance of which, like a reflex of physical light upon human faces from 'the land which is very far off,' we may trace from Giotto onward to its consummation in the work of Raphael—the serenity, the durable cheerfulness, of those who have been indeed delivered from death" (pp. 52-53).

15. Like Arnold, Pater seems to have seen certain lineaments of John Stuart Mill in the image of Marcus Aurelius—the genius of a severely limited man.

16. There are numerous images suggestive of a metaphoric role-transfer between Marcus Aurelius and a medieval Pontiff.

17. Marius speculates on a theme recurrent in Hardy—the correlation of pain to consciousness: "I wonder, sometimes, in what way man has cajoled himself into the bearing of his burden thus far, seeing how every step in the capacity of apprehension his labour has won for him, from age to age, must needs increase his dejection. It is as if the increase of knowledge were but an increasing revelation of the radical hopelessness of his position" (Chap. 25, p. 182).

18. "The Place of Pater: *Marius The Epicurean,*" in *The Ringers in the Tower* (Chicago: University of Chicago Press, 1971), p. 192.

19. For highly suggestive treatments of Pater and modern poetry, see Frank Kermode, *Romantic Image* (London: Routledge and Paul, 1957), *passim,* and Harold Bloom, *Yeats* (Oxford University Press, 1970), pp. 23-37 *et passim.*

20. The visibility of Keatsian models in various of Arnold's poems is quite another matter.

21. "The Victorianism of Victorian Literature," *NLH,* 6 (1975), 607-627. In this thoughtful, carefully argued, necessarily controversial article, Professor Timko does not refer to Pater.

22. The quotation is from G. H. Hartman, as cited in Timko, p. 614.

13.

Déjà vu Inverted: the Imminent Future in Walter Pater's *Marius the Epicurean*

Marius the Epicurean: His Sensations and Ideas is an extraordinary literary text, an apex-document, a mainliner in the efforts of the nineteenth century to convert itself into literature. In *Marius,* Pater continues to employ with unabated vigor the creative energy, the literary experimentalism, the confrontation of the geniune issue of the modern relevance of modern letters engendered by Carlyle, especially in *Past and Present,* where, according to Emerson, Carlyle converted an era into a style: "Carlyle is the first domestication of the modern system, with its infinity of details, into style." [1]

To some readers, perhaps, Pater's "infinity of details" will seem very different from Carlyle's, and *as details* they are very different. But both authors are working through that "infinity of details" to many of the same monitoring concerns: the character and usability of history, varieties of religious experience, the nature of man and his psycho-cultural linkages, perception and the barriers to reality that one's peculiar conventional heritage can impose upon his consciousness, the mythohistorical imperatives of imaginative literature and the indispensability of literature for casting a "white sunny Light" [2] into the dark spaces of human experience, the im-

periousness for modern man of a subjective affirmation of perceived truth, and thus the special urgency for modern letters to
discover new imaginative structures that will enable the modern
reader to participate experientially in the writer's evolving apprehensions in a way analogous to his own participation in them.
That these are central concerns of both Carlyle and Pater is a fact
not to be disguised by the very different imaginative structures
through which they draw their readers close to their insights-
in-the-making. Both were "rhetoricizing the conspicuous objects"
(another of Emerson's phrases about Carlyle)[3] for England and
Europe, and both had as their object the transformation and salvation of post-Enlightenment man.

Marius the Epicurean embodies a thoroughly new imaginative
structure, and in that respect it represents a clear advance upon
the bold experimentalism of *Past and Present*. Pater has distanced
his style from the strategic rhetorical inflations of Carlyle, from the
florid rotundities of Ruskin, even from the crisp ironic suresnesses of
Arnold; and he has done this largely through imaginative structure. Since his subject is the human understanding in a state of
directed motion, consciousness negotiating history, he creates in
Marius a structure of awareness that carefully dislocates all possibility of a dogmatic center and places the protagonist, the narra-
tor/commentator, and the reader in a state of spiritual community
in that they are all on their own, all fallible, and all engaged (while
the book lasts) in a conscientious effort at personal renewal. Even if
one's private response to the book as literary experience is negative—if he feels, for example, that its experiential world is her-
metically sealed or that its awarenesses are relatively negligible in a
brutal universe—he has simply disqualified himself as a companion
of Marius and his "miniature Boswell" and has confirmed the
book's method. On the other hand, the reader who can willingly
join this company adopts for himself a state of being in which
metamorphosis is the primary expectation and to which personal
inadequacy is a constant threat. Failure—for protagonist, narrator/
commentator, and reader alike—is a persistent possibility: a real
aspect of the book's methodological open-endedness is the ever present danger of collapse. The very genre-evasiveness of the book—
philosophical romance, historical novel, imaginary portrait, *journal*

intime, prose poem, culture epic, critical essay turned inward and personal—disavows even literary-conventional solutions to the problems the book explores.

Between Carlyle's signal to his generation that modern literary relevance requires nothing short of modern man's imaginative self-renewal and Pater's restatement, in *Marius,* of essentially the same theme, there has been an enormous shift in literary strategy. The relativism of the age has thoroughly reconditioned the aesthetic of the age: the participatory structure of Pater's book, prepared for over several decades by the literary transmutations effected by such texts as *In Memoriam, Maud,* and *The Ring and the Book,* provides an unparalleled insight into the ways in which modern man, forced afresh to a state of zero spiritual budgeting by the changed conditions of his culture, can work out for himself a dignified dénouement. Dignified, worthy of his humanness, but not romantically climactic: like Marius, he may have epiphanic moments as his mythic reassurances occasionally inflate, but as those moments are clustering, they are scattering too. At an eclipsed level, the narrative experience formalized in *Marius the Epicurean* is comparable to the narrative results of that spiritual hunger given a moment of explosive epic reality in Tennyson's *Ulysses,* concerning which the following provides a glancing insight:

> I am a part of all that I have met;
> Yet all experience is an arch wherethro'
> Gleams that untravell'd world whose margin fades
> For ever and for ever when I move.
>
> (18-21)

Life as a series or pile of solidifed blocks of experience, of frozen stagings however gratifying, has been dissolved into a renewed perceptual reality in which man is eternally voyaging into new spiritual spaces, is experiencing, with a rapidity that outstrips the inductive consciousness, a perpetual bombardment of deaths and rebirths, is constantly transforming the past, both the personal past and the cultural past, into the future.

All failure to recognize this truth of the human condition, a truth of man's physical as well as his cultural environment, smacks of the stereotypical. Even art itself—at its best the quintessence of man's formal awarenesses—necessarily freezes time and threatens to induce a false perceptual reality. Art frees itself from time when it releases in its *devotées* the capacity to perceive even art *sub specie aeternitatis,* the frozen image being only the most immediately conspicuous dimension of art *(art as artifact),* art's latent capacity to release psychic motion, to trigger inexhaustible possibilities, to make thinking men think (Carlyle) and intelligent men more intelligent (Arnold), being its essential character *(art as an embodiment of the soul's becomings).*

Even Pater's sentence structure in *Marius* forgoes rhetorical neatness in favor of perceptual precision: he allows his sentences to wander from a norm of classical balance in search of the minutely qualified revelation. "The privilege of augury itself, according to tradition, had at one time belonged to his race; and if you can imagine how, once in a way, an impressible boy might have an *inkling,* an inward mystic intimation, of the meaning and consequences of all that, what was implied in it becoming explicit for him, you conceive aright the mind of Marius, in whose house the auspices were still carefully consulted before every undertaking of moment." [4] This sentence is obviously germane to the way history is thematically handled in *Marius,* but it is equally indicative of the apprehensive tone of the book, of how respect for perception weights narrative language. Fairly reflective of the stylistic "feel" of the book, the sentence backs and fills and qualifies until it has made its revelation without any effort to subjugate that revelation to a rhetorical predisposition, a preconceived structural formulation. It is a style so "sincere" that it carefully avoids interposing between the truth with which it deals and the reader's (or the narrator's) consciousness any factitious heightening and distraction.

What is true of the individual consciousness is true also of the historical consciousness. The story of the race and the biography of the individual share a common pattern: "the composite experience of all ages is part of each one of us: to deduct from that experience, to obliterate any part of it . . . is as impossible as to become a little child, or enter again into the womb and be born. But though it is not possible to repress a single phase of that humanity, which,

because we live and move and have our being in the life of humanity, makes us what we are, it is possible to isolate ourselves in our
zeal for it; as we may hark back to some choice space of our own
individual life." [5] History is, therefore, not a "vain antiquaria-
nism," but a discovery of the pattern of the past in the self and a
chief object of man's poetic concerns. To be deep in empirical
introspection, to be radically in touch with one's own "sensations
and ideas," is to be deep in history. The macrocosmic cautions are
thoroughly consistent with this perspective: a monistic fixation on
any phase of human history of and for itself (a singular time-frame,
a special cultural manifestation, an all-consuming thesis) is personally self-destructive in that it divides us against our holistic
selves and diminishes us, just as to be frozen (like the protagonist
in *Maud)* into some moment in personal time would cause psychic
shrinkage.

Marius the Epicurean: His Sensations and Ideas is thus a brilliant
experiment in personal-historical narrative in which Pater draws
the reader deep into *the idea of history* (history's history) through the
precariously balanced creation of a narrator/commentator who
tries to embody in the form of a tale the radical self-awarenesses of
a soul's becomings (or, from the macrocosmic perspective, history
watching itself evolve).[6]

A crucial illustration of just how Pater's precariously balanced
creation works occurs in Book I, Chapter VII, "A Pagan's End."
The subject is the deathbed verse composed by a brilliant young
pagan dying of the plague:

> In the expression of all this Flavian seemed, while making it
> his chief aim to retain the opulent, many-syllabled vocabulary
> of the Latin genius, at some points even to have advanced
> beyond it, in anticipation of wholly new laws of taste as re-
> gards sound, a new range of sound itself. The peculiar resul-
> tant note, associating itself with certain other experiences of
> his, was to Marius like the foretaste of an entirely novel world
> of poetic beauty to come. Flavian had caught, indeed, some-
> thing of the rhyming cadence, the sonorous organ-music of the
> medieval Latin, and therewithal something of its unction and
> mysticity of spirit. There was in his work, along with the last

splendour of the classical language, a touch, almost prophetic, of that transformed life it was to have in the rhyming middle age, just about to dawn. The impression thus forced upon Marius connected itself with a feeling, the exact inverse of that, known to every one, which seems to say, *You have been just here, just thus, before!*—a feeling, in his case, not reminiscent but prescient of the future, which passed over him many times, as he came across certain places and people. It was as if he detected there the process of actual change to a wholly undreamed-of and renewed condition of the human body and soul: as if he saw the heavy yet decrepit old Roman architecture about him, rebuilding on an intrinsically better pattern.

(pp. 113-114)

History as perceived organic metamorphosis (time's sensuous story) is at the center of what is going on here, and Pater's imaginative structure brings us to a precise locus of illuminative understanding: we as reader-witnesses are watching a creator-witness (say Pater) watching the protagonist watching Flavian, a death-resurrection figure through whom time is sensuously, perceptibly evolving. Marius' own role is quintessential, of course, but each witness plays both an individual and a generic role, and each is induced to believe that Flavian's role-playing is both very special and very typical: we are all death-resurrection figures, and the more keenly we witness ourselves, the more keenly attuned we are to that poetic note-catching called prophecy. Through the instrumentality of the book, both as the story of Marius and as an imaginative structure, we, in whatever century, see our past futuristically: we witness both the *what* and the *how* of the making of us and hence the *what* and the *how* of history. Flavian is the inevitable product of the past that needs renewing, and by attempting to get in touch with the original genius of his particular instrument of creativity, language, he releases the new phase of that original genius—releases the future. It is a necessarily specialized process (music renewing music, art art, literature literature, language language) since the process is truly organic, but it is also as large as human nature: "Here, as elsewhere, the power of 'fashion,' as it is called, is but one minor form, slight enough, it may be, yet distinctly symptomatic, of that deeper yearning of human nature toward ideal perfection, which is a continuous force in it; and since in this direction too human nature is limited, such fashions must necessarily reproduce themselves" (Chap. 6, p. 98).

That Pater's metaphors are broadly symptomatic does not obscure the fact that they are highly specialized: his figures are apex-figures, figures at the cutting-edge of spiritual movement, creating, or observing the creation of, the language, literature, art, music, religion (for them, the "culture") of the future. The clarity of what he is doing depends considerably upon this narrowness. Cultural history as such is only the machinery through which, in a literary artifact, he enables his merged historical-personal consciousness to surface and process itself. But it is literature, not history, that we must watch most attentively: how the literary imagination perspects man surviving in time (the spirit negotiating its renewals) is the critic's necessary focus in dealing with *Marius the Epicurean.* It is as literature that the book has an impressive reality: history facilitates mythic apprehension and is thus made usable. Pater might have placed any one of the figures who play a significant part in the book at the center of a myth (Flavian, Marcus Aurelius, Cornelius, Cecilia), but each case would have required a very different tale. He chose Marius, his own imaginary *persona,* for reasons similar to those for which Tennyson chose the *persona* of *In Memoriam*—to make a certain kind of mythic process credible. *Marius,* like Tennyson's *persona,* is a hieratic personality predisposed to a belief that will give him some sense of what lies beyond the world's horizons; he is possessed, furhter, of a finely tuned imagination capable of extrapolating his experiences and of translating one order of experience into another; and he is blessed with a miraculous happening that, at the level of imaginative rather than dogmatic awareness, fully catalyzes him. If any one of these essential ingredients were missing from Marius or from his life-experience, the book's myth would be immeasurably altered. Thus one of the perceptions the book turns on is that an indispensable element in the pattern of this historical-personal consciousness is spiritual fatigue turning to hope and hope eventually turning to belief: human nature, through the instrumentality of individuals weary of their exhausted heritage, believes itself into the future; and its beliefs are most trustworthy when they emerge from a thoroughly empirical observation of one's self and one's time.

The two characters at the center of Pater's exploration of process, his history of history, are his persona *Marius* and the Emperor Marcus Aurelius; and the approximations and divergences of these two characters, the spiritual measurings made possible by their juxtaposition, diversify an admittedly narrow concentration. They relate to each other in doppelgänger fashion, like two halves of an imminent event both personal and historical: "Here, then, under the tame surface of what was meant for a life of business, Marius discovered, welcoming a brother, the spontaneous self-revelation of a soul as delicate as his own,—a soul for which conversation with itself was a necessity of existence. Marius, indeed, had always suspected that the sense of such necessity was a peculiarity of his. But here, certainly, was another, in this respect like himself; and again he seemed to detect the advent of some new or changed spirit into the world, mystic, inward, hardly to be satisfied with that wholly external and objective habit of life, which had been sufficient for the old classic soul" (Chap. 18, pp. 46-47).

Marius and Marcus Aurelius share the fatigue of spirit to which an exhausted past has brought their culture, and they are both bearers of the future. Their spiritual companionship, though limited, is very real: *"Before all things examine into thyself: strive to be at home with thyself!*—Marius, a sympathetic witness to all this, might almost seem to have had a foresight of monasticism itself in the prophetic future. With this mystic companion he had gone a step onward out of the merely objective pagan existence. Here was already a master in that craft of self-direction, which was about to play so large a part in the forming of human mind, under the sanction of the Christian church" (Chap. 18, pp. 50-51). But what they have in common, their pagan fatigue and their keen and delicate techniques of self-awareness and self-direction, is minor relative to the life-apprehensions with which, through them, the past is inducing the fugure.

Marcus Aurelius is the angel of asceticism: *"Abase yourself!* . . . With the ascetic pride that lurks under all Platonism, resultant from its opposition of the seen to the unseen, as falsehood to truth—the imperial Stoic, like his true descendant, the hermit of the middle age, was ready, in no friendly humour, to mock, there in its narrow bed, the corpse which had made so much of itself in life" (Chap. 12, pp. 200-201). The spiritual children of an ascetic Platonism are about to capture the world; and the "reality of the unseen" is about to assert its dominance anew, the spirit once again to be entombed in abstract expectancy. It is the renaissance of the death-wish and very, very real.

Marius, on the other hand, the visual concretist, the uncompromising empiricist, is the embodiment and messenger of Marcus Aurelius' spiritual counterpart in the coming age. To Aurelius' *Tristitia* he opposes an eagerness "to taste and see and touch" (Chap. 12, p. 201); instead of the self-abasement of the future, "Marius felt as if he were face to face, for the first time, with some new knighthood or chivalry, just then coming into the world" (Chap. 10, p. 170); the renaissance that he experiences and bears forward is that of the blithe, graceful, debonair aspect of the original pagan genius translated through the Christian jubilee into a new metaphor of hope: his vision is "of a natural, a scrupulously natural, love, transforming, by some new gift of insight into the truth of human relationships, and under the urgency of some new motive by him so far unfathomable, all the conditions of life. He saw in all its primitive freshness and amid the lively facts of its actual coming into the world, as a reality of experience, that regenerate type of humanity, which, centuries later, Giotto and his successors, down to the best and purest days of the young Raphael, working under conditions very friendly to the imagination, were to conceive as an artistic ideal" (Chap. 22, pp. 109-110). Gradually, as his experience of this wonderful new dispensation of the human spirit deepens, as his psyche becomes fully attuned to its historical correspondences, Marius becomes a witness rather than a prophet of the future:

> The reader may think perhaps, that Marius, who, Epicurean as he was, had his visionary aptitudes, by an inversion of one of Plato's peculiarities with which he was of coure familiar, must have descended, by *foresight*, upon a later age than his own, and anticipated Christian poetry and art as they

came to be under the influence of Saint Francis of Assisi. But if he dreamed on one of those nights of the beautiful house of Cecilia, its lights and flowers, of Cecilia herself moving among the lilies, with an enhanced grace as happens sometimes in healthy dreams, it was indeed hardly an anticipation. He had lighted, by one of the peculiar intellectual good-fortunes of his life, upon a period when, even more than in the days of austere *ascêsis* which had preceded and were to follow it, the church was true for a moment, truer perhaps than she would ever be again, to that element of profound serenity in the soul of her Founder, which reflected the eternal goodwill of God to man, "in whom," according to the oldest version of the angelic message, "He is well-pleased." (Chap. 22, pp. 116-117)

The *déjà vu* inversion through which patterns of historical incipience have been experienced, encapsulated, in the individual are now neutralized in the event: expectation is fulfilled; the future has become for the moment the present; and the *déjà vu's* of another era are implanted in personal-historical time.

Marius the Epicurean, then, is Walter Pater's history of history, his narrative experiment in personal and historical metamorphosis. In evolving his experimental narrative model, he carefully blended the past with the present *(perenniality)* and fact with fiction *(myth);* and he so layered the witnessings of the book's events that it becomes essentially a process of watching and wondering to which nothing (not style, not characterization, not story-line) brings a climactic conclusion. Everything is experientialized: every event, every thought, expectation, "disease of the spirit" is registered on personality, and each of the book's personalities plays a visible role in the historical transformations thus sensuously, tactilely rendered. Indeed, the power of the man and the power of the moment are so totally fused that the issue of cause and effect is thoroughly mooted. At the heart of the book is a firm belief in the organic regeneration of men and their cultures; and that belief is translated into an imaginative structure that enables the reader, during the relatively short time he spends with the book, to participate personally in that regenerative process.

Notes

1. *"Past and Present." Emerson's Complete Works* (London: The Waverley Book Co. Ltd., 1893),XII, 247-248.
2. *Past and Present,* Book III, Chap. XV.
3. *Journals and Miscellaneous Notebooks of Ralph Waldo Emerson,* ed. W. H. Gilman and J. E. Parsons (Cambridge, Mass.: Harvard University Press, 1970), VIII, 408.
4. Walter Pater, *Marius the Epicurean: His Sensations and Ideas* (London: Macmillan, 1910), Book I, Chap. II, p. 16. Future references to the novel are to this edition and are given in the text in parentheses.
5. Walter Pater, *Appreciations* (London: Macmillan, 1910), pp. 223-224.
6. The critical adjustments necessitated by this view of *Marius* are fundamental: the "Marius-Pater" rubric, a staple of criticism of the book, converts to "Marius-Everyman"; the comparisons between *Marius* and such historical novels as *Hypatia, Callista, Pompeii,* and *Fabiola* become essentially irrelevant; the manifest subject of the book ceases to be its central critical concern.
7. The narrator/commentator, though he sees monasticism, with its austere rubric of self-contemplation, projective in Marcus Aurelius, compares him unfavorably even with medieval asceticism since he suffers from *Tristitia,* "which even the monastic moralists had held to be of the nature of deadly sin, akin to the sin of *Desidia* or Inactivity" (Chap. 18, p. 51).

14.

The Dark Space Illumined: A Reading of Hardy's "Poems of 1912-13"

The emergence, finally, of Thomas Hardy as a major modern poet—indeed as one of the conspicuous foundation-figures of modern poetry—has radically changed the rules of Hardy criticism. The slightest suggestion of a patronizing air, evident for so long even among his ardent well-wishers, is simply no longer acceptable. We have all been alerted to abandon critical clichés about Hardy, about his attitudes toward this and that, about the subtlety of his poetic procedures, about the sophistication of his metrics and the significance of his narrative structures—and to observe as attentively as we possibly can what this subtle and innately literary man, this habitual concealer of the tricks of his genuine trade, offers us by way of artistic experience. Hardy is a mainliner in English poetry: he is continuous with Tennyson as the profounder side of Tennyson is continuous with Wordsworth. Hardy employs notably simple but fully adequate literary rituals to release keen and penetrating human awarenesses. Imaginative articulation engenders perception; poetry promotes authentic poise.

The imaginative imperative was so much a part of the literary texture of the nineteenth century that Hardy did not need to credit any single writer with influencing his highly developed realization that modern man, if he would survive with something more than coupling and battening in the wilds of time, must cultivate a strong imaginative sense of reality, a personally functional psychic ambience in which spirituality and rationality can be creatively joined. Like Tennyson, Hardy proceeded poetically through a double persuasion—that the inherited myths of his literary culture were essentially true and that his own awarenesses, however personal, must be so rendered poetically as to induce for them a mythic subtext that would enable the author to render them fully and allow the reader to share with heightened empathy the inner stresses of their *personae*. Thus Hardy's insistence, reiterated throughout his prefaces, that his poems are in "large degree dramatic or personative in conception; and this even where they are not obviously so"; [1] thus, too, his assertion that the concealment of his "art" is one of his persistent practices.[2] Mythic, personative, craft craftily hidden—poetic concepts in no sense esoteric, but also concepts that criticism cannot ignore without falsifying Hardy's character as a modern poet.

The "Poems of 1912-13" are monitored by a mythic subtext that enables the author to gain distance from the complex emotions energized by the sudden death of Emma Gifford Hardy. This mythic subtext provides the imaginative strategy by which the author can conceive of his private responses generically—moves personal emotion to an impersonative plane. The reader in turn, even if he does not consciously identify the mythic subtext, is affected by it in that he can enter into the strategies of coping which have been made imaginatively authentic and accessible through its presence as a substratum in the poems.

Several mythic subtexts were available to Hardy for his elegy,[3] and we can hardly doubt that he carefully considered at least three [4]—Tristram and Iseult, Aeneas and Dido, and Orpheus and Eurydice. The story of the tragically fated lovers of "sunk Lyonesse," widely current in the nineteenth century, was clearly relevant to Hardy's elegy about love and death, and it may have been influential in the poet's careful avoidance of blame in acknowledging "the dark space" of his lovers' recent years together; but even if, in these peculiar circumstances, he could have given literary decorum to the personal use of the myth of Tristram and Iseult, it was ultimately inadequate to the central cohering perception that emerged in Hardy's elegy. It would have required a role-reversal and a dying for love contradicted by both the facts and the fiction of the elegy.

The Aeneid offers more complex and provocative possibilities. Hardy's epigraph is taken from Virgil, he had a pronounced fondness for *The Aeneid (Life,* p. 59), and the note of sadness dominant in the sequence of lyric probings as a whole may be fairly called Virgilian. The narrative involving Aeneas and Dido is, of course, the point of fictive contact, and there are important veiled parallels to Virgil's fiction in Hardy's elegy: the brief fullness of their early love, the dark fate (or destiny) that separated them, the inevitable connection between love and death, the journey to the underworld, the effort at reconciliation beyond the grave.[5] Indeed, there may be in these parallels, over and above the confirmation that Hardy's elegy is mythically conceived, the hint of an explanation (certainly not a judgment, no more than a hint) of what separated Hardy's lovers in the first place—namely, the beloved's refusal to accept the poet-speaker's imperious vocation and the love-suicide consequent upon that refusal. If accepted as an authentic possibility, such a hint resonates throughout the elegy in a most significant way: had he, under the influence of his beloved, abandoned his imperious vocation, had he failed to remain "just the same as when / Our days were a joy, and our paths through flowers" ("After a Journey")—in short, had he died for love—they would both have been abandoned to a conspiracy of silence; and the poetic act, the lyric reconciliation being enacted in this elegy, would have been impossible, itself the victim of a silent and spiritless sterility. Thus the speaker of the elegy as a poet with a poet's imaginative resources becomes a postulate of the incremental procedures in the poems.

The psychological-imaginative division that both requires and promises lyric reconciliation is rather fully sketched in the initiating poem, "The Going." In a narrative/dramatic, colloquial/lyrical voice that orchestrates an interwoven complex of emotions—shock, lamentation, guilt, querulousness, dismay, incredulity, heightened nostalgic retrospection, plaint, and self-enforced resignation—the speaker projects the terms of the action (in a very spe-

cial sense, the plot) [6] upon which the elegy will turn. "Life" had at
one time—more than forty years ago—"unrolled" for the speaker
and the deceased "its very best." For reasons only obliquely hinted
at, they had allowed that moment of incomparable quality to atrophy and die (the first "going") and had failed to seek, through
language ("did . . . not speak," "might have said"), that precious
time's renewal. Now that she has literally "vanished" (the second
"going"), the speaker suddenly fears that all is "past amend / Unchangeable"—that she is now truly gone where he cannot follow,
even "With wing of swallow."

This curiously phrased and strategically placed metaphor
("Where I could not follow / With wing of swallow / To gain one
glimpse of you ever anon!") appears to be a signal to the reader, in
the first stanza of the first lyric, that poetry itself is a primary
theme of the elegy. It may not be a reference to Tennyson's "short
swallow-flights of song" (*In Memoriam,* XLVIII), though it is
tempting to see it as one; but it does seem to be an allusion to the
myth of Philomela and Procne as Swinburne had used the myth in
his dramatic lyric "Itylus" (1866):

> Sister, my sister, O soft light swallow,
>   Though all things feast in the spring's guest-chamber,
>   How hast thou heart to be glad thereof yet?
> For where thou fliest I shall not follow,
>   Till life forget and death remember,
>   Till thou remember and I forget.
>
>   (25-30)

Swinburne's poem, which Hardy certainly knew,[7] has a theme
summed up in the line "The heart's division divideth us" (1. 44);
and though spoken entirely by the nightingale, it characterizes
opposing responses to tragic experience—that of the swallow, "light
as a leaf," and that of the nightingale, "a molten ember." The
several oppositions in Swinburne's poem—remembering/forget-
ting, winter/spring, grief/joy, elegy/jubilee—all have relevance to
"Poems of 1912-13," but the chief common denominators are the
recognitions that a complex response to a tragic event is inevitable

in a genuinely imaginative survivor and that poetic expression rather than poetic silence is the chief hope for spiritual renewal.

"Itylus" is a wholly individual poem, whereas "The Going" is the first in an elegiac series of poems. Hence Hardy's lyric monologue, being prophetic of the narrative curve of the elegy, renders a counterpoint of perceptions relevant to the poems as a coordinated poetic process. Thus the speaker's defeatist sense of self at the end of "The Going"—"I seem but a dead man held on end / To sink down soon"—is set against the overall impact on the reader of his other awarenesses in the poem—the intensity with which he feels his loss, the dramatic vividness of his memory, the acuteness with which he perceives why their great love failed, the highly developed tendency of his imagination to fill "The yawning blankness / Of the perspective" with visual imagery, the very rituals of rhythmic language with which he intones his complex responses. Thus, the *persona* of the elegy is characterized in considerable depth, and the resources with which he will cope with his loss are implicit in his initial responses to that loss.[8]

Recognition that the basic movement of Hardy's elegy is toward imaginative reaffirmation of the power of lyric poetry, coupled with the double-death motif and the central gesture of looking backward, suggests that the primary mythic subtext for Hardy here is the myth of Orpheus and Eurydice.[9] Hardy, of course, was too practiced a concealer of his art to require that a right reading of his lyric sequence be initiated by a recognition of the relevance of this myth to his poetic procedures; and he was sufficiently relativist in his aesthetic perceptions to recognize that a poem might have a long and happy career among an intelligent and appreciative readership even if one of its monitoring perceptions went unrecognized. Further, it is wholly consonant with Hardy's deft poetic procedures that the mythic analogue is implicit rather than explicit,[10] sufficiently insinuated for his purposes by nonmechanical, noninsistent devices such as, in "The Going," the image of the quick vanishing "At the end of the alley of bending boughs," coupled with the motifs of the second death and of the stunned and seemingly inconsolable state of the speaker.[11]

In Hardy's elegy, the quest for a lost spouse has, like T. S. Eliot's use of the myth of Alcestis in *The Cocktail Party,* a psychological center: how the speaker can sort things out and come to "know some liberty" from a certain burden of the past is the chief concern of the elegy. Like Eliot, too, Hardy focuses so particularly on the resurrection of the dead through memory that the speech of the Unidentified Guest in *The Cocktail Party* reads almost like a gloss on the "Poems of 1912-13":

> *Guest:* Ah, but we die to each other daily.
> What we know of other people
> Is only our memory of the moments
> During which we knew them.
> (1, 3, 23-26) [12]

This being the chief concern of his elegy, Hardy re-orders the Orphic fiction: the second death of Eurydice comes at the moment when Orpheus has almost succeeded in bringing her back to the land of the living; the speaker in Hardy's lyric sequence makes his journey to the land of the dead long after the second death of his beloved in an effort to overleap "the dark space" of the more immediate past and "to seek / That time's renewal" which lies visible but unrecaptured in a yet deeper past. Thus one valid formulation of what the poet is attempting to do suggests patternings that were generic in the nineteenth century: like various imaginative efforts of Scott, Wordsworth, Carlyle, Tennyson, George Eliot, Ruskin, and Matthew Arnold, for example, Hardy's elegy stages an imaginative process by which an intermediate time of "derision" is transcended and a time "forty years since" [13] is restored in all its affective luminosity, a spot of personal time of incomparable quality.

In this imaginative process, "After a Journey" is the transformational center—the dramatic/lyric experience by which a response primarily stressful is turned toward a primarily affirmative response. Throughout the elegy, the speaker's consciousness is in a state of dynamic evolution, impelled by the motion of quest. Each of the lyrics preceding "After a Journey" embodies a strategy of that consciousness in coping with the complex emotions confronting it—grief, guilt, confusion, generosity, half-remembered joy, painful honesty, and so forth. The speaker, in an effort to place his living consciousness in a satisfying relationship to the dead, enacts various rituals of language—addresses her directly, refers to her in the third person, speaks of her "as one who was not," sets up dialogues with her, imagines her as soliloquizing in varying voices of peremptoriness, bustling hauteur, matter-of-factness, and haunting generosity:

> Yes, I companion him to places
>   Only dreamers know,
> Where the shy hares print long paces,
>   Where the night rooks go;
> Into old aisles where the past is all to him,
>   Close as his shade can do.
>   ("The Haunter")

These experiments in transformation of the spirit through the rituals of language reflect one of the most complex concerns of the elegy: the first death, or "going," was the result of a failure in communication and verbal renewal ("The Going"); the shock of the second death is greatly magnified by the realization that the remedy of communication is now, in one sense, lost ("The Going"); the failure of the voices of both the living and the dead to penetrate the consciousness of each other is a reiterated postulate of the elegy ("The Voice" *et passim*); [14] and the enveloping awareness of these dramatic lyrics as a whole is the self-conscious theme that poetry (dramatic/lyric language) enables the memory to purify itself and to salvage for the future the authentic, restorative past.

The journey to the land of the dead as a painful but unavoidable necessity is forced upon the speaker both by his imperious need to resolve his intense conflict of memories ("The Voice") and his recognition that his efforts thus far have ended in failure, resulting in a resurgent negativism ("His Visitor") or a dry satiric irony ("A Circular"). On the other hand, his recognition of the needs for the journey fills him with such intense anxiety that he is driven to an inflated questioning of the very reality of the past—its people and its places. He is approaching the crisis-point, and the precariousness of the possible outcome drives him to psychic rituals of half-denial, false but wholly understandable:

> Why go to Saint-Juliot? What's Juliot to me?
>   Some strange necromancy
>   But charmed me to fancy
> That much of my life claims the spot as its key.
> . . . .
> Does there even a place like Saint-Juliot exist?
>   Or a Vallency Valley
>   With stream and leafed alley,
> Or Beeny, or Bos with its flounce flinging mist?
>   ("A Dream or No")

An aspect of the Orpheus myth found in Plato's *Symposium* seems to be adapted to "After a Journey." Plato contrasts Alcestis' love for Admetus with Orpheus' love for Eurydice:

> Alcestis' sacrifice for her husband was given as an illustration of a lover willing to die for her beloved. But not so Orpheus; unlike Alcestis he did not dare to die for love. Instead, according to Plato's interlocutor Phaedrus, he contrived to enter Hades alive, a mere lyre player, and the God punished Orpheus by presenting him with a phantom in place of his wife. (Mayerson, p. 272)

Hardy's speaker, like Orpheus in this critical version, has also refused to die for love at the first going, perhaps for reasons suggested above; and at the second going, the nature of his love has become so obscured by the intervening past that dying for love is simply not an option. So it is a phantom—a "voiceless ghost," a "thin ghost"—that he comes to "view" and "frailly follow." But the speaker's sudden recognition of the validity of his beloved's voiceless answer suggests that they have long been victims of "misconceits" and "divisions dire and wry," of "horrid shows" and "long-drawn days of blight" ("The Spell of the Rose") for want of a language with which to release them from the hellish prisons of themselves—that like Alcestis they have suffered from an inability to speak until they will have paid off their debts to the gods of the underworld (Mayerson, p. 134). The question is the persistent one:

> What have you now found to say of our past—
>   Scanned across the dark space wherein I have lacked you?
> Summer gave us sweets, but autumn wrought division?
>   Things were not lastly as firstly well
>   With us twain, you tell?
> But all's closed now, despite Time's derision.
>
> ("After a Journey")

The answer is experiential, rather than expository; she re-immerses him in the unmediated past, shows him the secret of re-initiation, enables him to become afresh "just the same as when / Our days were a joy, and our paths through flowers."

> I see what you are doing: you are leading me on
>   To the spots we knew when we haunted here together,
> The waterfall, above which the mist-bow shone
>   At the then fair hour in the then fair weather,
> And the cave just under, with a voice still so hollow
>   That it seems to call out to me from forty years ago,
>   When you were all aglow.

The speaker is now ready for the third and succeeding deaths ("Soon you will have, Dear, to vanish from me, / For the stars close their shutters and the dawn whitens hazily"); for while there is "the dark space," there is also the dawn, and at the imaginative level of mythic apprehension, time has been transcended and love's renewal realized.[15]

Thus, "After a Journey" accomplishes its complex functions with amazing brevity. It orchestrates the historical (Hardy did make the journey), the mythic (the speaker again assumes Orphic lineaments), and the psychological (the landscape is that of the mind, and the drama enacted an internal one). It is the deceased beloved who plays for him the Virgilian role of guide and instructress. It is through her that memory is purified and the original glow of affection renewed.

The poems following "After a Journey" are all deeply affected by the revelation achieved there. "A Death-Day Recalled" returns to the day of the second "going" and asks with a detached but intense lyricism a conventional elegiac question in which the conceit of the question is the implicit answer: Why didn't places in nature commemorate the passing of one who loved them so? The answer—that poets celebrate places—is then orchestrated in the next four poems, in which places magnified by the lovers in the springtime of their love are jubilated—Beeny Cliff, Castle Boterel, the Three Towns, the river Hoe, Boterel Hill, "that shagged and shaly / Atlantic spot"—and the speaker makes a forthright confession of the joys of memory / myth / metaphor:

> one there is to whom these things,
> That nobody else's mind calls back,
> Have a savour that scenes in being lack,
> And a presence more than the actual brings.
>
> ("Places")

"The Spell of the Rose," an allegory of renewed fidelity, returns the sequence to a latter-day domestic frame but imagines the deceased in generous terms attempting to " 'mend these miseries' " and resting in the faith that the "mis-vision" has been "couched." In the last two poems—"St. Launce's Revisited" and "Where the Picnic Was"—another kind of acceptance is emphasized and thereby a possible confusion of awarenesses avoided. Although at one level the elegy rises to an imaginative inflation of memory / myth / metaphor, the speaker is very careful not to let the myth harden into fact: all of those associated with that wonderful spot of personal time are "banished / Ever into nought!" ("St. Launce's Revisited"), and that special "one" "has shut her eyes / For evermore" ("Where the Picnic Was"). Thus, the poet carefully avoids a mistranslation of his basic perception. There is an authentic sort of classical immortality apprehended in the elegy—the immortality of personal memory among the living; and this is given a heightened and endlessly extended reality if, as here, the deceased has the good fortune to "immortalized" by a poet. And although few readers would be inclined to strip the elegy of such pleasing, if conventional, acceptances, these do not constitute the central awareness of "Poems of 1912-13."

Hardy's unwavering concern in his elegy is with the living rather than the dead. The central conflict persisting painfully beyond death is the speaker's conflict; a reconciliation of warring memories is his desperately felt need. He achieves this reconciliation through poetry—through a relentless probing in ritualistic langauge (lyric, dramatic, meditative, elegiac) of the coordinates of experience and a rediscovery, through purified memory, of a lost past (in this case a lost paradise) not adulterated by the intervening dark spaces of blighted years, but illumined and magnified through the mythic archetypes in whose company it belongs. Thus the speaker can finally accept "Quite readily" the "burnt circle" of a literally matter-of-fact mortality, can forego a literally matter-of-fact immortality. And he can do this because through lyric / dramatic poetry —through the literary text entitled "Poems of 1912-13"—he and his beloved have gained access to the springtide world of Tristram and Iseult, Aeneas and Dido, Orpheus and Eurydice, Alcestis and Admetus, Tithonus and Aurora, where, like light-hearted gods together, they look down upon, as if "in a nether sky," "the opal and the sapphire of that wandering western sea"!

Notes

1. Preface to *Wessex Poems and Other Verses* in *Complete Poems of Thomas Hardy*, ed. James Gibson (New York: Macmillan, 1976), p. 6. All subsequent references to the poems are to this edition.
2. Hardy strove after "the simplicity of the highest cunning" that he found in the Bible narratives—watchful though disguised. See *The Life of Thomas Hardy* (New York: Macmillan, 1962), p. 170.
3. I use the term *elegy* because I perceive the "Poems of 1912-13" as a carefully integrated poetic process rather than a poetic bundling. The final number of lyrics might have been different, as might the poetic texts themselves, had Hardy chosen to make them so; but after some alterations, he left them as we have them in the collected poems. Thus they provide our only dependable access to the poet's central apprehensions.
4. As will be shown below, the myth of Tithonus and Aurora is an aspect of the

author's consciousness in the elegiac resolution; but, judged by the elegy itself, it seems to offer less of a mythic envelope than the others.

5. Tom Paulin's assertion that "Aeneas's journey to the underworld in book six is one of the inspirations behind the 'Poems of 1912-13' " is not sufficiently pointed and discriminating. See *Thomas Hardy: The Poetry of Perception* (Totowa, New Jersey: Rowman and Littlefield, 1975), p. 49.

6. "Plot" as an organic aspect of lyric poetry is persistently reenforced throughout the nineteenth century—from *Lyrical Ballads* onward—and is part of the personative tradition in which all the major Victorian poets worked and which Hardy both inherited and welcomed.

7. There are numerous references to Swinburne in the *Life,* several of them based on intimate personal contact between the two poets. Hardy memorialized Swinburne in "A Singer Asleep," recalling the excitement of reading *Poems and Ballads* (1866) "with a quick glad surprise / New words, in classic guise," and he repeatedly identified with Swinburne as the other writer of his own generation dealt with most brutally by the critics.

8. There is full poetic precedent for what Hardy is doing here in the opening section of *Maud:* everything the speaker in Tennyson's poem explicitly tells us about himself is dislocated by what the quality of the verses he recites tells us too, for in them we can clearly perceive the imaginative resources—visual intensity, spiritual engagement temporarily inverted, a keenly functional lyrical/dramatic imagination—by which he is likely to redeem both his past and his present. There are also several valid analogies between *In Memoriam* and "Poems of 1912-13." They were written alike—at various times and under pressure of differing moods. Both Tennyson and Hardy placed a very high premium on psychological and imaginative sincerity, allowing the individual lyrics to emerge out of authentic moments (natural structures) of "vision" (memory, fantasy, analogy, dream, visual reconstruction, and so forth) unforced by a conventionally imposed ordering. Of both *In Memoriam* and "Poems of 1912-13," it is fair to say that the poets, though they recognized a severe obligation to place every syllable within a well-wrought poetic context, trusted their imaginative intuitions (and those of their readers) in the matter of the valid narrative drift of the sequences as a whole. And in all three instances *(In Memoriam, Maud,* "Poems of 1912-13") the poet apparently assumed that the official ordering—the narrative curve the lyric experiences have in the final version—is authentic and meaningful rather than rigid and mechanical.

9. My perspectives on this myth owe a debt to Philip Mayerson, *Classical Mythology in Literature, Art, and Music* (Waltham, Mass.: Xerox College Publishing, 1971), pp. 270-279 *et passim.*

10. James R. Kincaid sees such an implicit analogue in Hardy's "Hap": "There can be no Promethus, he says, since there is no tormentor." See " 'Why Unblooms the Best Hope?' Victorian Narrative Forms and the Explanation of Calamity," *VN,* no. 53 (Spring 1978), p. 1.

11. The cluster of images at this point in "The Going" suggests a painter's view

of the scene from which Eurydice has just disappeared: "Till in the darkening dankness / The yawning blankness / Of the perspective sickens me!"

12. The text is that of *The Burns Mantle Best Plays of 1949-1950,* ed. John Chap-
man (New York: Dodd, Mead, 1950).

13. Each of the authors cited rings some variation on the time-frame, of course.
Silas Marner's recovery of a past, despite the sharp differences in the fictions,
seems especially germane to Hardy's perspectives.

14. There is no contradiction here of the classical law of the netherworld that
"only the voice could penetrate the realm of the departed" (Mayerson, p.
274): these dramatic lyrics are surfacings within the psyche of the speaker
and reflect formally sequential impetuses of that psyche.

15. There seems to be here an incorporation and redesign of the myth of
Tithonus and Aurora. The speaker has broken through the mortality/im-
mortality syndrome and is reconciled to the quotidian rhythms of darkness
and dawn. He has again recognized and named his personal continuity and
integrity and has accepted, at the imaginative level, the eternally reenacted
death-rebirth of his beloved. The "thin ghost" of "After a Journey" then
becomes the phantom of "The Phantom Horsewoman" in yet another
Tithonus-Aurora vignette. Here the more traditional metaphors of age versus
agelessness are used:

> And though, toil-tried,
> He withers daily,
> Time touches her not.

On the other hand, this "sweet soft scene" out of the cradle of the past has
become, through "his own figuring," more "Warm, real, and keen" even than
the present day; and in his mind's eye he takes it with him everywhere "As if
on the air / It were drawn rose-bright." Thus, the "ghost-girl-rider" has become, through imaginative translation, an aurora-figure; and having made
the imaginative conversion, the Tithonus-protagonist of the little fiction
lives, not with the pain of his own very real mortality, but with the vivid,
happy memory/myth ("In his rapt thought") of natural beauty and vitality
personally perpetuated.

15.

Thomas Hardy's "chronicle-piece" in "play-shape": An Essay in Literary Conceptualization

Any aesthetic theoriest working with the literary canon of Thomas Hardy must ultimately deal with the place in that canon of *The Dynasts*. It was, after all, the chief fruit of Hardy's imaginative effort—the subject that haunted him longest, on which he worked most elaborately and conscientiously, for which he created his most distinctive and complex literary structure, and in which he had most faith. In *The Dynasts,* Hardy tells us, he took as his shaping motive "the modern expression of a modern outlook" ("Preface," xxv),[1] and the ramifications of that assertion are endlessly fascinating. The very ordering of Hardy's phrases, considered in terms of their date (1903) against the background/foreground of the literary experience of the nineteenth and twentieth centuries, sends out a signal of the utmost literary importance: the first consideration is aesthetic rather than ideological, structural rather than thematic. As an artist engaged in supplying a rationale, for himself as for his readers, of his chief work, Hardy placed primary emphasis on literary form, imaginative structure, aesthetic procedure. It is an emphasis that critics have been reluctant to allow Hardy, and thus both its specific and general meanings need to be

310

examined in detail and with the critical attitude that Hardy is to be taken very seriously.

Hardy's own thoughts about this great new literary adventure are rendered with a deep and resonant profundity (though in a characteristically modest and understated manner) in the brief preface written on the eve of the publication of Part First. This preface requires very careful watching, so heavily weighted and precisely turned are its dozen brief paragraphs. For purposes of the present effort at literary conceptualization, it is indispensable to note that all of the issues raised in the preface either have a *prima facie* aesthetic center or dissolve into a principle that is primarily aesthetic.

The preface begins with a one-sentence paragraph stating that the primary aesthetic character of the piece is "Spectacle," a dramatic category for which Aristotle held no great brief but one that Hardy found indispensable to his modern imaginative expression.[2] The visual imagination, the "authority of the eye," had become a dominant assumption of modern aesthetics and certainly could not be ignored in a simulated drama intended for "mental performance" in which the poet's powers of visual creation would be crucial. Designation of the piece as "in the likeness of a Drama"—rather than simply a drama—suggests further departure from strict Aristotelian principles but makes careful reservation for the piece of a strictly literary character, however idiosyncratic. Thus, while Hardy would save the piece from irrelevant critical tests, he would save it too from irrelevant "historical" tests, tests other than strictly literary tests. The tragic aspect so central to *The Dynasts* ("Great Historical Calamity") absorbs the drama's character as Spectacle and is not to be measured by strict rules of tragedy of character; but it does have a genuine tragic center since the calamity itself was "artificially brought about," need not have been.

Paragraph 2 tells us some very important truths about the character of Hardy's involvement in this "matter of Napoleon." Although he has certainly had to work his subject up like a research historian, all his data have been converted to a keen sense of personal understanding more penetrating than intellective understanding. His feelings about the subject have a strong "tribal" aspect—he grew up amid tales of a time and events vividly remembered and repeatedly told by the grandfathers of his generation whose existences were actually touched by the Napoleonic matter on a day-to-day basis; their very home-lives moved in a Napoleonic medium. For them the matter had a geography of mind and of place, specific times and tensions. This tribal feeling got deep into family (Captain Hardy, "Nelson's flag-captain at Trafalgar") and, coupled with the mystique of having been both at the red heart of great affairs and in tribal jeopardy, gave an incomparable species of imaginative authority to a tribal spokesman qualified to give literary permanence to oral traditions in imminent danger of being lost to the human record. That tribal spokesman was Thomas Hardy, Wessex man and man of letters, too.

In paragraph 3, this tribal element undergoes enlargement and de-personalization. *The Trumpet Major* (1880) was an early and fragmentary rendering of this tribal fascination, but it suffered from the lack (through the author's then-deficiencies) of four essential ingredients now thought to be adequately reflected in *The Dynasts:* an adequate plan (a sufficient literary structure); adequate knowledge (a carefully researched understanding of this "vast international tragedy"); adequate opportunity (freedom from the burdens of novel-writing); and adequate motive. The motive is an English motive (to "re-embody the features of [English] influence [and action] in their true proportion") and hence a national motive. This movement from a tribal to a national motive is analogous to the movement from ballads to epics, from individual tragic laments to a literary celebration of genuine epic proportions. And this new definition of motive clearly associates *The Dynasts* with the traditional nationalism or national pride of the inherited epic. There is no jingoism in his "Englishing" of the Napoleonic war: England's role as a manipulator and inept but persistent purchaser of Europe's dynastic alliances is handled with unmistakable ironic deflation.

The rather elaborate claims to historical fidelity in paragraph 4 lead to some firm insights into the imaginative assumptions out of which the literary procedures embodied in the poem evolve. What Hardy has attempted to do is create the illusion of a densely textured fabric of historical contemporaneity, and to do this, he has drawn upon every known resource: he has recovered bits of actual language, visited some of the settings where contentions ran their course, had chats with pensioners, tried to establish from among the "authorities" an authentic imitation of the way the *dramatis personae* actually perceived themselves and their ambience. He clearly would have spared no labor in providing as factual a version of the relevant persons and events as possible. He was as concerned with the *Wahrheit,* the literal truth, of his piece as were, for example, Tennyson in *In Memoriam* and Browning in *The Ring and the Book.*

But also like Tennyson and Browning, Hardy was concerned with the *Dichtung* too, with an order of truth created by the poet out of the raw data of a so-called literal historicism. Between *The Dynasts* as *Wahrheit* (literal historical truth) and *The Dynasts* as *Dichtung* (imaginative mythohistorical perception) stands a poet who believes that truly significant patterns are to be discovered, not in fantasies, but in conscientiously reconstructed approximations of truth, the more literal the more usable by an authentic imagination dedicated to perceiving rather than reshuffling reality. For a poet like Hardy (for a poem like *The Dynasts),* perception (how men suppose and state fact) is a matter of ever widening significance: how we the reader-spectators perceive him the author patterning them the principals perceiving what is happening to them and their world of 1805-1815 is the source of the aesthetic dynamism of the piece as a whole—its humor, its pathos, its irony, and its awesome terror. But the transformational magic by which historical truth (illusion) is converted to mythohistorical truth (truth saved from repetitive illusion by being released into the timelessness and spacelessness of a universalizing consciousness) depends upon the literalness, however illusionary, of the historical truth dealt with.

Paragraphs 5 and 6 take up the crucial matter of the Spirit machinery of *The Dynasts.* Upon one's full and implicit understanding of this aspect of the poem's literary procedure depends his capacity to deal with Hardy's imaginative apprehensions at any level of genuine sophistication. The Spirits are "impersonated abstractions," "contrivances of the fancy merely." It is chiefly hoped that "they *and their utterances* may have dramatic plausibility" (emphasis added) under the Coleridgean rubric of "a willing suspension of disbelief." They are not, like earlier mythologies, channels of causation; and the degree to which they are successful is proportionate to their capacity as imaginative metaphors to engender imaginative awareness.

The monism of the piece, centered in the metaphor of the Immanent Will, is an assumption, not of the author, but of the culture addressed ("this twentieth century") and is an index to the difference between *The Dynasts* as history and as literary, experiential processing of mythohistoricism: the poem constitutes history converted to permanent imaginative relevance through literature. Hardy has carefully enabled the poem as a total perceptual process to be monitored by twentieth-century monism, not by late Christian theism or by early pagan polytheism. Hence even the Immanent Will is a cultural metaphor, in no sense an authorially endorsed doctrine, and has only a literary function (metaphoric, imaginative) in this "likeness of a Drama." Against this central metaphor of cultural/perceptual monism is in turn counterpointed the cultural/perceptual pluralism of the several spectator-Spirits, also metaphors and also aspects of the imaginative procedure of the piece, a procedure sustained by resonant metaphors without equation with authorial belief.

Pities "approximates to 'the Universal Sympathy of human nature—the spectator idealised' [Schlegel] of the Greek Chorus"—is "impressionable," "inconsistent," "sway[ed] hither and thither" by events. Years "approximates to the passionless insight of the Ages." The *approximations* to which Hardy repeatedly refers presumably relate to Pities and Years as metaphors, since the ideas they impersonate are clear enough; hence Hardy is undercutting excessive and rigid demands made on them as actors or impersonators and insisting that their fluidity of performance is an important dimension of his own attitude toward the workings of such imaginative machinery. The experiential freedom thus awarded them dissuades the reader from imposing on them rigid allegorical equivalencies that have an essentially ideological rather than an imaginative rooting. Thus viewed, *The Dynasts* is *in its length and breadth* to be looked upon as a literary rather than an intellectual structure: it functions within a firm design, but its coordinates are not syllogistically drawn. The literary structure evolves by such devices as "the scheme of contrasted Choruses and other conventions of this external feature"; but it develops incrementally through hundreds of other approximations and contrasts too; and there is a great tonal difference between a "contrast" and a dialectic, as there is between an "approximation" and an equivalence. Thus the very form of *The Dynasts* dissolves rigidity and implicitly bombards the habitual human tendency prematurely to solidify perception.

In Paragraphs 7 and 8, Hardy again insists on the special character of *The Dynasts* as Spectacle ("a panoramic show like the present"), but he insists unequivocally, too, on the role of the reader-spectator as imaginative co-creator of the piece: the reader-spectator must complete the action and make it intelligible with "supplementary scenes of the imagination"; and he must "combine the scenes into an artistic unity." Hardy's design of *The Dynasts* as a reader-participatory structure is an aspect of its "modern expression": like Tennyson, Browning, Arnold, and Swinburne, Hardy had helped to shape the new experiential poetry in which author and reader occupy analogous relationships to the created work from which the author has consciously withdrawn as mediator or meaning. And although he cites the authority of Aeschylus, Hardy seems to call upon the modern aesthetic sophistication requisite to the proper functioning of such reader-participatory structures: if "the mental spectator [is] unwilling or unable" to participate along the co-creative lines indicated, then the work as designed "becomes in his individual case unsuitable."

Just what kinds of responsibilities is Hardy asking the reader to assume? First, the richness of the imaginative experience provided by *The Dynasts* will depend to a degree upon the reader's understanding of Napoleon and his career in Europe. Much of the bedrock history the poem itself provides, but this is subject to endless supplementary reenforcement, with ever increasing richness of response, and can be considered trustworthy but, as actually provided in the poem, highly selective. Each reader will bring a different degree of understanding of the Napoleonic era to his first reading of *The Dynasts,* as each playgoer had his peculiar level of knowledge of the stories used by the Greek tragedians; but the authorial assumption is the same in both cases. Ignorance is inadequate as a guide to aesthetic experience: the more you know, the more likely you are to understand what is being enacted before your mind.

Second, Hardy has devoted years to the invention of an appropriate literary structure for his "Iliad of Europe," and the "chronicle-piece" in "play-shape" was a delicately devised machinery of the imagination designed to give "modern expression to a modern outlook."[3] He had finally called it an "Epic-Drama," frankly combining in his structure the examples of Homer and Aeschylus and the theories and evaluations of Aristotle. The individualizing marks of *The Dynasts* as a literary procedure are the dramatic multiplicity consequent upon the extraordinary number of characters and scenes and the sense of perspective, real or illusionary, resulting from the use of the Spirit Intelligences as spectators-in-residence. It is a procedure meticulously in place, but dependent too for its proper functioning upon a quality of looseness and fluidity—upon what one might call a "good read." [4] Hence, Hardy's abiding principle that art properly conceals art is operative in a general way here as elsewhere. On the other hand, it would have been coy on Hardy's part to deny the obvious about *The Dynasts:* it is a thoroughly complex and sophisticated literary procedure to which the reader must bring, besides knowledge of its subject matter, large experience of literary procedure itself, including some sophisticated thoughts about how cultural ambience and literary procedure condition and shape each other.

Finally, Hardy would have to expect the reader-spectator to bring to *The Dynasts* a large experience of human nature, especially a knowledge of the sort taught by his own stories in prose and verse—rituals of role-playing and self-deception, ironic discrepancies between reality and perceptions of reality, the wasted sincerity of many people's lives, the hardly thinkable but terrifying intimation that, by simply removing the backdrop of our enclosed reality, we would be faced with absolute nothingness. This last begins to touch upon the mad fringes of the poem's awarenesses, but Hardy's generation had indeed begun anew, as Aeschylus' generation had begun thousands of years ago, to be perplexed by "Riddles of Death Thebes never knew."

Hardy concludes his preface (paragraphs 9-12) with some remarks about the formal peculiarities of his Epic-Drama. He insists
that the fact that it is intended "simply for mental performance"
does not dissociate it from the finest tradition of serious drama in
that mental performance has become increasingly serious drama's
manner of functioning with a modern readership, while at the
same time he insists that the form of his piece is *sui generis*—a form
without brief definition and resembling a play only superficially.
And then he gives a central explanation as to why he evolved his
special form for *The Dynasts*. The basic motive was Hardy's sense of
the atmosphere, the spiritual ambience, of his time:

> the meditative world is older, more invidious, more nervous,
> more quizzical, than it once was, and being unhappily per-
> plexed by—
> Riddles of Death Thebes never knew,
> may be less ready and less able than Hellas and old England
> were to look through the insistent, and often grotesque, sub-
> stance at the thing signified.

This cultural apprehension is counterpointed through the literary
memory against recollections of the "triumphs of the Hellenic and
Elizabethan theatre in exhibiting scenes laid 'far in the Unapparent,' " with the inevitable creator-question as to "why they
should not be repeated." They are, in a sense, repeated in *The
Dynasts*, but with the mutations necessary to accommodate them to
the spiritual/imaginative needs of the modern "meditative world"
as Hardy perceived it. It is clear from these final paragraphs that
Hardy hoped by means of this unique design to incline the twentieth-century reader, despite his spiritual disinclinations or in-
capacities to do so, "to look through the insistent, and often
grotesque, substance, at the thing signified."

The Fore Scene, with its initial dramatization of the inhabitants
of the Overworld, brings us directly into the dress-circle of the
world-theater in which we as reader-spectators are going to watch
these spirit-spectators watching hundreds of men and women a
century since, in an archetypal fiction, involved in their own rituals
of perception/misapprehension. The reader-spectator's poetic faith

is given its classic test in this phase of the total literary experience, where the principles of the preface are put into dramatic motion: he is asked to suspend disbelief, to observe what emerges with heightened imaginative attentiveness, and to accept the promise that his own destiny will, through this extraordinary machinery of consciousness-raising, be made somewhat clearer to him. The fact that these Spirit Intelligences (really temperamentally distinctive personalities) represent diverse readings of life, are persistently fascinated with "the Immanent Will and Its Designs," and bear witness to the crucible of human experience represented by Napoleon and his Titanic wrench of modern Europe, endears them to twentieth-century readers since the readers too are possessed of a cultural positivism that demands knowledge of large and small alike. Moreover, the Spirits seem likely to make this whole literary adventure more interesting: there is just enough edge to their perceptual contentiousness to make the spectacle promising, and they have some fantastic powers of trajection, visualization, and telescoping Time that appeal to a science-fiction mentality eager to cut through ponderousness and start afresh. Moreover, when the "General Chorus of the Intelligences" brings its music of the spheres to a harmonious crescendo at the end of the Fore Scene, it formulates a perceptual ambition and tentativeness that are wholly sympathetic to the ambition and tentativeness of the mythicist poet-designer and hence to his aspirations for the transformational experiences of the reader-spectator:

> We'll close up Time, as a bird its van,
> We'll traverse Space, as spirits can,
> Link pulses severed by leagues and years,
> So that the far-off Consequence appears
> Prompt at the heel of foregone Cause.—
> The PRIME, that willed ere wareness was,
> Whose Brain perchance is Space, whose Thought its laws,
> Which we as threads and streams discern,
> We may but muse on, never learn.

The After Scene in the Overworld that balances the Fore Scene and rounds out the literary experience of *The Dynasts* is designed to tease the consciousness of the reader-spectator toward affirmations that everything to which he has been witness contradicts. Like Pities and Years, he has watched close-up and relentlessly coordinates of human chaos, and like Pities and Years he would eagerly affirm an alternative solution to what accretes as cosmic madness—beautiful, patterned, terrifying. Indeed, so deeply affected is Pities by what he has seen that he rises in desperation to a magnificent lyric celebration of benevolence that is moving to all who hear it—a glorious modern "Magnificat." Even Years is triggered into a memory-voyage that touches a time in his own innocent past that corresponds to the benevolent inflations of Pities. But experience of the Epic-Drama itself has not changed Years' mind, though it has induced in him inflations of consciousness too, images of a

> web Enorm
> Whose furthest hem and selvage may extend
> To where the roars and plashings of the flames
> Of earth-invisible suns swell noisily,
> And onwards into ghastly gulfs of sky,
> Where hideous presences churn through the dark—
> Monsters of magnitude without a shape,
> Hanging amid deep wells of nothingness.

These wild, primitive, inhuman possibilities constitute one "insistent" and "grotesque" variation on the incomprehensibility of which "the flimsy riband" of war with Napoleon is another. But the psychic state finally induced is that of a penetrating sense of awe, from which Sinister is finally omitted and about which Ironic utters a summary deflation:

> As once a Greek asked, I would fain ask too,
> Who knows if all the Spectacle be true,
> Or an illusion of the gods (the Will,
> To wit) some hocus-pocus to fulfil?

For their parts, Years and Pities, who have become cosmic comrades-in-arms during the poetic process, reaffirm their initial positions, though with deepened awarenesses. They face off like

Experience and Innocence still, one with an "eternally" won detachment, the other with a lyric ardor for reconciliation that will finally convert all this incomprehensibility into consciously designed benevolence. Despite their moments of impersonator-bickering, the Spirits ultimately come to poise as bearers, not of arguments, but of states of being, as archetypes of awareness that are thrown into contention (complicate the play) whenever we "muse on, never learn" the true meaning of our lives in our limitless universe.

Hardy has disturbed the balance of the Spirits as simple ideologues by allowing them to approximate, in their dealings with each other and in their reactions to situations, personalities too. That there is a good deal of playfulness about them is clear from the way in which they use their gifts of preternatural awareness to twit various characters, including Napoleon, to remind them that their inner-most anxieties and their outer-most pretensions are in fact transparent. It is not always clear as to whether a Spirit has intruded or only appeared to be the cause of psychic surfacings. But ultimately it does not strictly matter: Hardy has not created a full-scale machinery to reveal varieties of spiritualism; he has simply given his Spirit-impersonators enough elbow room to make them interesting as characters through their ability to play games and, in their playfulness, avoid questions of metaphysical consistency.

Likewise, the critic can simply oversophisticate Hardy's intention in the series of transparencies with which *The Dynasts* is punctuated.[5] There is a touch of science fiction about the way in which Years, whose gift it is to visualize the mode, depletes his battery in the process, but the science and the fiction are put to serious perceptual uses: Experience is attempting, fruitlessly enough, to instruct Innocence in the *vrai verité* of scientific reality. Such visualization of the mode is also a painterly act, and in these visualizations Years shares a most crucial function with the poet-designer of the scene-paintings and dumb shows (motion-paintings)—exhibition of the authority of the eye as a primary instrument of imaginative reality. Pities, unlike Years, is a conceptualist rather than a visualist, an idealist rather than an empiricist, and has little sense of the true dimensions of things, lacks sensuous perspective.

It should be noted that the Spirits Ironic play a centrally signifi-

cant role in the drama even though Hardy seems to give top billing
so exclusively to Years and Pities in the preface and in their dramatic tensions over perspective that there is a tendency to under-
value the part of the Spirits Ironic. Such undervaluation requires
very considerable redress. It is Ironic who sings most effectively the
central Chorus over Austerlitz, perspecting, as his failed education
does not enable Pities to do, present and ensuing events against the
eternal history of experimental creation and erasure (I, VI, III,
118-120). He points out, too, the startling overtones of the placid
scene between Napoleon and Francis (I, VI, V, 121-125): after all
the agony of Austerlitz, the two talk amicably as though there had
been but the slightest misunderstanding, now fully cleared up! The
Spirits Ironic create an imaginative medium of low-mimetic undercutting in the scene (II, I, VI, 165-166) in which Napoleon,
both his emotions and his verbiage in a high state of inflation,
declaims his embargo against English shipping; and they are absolutely right in their perception of the scene in the cellar on "A
Road to Astorga" (II, III, I, 206-210) as the "Quaint poesy, and
real romance of war!" In those scenes in which Ironic is placed in
contention with Pities, Ironic always seems to be trying to keep
open the question that Pities is attempting to close down. For
example:

SPIRIT OF THE PITIES

Something within me aches to pray
To some Great Heart, to take away
This evil day, this evil day!

CHORUS IRONIC

Ha-ha! That's good. Thou'lt pray to It:—
But where do Its compassions sit?
Yea, where abides the heart of It?

Is it where sky-fires flame and flit,
Or solar craters spew and spit,
Or ultra-stellar night-webs knit?

What is Its shape? Man's counterfeit?
That turns in some far sphere unlit
The Wheel which drives the Infinite?

SPIRIT OF THE PITIES

Mock on, mock on! Yet I'll go pray
To some Great Heart, who haply may
Charm mortal miseries away!

(II, VI, V, 306)

Ironic is not mocking. He is simply attempting to do what Pities is conspicuously incapable of doing—make perceptual assertion accountable by asking, what exactly are you saying? In the final crucial scenes especially (III, VII, VIII-IX, and After Scene), Ironic plays a role that challenges the *either-or* construct by which Years and Pities contend. It is Ironic's Chorus (517-518) that contains the briskest and most pointed insight into the overall nature of the total experience of *The Dynasts,* neither sinister nor sentimental, neither ponderous nor flippant, but detached, penetrating, nondogmatic. In the final secne, he cuts through the verbal pomposities of Years and the self-serving subterfuges of Napoleon with the central question:

Nothing care I for these high-doctrined dreams,
And shape the case in quite a common way,
So I would ask, Ajaccian Bonaparte,
Has all this been worth while?

There is sting in the question, but it turns Napoleon away from the collusive explanations of Years and brings him to such degree of honest recognition as he is capable of. Finally, it is Ironic in the After Scene (524) who declines a dogmatic answer and wonders, with Aeschylus, if it has all been an illusion, a hocus-pocus of the gods.

Thus if Hardy's purpose is to open the reader's eyes rather than to close them, to enlarge rather than shrink his perception of possibilities, Ironic clearly plays a crucial role in the literary procedure of *The Dynasts;* and the fact that he is somewhat sidelined and less prominently featured than Years and Pities rather enhances his importance, ironically, in Hardy's oblique, open-ended manner.

And this leads to a rather unorthodox view of Pities. Although Pities is paired with Years in a counterpoint of contrasting points of view (the *either-or* construct referred to above) and is given the abstract designation of an approximation to " 'the Universal Sympathy of human nature—the spectator idealized,' " the reader's sympathy for Pities is itself subjected to a subtle but relentless game-plan of erosion and alienation. We have just seen an instance in which Ironic places Pities in a wryly untenable light, developing a rational context in which Pities looks a bit absurd; and elsewhere he turns a penetrating light on the difference between Pities' irrational idealizations of the Will and "the dreaming, dark, dumb Thing" itself (After Scene, 524). And Pities' reactions from the beginning are deeply faulted in what amounts to a whole catalogue of failed perspectives: solipsism (I, I, VI, 36), pathetic fallacy (I, IV, III, 72), well-intentioned silliness and philosophical pretentiousness (I, V, IV, 99), sharply limited metaphysical acumen (I, V, VI, 105), equivocation (I, VI, III, 118), simplistic mentality— "one thing necessary" (II, I, II, 152), lack of balance and healthy perspective (II, I, VIII, 177), ineptness (II, I, VIII, 179), irrelevance (III, IV, IV, 414), dogged close-mindedness (III, VII, VII, 505), indiscriminate feeling (III, VII, IX, 521). Thus, it is difficult for a reader-spectator who is himself undergoing the process of consciousness-raising induced by the poem not to be thoroughly alienated from Pities by the end of *The Dynasts* and not to see the final positioning of Pities as one of the most cutting ironies of the whole literary construct. All of the pain witnessed in *The Dynasts* has taught Pities nothing, has been wasted pain; and Pities thus becomes a magnified model of those who, however harrowing and relevant their experiences, alter ther perceptions of reality hardly at all. It forces one toward this conclusion, at least tentatively: Hardy used a carefully modulated literary procedure that actually undercut his *manifest* intention with Pities and revealed it as a perceptual delusion of considerable magnitude.[6]

Thus, wherever one glances, the central concern of *The Dynasts* is with perception, and how Hardy orchestrates the perceptual complexities of the poem is the most encompassing aesthetic issue—the central issue of literary procedure—with which the critic must deal. What the reader-spectator learns from the experience of the poem is that men order their worlds through perception, but that misapprehension is their more habitual state and hence that their world is characteristically a world of perceptual chaos. Further, Hardy seems to make the very meaning of *The Dynasts* itself a central perceptual challenge to the reader (what *is* "the thing signified"?) and thus to press the reader into a dynamic relationship to the poem that disallows a passive reading and urges him, as it were, to play "the glass bead game."

In the broadest strokes of character and action, everyone in *The Dynasts* is made vulnerable to delusion, if not actually deluded. The dynasts themselves (that is, the current embodiments of old and royal bloodlines) are the least competent people in the whole poem. Their incapacity to do anything right has created the power vacuum that has made Napoleon possible, perhaps inevitable. From George III's petulant, clichéd "Hey, what?" to Queen Louisa of Prussia's extravagant melodramatic efforts ("the stormily sad air of a wounded beauty") to secure the toys in the attic (Magdeburg) and then on to the play-soldiers like Archduke This and Archduke That, the dynasts hover on the ironic edges of parody, only occasionally, as in the case of the broken George III, being drawn into the compensating circle of deep human pathos. Indeed, so near parody are the dynasts as portrayed in the poem that the inevitable ironic question has a circus quality to it: Why bother to prop upon such exhausted anachronisms? The answer, of course, is perceptual: the *ancien régime* is incapable of perceiving an alternative to itself except world chaos; it is the system in which Europe is, for the moment at least, intent on imprisoning itself.

At the opposite end of the social scale, the dynasts have their delusive correspondences. In the very first scene in the Underworld, a group of strangers traveling together in a coach work themselves up to a fury of charges and countercharges climaxing in the unpacking of pistols as a result of a collision of perceptions *about a collision of perceptions* that suddenly solidify into adamant face-down positions. In treating "England's humblest hearts," the poet-designer lets the farcical element become more transparent, abandoning the tongue-in-cheek solemnity with which the gyrations of the dynasts are narrated. It is genial farce, for the most part, frequently turning on the notion that rustic humor derives from being "sharp enough in the wrong place," but the supposing and stating of fact is at the center of the poet-designer's interest. After some night-time talk on Egdon Heath about Napoleon's victuals—"rashers o' baby every morning for breakfast," perhaps at least pagan babies in the desert if not Christian babies at home— the woman speaker caps it all as follows:

> Whether or no, I sometimes—God forgie me!
> —laugh wi' horror at the queerness o't, till I
> am that weak I can hardly go round house. He
> should have the washing of 'em a few times; I warrant
> 'a wouldn't want to eat babies any more!
>
> (I, II, V, 52)

This geniality is maintained in the broadly farcical scene in which a rustic expects to see Napoleon actually burned alive at Durnover Green (a scene that might otherwise have had a doubly turned cruelty to it) by being filtered through the stabilizing sensibility of the Reverend Mr. Palmer, the pipe-smoking, spitting, musing, gently cursing vicar of the parish (III, V, VI, 449-453). The difference, then, between the delusions of the dynasts and those of the humblest citizens is not so conspicuous as is the difference in the literary manner in which the poet-designer treats them—parodic solemnity versus genial farce; and since he avoids evaluative comment, it is on the manner, the right note-catching, that he depends for getting his awarenesses across to the reader-spectator. He uses a different literary manner, too, with each of the principal characters through whom he reveals coordinates of his concern with perception/delusion.

Any romantic attachment that might accrue to Csar Alexander—his youth, his accomplished manner, his heart-warmth for Queen Louisa of Prussia and his intercession on her behalf with Napoleon—is dissipated in the venality with which he so readily plays the mouse to Napoleon's cat (II, I, VIII, 170-173). Napoleon, of course, leads from great strength, and Alexander lacks both strength of character and strength of political position. But with

Napoleon he is more pliable than Louisa herself: he "shows mortification," gets all "stirred and flushed," gushes "with naive enthusiasm," reddens ingenuously. It is a regular wooing, and he pledges his hand, a victim of raw flattery and dreams of limitless bounty:

ALEXANDER (stirred and flushed)

I see vast prospects opened!—yet, in truth,
Ere you, sire, broached these themes, their outlines loomed
Not seldom in my own imaginings;
But with less clear a vision than endows
So great a captain, statesman, philosoph,
As center in yourself; whom had I known
Sooner by some few years, months, even weeks,
I had been spared full many a fault of rule.
—Now as to Austria. Should we call her in?

NAPOLEON

Two in a bed I have slept, but never three.

The psychosexual image emerges with great naturalness in the fictive verbal structure that the poet-designer has created, and its unmistakable presence here releases a renewed awareness in the reader-spectator that all of the negotiations in the book—the love-duets, the parliamentary debates, the Spirit-contentions, the frequent disagreements over perception and logistics, and so forth—are strategies of dominance having a clear analogical relationship to the central metaphor of war. And that Alexander can be so easily seduced by Napoleon stirs in us, on the one hand, thoughts about gentleness, cordiality, religiosity, and good manners (all qualities that Pities would admire) and, on the other hand, thoughts about basic integrity.

The reversal in Marie Louise is even more dramatic and can be seen without shading in two contrasting passages. What she actually said when confronted with Napoleon's proposal of marriage as conveyed diplomatically was this:

My wish is what my duty bids me wish.
Where a wide Empire's welfare is in poise,
That welfare must be pondered, not my will.
I ask of you, then, Chancellor Metternich,
Straightway to beg the Emperor my father
That he fulfil his duty to his realm,
And quite subordinate thereto all thought
Of how it personally impinge on me.

                                        (II, V, IV, 272)

When, however, confronted with the choice of whether or not to
join Napoleon after his escape from Elba and the declaration of his
outlawed state, she remembers her role in the nuptial alliance
quite differently:

A puppet, I, by force inflexible,
Was bid to wed Napoleon at a nod,—
The man acclaimed to me from cradle-days
As the incarnate of all evil things,
The Antichrist himself.—I kissed the cup,
Gulped down the inevitable, and married him;
But none the less I saw myself therein
The lamb whose innocent flesh was dressed to grace
The altar of dynastic ritual!—
Hence Elba flung no duty-call to me,
Neither does Paris now.

                                        (III, V, IV, 143)

Since the discrepancy between the two perceptions or readings of
history is not really ambiguous, one can assume that the poet-
designer's interest probably lay elsewhere, as indeed it did. Marie
Louise has begun to feather a different nest, and, in addition to
vestiges of her own childhood attitudes, she is orchestrating everything that she has learned from her late mentor, Napoleon, to be
rid of her current embarrassment, Napoleon. It is he who taught
her that marriage is not necessarily for life—that for reasons
thought personally persuasive one can get a fresh nuptial partner.
It is one of the most penetrating ironies of the poem that the King

of Rome, the would-be dynastic child, should be shared by Marie Louise and Napoleon for their comparable but disparate actions. The King of Rome was to have been Napoleon's way of shoring up the future, a goal to which he sacrificed Josephine; Marie Louise now wishes to shore up her own and the King of Rome's future, a goal that is symbolized by the Duchy of Parma, to which she has decided to sacrifice Napoleon. Further, it is from Napoleon that she has learned all that talk of puppetry and a "force inflexible" that ruled her destiny; having been well schooled, she can now turn the lesson against Napoleon and justify, by his example, her present convenient action. The irony gets even deeper: Marie Louise has actually absorbed into herself the Christ-imagery with which Napoleon had sought to sanctify his life and that of his son and here uses it to cleanse herself of all secular obligations that extend beyond her personal desire. The new Christ thus rejects the Antichrist who has lessoned her so carefully in his Christ-identity ways! Such image-building and role-playing resonates inexhaustibly through the literary procedure named *The Dynasts.* And it is a fit introduction for Napoleon himself.

Napoleon, as presented by Hardy in *The Dynasts,* is an extraordinary literary phenomenon having no genuine analogues in literature: he is not even much like his literary prototype, Achilles. He is the center of a myth, but it is not a romantic myth; he is the latest energy in a world visibly losing energy as his myth works out its curve. He is a bundle of caprices and magnetisms and contradictions and brilliances. He is a failed Prometheus and a momentarily successful Jupiter. Measured by the people around him, he emerges with proportions undeniably colossal: he is the *primum mobile* of a Europe called Napoleonic. Looked at in isolation, he threatens to shrink to something almost dwarfish: vulpine, saturnine, a sort of bully-in-charge, "Boney," as he is called by the lower orders in England. Indeed, there is hardly any consistent coordinate in Napoleon except the lust to imprint history with a Napoleonic image—to reengineer the past by "shoulder[ing] Christ from out the topmost niche / In human fame" (III, VII, IX, 520) and to manage the future by establishing a dynasty with a futurity as persistent, in retrospect, as that of the Holy Roman Empire. Everything else about him ultimately collides in contradiction.

The literary distinctiveness of Hardy's Napoleon derives from the imaginative mix out of which Hardy created him. He is conscientiously historical—a *real* Napoleon; magnificently *metaphorical*—a stand-in for human nature caught in some intricate and self-destructive toils; and persistently *ironical*—placed in an apprehensive medium in which his heroic qualities and his shabbiness are counterpointed. He is that curious modern hybrid—the low-mimetic protagonist of an epic literary structure.

It is difficult to know, in the broad sweeps Hardy uses, whether Napoleon is genuinely self-deceived, capable of foxlike subterfuge in disguising some relatively clear perceptions about himself, or such a thorough-going cynic that he simply jettisons with abrupt finality a past that would torture such characters of Pitt, Villeneuve, and Nelson. He can set aside Josephine, abandon his remnant army in Lithuania, make and break alliances, bolster his men's morale with an outright lie concerning reenforcements, and play games with the idea of the Immanent Will without apparent distress of conscience so long as no one shows the bad taste or bad judgment to remind him of his failures after he has chosen to be rid of them.

There is one conspicuous exception to this, and in it may lie the key to the grand deception of the Emperor's life: Napoleon's abandonment of his early mission as Savior of the Revolution. This is the subject of the earliest chiding of his conscience by Pities:

> Lieutenant Bonaparte,
> Would it not seemlier be to shut thy heart
> To these unhealthy splendours? helmet thee
> For her thou swar'st-to first, fair Liberty?
> (I, I, VI, 35)

And it is the subject most conspicuously absent from Napoleon's recognition-scene in the wood of Bossu. Yet, it can be fairly said that, despite Napoleon's multiple-seeming recognitions there, he never enunciates the basic truth: that the day he abandoned the cause of the people and the basic principles of the Revolution and was drawn into the network of dynastic strategies was the day his genuine fame was eclipsed and his equivocal destiny determined. It is the central fact of Napoleon's magnificent metaphorical stand-in for human nature: a young charismatic officer with a great flair for timing, he became the man of the hour; but power corrupts, and absolute power corrupts absolutely. So Napoleon fell victim to the very disease he was pledged to fight: he became the dynast of dynasts, "churning to a pulp within the maw / Of empire-making Lust and personal Gain" realms, laws, peoples, dynasties (I, VI, VI, 128). This failure to be true to his initial mission he cannot bear to recognize because in this, had he pursued it, he would indeed have challenged, not only "Nelson, Harold, Hector, Cyrus, Saul" or even Christ, but that great original and savior of saviors, Prometheus. Man is imprisoned in a systemic condition analogous to that in which Prometheus first found him. The French Revolution, before it fell into the hands of buccaneers and predators, promised a way out of the system. Even at the late hour of Napoleon's appearance on the scene, it could have been saved and by him. But he very quickly developed the systemic infection and became himself systemic with a vengeance. And yet it is just possible that, had he held true to his intial dedication, had he learned, like Prometheus, to "endure eternally," he might in fact and without arrogant consciousness thereof, have "shouldered Christ from out the topmost niche / In human fame"—mythically, he might have launched a new era of human liberation analogous to that launched in the imperious imagination by Prometheus.[7]

Napoleon, then, is the central image in a literary world which Hardy called *The Dynasts* and in which men, for the most part, occupy space in a bedlam of failed apprehension. Sometimes simply blind to the true truth, however quotidianal; sometimes, like Alexander, backing into self-deception out of weakness and romantically induced fantasy; sometimes, like the Empress Marie Louise, through a combination of wilfulness and some very careful lessoning; more universally like Napoleon, through an obsessive desire to cover over our half-hidden germ of failure and to obscure, in a fury of role-playing, a buried self. In these two selves that gaze at each other over what appears to be an ontological gulf created by a soiled personal history (the self that was and the self that is reciprocating an image of the self that might have been), Napoleon touches universal chords and induces in the reader-spectator a tragic sense of failure with which he can identify. Tragic, but not romantic, so that all inflation is undercut and acceptance takes place at a level of ironic ordinariness that is relentless rather than harsh in its stripped truth-telling.

Finally, on the overall subject of literary conceptualization, a word needs to be said about the narrative technique of the Epic-Drama. What Hardy seems to do in the scene-painting and motion-paintings (dumb shows) that are so prominent a feature of *The Dynasts* as panoramic spectacle—dramatic visualizations on an incrementally grand scale—is to synthesize several prominent features of nineteenth-century aesthetic experience. One of these is the picturesque, itself a synthesizing tendency among the arts, through which a practitioner in the verbal arts, especially poetry, attempts to structure his visual effects in a painterly fashion by rather strict analogy with painting itself. Another is the staged spectacle, framed by a proscenium and designed to give the illusion of a dramatic picture or motion-painting. A third is the staged poem, another form of motion-painting, particularly represented by the dramatic monologue, in which person, place, and crisis are given a paintinglike dimension and concentration. To these must be added the grand tradition of nineteenth-century illustration—in which the writer and the artist attempted to knead their perceptions together—and the new excitement brought to the drama of seeing by the late Turner and by Ruskin. A combination of visualness and vibrancy is what Hardy seems to have recognized as a rather imperious dimension of the modern aesthetic expression/outlook and what he attempted to capture in the scenes and shows of his design. But here again we must avoid forcing even Hardy's painterliness into overwrought rigidities. He was not *being* a painter: he was drawing from painting, in a well-developed tradition of the picturesque, certain *literary* procedures that emphasized the authority of the eye and sent out important signals concerning the reader-spectator's experiential relationship to the artifact called *The Dynasts*.

And what signals does this painterliness send out to the reader-spectator? Essentially a cluster of aesthetic/consciousness reenforcements: insight into the thing signified by this chronicle-piece ultimately depends upon the clarity with which we as human beings see things as they in fact are; even though there may be a hidden germ of failure in us all (poet-designer, reader-spectator, Spirit Intelligences, historical principals), there is no mechanical way of shortcutting the false starts and self-deceptions and endless winnowings through which a keener sense of reality, though hard-won and but partial at best, can be achieved; the artist, through his reliance on disproportionings and seemings rather than on literalnesses and dogmatisms, changes the rules of habit, moves the dial just enough off-center to insinuate distinctly altered conditions of spiritual accommodation, involves the reader-spectator in the imaginative process of *"mak[ing] a philosophy for himself out of his own experience"* through this participatory transformation of action into metaphor and history into myth. Painterliness is one of the conspicuous coordinates of Hardy's imaginative structure that reminds the reader-spectator that the experience of *The Dynasts* is essentially an aesthetic experience.

And it has been on *The Dynasts* as aesthetic experience that this essay has concentrated. Therein lies no capricious disregard for the "philosophical" inquiries and debates that have been the staple of the commentaries on the poem, and there is no presumption that these few brisk pages will counterpoise the rapidly growing canon of ideologically oriented exegesis of the poem. It is simply a matter of literary value and literary perspective. To one who thinks of Hardy as a great literary artist and, as an artist, a great engendering consciousness, ideas per se drift downward on the value-scale. When there is so much to explore and so little time, why, frankly, would one go to Hardy for Schopenhauerian ideas when he can go to Schopenhauer? Or to Carlyle for Kantian ideas when he can go to Kant? Unless, of course, we are talking about imaginative metamorphosis. Then the matter becomes deep and fascinating: how Hardy the artist transformed readings of life which he found in the pennings of others—Homer and Aeschylus as well as Schopenhauer and von Hartmann—into fictive configurations of representative human experience intensified and enriched by the literary strategies of metaphor, structure, myth that he found so effective in his predecessors in the literary line and which, through his startlingly tactful aesthetic sensibility, he converted to his own original artistic uses. But now we are rather far removed from ideas as such and are contemplating imaginative apprehension rather than philosophy, except in the most experientialized terms. No critic would wish to foreshorten Hardy's awarenesses, including his awareness of ideas old and new; indeed, it has become necessary to be very tentative in one's assumptions about what Hardy did not know. Thus, availability to surprises is an advisable spiritual condition for the critic of Hardy. But one cannot usefully ignore the fact that Hardy was primarily an artist, not a thinker; and although he habitually imagined a "terrible beauty," beauty was yet to Hardy truth's engenderer.

Notes

1. All quotations from and references to *The Dynasts* have as their basis *The Dynasts: An Epic-Drama of the War with Napoleon,* by Thomas Hardy (New York: St. Martin's Press, 1977). Passages are identified by part, act, scene, and page and are given in parentheses in the text as appropriate. This is a reprint of the text of the edition issued by Macmillan in 1924 with the same consecutive pagination throughout, and quotations used have been checked against the 1924 text. I have followed recent practice and suspended use of italics with the speeches/songs of the Spirits.

2. Despite Walter F. Wright's unsupported assertion that Hardy "did not take Aristotle for his guide" (*The Shaping of The Dynasts* [Lincoln: University of Nebraska Press, 1967], p. 83), the marks of the *Poetics* linger all over the face of *The Dynasts*. The six parts of tragedy to which Aristotle refers—plot, character, thought, diction, melody, spectacle—have pervasive relevance to what Hardy has done in the work, including the dramatic rather than the epic relevance of melody and spectacle. Further, the four literary species ommon to tragedy and the epic—"either simple or involved or concerned with character or pathetic"—energize critical considerations of a literary kind basically germane to what Hardy has done in his Epic-Drama. Hardy probably also took from Aristotle his cues for the role of the Chorus, the author's distance from his imitation, the subordinate role of diction, and the special sorts of effects for which the *Iliad* and the *Odyssey* were incomparable literary models: "magnificence of effect, variety for the reader, and the weaving of dissimilar episodes into the action." Of course, Hardy, like Shelley, felt free to adapt Aristotle to his own uses.

3. It seems clear that Hardy, at the time of working up an adequate literary structure for *The Dynasts,* reread Shelley's *Prometheus Unbound* and such associated documents as Shelley's preface to his lyric drama and *A Defence of Poetry.*

4. A passage that Hardy marked in Gibbon's *Decline and Fall* is precisely apt here: "instead of an indivisible and regular system, which occupies the *whole extent of the believing mind,* the mythology of the Greeks was composed of a thousand loose and flexible parts." See Wright, p. 6.

5. Susan Dean seems to be guilty of such oversophistication to very little inter-pretive purpose in *Hardy's Poetic Vision in "The Dynasts": The Diorama of a Dream* (Princeton: Princeton University Press, 1977), pp. 48-65.

6. Traditional commentary on *The Dynasts* takes a very much more sympathetic view of Pities than mine, of course. The latest commentator to sanctify Pities even at the expense of Years is Susan Dean, esp. pp. 163-167. But Professor Dean, it seems to me, merely lays unction to a very traditioñal insight, voic-ing Pities' voicings in rather cultish fashion.

7. This observation suggests that Hardy was actually thinking of Shelley's treatment of the Prometheus-Jupiter struggle as a model of a kind of dualism that can be personal as well as cosmic and that he saw Napoleon, in a glancing sort of way, as an internalization of such a dualistic metaphor. His wild career in Europe would be the coordinate of his Jupiter phase, released perhaps by his strangulated Prometheanism.

16.

"The Thing Signified" by *The Dynasts:*
A Speculation

Despite differences of perception and emphasis among the critics of *The Dynasts,*[1] critical orientation toward the poem's "outlook" has been essentially ideological, centering on the nature of the poem's metaphysics and the degree of Hardy's intellectual assent to the monism figured in the Immanent Will. An interest centered in these matters has naturally, perhaps, led critics to assume that, when Hardy spoke in his preface about "the thing signified," he was pointing the reader's attention toward such ideologically ordering concepts. But if one assumes that these ideological issues, being so large and reiterative a part of the simulated drama itself, are aspects of "the insistent, and often grotesque, substance," then he is forced to look further for "the thing signified."

That Hardy meant to unveil, at least fleetingly, matters somewhat different in kind from ideological or metaphysical perception is surely suggested by the vibrations he sets in motion by phrases like "scenes laid 'far in the Unapparent' "; the "older, more invidious, more nervous, more quizzical" unhappy perplexity of the modern "meditative world"; the "Riddles of Death Thebes never knew." Such phrases induce, not analytical poise, but experiential

335

disquiet. And even experiential disquiet has to be transformed to cosmic terror the more we reflect upon the perpetual bombardment of awarenesses to which we have been subjected throughout *The Dynasts*. We, *homo agonistes,* have certainly been treated to some harsh lessoning in the course of the poem: that we are without any control over our lives, the puppets of an unconscious energy that evolves morally valueless patterns; that even our most magificent representatives—our greatest heroes—are no more significant, historically perspected, than the most minute insect on the most mutable leaf; that our dynasts, remnants of the old order and restored monitors of our social and political lives, are conspicuously incompetent, even though we of the masses are still in life-and-death service to them; that there is likely to be little correlation between the truth of our perceptions and the ardor with which we hold them; that people alter their perceptions of reality hardly at all even in the face of the most harrowing and relevant experiences. It would be an intimidating programme of human diminution if it were coherently articulated by a centered authority in the poem, and even as a cluster of possibilities with which the reader-spectator, as ultimate judge, must deal, these perceptions of the human situation in the universe dislocate most of the traditional devices and structures by which we have sought to give ordered and self-satisfying expectations to our world.

Perception in its infinite aspects, how people suppose and state fact, is perhaps the central exploratory awareness upon which *The Dynasts* turns. But one aspect of human perception, intimately related to man's sense of anxiety in his universe, is so inevitable a dimension of experiential reeforcement that it is insinuated into the reader's consciousness in a relentless way. The poet-designer of the piece is determined to maintain the integrity of *The Dynasts* as an aesthetic structure, but he is also insistent that the reader-spectator be brought face to face with all the realities of war. Those realities go far beyond the hellish horrors and lurid rituals of eyeball-to-eyeball death-dealing. They include pageantry, gamesmanship, power-broking, the basic concepts of alliances and jealous regard for national borders, the balance of power, the establishment of new and the maintenance of old dynasties, and so forth. The fragility of such arrangements and the confrontal consequences of their collapse keep even older civilized centers of the world poised on the brink of war; and ancient discontents and a ruler's personal ambitions may alike upset the precarious balances and draw clusters of nations into conflict.

Hardy realized, of course, that it was beyond any writer's capacity to affect directly the international arrangements that seemed to increase the likelihood of war, but he knew too that it was not the people at the top of the social scale (the dynasts themselves) who were likely to suffer war's actual brutalities. War was induced by dynasts, but fought by soldiers; and soldiers at the very lowest echelon were likely to be the greatest bearers of war's devastation with the least access to such spiritually compensatory roles as leadership and individual charisma. Hence, the lowliest foot-soldier became generically the genuine victim of the games dynasts play. Like the cavalry horse itself, he could find least reason to justify his wounds. This awareness of the penetrating irony of those who had the least to gain suffering the most became a way of perceiving the hellish disproportion and madness of war and the object of a special sort of literary endeavor.

To the perceptual possibility of an abrupt and all-pervasive diminution of human significance is thus added a massive demonstration of raw, undeniably real human pain, brutal and unreasonable. Man emerges as negligible, largely deluded, and tortured. It is a crushing perceptual cluster capable of casting over the human prospect a terrifying light.

Further, one's attempts to define "the thing signified" by *The Dynasts* demand that he weigh in the significant accumulation of symbolist images of absurdity in the poem, oblique suggestions that are inexhaustibly disturbing. The poem's apprehensive tone is so keenly ironic that its potentialities as a grand spectacle of the absurd are insistently present throughout: the poet-designer could have screamed with grotesque laughter at almost every turn. Hardy chose a different aesthetic center: he counterpointed the manifest examples of absurdity with equally manifest examples of genuine degrees of heroism, pathos, fidelity, high purpose, and authentic tragedy. Hence, the very tangible strain of the grotesque in the piece is serious rather than light, tragic rather than comic.

The images of absurdity are numerous and very real, functioning within an aesthetic medium in which the discrepancy between reality and perception or between perception and perception constantly threatens the consciousness with absurdity of mind-blowing proportions. An all-pervasive discrepancy of this sort is that between men's sense of themselves as responsibly engaged in a moral contest called life and Years' visualization of them as simply particles of vitalized matter "writhing, crawling, heaving, and vibrating in their various cities and nationalities"—their habitats and subspecies. A more localized but quite grotesquely absurd discrepancy is implicit in George III's capricious response to Pitt's request for the personal relief and national unity of a coalition government: he thrusts himself like a colossal anachronism between the exhausted Pitt and his frustrating but fortitudinous efforts to create in Europe a sufficient international counterpoise to paralyze Napoleon's aggression. It is dynasties like George III's that are at stake, yet the King prattles on about the strains of his own office, "Our just crusade against the Corsican," the divine right of kings, the soundness of reasons never in fact thought of, climaxing with a royal petulance: "Rather than Fox, why, give me civil war! / Hey, what?" (I, IV, I, 67-68). At the end of their totally deflating conversation, Pitt makes polite reference to a "curious structure" outside, to which the King replies as follows:

> It's but a stage, a type of all the world. The burgesses have arranged it in my honor. At six o'clock this evening there are to be combats at single-stick to amuse the folk; four guineas the prize for the man who breaks most heads. Afterwards there is to be a grinning match through horse-collars—a very humorous sport which I must stay here and witness; for I am interested in whatever entertains my subjects.

The flatulence of the King's reply in juxtaposition to Pitt is itself disquieting, but the succession of images that George unwittingly releases become symbolist implants of absurdity: (1) life is a stage (2) on which men are paid for breaking the most heads (3) after which people play the amusing sport of grinning through horse-collars. It is inexhaustibly disturbing because of the wry truth of it, the piquant irony of the context in which it is released, and the essentially unmediated imagery from which it draws its memorableness.

The reader may shudder at the full reverberations set in motion by this scene between Pitt and George III, but the cumulative effect of such images of absurdity is greater than the sum of them individually; and they do darken as the poem progresses. The story of how the crew "broached the Adm'l" reveals a considerably darkened image of absurdity. The broad humor with which the FIRST BOATMAN tells how the crew of the "Victory," when they "brought the galliant hero home," "fairly saved their lives" by puncturing his casket and drinking him dry—that is, consuming the alcoholic spirits in which his body was being preserved on the long journey home—is counterpoised by the inevitable realization, however delayed, that a cadaver thus preserved would release into the preservative its body wastes (residual excrement, urine, semen, and a host of body chemicals and stored substances), thus converting the broad humor intended by the teller into a symbolist image of a grotesque and psychically distressful sort. The dark side of this image is then deepened in the direction of the authentically tragic by the song that closes the fifth act, "The Night of Trafalgár," in which images of futility sweep over images of heroism:

> Dead Nelson and his half-dead crew, his foes from near and
>   far,
> Were rolled together on the deep that night at Trafalgár!
> The deep,
> The deep!
> That night at Trafalgár!

These symbolist implants accrete rapidly. An indelible image is imprinted on the mind when, at Austerlitz, Napoleon quite capriciously and "with a vulpine smile" has the battery turned on the frozen lake which two thousand Russians are crossing: "A ghastly crash and splashing follows the discharge, the shining surface breaking into pieces like a mirror, which fly in all directions. Two thousand fugitives are engulfed, *and their groans of despair reach the ears of the watchers like ironical huzzas"* (I, VI, IV, 121, emphasis added). Even the mirror metaphor is symbolic since it reflects the multifarious tragedy that will be served up to Napoleon in his Moscow adventure; and the description of the Russians then in turn mirrors *his* action here: "My God, they are Scythians and barbarians still!" (III, I, VIII, 349) That Pitt should receive the news of Austerlitz while he is in the Picture Gallery at Shockerwick House having highly cultivated talk of Gainsborough and Sir Joshua Reynolds, Churchill and Quin stuns the nerves with a penetrating awareness that Pitt himself points up. Against the elegant perpetuation motif of eighteenth-century literary and artistic decorum is set Pitt's total sense of personal dissolution:

> So do my plans through all these plodding years
> Announce them built in vain.
> His heel on Europe, monarchies in chains
> To France, I am as though I had never been!
> (I, VI, VI, 128)

One of the most complex symbolist images imprinted on the mind is that of the war as perspected by a group of English deserters in a house-cellar on "A Road Near Astorga." The grotesque humor with which the scene is projected by the several deserters cannot disguise the bizarre low to which their world has degenerated, nesting as they are in wet straw among dead or drunk or naked men, women, and children and looking out upon a civilization in reverse motion—"dying downwards," as it were. What they see is horses falling from exhaustion, being pistoled in the head; soldiers who have pillaged being executed by lot; people who have died in transport being laid out beside the road with "some muddy snow scraped over them"; a momentary display of soldierly behavior in absurd pantomime. This is what, from inside the English ranks, the war looks like—a complex image burnt deep into the reader-spectator's consciousness without authorial interpretation or judgment.

Walcheren represents a different kind of nadir to the English. That it is authentically historical in no way detracts from its massive metaphorical quality: one of the inevitable dimensions/possibilities of war is that one may, like the speaker in "Hap," have to forego the satisfaction of a combatant, may have to forego one's personal Prometheanism for lack of an available tyrant. One is perhaps fairly reminded of the soft, nerveless, pithless, misty world of Lotos-land as an ironically reversed analogue: the narcotic-laced Lotos-eaters crave a death-in-life state, while the soldiers sinking into the sediment of Walcheren, sliding toward an inertia-point of human mistery, crave but the chance to "yield their lives" in fair fight within sound of the echoes of "the aggressor's arrogant career." It is the most haunting error of English strategy, and it is the victims' fear that

> Our country's chiefs, for their own fames afraid,
> Will leave our names and fates by this pale sea
> > To perish silently!
> > > (II, IV, VIII, 251-252)

But of course the most devastating images of a grotesque absurdity are implanted in Napoleon's Russian campaign (III, I); and there, if anywhere, we can expect to find a revelation, however oblique, of "the thing signified."

The first scene of Part Third, in which massive anxiety is projected, functions at two very different levels—that of the *dramatis personae* and that of the reader-spectator, the latter having gradually learned through the literary procedures of the piece to translate even its denotative action into symbolist awareness. Napoleon himself is the primary dramatic personage in the scene, so what we are essentially faced with is Napoleon's view of himself versus our view of him. That he is somewhat shaken though defiant, is overwrought and has lost his fine-tuning, begins to see history as closing in on him, feels fated even against his "better mind," but faces his gloom in a spirit of grim irony—these aspects of his self-hood we perceive and can believe that he perceives them too. But there are dimensions of our awareness that he does not share, and these move the experience of the scene for the reader-spectator to a deep ironic level. Napoleon is beginning the long slide toward moral and psychological shabbiness, and he is blinding himself to glaring contradictions in his self-projection: his haughtiness toward the

Russian sense of destiny countervenes his own oft-repeated claim of a manifest destiny; he attempts to equate the disastrous strategy of invading Russia at an inopportune time of the year, wholly his willful error, with the need to lesson Russia in French insuperability; he falls back upon the "force" that moves him "inexorably" to offset the sense of ominous foreboding that has enveloped his psyche. But it is the images induced by the scene that scarify the mind. Napoleon's version of the "Malbrough" air projects his self-serving return after abandoning his troops starving and freezing in Lithuania, while Sinister's revision of the same air projects the chaotic destruction of half-a-million men *"dead and buried"*—at least till the coming of spring! This is then immediately followed by an image of this "Christ of war" shrinking, shrinking to the aspect of a doll while the heavens burst with thunder and lightning and torrents of rain as if a divine dispensation were in fact ending. It is a literary realization worthy of Aristophanes.

The scene in "The Open Country Between Smorgoni and Wilna" (III, I, XI, 357-359) that closes the Russian sequence is widely recognized as the nadir of horror represented in *The Dynasts,* and it deserves that recognition because of the literary manner Hardy brings to it. The symbolist technique is complete. "These striken shades in a limbo of gloom" perambulate as tattered skeletons (scarecrows) in a merciless wintry desert of which there is no beginning and no end, no alpha and no omega. Like Dante's limbo-inhabitants, they are without hope, and they move about like iced automatons building their bivouac fire and having their meal of horse and rat. Word that Napoleon has abandoned them drives them variously into paroxysms of "grief, rage, and despair," some sobbing like children, some becoming wildly insane. The "Mad Soldier's Song" becomes their aria of ironic salvation since they have reached a state of being that has finally exceeded pain as ordinarily understood. Then they gather in their physical exhaustion for the ultimate symbolist tableau of *The Dynasts:* the last survivors of the Grand Army gathered around the bivouac fire, pressed close for shared body heat, cindered in front, caked hard with frost in the back, with the tears on their cheeks "in strings of ice." Thus they are found by Kutúzof and his men; thus they are left to be buried by the falling snow. And the reader-spectator is spared intrusion in his awed contemplation of the scene.

What happens within this symbolist envelope provides the chief key to "the thing signified" by *The Dynasts*.

It should be noted that, when Napoleon arrives at Moscow, he has been seriously depleted: the ardors of the march and battle-butchery have already destroyed three-quarters of his army. As he says, "And it was time." Thus he is ill-prepared, in physical or psychological resource, for the failure of expectation that Rostopchin and Kutúzof have prepared for him. Here he is, the supreme European, face to face with Asia, and Asia has prepared a bag of "foul tricks" for him: "My god, they are Scythians and barbarians still!" For Napoleon to arrive, after such hardship, at an abandoned Moscow is as bizarre as for Marlowe, in Conrad's *Heart of Darkness*, to witness a French man-of-war firing into the continent of Africa: it is surreal, defying comprehension by the highly coded European mind. It is a "crazed act," an "infernal scheme" which some "Satan" has devised. This Europe-Asia dichotomy is made explicit, in Hardy's oblique, ironic way, on Napoleon's journey to Elba. He says to Bertrand, "Yes—all is lost in Europe for me now!" Bertrand replies, "I fear so, sire." Then Napoleon: "But Asia waits a man, / And—who can tell?" (XXX, IV, VI, 420). And just before this (III, III, II, 383), the poet-designer has noted, "Nationalities from the uttermost parts of Asia here meet those from the Atlantic edge of Europe for the first and last time."

This climactic revelation—that for the coded European mind to look into Asia is to look into a vast mystery, an incomprehensibility, with which it is not prepared to cope—is a perception that has haunted the twentieth century. Hardy suggests it somewhat circumspectly, to be sure; but it is highly significant as one of a cluster of perceptions that draw us to the terrifying conclusion—perhaps "the thing signified" in *The Dynasts*—that the modern European is possessed of a whole repertoire of strategies for coping that are simply irrelevant to the things to be coped with; that his reality is a preferential disposition, not the true truth; that beyond the painted shell of his privately packaged universe there are "deep wells of nothingness" with which he has no capacity to deal. It is a frightful vision, and if one takes Hardy's epic analogy seriously, *The Dynasts* spells the doom of modern Europe as surely as the *Iliad* spelled the doom of ancient Troy.

But Hardy does not seem to have been inclined to translate these dire imaginings into a voice *in propria persona* and to assume the role of a modern vates. Like his own, the preceding, and the following generations of poets, he was "dramatic," "personative," creating structures in which truth was not authorially mediated but authentically explored through the aesthetic placement of a reader-spectator who is not infallible in a position analogous to that of an author who is not infallible watching a protagonist who is not infallible. Such structures could be as comparatively simple as the dramatic lyric in sonnet form entitled "Hap" or as epically direct, dramatically complex, and aesthetically inexhaustible as *The Dynasts*. But the mark of their modernism, being attitudinal, is the same. The modern artist has no obligation to dismantle the past, however anachronistic it may have become; indeed, the modern artist, as Arnold said, does not deal in pastness or presentness, but in relevance; he makes the past and the present creative bedfellows to the degree that he makes his individual talent and his inherited literary traditions organic. Thus both modernism and the modern artist are in a perpetual state of becoming. Like the Immanent Will, in many ways a fit analogue to the artist right down to the unconscious center of his creativity, the modern poet-designer is an instrument of creative evolution, his aim "to alter evermore / Things from what they were before" (III, VII, VIII, 518); or, to translate this into words from Hardy's preface to *The Dynasts,* to adopt as one's single aim "the modern expression of a modern outlook."

Thus the modern poet puts a premium, not on action, but on awareness: consciousness-raising (spiritual transformation, imaginative elevation) is the goal to which everything else he does is subordinate. His faith is not in social arrangements or in political or religious creeds but in metaphors and myths because they are his instruments of metamorphosis. The imagination, he knows, is an organic part of Everyman; and the cultivation of the imagination, for which the poet-designer has special gifts, is an organic cultivation promising organic (and hence permanent) results. Every dimension of man's consciousness—from day-to-day perception to loving-kindness to cosmic symbolism—is dependent on the state of cultivation of that man's individual imagination.

What we have in *The Dynasts,* then, is a frightful vision set against an irrefragable faith. The *vrai verité* of a universe that very quickly outstrips rational comprehensibility (a universe centered in the consciousness as well as in the cosmos) is juxtaposed to an aesthetic way of ordering reality, a way exemplified by both *The Dynasts* and its analogue, the *Iliad.* At the time Hardy published his epic-drama, the *Iliad* and *The Dynasts* constituted, for the moment, a literary frame, an alpha and an omega of sorts, of man's imaginative efforts to deal with his woes and to establish, at least suggestively, a symbol of reconciliation to his frightful condition. That symbol became literature itself, *The Dynasts* and all those instruments of imaginative awareness, from Homer and Aeschylus and Sophocles to Dante and Shakespeare and Shelley, through which man has been enabled to perceive imaginative coordinates in what would otherwise be a chaos both within and without. Like Shelley, in whose *Defence of Poetry* he found the text, Hardy seems to have endorsed Tasso's perception—*Non merita nome di creatore, se non Iddio ed il Poeta* [*No one deserves the name of creator, except God and the Poet*]— with this fundamental difference: that by the time Hardy wrote *The Dynasts,* the poet stood alone.

It should be clear from the foregoing that anyone who does not know *The Dynasts* simply does not know Hardy. To ignore his epic-drama is to ignore his efforts to create a truly monumental work, to wed his individual talent and his keen sense of contemporary spiritual ambience to the most ancient theory and practice of the Western literary tradition, to convert history into myth and thus to place the nineteenth century in Europe in the literary pantheon of the Indo-European ages. It is to ignore, too, a fine literary achievement that, in retrospect, is more and more seen as the twentieth century's prototypical literary formulation, the aesthetic structure that gathers in the fright and the fragments, the pulverizations and the importunities, the inheritances and the alienations—the epic, narrative, dramatic, lyrical, elegiac, symphonic, panoramic, picturesque, impressionistic, grotesque, symbolist artistic expectancies and despairs of "these disordered years of our prematurely afflicted century. . . ." Hardy brings to bear on the literary procedure of the poem his complete literary repertoire as he tries to create a massive artistic structure in which there is a place and function, not only for the sweeping panoramic spectacle, but also for the thousands of bits of individual dramatic role-playing, in high and low alike, that go to make up a densely textured, Breughel-like, vibrant representation of life. And he does this, in what must be called a grand literary paradox, Homerically rather than Miltonically: he overleaps the whole Christian experience in literature and finds his analogical mirror in a literary text that, as Hardy read it, did not depend on "an indivisible and regular system, which occupies *the whole extent of the believing mind,*" but is "composed of a thousand loose and flexible parts."

The Dynasts represents, in a quite new degree, a break-through from systematic ideology to genuine metaphoric awareness, even from a closed system used metaphorically to a metaphoric open-endedness in which one's own system-making can undergo fundamental restructuring and renewal. It is authorially nonjudgmental as a literary work, and in it even the soul-warts of representative modern men are allowed to surface and show. It is a work that creates a massive collision of individual "systems"—some austere and disciplined, some soft-headed and limply sentimental, some conscientiously researched, some got up on the run and for the occasion—for the singular purpose of exposing in the raw and in the mass modern man's perceptual resources and perceptual techniques; and against these are set relentless exposures of man's perceptual needs if he would hope, with anything like the "complete rationality" necessary for human survival, to reconcile himself through his individual consciousness to his cosmic situation.

Twentieth-century poets have long since recognized that Hardy had discovered in his long dramatic poem a "modern expression of a modern outlook" that was eminently usable by pursuers of their craft. Twentieth-century critics have been slower—perhaps because they have been imaginatively duller, perhaps because they have felt no need, in the pursuit of their craft, for the recognition. Nevertheless, it has been an unfortunate critical short-sightedness, allowing one of the pedestal documents in modern literary transmutation and definition to lie gathering dust in the full but glazed sight of all.

The critic who presses *The Dynasts,* however belatedly, upon the attention of the student of the twentieth century's imaginative life must be cautioned by Hardy's judgment that, for a certain type of reader, his poem was unsuitable—specifically the reader "unwilling or unable" to participate along the co-creative lines designated. Reversing the implications of Hardy's astute judgment here, one can perhaps identify the type of reader for whom *The Dynasts* is most suitable. He is a reader who knows that a literary experience worthy of our best efforts is a complex and strenuous activity demanding full use of the enriched resources of writer and reader alike; that, with few exceptions, it is an experience that must be repeated several times before he gets a practiced feel for the individuality of the work being assayed and the literary traditions upon which it is drawing; and that the experience is its own end, the exercise of some of the most refined and pleasurable resources of his consciousness for purely organic reasons having little to do with political or cultural or philosophical direction or wisdom. For such a reader, *The Dynasts* should be an extraordinary adventure. An ambitious poem monitored by a pervasive awareness that poetry itself has become the chief instrument of order and significance in a godless modern world, Hardy's "Iliad of Europe" has an open aesthetic center out of which hundreds of individual poetic structures emerge in an incremental but flexible surfacing of varied human efforts to systematize reality through or in response to language. These poetic structures in turn become metaphors of human reality (perceivers perceived perceiving) within a symphonic magnitude of complex variations that absorbs these individual poetic structures into a densely configured awareness of epic proportions and significance. The historical subject—a decade of Pan-European struggle—is translated into a modern myth having a genuine analogue in the *Iliad;* the human subject—how people suppose and state fact or the head-games people play with reality—is gradually enriched through poetic technique in this mythohistorical structure until ultimately two of the most insistent subjects of both historical and modern man come to dominate the poem and, through their interlocking, define its central concern: war and peace, perception and truth.

How well Hardy sustains such a challenging concern in the working out of his literary procedures is ultimately a judgment to be made by the individual reader; but obviously to anyone who thinks that he sustains it superbly, every other item in the Hardy canon will be seen in literary magnitude and importance as secondary to *The Dynasts*.

Notes

1. All quotations from and references to *The Dynasts* have as their basis *The Dynasts: An Epic-Drama of the War with Napoleon,* by Thomas Hardy (New York: St. Martin's Press, 1977). Passages are identified by part, act, scene, and page and are given in parentheses in the text as appropriate.

17.

Thomas Hardy's Illusion of Letters: Narrative Consciousness as Imaginative Style in *The Dynasts, Tess,* and *Jude*

I

It is obvious to anyone who mediates on such matters that Thomas Hardy has taken extraordinary hold on the literary imagination of the late twentieth century. He has not only survived; he has prevailed. Every individual gesture of his long literary life—his notebook jottings, his short stories and sketches, his very occasional essays, his "thousand" poems, his "Iliad of Europe," his novels and fantasies, his staged autobiography—has become a metaphor, a characteristic, fascinating reflection, of the man who, more than anyone else in English, acculturated imaginative letters. The whole movement of the nineteenth century had been in Hardy's direction—from Wordsworth's efforts to return to the actual language of men in ordinary life through Dickens's efforts to gain unlimited popularity and Tennyson's efforts, particularly in *Idylls of the King,* to create a universal reading act; but it actually succeeded only in Hardy. Hardy created the illusion of total availability to anyone who could read. His only genuine predecessor in anything like the same complex simplicity—poetry and prose, fable and history, paradigmatic model and experimental form—had been the vernacular Bible, which may have been his unconscious model; and he has had no genuine successor. With the inevitability and lack of self-acclaim of unwritten history itself, Hardy brought the illusion of letters and the illusion of life as near to merger as it is perhaps possible to do and still keep the illusion of letters intact, unfoundered on the very life which is its nurture but to which it yields degrees of its distinctiveness only at its own peril. The illusion of letters is the secret sharer of Thomas Hardy's life.

The illusion of total availability, though clearly the chief source of Hardy's strong hold on a popular readership and a crucial thrust of his practice of letters, has monitored the emergence of his critical reputation. Henry James's infamous phrase "good little Thomas Hardy" is the misguided but wholly understandable judgment by one of the great literary formalists on one of the great literary casualists: James simply mistook Hardy's illusion of availability as the measure of Hardy's whole literary cloth; and that, with altered metaphors, has been the story of Hardy's reputation even among modern professional readers of his works (reviewers, critics). It can even be reasonably argued that James's implicit judgment that Hardy was a simple-minded fabulist—a sort of domesticated moralist hanging in a rich cluster from an Aesopian vine, shockingly rebellious perhaps but ultimately yielding to an orthodox tradition through an unorthodox view—has persisted into the present. The critical arguments have been sophisticated in a most elaborate and stimulating way, and the attitude of pained superciliousness has almost totally evaporated; but even the most sympathetic of modern critics insist on closing Hardy's options. D. H. Lawrence, Albert Guerard, and J. Hillis Miller [1] have opened access routes to Hardy that had never been available for general passage before them, but they too have ended by closing, in however ingratiating a fashion, Hardy's options: in each case, their pioneering brilliance has reached a critical terminus that is not coterminous with Hardy's imaginative country. All three have moved away from such old-fashioned, obviously inadequate techniques of appraising Hardy's availability as *naturalism, pessimism, realism, necessitarianism;* but each has ultimately found an outpost for his critical patternings that is self-satisfying rather than fully encompassing, essentially critic-centered rather than author-centered.

J. Hillis Miller's *Thomas Hardy: Distance and Desire*—to elaborate but one imposing and crucial example—may be the most truly stimulating book ever published on Hardy. But the creative mind, urbane manner, and refined sensibility at work in the book's invariably interesting methodology cannot disguise the fact that the author has ultimately taken a respectable leap into critical closure. It might be reassuring, in a self-congratulatory sort of way, if some of his conclusive assertions were so. But they may not be so, and until the individual reader determines whether or not there is a reasonably exact overlay of the perceptions of the critic on the perceptions of the author, Hardy must be left in imaginative solution.

Part of the difficulty is inherent in Professor Miller's assumption that criticism is an enclosed language-game: "If there is no escape outside the text, if language is as much the source of consciousness or of history as consciousness or history is the source of language . . ." (p. viii). There is a *non sequitur* here, surely. If there is this equal ("as much") interpenetration of language with consciousness or history, then the critic *must* "escape outside the text" to some degree unless he thinks life can be adequately lived within a faulty syllogism. He must undertake to appraise the consciousness and history that impinge upon this particular language-cluster, and he must return himself to that exquisitely painful / joyful space to which life has destined the best of critics (and the best of men), a space pinpointed with magnificent economy by Alexander Pope. He must "[hang] between":

> in doubt to act, or rest;
> In doubt to deem himself a god, or beast;
> In doubt his mind or body to prefer;
> Born but to die, and reasoning but to err. . . .
> *(Essay on Man,* II, 7-10)

He cannot escape *from* the text so long as his labor as a critic takes a literary work as the object to be seen; but since he is himself outside the text, he cannot escape into it, and since the author is outside the text, the two most crucial parties to the text (creator and critic) are outside it; and the critic must not attempt to accommodate a complex problem too simply even if that simplicity promises great and immediate rewards. As Einstein said, we must keep it as simple as possible—but not simpler. So the "autonomy of the text" is either a metaphor or a fallacy: as a metaphor, its function is to minimize irrelevance; as a fallacy, it tempts us to play with language in such a way as to compound the critical problem, however brilliantly, without really attacking it. And when we extend the metaphor to include the *oeuvre*—the autonomy of the *oeuvre*—we have both collapsed the integrity of the original metaphor (to call a text "autonomous" in two different senses is a quibble) and increased our opportunity for brilliance at the expense of logical clarity and ultimate (as distinct from intermediate) relevance.

In another place, Professor Miller asserts that "In Hardy's intuition of human existence there are no fixed celestial archetypes of which each particular is an incarnation. There are only the particulars in their mutual generation of meaning" (p. xi). The wording is vague enough and right-minded enough to provide quicksand for the critic who feels uncomfortable with it; but it seems to mix what may be true with what may not be ture. Hardy de-constructed archetypes of which his imagination was clearly conscious (Clym Yeobright, Michael Henchard, Napoleon) because he was undogmatizing even the imagination; but the fact that those archetypes were dismantled is evidence, not of their absence, but of their peculiar presence in his work; and simply to deny their existence because they do not exist in a traditional, full-bodied form is to make things simpler than possible. Moreover, although Hardy was invariably struck by the distinctiveness of each individual, even his chief protagonists bearing in their individuality no more than a fragment of an archetype, the situations which he uses, while not literally repetitive, are formulaic: his "plots" or "fictions" turn upon such a limited number of patterns that one can hardly avoid thinking of a typical Hardy situation. What distinctive people do (what one's consciousness does) in a more or less typical situation is the persistent imaginative focus in Hardy's writings; and this is so pervasively true that it tends to erase the difference between Hardy the poet and Hardy the novelist. His poems are mostly short stories in verse, and his novels are made up of thousands of poems in prose. There is a Hardy poem on almost every page of the major Hardy novels, and there is the germ of a short story or novel in hundreds of Hardy's poems.

At the heart of this matter is another highly significant aspect of Hardy's manner: his dismantling of classicism. Hardy never lost sight of the importance of the "action" to the making of a poem in prose or verse. Aeschylus, Sophocles, Aristotle were unwithdrawing presences in his imagination; when he came to write his climactic work, he took Homer as his imaginative model; and he repeatedly invited the readers of his novels to apply to them classical (say, Aristotelian) principles. But just as it would be too rigid and hence critically unserviceable to overdraw Hardy's consciousness of archetypes, it would freeze his novels into somewhat shrunken artifacts to overdraw his Aristotelianism. On the other hand, one's care not to overdraw Hardy's classicism should not lead to a denial of its presence, however dismantled. Hardy's more representative works—his novels and poems of character and environment—have at their center "a fitting action" "with the feeling" of whose "situations" the author has deeply penetrated himself [2] and from which everything else follows; and at that center Hardy's classicism is intact. But the response of his characters to those situations, their part in the total "action," is characteristically magnified, however confused or paralytic or tentative or dogmatic or fantastic. That is the author's emphasis—how people feel about the situation with which they are confronted and the myths they make as a way of coping—and it is to that that our attention is drawn. There is an inexhaustible energy of myth-making that permeates every dimension of Hardy's texts: that is the poetry of life to which he is fully attuned. People cope with situations by more or less imaginative mythic strategies. Thus, Hardy's "actions" are expanded inward, undergoing a process of inflation by the individual psyche until our consciousness of the process draws our eye away from the action that is, however, still intact. He thereby dismantles classicism without abandoning it, and the precarious balance which results constitutes what, in the Preface to *The Dynasts,* Hardy calls "the modern expression of a modern outlook"—classicism, which was a full exemplification of the human situation, transformed to modernism, which is a full exemplification, too.

Professor Miller also argues that Hardy's texts are made of Hardy's texts—each new text being "a differential repetition of the others . . ." (pp. xi-xii). This autonomy of the *oeuvre* leads him to reassert his view of criticism as an enclosed language-game: "This circling, or coming and going of fibers of meaning, has no center or fixed point of reference outside the weavings and interweavings of the tissue of words, and the critic can do his job only while he remains caught within this web, following its filaments." Again the central issue has been shuffled away so far as Hardy is concerned. Hardy has forgone the two customary "fixed point[s] of reference outside the [text]"—authoriality (where he stands, what he thinks) and thematic summary (concretion of a reasonably official view of the matter); but this is the implicit metaphor (inverted in Hardy's procedures) of a fixed (or unfixed) point of reference outside the text—namely, that there are no fixed points of reference outside *or inside* the text. Unfixing points of reference is "the ruling passion" of Hardy's "whole mind." That is the "unthinking" at the center of Hardy's imagination which makes everything else possible; that is the product of history and consciousness that came to fruition in such a unique way in Hardy that it makes him at once simple and profound, elusive and fascinating, magnetic and terrifying, the grand heretic of the literary imagination whom only a new age of dogma can have the motive to burn at the stake. The fixed point of reference outside the Hardy text—what he brought to it, what we go away from it with—is the unfixing of points of reference or the imaginative revelation of the illusionary fixing of nonpoints of nonreference. It was out of this "leading sentiment of his mind" that the need to create fallible narrators of his fictions grew: their sympathetic untrustworthiness, the transparent inadequacy of their closure, removes the final authority on experience, *including artistic experience,* and returns reality to eternally tempting incomprehensibility. Thus Hardy's imagination, like everyone's imagination, is at work everywhere and conclusive nowhere.

This leads to a view of Hardy's fundamental effort as a writer very different from Professor Miller's, who says (p. xiii) that Hardy's "writing attempts to close these fissures ["within time itself"], to bring the persepctive of narrator and character together, to reconcile then and now in the poetic persona's life, or to possess all time in a single moment, as do the choruses of spirits in *The Dynasts.*" On the contrary, Hardy's writing does not attempt to do "as do the choruses of spirits in *The Dynasts.*" He was not attempting to refine or civilize or humanize dogma, either through such imaginative metaphors as the spirits in *The Dynasts* or through exact overlays of imaginative perspectives. He knew, rather, both that such "exact" overlays sometimes occur and that such overlays multiplied to the nth degree would initiate a new age of dogma; and the spirits' capacity to "close up Time, as a bird its van / . . . traverse Space, as spirits can" (Fore Scene) is no solution to anything except the epic-dramatist's imaginative need to give fallible perspectives of "eternity" (ultimate imaginings) to his "Iliad of Europe." What Hardy was trying to reconcile men to was the fact that they had an imperious compulsion to make myths, that myth-making was an obsession of the human mind, but that there was little necessary connection between the myths they made and the lives they hoped to live by them or between the lives they lived and the "reality" (measured relatively by their inadequate myths) of the world around them. The excitement in Hardy's work is generated, not by reconciliation, but by discrepancy, and his "truth" is that illusion recognized helps us to avoid disillusion by reconciling us only to discrepancy. Reconciliation is a coincidence of harmony just as imaginable as coincidences of discord, and they happen in life as well as in letters; and to measure Hardy's ultimate purposes as a writer by their infrequent occurrence in his work is to strip him of his highest imaginative courage and to make him, in however small degree, just another Romantic.

And it would be unthinkable that Hardy did not apply to the artist (poet, novelist) the rules of life in this world as he perceived them. So to say that "the poet's eye and the eye of eternity are one" (Miller, p. 254) or that "A work of art is objective in the sense that the thread has existed all along in the confused tangle of reality" (Miller, p. 259) or that "Such an art [as Hardy's] is a resolute confrontation of reality and its injustice" (Miller, p. 262) is to create a new fissure between "us" (the artist, the critic) and "them" (the rest of mankind). It is a new breed of aestheticism that makes of the artist the new Jehovah and of the critic his high priest. This is an "escape outside the text" with a vengeance because no combination of words inside the individual text or the *oeuvre* of Hardy substantiates any such view. Hardy was a writer of impressions and seemings, not a perorative aesthete. He knew nothing about the "eye of eternity" and said so repeatedly. He followed the threads of designs as he perceived them, but he made no pretense to objectivity in any essential sense, and he knew that "reality" is an illusion for the artist as for everyone else and that justice, like injustice, in any absolute sense is simply an obsession of all men's imaginations. His whole effort was to see things as they in fact are, and if he had a design on his reader it was to enable him in some small individual degree to know a little the world he would leave so soon. And things as they in fact are are not "things" at all but perceptions of things, translations of stimuli into the maneuvers of consciousness—the poet's, every man's. Language is a shaper of history as consciousness, both a revelation and a concealment. Characters in poems and novels use it that way, as do poets and novelists; and just as the linguistic shapings of characters in texts are both true and false, the linguistic shapings of authors of texts are subject to the same kinds, if perhaps not the same degrees, of inadequacy. The poet, the novelist, has a special but not an absolute talent; and like most of us, he is better at seeing other people's weaknesses than his own. Hardy knew this better than most: his breath-taking modernism is centered in it. He carried the individualism, subjectivism, relativism of his century to an authentic open-endedness that pointed outward toward "the roars and plashings of the flames / Of earth-invisible suns," toward "Monsters of magnitude without a shape, / Hanging amid deep wells of nothingness" (After Scene, *The Dynasts,* p. 522). He shaped what he could—tirelessly, ambitiously, effectively, but he never confused himself with God; and the critic who is content to be "caught within [his] web" is content in a way Hardy never was.

II

The growing tendency among Hardy critics to use *The Dynasts* as the chief confirmatory text for points of view about his novels and poems makes it imperative that that crucial work be taken out of the closet and subjected to the same penetrating scrutiny that some of the individual novels and poems have received. Otherwise, doubtful readings of *The Dynasts* will increasingly be used to confirm doubtful readings of the novels and poems. *The Dynasts* is to Hardy what *The Ring and the Book* is to Browning: the text to which all of his efforts as a writer finally lead and the model by which our larger perceptions of Hardy's imagination are to be tested. Hardy is conspicuously absent from *The Dynasts* as Browning, somewhat genericized, is conspicuously present in *The Ring and the Book* (Books I and XII). But this would seem to be the aesthetic position to which Hardy had finally come and the implicit perspective that he wanted his readers to adopt toward his work as a whole. Nor should the special subject matter of *The Dynasts*—the "War with Napoleon"—divert us from the poem's serviceability as an aesthetic guide to the Hardy canon: the poem was so designed as to encourage the reader "to look through the insistent, and often grotesque, substance at the thing signified," [3] and such encouragement has relevance to Hardy's work as a whole.

If *The Dynasts* is in truth the model by which our larger perceptions of Hardy's imagination are to be tested, then we must be chary of citing the arguments of individual characters, including the spirits and choruses of spirits, as if they had an independent authority. At the imaginative center of the poem is the metaphor of war, and that metaphor catalyzes the vast collision of metaphors that permeates *The Dynasts* as a work of the literary imagination. Behind the work is the conscientious historian, and the research-ingredient in the poem—"unimagined" fact carefully "verified"—is one of its assumptions. But even history, however carefully wrought, ultimately yields to illusion, and what we have in *The Dynasts* is not fact, but an imaginative sense of fact—fact mixed with fancy and thereby moved into a sustaining, because living, medium.[4] History yields to myth, and the very conscientiousness of the imaginative historian is a poetic act of faith: all truth relentlessly seen moves toward emblem. If facts even the most stubborn have their sustaining life in perception, then reality itself as a function of life is perception; and if imaginative perception is poetry, reality moves toward universality (life sustained to the nth degree, life enabled to violate our ordinary sense of Time and Space as modes of consciousness) in proportion to the strength and purity of the imagination that perceives it. All of this is relative, of course—the perceiver also being subject to perception; and one must make a choice as to how far he will pursue the metaphysical implications of this line of thought. Hardy was a subtle and globally curious man, and it would arbitrarily enclose him to say dogmatically that his mind did not play out the analogies in metaphysics. But the emphasis in this essay is on the aesthetic rather than the metaphysical, on the metaphoric interplay between fact (history in its multiple shadings), consciousness (history perceived), and poetry (the transformation of fact as consciousness, history as perception into a formal / casual structure of symbolic language).

The war-metaphor at the center of *The Dynasts* projects a retrospective / imaginative perception of a "Great Historical Calamity"—the quintessential belaboring of Europe in the nineteenth century, both inevitable and unnecessary. Like the ten-year war at Troy, its mythic analogue in Homer's *Iliad,* it made a slaughterhouse of the broad human stage on which modern civilization had reached its apex. At the center of the war-metaphor is the figure of Napoleon, once a young charismatic artillery officer with a great flair for timing who converted his original lust to save the Revolution into an imperial lust to imprint history with a Napoleonic image by establishing a dynasty with an imagined futurity as persistent, in retrospect, as that of the Holy Roman Empire. That is the perception that initiates a might collision of perceptions, counterpointed against a swollen ground-tone of dumb impercipience, which make up the "Quaint poesy, and real romance" of the Napoleonic war (Part II, Act III, Scene I, p. 210). The ironies roll like thunder through the poem: Napoleon, had he learned like Prometheus to "endure eternally" in his original intuition, might metaphorically have "shouldered Christ from out the topmost niche / In human fame" (Part III, Act VII, Scene IX, p. 520); the desperate effort of all Europe outside of France is to prop up a group of exhausted anachronisms and to imprison Europe once more in the incompetence of the puppet-outcroppings of the *ancien régime;* and the hundreds of thousands of faceless soldiers who die in the Peninsula or at Austerlitz or in the Russian campaign perceive only that some dynast perceives that they should be there doing what they are doing.

But there are two perceivers or groups of perceivers of the action of *The Dynasts* besides those who play a part—great or small, central or peripheral, informed or ignorant—in the action itself.[5] These are the celestial spirits and the master of all ceremonies, the encompassing intelligence who sees all, hears all, knows all, tells all. He is the imagination itself, the universal consciousness of the piece. He is, in some respects, the exact opposite of the Immanent Will, knowing all and causing nothing as the Immanent Will knows nothing and causes all. But like the Immanent Will, he is a metaphor, a mythic intelligence, "Which we as threads and streams discern, / We may but muse on, never learn" (Fore Scene, p. 7). He is an awareness, not a judgment; and although he shares his knowledge fully, he does not take an imaginative leap into critical closure.

Since he is the universal myth-maker, the poet as ultimate metaphoric perceiver, he creates such myths of imaginative perception as the Immanent Will, an illusive orderer in both the macrocosm and the microcosm; but he fully recognizes his creation as a myth, an imaginatively useful illusion which enables the fiction upon which he is concentrating to have outreaches which it could not have (and does not have) in imaginings less far-flung. He has not, he knows, explained the mystery of the universe; he has only created an imaginative myth that makes other imaginings possible. The celestial spirits are emanations of the Immanent Will, the progeny of the universal myth-maker's primary myth, the children, therefore, of both the myth and the myth-maker. They are the chatterboxes of eternity, a group of siblings on a "Walking-tour" in Time without being Time-bound. They do not know, as we do, that they do not exist except as perceptions of the myth-maker, thinking that they are the children of "the gods (the Will, / To wit)"; and with a like irony, they are dogmatic critics of humanity in ignorance of their total anthropomorphism. Big Brother (Years) is in charge of their expedition, and he keeps their boisterousness within bounds and their criticism of Big Daddy (the Immanent

Will) within reasonable limits of decorum. But their capacities—of action, knowledge, and personality—are entirely endowed by the myth-maker, and they clearly mirror macrocosmically microcosms of human thought. So while we yield them, as required, "that willing suspension of disbelief for the moment which constitutes poetic faith," we do not fall foolish into the notion that they constitute a serious explanation of the matter at hand. They exercise our imaginations, not our judgments; and we finish the poem with a heightened imaginative awareness that frees us from overstructured analogues (more or less rigidly codified dogmas) in our own perceptual illusions. The imaginative inflation of *The Dynasts* has as its purpose to deflate our dynastic delusions—eschatological, political, personal—and to leave us with a chastened wisdom that will assist us, perhaps, in making the inevitable myths that we inevitably live by severer and less delusionary.

The truly mind-blowing imaginative perception of *The Dynasts* is that at both imaginative extremes of its perceptual reality is mere puppetry. The great masses of people, including the armies that move back and forth across Europe, have no control over their lives, but are the automatons of the next-ranking automaton; they are seen from the Overworld as "writhing, crawling, heaving, and vibrating in their various cities and nationalities" (Fore Scene, p. 6). But the Immanent Will, the grand puppeteer in the poem's metaphysics of the imagination, is a puppet too. He is "The PRIME" because that is as far as the imagination can go without simply replicating him in an infinite search for origins; so he is not explained, only created. And, once created, he has no more control over what he does than the lowliest, most faceless foot-soldier in Napoleon's Grand Army of the Republic. He is wholly nescient and "works unconsciously . . . / Eternal artistries in Circumstance" "by wrapt aesthetic rote" (Fore Scene, p. 1). He is the puppet puppeteer, and the least of men and the Prime Cause of all mirror each other across all imaginable Time and all imaginable Space in their common helplessness. That is the "Quaint poesy, and real romance" of life. And while it may be wholly terrifying, it can be wholly satisfying too, encouraging us perhaps to shape both our illusions and our language (our illusion of letters) in a spirit of mutual, if chastened, sympathy.

But it would be foolish, a misuse of spirit, to expect the universe itself to change, and the inclination of some commentators to sentimentalize the promise of *The Dynasts,* to pick it for pithy reassurances or for passionate protests against "reality and its injustice," runs quite counter to the careful way in which Hardy has isolated his stern imaginings by stripping the poem of personal authoriality. And it counters, too, the truths of human experience implicit in the way in which he deploys his Homeric analogue. *The Dynasts* is a metaphoric omega to a curve of *human history perceived* of which the *Iliad* is a metaphoric alpha; and even if Hardy does not intend in his poem to spell the doom of modern Europe as Homer in his spelled the doom of ancient Greece and its Panhellenic world, there is certainly little foundation for sanguine unction in the historical record if man in the nineteenth century A.D. can repeat the equivalent holocaust of man in the twelfth century B.C.

What, then, are the chief lineaments of Hardy's imagination as they emerge in *The Dynasts?* What are its indices to "the ruling passion of his whole mind"? Certainly not that he was a language-man weaving a "tissue of words" within whose web the reader most fully caught could most fully flourish. Rather, he saw reality as a Thing-in-itself as unknowable, while at the same time he saw "knowing" as an irresistible imperative of the human mind. An obsession to know the unknowable leads inevitably to imaginings, myths of reality, illusions. That is the way the human consciousness copes with its need to know. But every individual is "sealed within the iron hills" of personality, and hence all myths are in some way distinctive, life in the human community thus becoming an acceptance or negotiation or collision of myths. In every microcosm of the human community this acceptance or negotiation or collision of myths takes place perpetually, and in every social microcosm there are those personalities whose illusion of knowing includes the illusion of knowing better: every hamlet, every household, has its dynasts. This results in a persistent, if muted, presence in the human community, however large or small, of the pressures of struggle and survival.[6] For the most part, these pressures are held in balance by a community myth (a contract) to which some myth-makers are willing to succumb and which other myth-makers are content to exploit. Occasionally, a Titanic myth-maker makes a myth that threatens all the other illusions of knowing better, and there is a mighty collision of myths. Such collisions have very little dramatic value in the perspective of timelessness; but then Time itself is an illusion, a mode of consciousness, and within its narrowing illusive frame, these collisions, mighty or minute, become explosively dramatic, the more dramtic the narrower the frame. *The Dynasts* embodies one of those mighty mythic collisions perceived by the imagination in four different perspectives: as historical memory, oral and written; as dramatic re-creation (then made now); as a myth of human rhythms in time (the *Iliad, The Dynasts*); and as a myth of timelessness. One is not more real than the other, and all are available to the human imagination according to its clarity and strength. Indeed, all men regularly employ all four perspectives in their daily myth-making—in their thoughts of the past, in their maneuvers in the present, in their general expectations of human behavior, and in their dreams of the future, whatever coloration their post-mortem thoughts may take. Therefore, it was not Hardy's purpose as a writer to introduce into men's awarenesses a wholly new revelation that would alter the human mix, to bleed eternity into time. He hoped only to lend his imagination out and thus, perhaps, to help men better understand their own illusions by measuring them against the illusions which his own imagination had shaped in the illusion of letters. Though his imagination did not elsewhere take so explicit a leap into the macrocosm as it did in *The Dynasts,* the macrocosmic awareness is a dismantled presence in his works as a whole; and the universalizing of the narrative consciousness in his epic-drama formalizes what he there perceives to have been an assumption of his art throughout its major phase.

Hardy's very special use of the narrative consciousness, including the variations he works on that use, is the principal metaphor of his imagination: it is both our chief access-route to the "leading sentiment of his mind" and the source of the ultimate excitement that the experience of one of his major works induces in us. This narrative consciousness operates in a submerged fashion in the major novels, but its patterning is implicitly modeled for us in *The Dynasts.* First, there is the fiction itself, the story-line or action of the novel as romance. The characters live in separate but overlapping worlds of action and consciousness, and each creates for himself an explanation (an illusion or myth) of the way things are according to his angle of vision (his placement in community) and his capacity to intuit meaning (his imagination). This is the novel as dramatic re-creation, including the drama of perception which the form of *The Dynasts* forces almost entirely into dialogue. Second, there is the interpreter of the fiction, a presence in the artifact but not a participant in the scenic action. He is a somewhat elusive presence, surfacing and submerging, moving between two identities: he is both commentator on the dramatic myth and product of the myth, freer than the characters in the basic action but not free of the fiction itself. He corresponds to the celestial spirits in *The Dynasts,* offspring of both the myth and the myth-maker, and he suffers from a fallibility that corresponds to their inconclusive multiplicity of views. In his efforts to enclose perception, to wrap meaning up, he frees perception by brushing against awarenesses that he does not fully understand. He is the imaginative trigger cast as the thematic bullet.

The Immanent Will of *The Dynasts* also has implicit correspondences int he novels. The Immanent Will is the enveloping metaphor of which the characters in the central fiction have little or no awareness [7] and of which the commentator has only a partial, fallible understanding. The Immanent Will is in one important sense extra-textual. No matter how thoroughly we suspend our disbelief in order to enable the poem to function, we carry into the poem our imperious need to know, to discover some coherent explanation of the meaning of things; that need then measures what we come to know about the Immanent Will against the analogous metaphors (beliefs, speculations) of our own minds; and we retain the Immanent Will as a reference point in our thoughts (positive or negative or neutral) about the ultimate meaning of life quite independent of Its formal place in the imaginative architecture of *The Dynasts*. The major novels also have enveloping metaphors which are in an important sense extra-textual. They are not "explanations," however metaphoric and illusionary, in the codified way the Immanent Will is; but they are immanences, atmospheres, spiritual / imaginative media in which the localized fiction unconsciously functions and which no one inside the fiction, including the commentator, quite understands. But the fourth dimension of the narrative consciousness (say, the author at a symbolic level)— the universalized imagination that enables all the rest to come into existence—understands them; and the reader who, as co-creator, takes a position analogous to that of the universalized imagination understands them too.

These enveloping metaphors, except in such an experimental structure as *The Dynasts,* cannot be made an explicit part of the literary artifacts (the novels) themselves because that would defeat their imaginative purpose, making them just another species or overlay of commentary and reintroducing therewith the very principle of authoriality which Hardy was trying to suspend. Our clues to their presence outside the text are embedded in the text, but they are themselves otherwise extra-textual. They are not "the meaning" of the novels, but they flood the novels with fresh meaning and enable the cooperant reader to "fill in the junctions required to combine the scenes into an artistic whole" (Preface, *The Dynasts*, p. xxv). Like *The Dynasts,* they assume "foreknowledge" on the part of the reader; and to the "mental spectator . . . unwilling or unable" to provide that foreknowledge, Hardy's novels in their ultimate imaginative outreaches become "in his individual case unsuitable" (Preface, p. xxv). But for the mental spectator or reader to whom this fourth dimension of the narrative consciousness in Hardy's novels is suitable, those novels become a revolutionary literary experience, so revolutionary in fact that they challenge the preeminence in modern fiction of the very writer who expressed such a negligent understanding of their import—Henry James. Working under the same pressures as James to create a truly "modern expression of a modern outlook," Hardy found a more imaginative solution than James. Like James, he placed in the fiction itself a *persona*-presence who is a commentator on the action. But Hardy's commentator is not, like James's, involved in the action; he is involved only in the myth that the action-clusters as a whole constitute and only as commentator. Moreover, Hardy's commentators, unlike James's, are conspicuously fallible and touch the large significances even of the inner mythic action in a customary and inadequate way. But this is only the raw material, the *Stoffen,* of the Hardy narrative consciousness. He has suspended the myth as action-clusters in an enveloping metaphor of which the commentator has only fragments of unconscious awareness, and he has created a universalized imagination that corresponds to this enveloping metaphor. By so doing, he has dissolved the issue upon which James was so dependent—the trustworthiness of the narrator—and has, in a very real sense, erased from his fiction the impediments of authoriality and infallibility. Instead, he has introduced into his fiction the modern equivalent of a classical aesthetic insight: the imagination is more vigorous and invigorating when the artist is *showing* something rather than *proving* something and when the reader's (spectator's) energy is concentrated on how the imagination in and of itself works rather than on some thematic bottom line.

The enveloping metaphor and its effect on the fictional procedure correspond in one sense to the extra-textual myth, with its penetrating universal significance, and the transformation of that myth and its signifiance into a localized forms by the chief classical dramatists.

And Hardy's enveloping metaphor / localized fiction achieves two of the principal aesthetic results of the classical formulation: it places the localized fiction in a medium of universality (macrocosm / microcosm), and it detaches the reader from the imperious demands of theme, freeing him to focus on the way in which the artist conducts his affairs (seeing the artist see life). But there is this stunning difference between Hardy and the classical dramatists: his enveloping metaphors are not inherited but are shaped in his imagination through his keen observation of life in his own time-frame and his extrapolation of those observations to the whole human condition, independent of particular time and particular place. Therefore, his enveloping metaphors are not archetypal fictive configurations of universally representative human experience transformed into a novel or play in the classical manner of a fiction (play) made of a fiction (inherited myth). Rather, his enveloping metaphors are myth-less, uncodified, unshaped.

They are perceptions of peculiar manifestations of the *Zeitgeist* which have universal relevance in the imagination. They are spiritual conditions under which people's lives have to be lived, and they have a mythic habitation only in those lives as people live them. It is only by the keenest observations of our individual lives that their patterns begin to emerge; but after we perceive them, we realize that the very possibilities of our lives are dependent on those patterns and that, although we daily fail to recognize it, our freedom from them is, to the degree that it exists at all, severely limited. Hence, Hardy's austere modernism represents a mythic reversal, a sort of mythic Baconianism; and although the very process is manifestly illusionary, it is also to a very high degree imaginatively cogent. Though life may ultimately make no sense at all, it does form what we see as patterns, metaphors, illusions of reality independent of the individual myths that people make to give order to their daily lives. The detached man of imagination (the philosopher, the historian, the scientist, the artist) verifies those patterns by initial observation and a quick intuition which he then subjects to a more exhaustive observation. Having verified that these patterns really exist, the man of imagination puts them to his special uses—the philosopher, historian, scientist to proof, the artist to the creation of a vehicle that will enable his audience (spectator, reader) to experience his discovery more economically, more complexly, and at an even deeper level of impact than the original process of discovery afforded him. But in a modern age of "keen Discovery," these patterns do not emerge in fabulous forms like those of the ancient myths which took their shape, their expression, from an age that did not, in the fabulous way it shaped its myths, have a "modern outlook." So the modern artist must proceed differently. Having verified these nonfabulous patterns in his imagination, having *seen* that they do really exist, he reverses the classical process and creates an inductive myth—a localized story— in such a way as to enable the imaginative reader to make an inductive leap into the enveloping metaphor of reality which corresponds to the inherited myths of the ancients. That enveloping metaphor is not an image or story: the image and story have only a local habitation and a name. It is a structure of the consciousness, a perception, a reading of life; but it is also an immanence, a pervasive sentiment of the imagination that makes the story and without which the story itself makes sense at only a severely limited level. The enveloping metaphor is that spiritual presence, that *Zeitgeist,* which sets the conditions under which life is to be lived. It has a strong contemporary component that suffuses, shapes, imprints an age. But that epochal imprint, though imperious, is never quite unique; it is repetitious in long rhythms, and the remnants (the ruptured patterns, the echoes, the shadows) of each age persist in all other ages. It is the "concurrence, renewed from moment to moment, of forces parting sooner or later on their ways"; it is "a design in a web, the actual threads of which pass out beyond it" (Walter Pater, Conclusion to *The Renaissance*).

III

Tess of the d'Urbervilles and *Jude the Obscure,* for example, resist all of our efforts to discover their secret power through traditional techniques of novel-reading. Each contains hundreds of significant thoughts *(motifs, leitmotifs),* but neither has a genuinely cohering theme; both are manifestly larger in their total affectiveness than any idea or reasonable combination of ideas. They defy dogma in even its most undogmatic sense: they are experiences, not teachings. Nor do we do much better when we try to make the total experience of the texts cohere around the protagonists. Both *Tess* and *Jude* project imaginative world-awarenesses with which Tess and Jude are not as characters co-equal. Angel Clare and Alec d'Urberville are closely connected with Tess in her story-line, but both occupy large spiritual spaces quite independent of Tess, and each could be the center of a meditative or melodramatic romance. Arabella and Sue Bridehead are dwarfed as characters by our temptation to subordinate them to the inner conflicts of Jude.

But they are massively larger than that, and their individual efforts to cope with life bring us into vivid contact with experiences of our own that Jude himself does not even resonate. Arabella may be a Circe-figure turning men to swine and provoking in Jude impulses which he finds both irresistible and disgusting; but Circe was also a shrewd lady, not to be measured simply by her design on Odysseus and his men, and Arabella has an unmistakable life-force that Jude lacks the inner capacity fully to appreciate or enjoy. Sue is one of the fascinating female figures in modern fiction, an elusive reference point for a type of character that she refuses identification with. Although Jude locks her in for a time in his search for fulfilment, she is in a perpetual state of breaking out; and the thing she does at the end—which crushes Jude's heart, his spirit, and his will to live—has a decisiveness and a solidity which he never evinces. Sue may not be bigger than Jude, but she certainly outruns any effort to make her a mere satellite in his life-story. She intensifies his fiction while enlarging in her own right the myth of which he is also a part. And the repeated assertion, by both the commentator and the characters, that Jude and Sue are two halves of a single self is more deflection than insight at the level of mythic action: he requires of her what she simply cannot give, and the compromises she makes end catastrophically. Sue brushes against extra-textual mythic reference points—the myth of Diana, the myth of Hermaphroditus; but she is wholly intact as a character of very large significance. The integrity of her desire to be the soul-mate of sensitive men is not violated by their inability to adjust their desires to hers. Her life is ravaged, not by her self-myth, but by her weakness in succumbing to the very chaos against which that self-myth was her one dependable intuition.

Little Father Time is a very special character in *Jude the Obscure* and in Hardy's fictions as a whole. He shatters the textuality of both *Jude* and the canon by the very violence of his metaphoric eruption, suggesting even that he puts a final exclamation mark to Hardy's career as a novelist long before any review of *Jude* had been penned. But it hardly needs to be argued, in the present context, that Little Father Time is in any simple way subordinate to Jude as protagonist of his novel: he turns the whole myth around and sets it on its final, devastating course. Moreover, the terrible beauty of their novels, while having a central focus in Tess and Jude, draws largely on the nature of the world they release in our imaginations—the dark spaces illumined by their presence in it that we might otherwise manage to leave in convenient shadows and the way that world, once seen in the illusions of Tess' and Jude's composition in time and community, enables us to reach toward the enveloping metaphors of which they are the topical, historical, mythic bearers.

Nor does our recognition of the basic technique by which the fictive worlds of Tess and Jude are imaginatively energized enable us to gain a wholly satisfying insight into their secret power. Each is set in motion by a rather shabby myth—*Tess* by Jack Durbey-field's inflation of Parson Tringham's information about his noble ancestry and *Jude* by Phillotson's off-handed remark about his " 'scheme, or dream' " of becoming a " 'university graduate, and then to be ordained.' " These initiating myths function very differ-ently in the two novels: Tess resists strenuously the invasion of her consciousness by the Durbeyfield-d'Urberville myth, while Jude yields to the Christminster myth so readily and fully that it be-comes an *idée fixe* which he cannot see disillusively even in the otherwise total disillusion of his shabby death. But in both novels they are relentless presences, and they provide the simple model of the total fictive procedures. As the novels are fictions, so the char-acters deal in fictive structures: *Tess of the d'Urbervilles* and *Jude the Obscure* are myths about myth-makers.

Tess is highly resistant to the popular myth-making strain. It is her peculiar illusion that she must keep herself free of the ordinary small-beer fantasies of Jack and Joan, that there is a knowable difference between fact and fiction and that it is incumbent on her not to delude herself. That, combined with her perpetual self-doubt and her absolute purity of intention, accounts for her over-whelming hold on us: she is determined not to seduce herself, to allow the wounds inflicted by others to heal, and to deal with life through an infinite capacity for sorrow and through rituals of self-reliance even in the most harrowing of circumstances. It is our last and purest myth, and though it does not finally work, it gives Tess' "Poor wounded name" a bed of lodgement in our own naked bosoms. *She* is *we* in the myth of ultimate retreat. But, though resistant, Tess is not immune, and the combinations begin to form against her from the beginning: Jack and Joan's myth of procrea-tive happiness, the Durbeyfield-d'Urberville myth, the myth of "the happy hour," the *nouveau-riche* myth of old Simon Stoke-d' Urberville, the *petit-riche* myth of Joan with her outhouse *Fortune Teller,* the satyr myth of Alec, the Bacchanalian myth of the work-ing community ("a multiplicity of Pans whirling a multiplicity of Syrinxes; Lotis attempting to elude Priapus, and always failing"), the myth of the Furies (dark Car the Queen of Spades and her sister Nancy the Queen of Diamonds in a night-riot of psychotic dislocation), the grotesque myth of the savior-seducer. This is the densely textured mythic fabric (the labyrinth) which the Daedalian artist has created for Tess and from which there is no escape even in integrity, only in death. Tess' integrity (the *"Pure woman"* of the subtitle) is bombarded on all sides and relentlessly by other people's myths, and it can be sustained only by an act of faith (the "Faithfully Presented" of the signature) on the part of the reader, who has to cope with the myths of his labyrinth too. On the one hand, it would destroy the vibrancy of Tess' fiction if the author or the reader leapt suddenly into an abstract absolute, into an immaculate conceptual myth of inhuman purity or its companion myth, equally abstract, absolute, and inhuman, of the virgin birth. On the other hand, it would lock the reader into a needlessly shrunken labyrinth—a labyrinth not really worthy of the name—if he allowed himself to be enclosed so entirely in the text that only its definitions and exemplifications had relevance to the issue. Indeed, both *"A Pure Woman"* and "Faithfully Presented" are themselves extra-textual. So the novel does all it can (the novelist does all he can) to shape an open question imaginatively and then releases the question, shaped but still open, into the larger waters of life represented by a million readers' consciousnesses.

The presence of Angel Clare in the novel greatly enlarges the frame of reference in which Tess' integrity is to be perceived and moves the fiction as a whole towards the enveloping metaphor in which the novel itself subsists. He, too, he thinks, is resistant to myths even the most sophisticated. He is that privileged young man who judges that he has seen into the truth of things; and, giving up the untenable myths of his elders and of an older, less enlightened culture, he has gone out to school himself, to touch wood, in the arts of farming so that he can realize the most persistent myth of all highly developed civilizations, the myth of the lost agrarian paradise, far away psychologically (close to the soil) and far away geographically (somewhere at the antipodes). He is the most lethal myth-maker of all—gifted, ingratiating, and self-deceived. He has no idea who he really is, and yet complete authenticity is the mythic measure he applies to those who take hold upon his attention. Liberated from one mythology, he sets to work immediately and unconsciously to create a new mythology. Imaginative, sensitive, ethereal, post-modern, he does an explosively ironic thing—he reverts to a medieval pattern and creates a secular Mariolatry, puts his romantic Virgin back into her sacred niche. And when he discovers that he has been deceived, he punishes, not his deceiver—himself—but his fallen Virgin, whom he has de-created as a person and created as a dream. The earlier mythology had been simply inherited, and he could let it go as easily as an Old Master from which his taste had become alienated; but he has himself been the Daedalian craftsman of this iconic center of a new mythology, and he rebels against its imperfection, its untenableness, with an adamant subjectivity: it just isn't the same; she was one person and now she is another. Having been created from outside herself, having been de-personalized and mythicized, Tess has no possible redress. She can simply retreat into the coordinates of which her personal integrity is made: that she knows the difference between this fact and this fiction; that although she is full of self-doubt, she does not doubt the purity of her intentions; and that she will deal with life, here as elsewhere, through an infinite capacity for sorrow and through rituals of self-reliance even in the most harrowing of circumstances. She does not exculpate herself for what she has done: she has given in to his relentless importunities and has, however anxiously, sung with him a duet in paradise. But she has never dehumanized him; has loved him for just what he appeared to be; and his ritualized confession of his fallen condition has only freed her to share the truth of herself. But the truth is not what Angel wants—he wants his myth; and when he cannot have it, this enlightened, liberated young man of the new age is as unyielding as the Inquisition.

But Tess and Angel, despite the vast differences between them and the faulty maneuvers of their consciousnesses, do occupy a common spiritual space: they have an all-encompassing need to believe in something in whose reality they can make a complete act of faith. And this draws the novel, the localized fable, into its eveloping metaphor. In a large but restricted sense, the enveloping metaphor of *Tess of the d'Urbervilles* is the metaphor of a Christianity in shambles and, enlarged further, of a world in which one does not know what to believe, perhaps has nothing to believe in. The novel is suspended in a perilous ambience of agnosticism in its all-pervasive sense—an ambience in which there is not only no god, but also no god-substitute. It is pervaded with anachronistic spasms, personal efforts to reassemble, in good faith or in bad, the shattered spars of a remembered Christian icon—Cuthbert and Felix, the itinerant sign-painter, even old Mr. Clare; and there are failed reenactments of ritual patterns having clear analogues in an intact Age of Faith—Angel's cult of the Virgin, Tess' efforts, when abandoned by Angel, to die the "little death" of the vowed nun, the series of epistles that Tess writes to her absent Lord, her Angelology, the conversion of the pagan Alec. But it is a chaos of Christian remnants held together by patterns of human struggle after a personal world-coherence having nothing to do with Christianity except that Christianity was initially put together through the same patterns of struggle, the difference being that then there was faith where now there is none. The degeneration of the d'Urberville family-line is analogous to the decay of Christianity, the once grand Age of Faith, itself; the brisk emergence of the Stoke-d'Urbervilles is the metaphor of an effort to graft wholly alien modern motives onto a decayed Christian trunk in the hope of giving them a patina of respectability; Jack Durbeyfield's fantasies are the romantic day-dreams of an age after its long-lost Christian identity; Christianity, like the authentic d'Urbervilles, lies entombed in a metaphoric Kingsbere. The "local Cerealia" with which the novel begins and the sacrificial altar at Stonehenge on which Tess enacts her final life-gesture measure the cultural timelessness into which Christianity has in truth slipped.

See, in the perspective of this enveloping metaphor, *Tess of the d'Urbervilles* as a work of literary imagination loses nothing and gains a great deal. The local myth is still full-bodied, and Tess' struggle to keep herself intact amid all the conscious and unconscious efforts to dismantle her is still suffused with the keenest dramatic poetry. But though still knitted in a time which any cultural observer can easily identify as today and yesterday and even tomorrow—so slowly does the twilight of Christianity fade into darkness, so almost imperceptibly does one of the highest of all mountains of faith sink below the horizon of slow-moving time—Tess and all her fable are suddenly transported out of particular time and become the metaphoric fiction of the human effort to cope with the rhythmic troughs of a recurrent faithlessness, a cultural timelessness that includes not only the collapsed myth of Christianity but also the blighted fields of Demeter and the last flicker of the Druid flame. In such twilight worlds, people spasm and scramble and call things by false names and deceive themselves. The purest, like Tess, deceive themselves as little as possible. They try to see things as they in fact are; they enjoy, within their limited capacities and despite the persistent pressures of self-doubt, such moments of happiness as are granted; and when, after a lifespan of sorrow barely surmounted through endless strategies of self-reliance, the end comes, they say simply, " 'I am ready.' "

The enveloping metaphor of *Jude the Obscure* is the next terrifying step in the long, circular pageantry of man: When he no longer knows what to believe in, when there is perhaps nothing left to believe in, how can he sustain the will to live? In its imaginative outreaches, *Jude the Obscure* subsists in the spiritual ambience of life-exhaustion, and Jude himself delivers the valedictory. He is both a perennial human type who feels life perpetually threatening to exhaust itself and a modern summation of a cumulative pressure toward death. Jude's is the story of the extraordinary and unsuccessful efforts of a young man not to die; and the " 'chaos of principles' " that he rationalizes at the end is, in the curve of the fiction itself, a magnificent grasping at straws. Jude is the inheritor of a death-prophecy, that of Drusilla-Sibyl; he is the carrier of a death-wish; and he is the progenitor of a death-child, Little Father Time. And when all his maneuvers to stave off death have failed—when "the fret and fever, derision and disaster, that may press in the wake of the strongest passion know to humanity"[8] all come to naught—he accepts the failure of his aims and, in his own oblique fashion, kills himself. Jude is the failed, desperate Apostle of a life "dying downwards."

Acceptance of this enveloping metaphor, which Little Father Time in a rupture of textuality draws the novel into, re-casts the reader's whole relationship to the inner fable. Jude is still a working-man with a dream that founders on both the system and his own internal incoherences; and the "deadly war . . . between flesh and spirit" is authentically "waged" on that personal / societal level. There is even a visible classical subtext by which we are invited to measure Jude's tragedy by traditional standards of *stat-*

ure, flaw, catastrophe, recognition, and *acceptance.* But that visible subtext is counterpointed against a struggle that dwarfs it, as it is itself
dwarfed, through conscious adaptation, by measure of the models
created by Sophocles and Aeschylus. Jude's ultimate struggle is not
with a role in life but with the very possibility of life. As Tess tried
to preserve her integrity in a world without faith, Jude tries to
preserve his existence in a world without reality; as hers is the
myth of ultimate retreat, his is the myth of ultimate dissolution.
Jude makes fantastic myths and retreats into transparent self-delusions because myths and self-delusions are his life-lines. He has
been placed in a spiritual / imaginative state in which even Tess'
admirable determination to separate fact from fiction is a luxury
which he simply cannot afford. He is trying to believe himself into
existence, to believe himself into life; and any little belief will have
to do in a crisis because when the belief (the myth, even the delusion) goes, the life goes too. He moves in a world of emblematic
death—his aunt's wish to de-create him, the severed pig's pizzle,
Arabella's falling hair, the stuck pig whose life is deflowered in
such a lurid way on the white, virgin snow, the rotting stones of a
darkened Christminster, his collapsing dreams—which he attempts to prevent from inundating him and sweeping away his
fragile hold on life by dreaming fall-back dreams, cutting stones,
restoring churches, writing letters, studying the pagan and Christian classics, making babies, baking cookies in the shapes of living
things. But even the possibility of holding onto life finally eludes
Jude; and when, in her psychotic recoil from Little Father Time's
genocide, his soul-mate Sue forces herself, in the pervasive sexual
imagery of the novel, into the role of a pig given up to perpetual
sticking, he abandons his fruitless life and dies.

As *Jude the Obscure* narrows the issue to the most fatal of human
truths ("to be or not to be"), so it narrows the fictive canvas and
concentrates the myth-making energy into Jude himself. Even Sue
as an alternative myth-maker is singularly chaste: her views of life
are fundamentally disillusive, and when she lets her authentic self-
myth go, she largely makes do, enjoying what she can, in her withdrawn, frigid fashion, of her daily life with Jude; and her ritual of
self-immolation at the end is mythic in only a disheveled sort of
way. She is determined on a self-defilement which is only half

believed in, and it can bring her no more peace than Jude's last Remembrance Day brings him. The rest of the characters, like Arabella and Phillotson, deploy myths that are much shorter-ranged and that have about them an edge of "innocent" brutality; they make such *ad hoc* adjustments as they think they must and get on from day to day, their lives little perspected by large dreams or spirit-crushing disappointments, never questioning whether they are alive in any genuine sense at all. Only Mrs. Edlin, Drusilla normalized, has a quality of honest, helpful matter-of-factness which keeps her free both of fixed ideas and helter-skelter reaffirmations.

But in appraising the final import of the novel, it is well to remember that Hardy was not making a generalized thematic comment on modern life and its immediate prospects. Jude is not a modern Everyman, but a perennial strain in all men that occasionally surfaces quintessentially in certain human types. He is the man who cannot find self-definition in the ordinary circumstances of life and must, if he would have any sense of existence at all, fabricate a self. It is a precarious undertaking, even if one can find no acceptable alternatives to do it; and it is the product of that perennially modern disease of restlessness which results from an increase in expectation concurrent with a decrease in stabilizing structures and traditions. And it is precarious especially for those most likely to be drawn into it—imaginative young people with a keen dissatisfaction with what they are but with little or no capacity to create what they would be. And the imaginative revelation of the enveloping metaphor of *Jude the Obscure* is that when one embarks upon the Daedalian fabrication of a new self in the labyrinth of life, the issue quickly shifts from *what* he will be to *if* he will be at all.

Hardy's next major literary effort after *Jude the Obscure* was *The Dynasts*. And to the degree that the suggested readings of *Tess* and *Jude* in this essay are persuasive, we must believe that Hardy's dissatisfaction with the critics of his last two major novels was not that they had misread details of those works but that they had failed to "read" them at all. His narrative consciousness had moved into an imaginative space to which contemporary reviewers were strangers; and having realized this, having perceived that "the ruling passion of his whole mind" was operating on matters the most penetrating in an essentially impenetrable way, he abandoned a craft which had, practically speaking, ceased to work for him even among his most practiced readers. He turned, instead, to the creation of his most sophisticated and challenging work, *The Dynasts,* which is at once one of the great experimental literary successes of the twentieth century and the literary structure in which students of Hardy's imagination can be most profitably schooled.

Notes

1. D. H. Lawrence, *Study of Thomas Hardy,* in *Phoenix: The Posthumous Papers of D. H. Lawrence,* ed. Edward D. McDonald (New York: Viking, 1936), pp. 397-516; Albert Guerard, *Thomas Hardy: The Novels and Stories* (Cambridge, Mass.: Harvard University Press, 1949); J. Hillis Miller, *Thomas Hardy: Distance and Desire* (Cambridge, Mass.: The Belknap Press of Harvard University Press, 1970).
2. Matthew Arnold, Preface to *Poems* (1853), in *The Complete Prose Works of Matthew Arnold,* ed. R. H. Super (Ann Arbor: University of Michigan Press, 1960), I *(On the Classical Tradition),* 7.
3. Preface to *The Dynasts* (New York: St. Martin's Press, 1965), p. xxvii. All references are to this edition, which is a reprint of the text of the edition issued by Macmillan in 1924.
4. The parallels between *The Dynasts* and *The Ring and the Book* in the imaginative transformation of dead truth into living truth are close and highly significant.
5. I am suspending for the moment the occasional invasions by the celestial spirits of the dramatic action itself.
6. There are analogous pressures observable in the nonhuman community of animals and plants, but any argumentative application of the results of those observations to the human situation, though almost irresistible, always leads to further confusion because it is an effort to clarify one situation which we do not fully understand through the application to it of another situation which we understand even less well. It may be useful as analogy or loose metaphor but never as argument.
7. Napoleon's ambiguous consciousness of the Will is inconclusive, suggesting at once rational self-exculpation and momentary flashes of insight, by one who has exhausted ordinary human myth-making, into suprahuman possibilities.
8. Hardy's Preface, 1895-1902. Other phrases in the following sentences are also adapted from the preface. The phrase "dying downwards" is from the poem "Nature's Questioning."

Index

Primary Names and Literary Titles

(The arrangement of this index is strictly alphabetical. Characters in *Idylls of the King* are indexed individually, and titles of literary works are italicized throughout.)

377